Quakers and the American Family

Quakers

and the

American Family

*British Settlement in the
Delaware Valley*

BARRY LEVY

New York   Oxford
Oxford University Press
1988

Oxford University Press

Oxford   New York   Toronto
Delhi   Bombay   Calcutta   Madras   Karachi
Petaling Jaya   Singapore   Hong Kong   Tokyo
Nairobi   Dar es Salaam   Cape Town
Melbourne   Auckland

and associated companies in
Berlin   Ibadan

Copyright © 1988 by Barry Levy

Published by Oxford University Press, Inc.,
200 Madison Avenue, New York, New York 10016

Oxford is a registered trademark of Oxford University Press

Library of Congress Cataloging-in-Publication Data
Levy, Barry.
Quakers and the American family.
Bibliography: p.   Includes index.
1. Quakers—Delaware River Valley (N.Y.-Del. and N.J.)—History.
2. Delaware River Valley (N.Y.-Del. and N.J.)—History.   I. Title.
F157.D4L48   1988   974.9'0088286   87-11126
ISBN 0-19-504975-6

1 3 5 7 9 8 6 4 2

Printed in the United States of America
on acid-free paper

For my Mother and Father
Lenore and Murray

Preface

This book began as an effort to describe Quaker families and communities that left seventeenth-century northwestern England and settled and developed colonial southeastern Pennsylvania. I hope the final product retains evidence of its origins as a trans-Atlantic study of a significant cohort of religious people and their descendants. As I researched this topic, I did become increasingly touched by the psychological insight, devotion to emotional truth, and exquisite, interpersonal morality of the farmers I was studying. During the course of this research, I have made every effort to understand both intellectually and emotionally the religious ideas and experiences of these Friends. While focusing on Friends' familial and economic life in the following work, I have positioned the Friends' religious experience as the central reality around which all their familial and social ideas developed. On the other hand, this is not an uncritical work. Whether biased by professional commitment or my own cultural heritage, I have remained skeptical about the ability of human beings to embody divine truth within the contingencies of daily life, especially without external, authoritative institutions.

Yet, from the early stages of research, I implicitly and then explicitly enlarged my purposes. Among the voluminous records of Chester County and Welsh Tract Friends at Swarthmore College, I found a book of seventeenth-century removal certificates, descriptions of the characters of poor, rural Welsh men and women who settled in Pennsylvania between 1682 and 1695. I was astonished to read repeatedly ideas about children, women, and marriage in these certificates which supposedly were not normative, much less so explicitly expressed, in Anglo-American life until the late eighteenth or early nineteenth century. Not only were these ideas expressed much earlier than I thought they ever could be, but they were being expressed by pious farmers from northern Wales, an area still regarded by cosmopolitan English people as being on the periphery of English culture. As a Suffolk visitor told me at a London bed-and-breakfast, the areas around Chester and northern Wales were places to go with camping gear to experience dramatic rustic scenery, not places to go with notebooks to study lasting cultural innovations. I realized that I would have to write a book simultaneously about transplanted Quaker communities, about the cultural significance of Anglo-American frontiers, and about the origins of American family ideology.

Miss Dorothy Lapp and Mrs. Lucy Simler have both rescued and made accessible the documents of early Chester County life upon which the history of early Pennsylvania has been and will be written. All early American historians, especially myself, are indebted. I must also thank the staffs of the Chester County Historical Society and the Chester County Court House (many of the records I saw in the court house are, thanks to Lucy Simler, currently safer in a new Chester County archives). I also owe a great debt to the helpful staffs of the Genealogical Library, Historical Society of Pennsylvania; The Friends Historical Library, Swarthmore College; Philadelphia City Hall and City Hall-Annex; Friends House Library, London; The Cheshire County Record Office, the Castle, Chester, U.K.; and the National Library of Wales, Aberystwyth, U.K.. I reached the British archives thanks to an National Endowment of the Humanities' Summer Stipend. An Andrew W. Mellon Faculty Fellowship at Harvard University gave me access to the Houghton and Widener Libraries, and time to write and think in an invigorating intellectual environment. The Charles Rieley Armington Research Program on Children and Values at Case Western Reserve University provided me with several small, but very timely and helpful, grants. A fellowship at the Bicentennial College, University of Pennsylvania, supported research on rural Anglican families in the Delaware Valley.

And while looking for seventeenth- and eighteenth-century Quaker communities, I also found the reality of a contemporary community of scholars. Many of the ideas upon which this book are based were first publicly tried out before members of the Shelby Cullum Davis Seminar at Princeton University, who provided a most encouraging, yet helpfully critical, experience. J. William Frost, Lucy Simler, Thad Tate, Mary Beth Norton, Gary Nash, Bernard Bailyn, Carl Ubbelohde, David Van Tassel, and Daniel Scott Smith read early and later chapters, and sometimes all, of the developing manuscript, and provided helpful criticism and encouragement. Sheldon Meyer, Rachel Toor, Judith Tucker, and Leona Capeless at Oxford University Press repeatedly and patiently gave me their advice. Bertram Wyatt-Brown not only critiqued the manuscript at a late stage, but provided me with a vital intellectual friendship, including discussions about how the honor ethic of the Southern United States and the Friends' emphasis upon the honor of Truth, though diametrically opposed, had related sources in England's remoter provinces. John Murrin's reading of the manuscript and insightful criticisms were of enormous help. His faith in the project, his example of dedicated scholarship, and his prodigious knowledge of early American history remain invaluable. By their examples, teaching, and friendship, accentuated by their differing styles, Michael Zuckerman and Richard Dunn made the University of Pennsylvania a special place to pursue imaginative scholarship within the context of empirical rigor. Michael Zuckerman adopted this project at an early date, when I was frightened by its implications, and nurtured it with warmly expressed enthusiasm, encouragement, praise, and criticism. With overt reserve, yet with constant sympathy and penetrating judgment, Richard Dunn helped me from the beginning to the end by his example and with advice, counsel, encouragement, and timely criticism. The project and I owe an enormous debt to these men—though the final interpretations and arguments remain my responsibility totally.

Jacquelyn Hinde Wolf, my wife, and Aaron and Amos Wolf Levy, my sons, lived graciously with me and the project—no easy task. Their presence informed me daily that the substance of the topics I was trying to write about—children, marriage, and love— still make life on the American frontier worth living.

B.L.

Contents

Quakers and the American Family

Intimate Frontiers

During the nineteenth century most Americans defined the "home" as a sheltered location where American women cultivated motherhood to nurture conscience in America's children. Similar ideologies affected Western Europeans. But domesticity's strain was purest in America. Many Americans held the conceit that the household should be a morally self-sufficient institution.

The moral influence and responsibility of the mother and of the household were limited in nineteenth-century English family ideology by the rise and influence of the public school. Respectable nineteenth-century boys continued to be taught the ethics of male honor in English boarding schools (Eton, Harrow, etc.) through peer group pressure. Nineteenth-century New England had boarding schools too, but they were newer institutions primarily attended by the children of rich urbanites who feared their children's moral corruption in the city. These schools were informed by the ideal of domesticity, and they were warmer and smaller places than their English counterparts.[1] The ideology of domesticity also helped create a body of family law in the United States that was quite different from Great Britain's.[2] The impact of the ideology of domesticity also inspired a body of writing with some unusual tendencies among the United States' best nineteenth-century male authors. American male writers had difficulties defining the wider meanings of relations between men and women. Perhaps in response to the burgeoning spiritual authority of women, they confined the sacred world of human relations to areas distant from the conventional moralizing wife and mother. Only on Melville's *Pequod* or in Mark Twain's touching relationship between Huck Finn and the runaway slave Jim on the Mississippi River, where women were absent, were human communions described as being truly possible.[3] The ideology of domesticity remains a major American cultural feature, and it continues to affect American men and women deeply, though it is assailed by critics, diminished economic expectations, and its own contradictions.

The new family prescription served Americans as a moral substitute for declining ministerial and communal institutions and as their haven in a harshly economically competitive and expanding republican society. This new ideology promised to allay the confusions and fears of nineteenth-century Americans, who were experiencing rapid landed expansion, commercial development, and early industrialization. Historians note that New England reformers played the central role in the definition and spread of nineteenth-century domesticity. Such an understanding, incorporated into a fine body of historical writing, is generally satisfying.[4] Nineteenth-century New England reformers dominated nineteenth-century family reform movements. The novels, advice literature, and periodical literature of liberal New England clergymen and New England women first spread the strictures of domesticity nationally. The evidence of the connections between family change and early industrialization and landed expansion, especially in New England, is undeniable. As new textile factories, new immigrants, and high rates of geographic mobility among New Englanders attest, nineteenth-century New England society was being transformed rapidly. Its patriarchal and minister-supported family system of colonial heritage had long been dying. Yet New England culture was a likely context for the development of domesticity. Seventeenth-century Puritan ancestors, by emphasizing the importance of family relations, had provided a firm foundation for nineteenth-century reformers' drastic moral burdening of the household.[5]

Yet, some questions remain. In order to be something plausibly attempted, much less to be truly effective, morally self-sufficient households require precise and stringent obedience to a complicated set of roles and rules. Did these roles and rules simply evolve from previous family forms, even with New England households' predispositions, under the pressure of social and economic change? Were they, in fact, self-consciously created by a morally intense subgroup over a long period of time? Given the complexity of the society they lived in, why did late eighteenth-century and then nineteenth-century reformers frequently cite the experience of rural seventeenth- and eighteenth-century Quakers (a phenomenon which will be illustrated below)? And why was domesticity so much more clearly the dominant ideology in America than in Britain, though both societies experienced notable social and economic change between 1750 and 1850?

An important, if admittedly partial, answer to all these questions exists in the realization that domesticity had a significant and widely acknowledged social incarnation in America well before it became the ideology of nineteenth-century New England reformers. A type of domesticity, almost identical to that later advocated by New England reformers, informed a major seventeenth-century folk movement and was the organizing principle beneath arguably the most socially and economically successful process of development in early American: the settlement and ensuing social and economic growth of colonial Pennsylvania. Quaker farmers in the late seventeenth century brought a type of domesticity to Pennsylvania, and it provided them with the animus for their rule over colonial Pennsylvania for nearly a century.

The Friends' great tenets and the outlines of their early history are widely known. Among the many religions born during the turbulent aftermath of the English Civil War of the 1640s, the Quakers were the most radical religious group to survive. Quaking when the power of Truth first struck them in meeting and rudely invading the pulpits of more staid Protestants, the early Friends believed that God's Truth, Grace, or Light was reborn on earth with the birth of every individual. They insisted that Truth in both individuals and society could only be hampered by excessive external coercion. They rejected intolerance, university-educated ministerial authority, and most forms of civil and international force. They were a clear threat to the English social order. After the Restoration in 1660, they experienced severe persecution and turned from direct political and religious confrontation to securing communal and familial survival. In England, during the eighteenth century, the Quakers declined in number, but many, like the founders of Lloyds and Barclays banks, became enormously wealthy. In North America, Quakerism grew during the eighteenth century. The Quakers were a considerable force in the middle colonies and

the third largest religious group by 1750 in early America. Their
numbers and power declined percipitously, however, after an internal reform movement from 1754 to 1790.[6]

Omitted from this outline of Quaker history is the contribution
which Quakerism as embodied in a powerful religious community
made to the extraordinarily rapid development of the Delaware
Valley, Pennsylvania. Nor has it been sufficiently emphasized that a
disproportionate share of the early Quaker farmers in Pennsylvania
came from northwestern England or from other areas of Britain
relatively untouched by the dynamic social and economic developments which transformed, during the seventeenth century, southeastern England. This fact was of the utmost importance. Early
Pennsylvania was a transplantation of upland, provincial, British
society, albeit profoundly modified by radical religion. Similar
physical and economic conditions complicated conventional efforts
to organize people through strong, centralized institutions in northwestern England and initially in frontier Pennsylvania.

Seventeenth-century northwestern Quakers were emotionally,
spiritually, and geographically among the most successful Anglo-
American frontiersmen and frontierswomen. Their emotional, spiritual, and geographic frontiers were intimately related. Partly because they had lived on the frontier of Great Britain's commercial
and political expansion, Quakers took to exploring the frontiers of
intimate relations. Largely because many transplanted themselves
in the richer American frontier, they were able to establish their
unique family system as an influential cultural force. The Quakers'
provincial experience, knowledge, and limitations propelled
Quaker farmers to emigrate to Pennsylvania and then made them
unusually able in the vast, lonely forests of North America. Having
faced problems of poverty and dispersion of settlement in England
between 1654 and 1681, English Quakers devised a new solution to
the question of social authority: they originated a form of domesticity based upon radical religious ideas. Northwestern Quakers who
emigrated to Pennsylvania found that their way of life provided an
unusually effective blueprint for North American settlement.

QUAKER FAMILY ideas were not much appreciated in England. Few
English Protestants during the seventeenth century suffered to tolerate, much less to admire, Quakers' social and religious ideas. Until
the 1670s, the popular London press described Quakers as an ugly,

enthusiastic people hostile to all civil and political restraint. By 1675 most writers admitted that Quakers lived righteously, but the popular London press then attacked them for devising a family system too spiritualized and feminized for use by sane English people. In the early nineteenth century, an English reformer Thomas Clarkson recommended Quaker family life as a model for all Englishmen. Clarkson's *A Portraiture of Quakerism* (1806) received polite attention by middle-class English journals, but Lord Jeffrey, speaking authoritatively for England's gentlemanly establishment in the *Edinburgh Review*, dismissed the Quaker family. He concluded that Quaker children were "inwardly chilled into a sort of Chinese apathy by the restraints in which they are continually subjected" and grew up to be adults who were "very stupid, dull, and obstinate . . . in conversation; and tolerably lumpish and fatiguing in domestic society: active and methodical in their business, and narrow minded and ill informed as to most other particulars."[7]

American Quakerism attracted more formidable intellectual champions in France, however. In the early eighteenth century Paris intellectuals began to praise Quakers and especially to celebrate the achievements of Quakers in Pennsylvania. These French intellectuals questioned the necessity and rightness of the excessive authority wielded by church and magistrate in Europe. They began to imagine alternative ways of organizing humanity. Some, most notably Jean Jacques Rousseau, projected new familial and educational relations which might produce happy civil men and women who did not require the external disciplines of the coercive state or authoritative, superstitious church. They hoped to make households nearly autonomous moral institutions, capable by themselves of morally sustaining republican or democratic states. Many of these men came to believe that Quakers, especially those in Pennsylvania, had realized the superiorities of just such a familial order. Cosmopolitan deists made Pennsylvania their favorite proving ground for Enlightened ideas.[8]

Voltaire, while in exile in England from 1726 to 1729, discovered the Quakers and Pennsylvania. He praised both extravagantly in the first four chapters of his *Letters on England* (1734). His description of William Penn, the Quaker proprietor of Pennsylvania, as a great lawgiver, of Pennsylvania as a utopia, and of the Quakers as humble people of remarkable civic virtue was restated almost verbatim in the great French *Encyclopédie* (1751–80). It thereby entered the mainstream of Enlightenment thought. Montesquieu called William Penn the greatest lawgiver since classical antiquity. When a Philadelphia artisan produced his widely acclaimed *Experiments and Observations on Electricity* (1751), this Benjamin Franklin confirmed all that had been said about Pennsylvania. A Quaker society, though primitively simple in manners, could support a first-rate scientist and philosophe. "If ever despotism, superstition, or war, should plunge Europe again into that state of barbarism out of which philosophy and the arts have extricated it," wrote Abbé Raynal, " the sacred fire will be kept alive in Philadelphia, and come from thence to enlighten the world."[9] Until coming to Pennsylvania in the sixth volume of his *History of the East and West Indies* (1784), Abbé Raynal had mercilessly documented the theory that nature, including and especially men, degenerated in the New World environment. He suddenly proclaimed in respect to Pennsylvania, however: "It is time to observe the dawnings of reason, happiness, and humanity, rising from among the ruins of a hemisphere, which still reeks with the blood of all its people, civilized as well as savage."[10] In eighteenth-century continental Europe, the marriage of Quaker domesticity and the philosophes made Pennsylvania the best known, most studied, and certainly the most appreciated of all the British North American colonies.

This extraordinary French response to American Quakers has been well described by scholars, particularly Edith Philips and Durand Echeverria. They judge it a projection of the philosophes' wishes.[11] There is much truth in this point of view; but the philosophes' disdain for evidence can be overstated. Voltaire never saw the Quakers in their Pennsylvania habitat, but during the early period of his English exile Voltaire lived among a Quaker community in Wandsworth and studied English with Edward Higginson, an assistant master in the local Quaker school. He read widely in Quaker literature and attended Quaker meetings.[12] Later, especially to Frenchmen inspired by Voltaire and influenced by Jean Jacques Rousseau, the Quakers were an irresistible object of direct study. J.P. Brissot de Warville and J. Hector St. John de Crèvecoeur did much ethnographic footwork in order to study Quakers in Pennsylvania. They visited Quaker social-welfare institutions, meetings, funerals, and marriages.[13] Brissot characteristically spent several days and nights in the household of a Quaker Chester County farmer in order to digest the domestic atmosphere of what he called "a true American farmer." He literally got a stomach ache, but retained his enthusiasm for Quaker family life. "In truth, I was never before so edified as I was in this house," he concluded.[14]

These investigators were curious about how the Quakers could produce toleration, prosperity, and civic virtue in Pennsylvania without an established clergy or privileged upper class. Brissot thought they even lacked an exciting form of worship. Brissot was unimpressed by the incoherent, nasal-speaking ministers and "atmosphere of lugubrious boredom" in Quaker worship meetings, as he described them. He was "astonished that this sect manages to survive and even to gain proselytes." Brissot's, and also Crèvecoeur's, answer to the Quakers' continuing growth and development of tolerance, virtue, and prosperity in Pennsylvania was the Quakers' ability to make the generation of public authority and morality intimate and attractive or, in other words, in "the reputation they have of leading a happy domestic life." As Brissot noted, "they devote themselves completely to their duties—to their wives, their children, and their business. Such is the picture which has often drawn to Quakerism men who laughed at it in their youth."[15]

Given the religious and cultural gap between the polished Frenchmen and the rustic Pennsylvania Quakers, it was an exotic discovery. Philosophes saw domesticity as a theoretical solution to the problems of a cosmopolitan, heavily institutionalized society. For them, the issue of domesticity involved not the growth of familial affection among middling people in Western society but the severe disciplining and spiritualizing of that affection in a manner which not only increased the allure of the household and privacy but also allowed the household and intimacy to bear alone the burden of producing and sustaining happiness and civic and economic virtue. In this way they hoped to render the established priesthood, intolerance, and an authoritarian upper class visibly unnecessary. The Quakers, needless to say, were not Enlightened deists who relied upon critical reason; they were religious zealots who relied upon revelation. And, although seventeenth-century Pennsylvania Quaker immigrants had thought through a religious form of domesticity and then actually realized it, they were largely faced by severely provincial conditions on both sides of the Atlantic.

The Pennsylvania Quaker settlers were a rural provincial people. A large share had come from the northwestern fringes of England, areas which in many ways were more culturally remote from Paris than was eighteenth-century Philadelphia. A recent accounting and analysis of the first purchasers of Pennsylvania land show

that of the 315 rural buyers of known origin, William Penn recruited the bulk of his colony's first rural European population
from upland, provincial British regions, most often characterized by
livestock farming, widely dispersed farmsteads, relative poverty, and
relatively low population densities. Welsh farmers and their Cheshire neighbors in northwestern England, who composed the largest
regional contingent of rural Quaker settlers in Pennsylvania before
1700, form the basis for the following narrative.

Concentration upon northwestern British Quaker settlers of
southeastern Pennsylvania and their descendants, specifically some
2,500 people from Cheshire and Wales, provides a good beginning
for the study of the origins of American family ideology. Northwestern British Quakers came from the region of England where Quakerism was first organized by George Fox and Margaret Fell. These
settlers' social and geographic environments in northwest Britain
were also similar to those of the great majority of other early
Pennsylvania settlers. Thomas Holme's famous survey map of
Pennsylvania (1687) depicts three counties filled with dispersed,
contiguous farmsteads, an English highland settlement pattern,
complete with highland place names: Radnor, Haverford, Darby,
Marple, Edgemont, Ridley, and Chester. Far fewer place names told
of lowland, fertile English origins: Chichester after a town in Sussex, or Kennet after a town in Wiltshire. An examination of nearly
six hundred early purchasers of Pennsylvania land confirms that
more of them (55) came from Cheshire in the northwest than from
another county, and that well over 60 percent came from the poorest
highland areas of Britain. Virtually no one came from richly developed East Anglia in southeastern England. The Welsh and Cheshire
settlers occupied good farmland just outside the intended port of
Philadelphia. They developed almost 20 percent of the settled land
in Holme's map (the Welsh Tract and eastern Chester County), and
they constructed in this territory powerful and influential rural
communities. During the first four decades they also accumulated
considerable economic and political power, promoting such early
leaders as Griffith Owen, the counselor; John Simcock, president of
the Free Society of Traders; David Lloyd, the speaker of the Assembly and chief justice; and Thomas Lloyd, the deputy governor.
Early Pennsylvania political history prominently features these
men, although their social origins and purposes remain obscure.[16]

The northwestern Quaker farmers cannot represent the phenomenon of Pennsylvania Quakerism or of Anglo-American Quak-

erism definitively, however. Study of these Quakers, for even stronger reasons, cannot substitute in the story of Pennsylvania's development for adequate study of other Pennsylvania groups like the Scots-Irish, Germans, Anglicans, Afro-Americans; or for broader economic study of all these groups together.[17] Yet, especially when sufficient attention is devoted to their British experience, the story of the northwestern Quakers provides the best focus available for the story of the social history of the ideas, people, places, and events which created, introduced, and partly established America's distinctive, major family ideology.[18]

THE QUAKERS' message and witness was universalistic, but the nature of northwestern British Quakerism was also influenced by the provincial context in which Quaker organization was developed. By 1640, the cosmopolitan core of England was the southeastern region; almost two-thirds of the English people lived there; it contained the largest cities; it was the center of rapid social change. It was a flat, fertile region which contained prosperous gentry and yeomen, who employed a growing laboring class—often the former smallholders of the region—in order to supply agricultural commodities to rapidly growing cities nearby. The southeastern region was also the center of English education and of a religious reform movement, Puritanism, that hoped to make the Anglican Church a purified institution that emphasized the moral and intellectual education of the British population through plain-spoken but highly educated Protestant preaching. Because of its emphasis on individual, internal, self-control, Puritan reform, many historians argue, offered a solution to the disorder in southeastern England caused by rapid commercialization and urbanization.

Puritan reform, before the Civil War of the 1640s, made little advance in northwestern Britain. After the war, zealous, talented, Puritan proslyters spread over these "dark corners." Though they were supported by Oliver Cromwell, the Rump Parliament, and a victorious Puritan army of occupation, they had only ambiguous success. Southern Puritan reform assumed human relations impossible to replicate in northwestern England's economy and society: a close and continuing relationship between university-educated ministers and their parishioners; and strong, patriarchal nuclear households in which fathers played domestically the ministerial role.

During the sixteenth and seventeenth centuries, northwest England, including northern Wales, had been slowly integrated into the English state and into English commerce, but with different consequences and problems from those experienced in southeastern England. Northwesterners continued to wrestle with a stingy environment remote from England's major markets. The relative poverty of northwestern households resulted in unmanageably large parishes. Northwestern "middling" people—yeomen, husbandmen, and artisans—were also much poorer than their southern titular counterparts. For the accomplishment of essential household tasks, particularly the promotion of children in livings, middling households in northwestern England depended more than comparable southeastern households on people outside their households, especially local gentry and kin.

When George Fox and other Quaker prophets appeared in these hills in the late 1650s, they appeared defiantly, yet plausibly, anti-institutional. Instead of relying on close pastoral relations and university-trained ministers, these frontier prophets tried to reach those "intricate and abstruse places" in the human mind where they believed divine authority most surely dwelled. The central medium of Quaker worship was not the reception of a well-produced sermon, as among the Puritans, but a silent meeting, a gathering where all social criticism or support was purposefully suspended to reveal and communicate the divine truths embedded in the spiritual human body—either by silent communication or by the verbal expressions of a spontaneously inspired "minister," a "vessel of the Truth." From these experiences, the Quakers developed a folk theory of divine language by which the Quakers promised to be able to form relatively inexpensive communities of the Holy Spirit. Each Quaker was an embodiment of the Word and therefore preached within or without meeting, or with or without words, to other Quakers or "tender" people.

The Quakers provided an exciting and seemingly plausible theory of the Holy Spirit capable of transforming dense northwestern middling familial connections into saving communities of holiness. Yet, these new spiritual clans of "holy conversation" also required a severe code and discipline to ensure their purified identity. Quakerism could easily degenerate into just another northwestern tribe (which Quakerism resembled in organization) unless exchanges within families were suffused with purity and love. Beginning in 1653, George Fox produced letter after letter advocating and designing the radical spiritualization of all household emotions and the redefinition of the Quakers as a holy tribe, "the family and household of God." This work prescribed the elimination of all symbols and gestures of honor from family life and human relations; the complete spiritualization of marriage; the redefinition and intensification of childrearing; and, perhaps most radically, the existence of rational, self-disciplined women in every Quaker household; and the demand that such women be encouraged to discuss and legislate on what Fox called "women's matters," including sex, child-birth, and childrearing, in specially designed and church sanctioned "women's meetings." Fox projected the most thorough familial reorganization yet witnessed in England. Quaker domesticity was partly a solution to the problems this new, radical religion faced in its provincial seedbed.

By 1675 northwestern Quaker monthly meetings applied Fox's code vigorously. Despite organization and effort, the northwestern British Quakers also experienced a destructive demographic crisis. Within just one generation from their religion's founding, the northwestern Quakers experienced a 49 percent reduction of their community. Northwestern livestock farmers, after becoming Quakers, could no longer give their children promiscuously to their kin or the local gentry. They now accepted a religious obligation to protect their children's gift of grace from "carnal talkers," not simply by protecting and cherishing them when young children but also by settling them in morally protected situations. This task required more wealth than most northwestern middling households had. Most of their children left Quakerism.

Northwestern Quakers were the best customers of Pennsylvania's Quaker proprietor, William Penn. By 1681, the year of Penn's charter, Quakers composed about one percent of the British population and were spread fairly uniformly throughout the realm. Yet Penn recruited his rural population very disproportionately from northwestern Britain and other outlying provinces. The plight of the economically pressed northwestern Quaker farmers suggests that the early Quaker, European peopling of early Pennsylvania was largely caused by the conflicts between the high costs inherent in radical Quaker domesticity, particularly the costs of controlling the placement and marriages of Quaker children, and the stringent economic limitations of its original, upland homelands.

Almost two hundred Cheshire and Welsh Quaker households arrived in the Delaware Valley between 1682 and 1700. Most of these households contained children whose spiritual safety was their parents' top priority. The northwestern Quakers found a lush frontier in Pennsylvania, and used their radical familialism as well as their provincial, northwestern heritage to design their settlement pattern, behavior, and success.

For example, by 1686 (only four years from the first Quaker settlement), Pennsylvania farmers were already producing a large enough wheat surplus to begin a lucrative flour trade to the West Indian sugar islands. This rapid development of the flour trade followed from the formerly upland settlers' desperate search for adequate profits to provide land and material to protect their children. This pursuit demanded agricultural innovation. Though Merionethshire and Cheshire immigrant farmers remained mixed farmers in Pennsylvania, they quickly and nearly uniformly changed their agricultural priorities from livestock raising to grain cultivation. The pressures of achieving Quaker familial ideals also led Quaker fathers to buy enormous quantities of land, which were devoted to their sons, and which they distributed generously. Indeed, although notoriously disorganized and fractious in politics, these early Quaker Pennsylvania settlers were remarkably uniform in familial economic policy.[19] In the 1690s a religious schism fractured the fledgling Quaker community and provided the basis for a vigorous Anglican challenge to the Quaker settlers' hegemony. Even these troubles revealed the rapid emergence of Quaker familialism in Pennsylvania as a powerful social and political reality. Dissatisfied with the sudden, almost totally encompassing, hold of Quaker familialism on almost every aspect of secular and spiritual life, a minority of Quakers ignited the Keithian schism. History is full of revolutionaries like the Keithians who become revisionists when their dreams emerge too quickly as fact.

The settlers' child-centeredness also greatly helped the Pennsylvania Quakers maintain a strong religious community. Their peculiar beliefs and commitments about nurturing and protecting children made piety, profit, and community compatible—at least initially. These Quakers had been poor farmers in northwestern England and had lost their children. In Pennsylvania, the Quakers became wealthier farmers and retained their children. The Pennsylvania monthly meetings reinforced the settlers' desire to become decently rich by encouraging economic virtues for the purpose of saving children. They also provided many forms of non-economic advice and intrusions to help parents save their children.

The Welsh Tract and Chester Monthly Meetings promoted both economic and communal development through the ethos of Quaker domesticity. The results were nearly spectacular. Although Voltaire did not emphasis the link between Quaker domesticity and Quaker prosperity, this theme was emphasized by later commentators, especially Brissot and Crèvecoeur. They thought the Quakers produced the quintessential republican economy in which domesticated relations united both impressive wealth production and the maintenance and fostering of civic virtue. Crèvecoeur constantly observed the virtuous economic prowess of Quaker domesticity, whether among the Quaker inhabitants of whaling Nantucket or on John Bartram's farm near Philadelphia. Crèvecoeur's quintessential American farmer was a child-centered father who increased his productivity by placing his "little boy on a chair which screws to the beam of the plough."[20] Brissot thought that thrift and attention to business—which he regarded the "two sources" from which "all private and civic virtues flow"—were best seen in Quaker domesticity. Speaking of the Quaker father, he noted, "if he has many children, he loves them and sees ways of planning for their future. Such a man is a good husband, for putting his whole happiness in his family life, he is forced to be good in order to be loved, and he can be happy only by making those around him happy."[21] When set among abundant farmlands, the Quakers' system seemed to promise centuries of happy republican economic development.

Though somewhat overinflated and unduly dismissive of the contributions of non-Quaker Pennsylvanians, these were plausible assertions. By the second half of the eighteenth century, when Brissot and Crèvecoeur made their direct observations, Pennsylvania, Philadelphia, and the middle colonies were all flourishing. The middle Atlantic region had become the first in British North America to build a successful regional economy on the agricultural surpluses generated by family farms. The middle colonies were where the virtuous and prosperous family farm of legend and lore actually existed. Although this phenomenon was primarily due to the superior farmland of the middle Atlantic region, Quaker domesticity did play a role. Delaware Valley Pennsylvania Quakers and their New Jersey neighbors were the leaders and pace-setters in the construction of a family-based wheat and flour trade.[22]

The Quakers' commitment to their special form of domesticity also encouraged Pennsylvania's famed pluralism. Because they thought public enunciations of religious doctrine ineffectual,

Quakers hardly feared them. They did fear and did legally ban cock-fights and theatrical performances, forms of public display which could corrupt private life. Quakers confined childhood education and nurturance largely to private spaces, and they made those spaces increasingly wealthy and enticing. Thus, Pennsylvania Quakers could maintain strong communities while tolerating the influx of a wide array of strangers.

This is not to say that rustic Delaware Valley Quakers and cosmopolitan French admirers always learned the same lessons from their observations of the Pennsylvania experience. Brissot and Crèvecoeur came upon the Quakers in the late eighteenth century during the Pennsylvania Quakers' great spiritual crisis, what Jack Marietta has called the reformation of American Quakerism. From 1750 to 1790, Pennsylvania Quakers disowned almost 50 percent of the rising generation of Quaker children; they abolished slavery within the Society of Friends, and the Quakers withdrew from government.[23] The Frenchmen generally ignored these events or merely regarded them as peculiar features of intense Quaker sectarianism that threw no shadow over the achievements or exportability of the Pennsylvania Quakers' marvelous social invention: domesticity.

The Frenchmen were wrong. At least among the descendants of the northwestern British Quakers, this crisis was caused by Quaker domesticity itself. After 1740, many Quaker farmers increasingly found that the Delaware Valley economy, although rich in raw wealth and opportunity, was becoming too complex for the successful transference of "holy conversation" to the next generation. Many Quakers were running out of land. The alternative of establishing their sons as independent, rural tradesmen, while economically feasible, also led to their sons' longer independence from their parents' households' intimate family relations. Many of their sons married non-Quakers or other Quakers outside of meeting. Thus, by the late eighteenth century Quaker meetings and parents faced difficult choices. They could either ease the Quaker discipline and the purity of their household ideal or disown a large share of their children. After much debate and resistance, Quaker leaders chose to protect their household ideal and to disown, in effect summarily, all those who married irregularly. The remaining Quakers formed an exemplary, upper-middling, smaller, intensely purified, less expansionist, and more introspective sect. Although Quakerism had grown in population dramatically between 1681 and 1750, it failed to grow after 1750 in pace with other American religions. The Quakers' reformation meant the end of Quaker hegemony in Pennsylvania.

Domesticity remained at the heart of the Quaker religion for surviving Friends. The Quakers were interested in forming special families to produce and perpetuate sacred lives, not to merchandise an alternative form of social organization for priest-ridden Europe or for the United States. Nonetheless, this early history might explain why it was the relatively inexperienced New England reformers who most vociferously promoted domesticity in the nineteenth century as a partly secularized ideology of American expansionism. Many Quakers supported the reformers and even provided experienced leadership with the thornier problems of a society of domesticity (women's rights, lunacy asylums, slavery). But Quakers tended to withhold unqualified praise and enthusiasm. Aside from being ambivalent about the secularization, sentimentalization, and mass production of their sacred family form, Quakers were ambivalent about domesticity itself. They alone had painfully experienced domesticity's moral and economic ambiguities.

NINETEENTH-CENTURY New England reformers also ignored the lessons hidden in the Quakers' reformation. After French politics quelled French enthusiasm for Quaker Pennsylvania, New Englanders perpetuated the image established by French philosophes. The English reformer Thomas Clarkson and a host of nineteenth-century New England intellectuals and family reformers continued to recommend the Quaker family model to encourage themselves and their audience that domestically engendered virtue, wealth, and republican American society were naturally compatible.

Although they have been correctly identified as original thinkers by historians, nineteenth-century family reformers and advocates of domesticity were themselves aware and often advertised that they were building upon a positive tradition of domesticity in American life. Largely because they so admired Quaker families and their methods of early education, major nineteenth-century New England intellectuals wrote the Quakers into the mainstream of American history and literature with resounding phrases. Evoking the earliest days of Puritan and Quaker hatred in the 1650s, Nathaniel Hawthorne's historical tale "The Gentle Boy" told how the life and death of a tender Quaker child informed seventeenth-century New Englanders' understanding of children and charity. Hawthorne did criticize early Quakers and Puritans for idolizing their peculiar convictions at the expense of human charity, but he was also careful to praise later communitarian Friends.[24] With less qualification, Ralph Waldo Emerson thought the Quakers forerunners of his religious reliance upon individual spiritual intuition. He packed his sermon against the Lord's Supper, marking his resignation from the Unitarian pulpit, with paraphrased sections of Clarkson's *A Portraiture of Quakerism.* He saw nineteenth-century institutional reform, including family reform, building upon Quaker inspiration. Writing of George Fox, Emerson noted that "one cannot look at the course of the great charities and best institutions of our age without following back their swollen stream until it begins in the little rill of this individual life at Drayton-in-the-Clay in Leicestershire."[25]

Quaker domesticity was essential to the development of democracy in the United States, proclaimed the great New England historian George Bancroft. The Quakers' rise in provincial seventeenth-century England, "one of the memorable events in the history of man," marked "the moment when intellectual freedom was claimed unconditionally by the people as an inalienable birthright."[26] The Quakers' philosophy of human relations, claimed Bancroft, laid the foundation for the popularization of the conscience and thereby of democracy itself. In his *History of the United States from the Discovery of the American Continent,* the standard and most widely read work of American history in the nineteenth century, Bancroft argued dubiously that the Quaker thought of William Penn was more important to the development of American republicanism than the philosophy of John Locke. "To Locke," noted Bancroft, "'conscience is nothing else than our opinion of our own actions'; to Penn, it is the image of God, and his oracle in the Soul. Locke, who was never a father, esteemed 'the duty of parents to preserve their children, not to be understood without reward and punishment'; Penn loved his children with not a thought for the consequences. Locke, who was never married, declares marriage an affair of the senses; Penn reverenced woman as the object of fervent, inward affection, made, not for lust, but for love."[27] Emerson relished this unabashed conflation of domesticity and republicanism. "The huge world has at last come round to George Fox and William Penn," he wrote in his notebooks, "time-honoured John Locke received kicks."[28]

The most appreciative New Englanders were nineteenth-century family reformers, advocates of domesticity. An early publicist of the feminized, domestic household as the prime and nearly exclusive source of republican virtue, Lydia Maria Child wrote she was much like a family she described, "a little Swedenborgian, but more Quaker, and swinging loose from any regular society."[29] Resettling in New York City in 1841 to edit the *National Anti-Slavery Standard*, she lived in the household of Isaac T. Hopper, a Quaker abolitionist and philanthropist, whose biography she published in 1853. In her popular *Letters from New York* she praised Quaker prisons, alms houses, and orphanages as models of proper reform strategy, and noted, "since the dawn of Christianity, no class of people have furnished an example so replete with a most wise tenderness, as the Society of Friends, in the days of its purity."[30]

It is important that many heroines of nineteenth-century New England fiction gained independence, abandoned their father's Calvinist authority and beliefs, and established more feminized, morally self-sufficient households by marrying Quaker men.[31] The ideology of domesticity was conveyed most effectively in nineteenth-century sentimental fiction. In the most popular description of American domesticity ever written, Louisa May Alcott's *Little Women*, the March girls did not wed Quakers. But "The First Wedding" in *Little Women* was almost a Quaker affair. "'I don't want to look strange or fixed up today,'" the bride said, "'I don't want a fashionable wedding, but only those about me whom I love, and to them I wish to look and be my familial self.'" Although a minister was present, he was only Meg's tongue-tied father, whose "fatherly voice broke down more than once, which only seemed to make the service more beautiful and solemn." The Marches forgot ceremony and formal service, "there was no bridal procession, but a sudden silence fell upon the room as Mr. March and the young pair took their places under the green arch." Representatives of old Puritanism and modern capitalism respectively, Aunt March and Mrs. Moffat, were scandalized and then charmed by the foreign scene. Meg appeared after the wedding, "looking like a pretty Quakeress in her dove-colored suit and straw bonnet tied with white."[32]

Mrs. March had prepared the March girls well for appearing in Quaker dress on their wedding days. She exclusively and tenderly coaxed, loved, and disciplined her daughters from their natural sins into pure Christian womanhood. Their father, a Protestant minister, was absent in the first half of the novel. He returned home during the second half of the book, but fell ill and silent. And during his real and psychological absences the pious March women never bothered to attend church. The March household needed no external institutional supports.

Little Women tells more about New England than about Delaware Valley culture. Alcott's domestic ideal involved her own family's history, nonetheless. In his youth Bronson Alcott traveled south to peddle shoes and found some Quakers in his territory. He spent two months selling shoes to, and learning from, North Carolina Quakers (the North Carolina Quaker communities were composed largely of the twice-migrant descendants of northwestern British Quakers). They and the books they gave him convinced Bronson Alcott that God's Truth dwelled within individuals, including young children. Alcott opened schools so informed in Connecticut. His ideas about the innate goodness of children appalled local Congregationalists. His schools failed. Two wealthy Philadelphia Quaker merchants, Robert Vaux and Reubin Hines, found Alcott a job at Germantown Academy, near Philadelphia. Louisa May Alcott was born in Germantown, Pennsylvania, on November 29, 1832.[33]

Louisa May Alcott paid homage explicitly to the tradition of Quaker domesticity in her novel *Work*, and her heroine then married a Quaker. An orphaned Massachusetts farm girl, Christie Devon, faced life and work as a domestic servant, an actress, a governess, a nurse-companion, and a seamstress—the restricted labor markets available to poor New England women. She became distraught. A group of Boston reformers wisely sent her to the rural household of a Quaker widow, Mrs. Sterling, and her farmer-florist son David. Mrs. Sterling's "look, the tone, the gentle 'thee,' went straight to Christie's heart; and [she] said to herself: 'Surely, I have fallen among a set of angels'."[34] The Sterlings' quaint home restored her faith in life and work: "As she lay in her narrow white bed, with the 'pale light of stars' filling the quiet, cell-like room, she felt as if she had left the troublous world behind her, and shutting out want, solitude, and despair, had come into some safe, secluded spot full of flowers and sunshine, kind hearts, and charitable deeds."[35] When asked by her minister-mentor Mr. Powers, how the simple life at the Sterlings contented her; "'I feel as if I had been born again; as if this was a new heaven and a new earth, and everything was as it should be,' answered Christie, with a perfect satisfaction in her face."[36] Christie married David Sterling, and she appeared at her wedding, predictably, "looking very like a Quaker bride in her gray gown with no ornament but delicate frills at neck and wrist, and the roses in her bosom."[37] Just as Catholic women adopt a new habit upon entering the highest religious vocation available to them, so American women, Alcott implied, should replicate the dress of the Quaker upon entering their vocations as women of American domesticity.

THE NORTHWESTERN British Quakers' story concerns the social and religious history of remote seventeenth-century British provinces, and the social and family life of a radical British religious group in a significant region of pre-industrial, early American society. Such a story can promise to increase understanding of the development of American family ideology, but should not be asked to replace or reduce the importance of later developments, particularly nine-teenth-century socio-economic change, or the campaigns of New England reformers. Study of Quaker farmers in Delaware Valley is chiefly the study of the origins of an influential form of domesticity in American life, not a study of why this particularly ideology was so successfully spread by New England reformers in the nineteenth century.

Yet, in the case of the American family, understanding its origins may be as significant as understanding the causes of its wider adoption. Producing and sustaining morally self-sufficient households in any age, much less in the late seventeenth century, was no easy or logical task. It demanded, for example, the thorough spiritualization of marriage, the granting of spiritual authority to women comparable with that of men, painful self-discipline in childrearing, and the creation of enormous amounts of wealth to give households the resources to accomplish such tasks.

Such a family system naturally provoked the ire of established and state authorities from England to New England who made Quakers targets of severe persecution from 1655 to 1689. Early Quakers vividly denied the moral authority of everything foreign to their spiritualized intimate relations—and early modern English and American social orders hardly relied on gentle intimacy. Even after toleration was granted, the horrible prospect of Quakerism

overrunning the British North American colonies motivated Thomas Bray in the 1690s to found the Society for the Propagation of
the Gospel. The reduction of Quakerism in North America was this
Society's first goal. And if creating domesticity was a notable and
difficult achievement, making the system practicable for a large
population was even more unlikely. Yet this was a major meaning
of the pluralism, prosperity, and rapid growth in Pennsylvania
between 1681 and 1760 under sustained Quaker rule.

Given the implausibility and social danger of assertions that
households and intimate relations could and should monopolize
the production of conscience and morality, it is little wonder that
domesticity was initially the creation, not of rational, elite social
engineers, or even of sophisticated, southeastern British theolo-
gians, but of radical, provincial, upland, religious zealots. The
Pennsylvania Quakers standardized and combined the goals and
tasks of thorough domesticity well before anyone else, including
most Puritans, who had attempted to spiritualize household relations more compromisingly. While nineteenth-century New England reformers and harrowing social change did cause the redis-
covery, adaptation, and nationwide spread of the ideology of
domesticity, the Pennsylvania Quakers originated and established
the institution of the morally self-sufficient household in American
society.

While the Frenchmen's and New England reformers' discovery
of radical Quaker domesticity was not without its misperceptions,
these reformers did understand that the origins of such a complex
and arduous system of human relations as domesticity required
appreciation of an unusual people. They failed to see the latent
flaws in domesticity, but these have really become quite apparent.
The most interesting irony in their discovery was that domesticity
originated in American culture less as an adjustment to modern
conditions—the conventional understanding—than as a series of
very radical solutions to the spiritual and moral problems of extreme provincialism both in Britain and in the New World.

PART ONE

The Birth of Quaker Domesticity

Northwestern England
1650–1700

Great things are done when Men & Mountains meet
This is not done by Jostling in the street
WILLIAM BLAKE

Geographical Origins of Rural First Purchasers, 1681-1685

SCOTLAND
2

Northumb.
4

Durham
2

Westm.
5

Yorkshire
13

Ireland, county unknown
← 9

WALES total 79

Lancs.
5

Holland
1 →

central Ireland
← 3

Flint
2

Cheshire
55

Derby
7

Germany
3 →

Caer.
1

Denbigh
6

Merion
26

Notts.
6

southern Ireland
← 9

Mont.
8

Salop
5

Staffs.
5

Cardigan
1

Radnor
14

Worcs.
6

Northants.
2

Suffolk
1

Heref.
2

Pemb.
8

Carmarthen
2

Glos.
2

Oxf.
18

Bucks.
17

Herts.
7

Essex
2

Glam.
4

Berks.
13

Mx.
20

Wales, county unknown
7

Wilts.
53

Surrey
11

Kent
10

Somerset
21

Hants.
7

Sussex
25

Cornwall
3

ENGLISH CHANNEL

0   20   40   60   80   100
Miles

CHAPTER ONE

Middling Roots

In order to understand the social development of early Pennsylvania and the development of the American ideal of domesticity it is helpful to examine the distinctive nature of middling life in seventeenth-century northwestern Britain, where Quaker organization was developed, primarily by George Fox and Margaret Fell, and from where a significant number of the early Pennsylvania settlers came. Historians, using evidence primarily from southeastern England and New England, have developed persuasive generalizations about seventeenth-century British middling families. These are misleading, however, in reference to northwestern society, Quakerism, and Pennsylvania. Historians have shown that a middling society emphasizing household autonomy developed in southeastern England by the early seventeenth century. Some have argued that domesticity originated as a modification of this household tradition.[1] Northwestern Quakers accepted middling northwesterners' emphasis on human relations, for neither Quakers nor typical northwesterners could afford alternative institutions. On the other hand, northwestern Quakers developed their family ideal in bold opposition to the customs of their native region. These tensions help explain why the Quakers were the first to develop a form of domesticity as part of their religion and why Anglo-American domesticity originated in remote and rugged terrain.

The "middling" part of early modern British society included those working people who kept some independence by owning a small business or by securely occupying a piece of land. This excluded the gentry and aristocracy, who failed to work, and laborers, who failed to have independence. It did include the great majority of late seventeenth-century northwestern Quakers, for they were chiefly rural artisans and tenant farmers on secure leases. Barry Reay has thoroughly examined the social positions of early Cheshire Quakers between 1657 and 1684. He found that 3 percent were gentry, 15 percent retailers, 8 percent artisans, 4.5 percent laborers, and 60 percent yeomen and husbandmen. He found that the average Quaker household contained 1.6 hearths, while the average, non-Quaker household contained one hearth.[2] The overwhelming majority of Merionethshire and Montgomeryshire Quakers also lived in one-hearth houses and cottages. Tithe seizures of 49 southern Welsh Quakers between 1662 and 1681 suggest that their average holding in livestock and crops was £18.[3]

The Quakers lived in the most remote and rural parts of northwestern England. Among the 266 Cheshire households recorded in the Quaker register between 1660 and 1686, most, 81 percent, lived in sprawling rural townships, particularly in the northern part of the east Cheshire plain, where the two neighboring Quaker strongholds of Pownall Fee and Mobberley, both with 21 Quaker households, lay. Only 29 (11 percent) lived in the five largest Cheshire towns, and only 30 (19 percent) lived in Cheshire's fourteen market towns.[4] The Welsh counties of Radnorshire, Merionethshire, and Montgomeryshire were totally rural, having market towns, but no cities. In 1670 the largest city in Merionethshire was Dolgellau, containing only 144 households and 720 people.[5]

The northwestern Quakers on the eve of Pennsylvania colonization appear exactly the kind of middling people so often featured in the literature of early American history. Such middling people, it has been argued, carried "middling" habits of thought to early America. Particularly as they were incorporated in "middling" families, their values, almost irrespective of any specific religious faith, were responsible for the relatively rapid and orderly development of British North America. Thus the "middling" connotations of the northwestern Quakers' social titles suggest that there was nothing remarkable about the rapid social development of the Delaware Valley, Pennsylvania, and that Quakerism itself played a secondary and supportive role to the settlers' middling *mentalité*.

It is also assumed, based on study of southeastern British middling households, that the seventeenth-century middling family was an independent unit grounded on economic necessity. This family was above all "a 'business'—an absolutely central agency of economic production and exchange"—as John Demos has written. "Each household was more or less self-sufficient; and its various members were inextricably united in the work of providing for their fundamental material wants."[6] Streamlined for production and consumption, the household was usually nuclear, composed of a husband, wife, and children—with perhaps a servant or two. Its economic centerpiece was land. The "middling" household ensured its autonomy by passing on its land or lease to one male child, while other children, in return for childhood work and obedience, received comparable money and goods to reach an equal, sex-appropriate level of independence and dignity. Most historians have agreed that continuity and autonomy, not merely the maximizing of profit, was the aim of the family's economics; so households were proto-bourgeois—"middling," not "middle class." In order to thrive, however, such households required self-denying, laborious parents and children. Appreciating such hard work in the pursuit of autonomy, one historian described American settlers as, "England's middling people—the most valuable cargo that any captain carried on his westbound voyage."[7]

In reality, northwestern middling society was economically impoverished, and most northwestern middling people did not display the kind of "middling" values emphasizing household autonomy so appreciated by historians. The appreciated "middling" values were created in northwestern society by religious fanatics like the Quakers, and they were so unworkable in the context of northwestern society that most Quakers had to leave. Thus the *mentalité* of seventeenth-century northwestern middling families, far from reducing the importance of religious beliefs and ideology, highlights the Quakers' zeal and the social impact of Quakerism.

SOUTHERN Puritans judged northwestern middling people as typical denizens of one of the "dark corners" of British society, areas where poor, superstitious people spent sinful lives. Northwestern Quakers, most of them formerly recent Puritan converts, partly accepted this jaundiced view of their own society. Contemporary southern British commentators with secular, not spiritual, emphases also harshly described northwestern yeomen, husbandmen, and artisans. The less subjective historical record of local economic and demographic evidence supports these critics' perceptions of the economic realities, though often refutes their harsher cultural and ethical criticisms.

Certainly contemporary southern Englishmen recognized, and even exaggerated, the peculiarities of life in northwestern Britain. Southerners often boasted that middling northwesterners, especially the Welsh, were much poorer than themselves. While touring England in 1705 in search of evidence of England's emergence as an economic power, Daniel Defoe, a Londoner from birth, groaned at the sight of Welsh mountains, scrawny black cattle, meanly dressed farmers, and minute towns. He described north Wales as "a country looking so full of horror, that we ought to have given over the enterprise and have left Wales out of our circuit."[8] E.B.'s *A Trip to North Wales* (London, 1701) was a typically nasty satire. He thought describing Wales was a worthy artistic test, "because a Titian, a *Michael Angeleo*, and a Van Dike equally display their art in portraying a loathsome dunghill, as in describing a magnificent palace." He described Welsh farmers living in one-room hovels packed with people and animals, "and who can say which are the greater brutes." He scoffed at Welshmen's social pretensions. In Wales, chortled E.B., "should a man have a chimney on top of his thatch'd mansion, he should stand in danger of being picked for high sheriff."[9] A Welsh youth was depicted in another chapbook piece as believing he had been "preferred" when he married a rich sow.[10] Southerners laughed at northwesterners' love of their poor region. Defoe was amused that Welsh gentlemen were so confused as to "believe their country to be the pleasantest and most agreeable in the world." In an effort at humor, E.B. concocted a vainglorious Welsh gent pointing to a ramshackle house "that the sun shown through in about five and forty places: 'Got knows (says my old gentleman) our family has flourished here these eleven hundred years.'"[11]

Southern Englishmen were bad ethnographers. But even Defoe and E.B. rightly understood that northwest England was not the arable, commercialized, competitive society of seventeenth-century southeastern England, the seedbed of English and American Puritanism. Southeastern yeomen and husbandmen usually farmed large farms, grew crops which they marketed nearby, heavily capitalized their farms, and kept a large labor force of out-living farm laborers. Symptomatically, laborers' households were common. In Clayworth, Devon, 32 percent of the householders in 1688 were laborers. In Terling, Essex, 56 percent of the householders in the late seventeenth century were laborers.[12] Symptomatically, few northwestern householders were identified as laborers. An inspection of 348 inventories between 1660 and 1681 in Cheshire, Radnorshire, Brecknockshire, and Merionethshire uncovered only five men who called themselves, or were called by the assessors, "laborer." Myddle, in Shropshire contained, throughout the seventeenth century, only three or four laborers' households, some 4 percent of the total.[13] Livestock required only a few laborers, preferably live-ins, to handle the animals' needs and emergencies. In any case, farmers of relatively unprofitable northwestern land could not pay many laborers. Though they had titles of well-earned dignity, northwest middling people—yeomen, husbandmen, and artisans—were generally poor and powerless.

Cold, wet winds buffeted a rocky land in Merionethshire, Montgomeryshire, and Radnorshire—the Welsh counties from which most of the Welsh Tract Pennsylvania settlers came. More than 58 percent of the land was well over 500 feet above sea level. Welsh middling farmers could not grow wheat. They ate toasted oatbread topped with cheese. They raised cattle, sheep, and goats, and exported black cattle and Welsh cottons (a cheap, coarse woolen cloth) to southern England for small profit. The Cheshire plain, just east of the northern Welsh mountains, broke comparatively flat, well-watered, and pleasant. However, glacial deposits of clay, ill-timed rainfalls, and a cool climate made wheat farming treacherous. Most seventeenth-century Cheshire farmers kept the land in grass, raised cows and cattle, and exported Cheshire cheese to southern England for better profits than the Welsh enjoyed. Most farmers in Wales and Cheshire lived on farmsteads on patches of arable land, organized into sprawling townships and enormous parishes. While southeastern parishes had one or two towns, Cheshire's usually had six or seven, and the County had the second and third largest parishes in all of England: Great Budsworth with 35 townships and Prestbury with 32 townships.[14]

Southern critics also described the tiny holdings of most middling Welsh farmers with rough accuracy. In a sample of 323 probate inventories from Cheshire, Merionethshire, and Radnorshire (1660–91), only the yeomen from Cheshire had personal estates comparable to those of yeomen in some southern English counties.

Margaret Spufford found that the inventories of 58 yeomen in Cambridgeshire, a county in the Midlands, had a medium personal estate in 1660 of £180 and ranged from £2 to £1132.[15] Fourteen yeomen in Cheshire in 1660 had a median personal estate of £150 and ranged from £65 to £595. In Cheshire, husbandmen were poorer than yeomen: a median of £70 compared with £171. Middling Welsh society was barely economically articulated by title: both titular Radnorshire and Merionethshire yeomen and husbandmen had similarly meager personal estates. The titular yeomen of Radnorshire and Merionethshire had median personal estates of £37 and £27 respectively, little more substance than many laborers' households in Cambridgeshire (see Appendix: Table 1).

No economic collapse in the late seventeenth century is needed to explain many northwestern middling families' tiny holdings. They had always been poor. A detailed analysis of the lay subsidy rolls of 1524 and 1585 has shown that the northwestern counties, when they were not exempted for poverty or border defense, returned only one to 9 shillings an acre, compared with 50 shillings an acre for such southeastern counties as Kent, Essex, and Sussex.[16] Such deficits in productivity continued almost unchanged into the middle of the seventeenth century. According to a correlation of the Ship Money evaluations of 1636 with acreage in each county, Cheshire earned an evaluation of one pound for every 400 acres, the north Welsh counties earned an evaluation of one pound for every 451.8 acres, and the southeastern counties of East Anglia earned much higher evaluations: one pound for every 52 to 200 acres.[17] By the late seventeenth century, economic trends were generally helping the northwesterners. Population growth in north Wales certainly caused middling households severe problems in relation to child support and promotion, but lower prices for arable crops after 1660 (though a worry to southern farmers) benefited northwest livestock farmers by lowering feed and food costs. The harvests were better than average by the time of the heaviest Quaker migrations to Pennsylvania. According to W. G. Hoskins, there were seven good harvests from 1665 to 1672, only four good harvests in the 1670s, and a string of good harvests between 1680 and 1685, the major years of emigration.[18] Whether the economy improved or slumped, however, the idea of establishing a "little commonwealth" society in the northwest remained a dream for most middling people.

The region supported many tenant farmers: the gentry had ample marginal land to let. In contrast to developments in southeastern England, northwest smallholders were not replaced by commercially enterprising farmers, but grew more numerous during the seventeenth century. There were only eleven farms in Cheshire, as late as 1851, with over 500 acres, and one-half of the 6,663 farmholdings employed no labor. In order to lure northwest tenants to use marginally profitable land, northwest landlords also offered relatively attractive leases. According to the above sample of 323 wills and probate inventories, only 24 percent of the middling farmers and artisans in Cheshire, 24 percent in Radnorshire, and 13 percent in Merionethshire held their land in fee simple. In Cheshire, however, most of the tenants held generous lifeholds or leases of 99 years determinable upon three lives (52 percent of the above sample). This form of land tenure remained common in western England until the middle of the eighteenth century, whereas it was largely replaced in wealthy, fielden, southeastern England by the middle of the seventeenth century by the rack-rent or lease on years. Despite high initial fines, these lifeholds gave tenant households more freedom than leases on years. Upon taking a farm on a 99-year lease determinable upon lives, a farmer gave the landlord three names (usually himself, wife, and eldest son) and a large fine, usually ten years profit of the farm, and paid thereafter only a small rent annually. At the death of any named leasee, the head leasee renewed the lease by paying a smaller fine and inserting a new name in the lifehold. A tenant household essentially worked for the landlord for ten years and for itself thereafter, pending the death of any named leasee, a better deal than constantly paying all profit after the expenses of subsistence.[19]

Landlords' tenants in the Welsh mountains were too poor to be granted such quasi-independence. On the Harwarden estate in Flintshire, on the border of Cheshire, three-lives-leases were common between 1630 and 1680 (40 of 47 leases issued), but the fines were low or absent and the annual rents high. Welsh mountain farming could not support large fines, so landlords often used a tenant-dependent type of lifehold. For example, on May 10, 1641, Thomas Ravencroft, Esq., leased a farm in Hope Parish, Flintshire, to Thomas Discus for three lives on a yearly rent of £5, two days' reaping, two hens at Christmas, a heriot of the best goods, and the customary renders and services. There was no fine, but a high annual rent. In a small sample of deeds from Montgomeryshire and Merionethshire between 1600 and 1680, only 19 of 59 deeds were for lives, most were for 21 years. Similarly, on the Crosswood estate between 1600 and 1680 in Cardiganshire in south-central Wales, only one of 52 leases were for lives. These tenants were tightly bound to their landlords by high annual rents and labor services. In 1677, Edward Vaughan of Trowscoed, Cardigan, Esq., rented a tenement to Felix Rees for twenty years at an annual rent of £7 10s, two hens, six chickens, a fat hog, two days' reaping, two days' carrying corn, two days' carrying turf, and responsibility to grind his corn at Vaughan's mill.[20]

The few benefits that scarcity provided the most fortunate tenants conspired to weaken northwest middling households as autonomous units. Sons not named in the lifehold could not hope that their parents could purchase a second lifehold. The initial fines were too expensive. They had to look elsewhere for a livelihood. If daughters hoped to marry a lifehold man, they similarly required large portions, for a lifeholder usually expected to capitalize his farm from his wife's portion. Northwesterners often had to violate the independence of their household units in order to help their younger children survive.

Middling northwest households' independence was especially sapped by the lack of positions for younger children in the northwest's poor economy. Even the commonest trades of southeastern English villages were often absent in Wales. "I need not describe Llanberis parish (Merionethshire) unto you," wrote a Welsh traveler in 1690, "in which neither miller, nor fuller, and any other tradesman but one tailor lives."[21] Cheshire's economy was only slightly more diverse. The hides of milk cows and cattle, supplemented by water and oak bark, supplied significant leather-working in northern and central Cheshire. Chester also had a small shipbuilding and linen industry, Nantwich a salt-making works, and Macclesfield a button-making industry.[22] The city of Chester looked impressive, "the largest city in all this side of England that is so remote from London," as Defoe described it, a walled, a cathedral town, with a population of some 7,500 people.[23] Chester flourished, not as an industrial powerhouse, but as an oasis of sophisticated services for the region, being the center of county government, regional courts, the county market, the local gentry's social life, and the ecclesiastical establishment. According to the 1664 hearth tax returns, only the gentry and ecclesiastics owned lavish houses—the bishop's palace had 17 hearths, Lady Calveley had 16 hearths, Lady Kilmorey had 16 hearths, and Sir Geoffrey Shakeley had 12 hearths, whereas the largest houses of Chester's leather masters and merchants had 7 hearths.[24] The few promising local opportunities available to middling children were expensive. William Stout's yeoman family paid £30 in 1678 just to apprentice him to a Lancaster ironmonger for seven years. They collected £129 more in 1687 to stock his first shop.[25] Such costs were beyond the reach of most northwestern middling households.

Most used their lease-land to survive and to help all their children, not to erect emotionally and economically stocked familial fortresses against society. Most northwest households were only temporary residences for children. And by themselves they gave little economic support to children after childhood. In this total region, the dairy-farmed Cheshire plain promised most to support a large number of autonomous "middling" households. Yet the demographic returns of 47 rural Cheshire households belie such a hope. These 47 households, formed by marriages between 1656 and 1681, were in seven different parishes, the majority rural. In order to gain complete data for analysis, a biasing criterion for selection was that either the husband's or wife's death, or a note of remarriage, be recorded in the parish register.[26] Such selection means that these people, remaining so long in one parish, were probably more stable and prosperous than the average. But even such statistically privileged Cheshire middling households failed to control the social place of their children autonomously.

Perhaps because of the bias of the sample, each of the 47 marriages lasted an average of 22 years. In every other way, however, these households appear weaker than possible "little commonwealths." They were less fertile, less healthy, and therefore smaller than similar southeastern English families in Terling, Essex.[27] The Cheshire parents saw most of their offspring drift away from home permanently. Among the 110 surviving children, 59 (54 percent) neither died nor married in their parents' parishes. They probably left home and the parish between the ages of eight and sixteen years for service. The children who did continue to live in their home parishes rarely gained independence or an opportunity to rear a household of their own children. Among the women who stayed or returned, nine or 41 percent never married, dying at an average age of 46 years. Among the men who stayed or returned, ten or 34 percent never married, dying at an average age of 53 years (only about 15 percent of the adult population as a whole remained single in England). The few children who remained and married in their home parishes married late. The Cheshire women married at an average age of 26 years, and the men at an average age of 32 years. In comparison with their Terling counterparts, the Cheshire women were one year and a half older at first marriage; the Cheshire men eight years older.

The situation was worse in mountainous north-central Wales where parents had a pitiful supply of resources for their children. The most revealing demographic source for late seventeenth-century Wales are the St. Asaph notitiae, which described households in most parishes in Montgomeryshire. Worried about his diocese's children in 1681 (the same year that many Montgomeryshire Quakers prepared to leave for Pennsylvania), William Lloyd, Bishop of St. Asaph, asked the ministers in his bishopric to provide him with the names of the heads of households in each parish, the number of people in each household, and the number and ages of all people, including servants, who were under eighteen years of age. The ministers completed their notititia between 1681 and 1687. A sample of sixteen of the 108 parishes included 1979 households, 5889 adults, and 3048 children.[28]

The percentage of the population under eighteen years of age in Montgomeryshire was much lower than in any other reported area of Great Britain. The seventeenth-century demographer Gregory King estimated that in the 1680s over 45 percent of the British population was eighteen years old or younger, that this age group composed 33 percent of London's population, 40 percent of other urban places, and 47 percent of the agricultural villages. King's estimates were probably close to accurate, as Peter Laslett's relatively recent analysis of lists in Lichfield and Stoke-on-Trent, Staffordshire (1695, 1701), show. In Lichfield, 47.5 percent of the population was nineteen years or younger, and in Stoke-on-Trent, 48.5 percent of the population was eighteen years or younger.[29] In the 16 Montgomeryshire parishes, however, only 34 percent of the population was under eighteen years. For example, the most populous parish, Guildsfield, contained 409 households with 1905 people, but only 627 or 33 percent were children; and the least populous parish, Hirnant, contained 26 households with 86 people, but only 21 or 24.4 percent were people under eighteen years of age.[30]

Economic backwardness was not the only reason, of course, for a local population to have such an unusual age distribution. King thought seventeenth-century London had a low proportion of children, in fact, just because London was a boom town. The great city was a disease pool, where deaths consistently outnumbered births each year. Yet some 6000 young adults, usually childless, (including many from northwestern Britain) flocked annually to London in search of adventure and wealth. People in Montgomeryshire were healthier than Londoners. Despite little, if any, immigration, Montgomeryshire's population rose from 18,972 in 1563 to 34,097 in 1670.[31] In a typical parish, Meifod (the home of the Quaker Lloyds of banking and Pennsylvania fame), 482 baptisms were registered between 1667 and 1680 against 443 burials, and not all who died were children. In 1693, an especially sickly year, 40 babies were baptized and 46 people were buried: 21 adults and 25 children.[32] Meifod parish gained 14 children even in this deadly year. However, a paltry 33.5 percent of the population in Meifod's notitiae were under eighteen years, and over 27 percent of its households had neither servants nor children under eighteen years of age. Meifod would have had a typical English rural age distribution, if children had remained in the parish.

In order to stay in a county without large cities or industry, children required places locally within the households of wealthier yeomen and gentry. But there were few wealthy yeomen, and the Montgomeryshire gentry, whatever their effort, could supply remarkably few positions. Lacking local economic alternatives, young servants grew old in gentry service and became old retainers, preventing local children from gaining places which were common sources of childhood employment and patronage in other parts of England. The 36 titled households in these 16 parishes were larger than average, 9.92 people compared with 4.5 people. Yet, only 24 percent of the people living in these big houses were under eighteen years of age. Children composed a higher percentage of people in the average middling Montgomeryshire household. Six gentry households, averaging 5.8 people, had no children whatsoever. Many of the largest servant staffs included few children. Mathew Morgan, Esq., kept nineteen hungry people in his thirteen-hearth seat in Aberhafesp, but just one person was under eighteen years of age.

Thanks to leaders like Bishop Lloyd, the Anglican Church began in the late seventeenth century to recognize the Welsh children's unemployment and under-employment as serious social problems. Under the auspices of the Society for the Propagation of the Gospel (SPG), it began to establish charity schools in the Welsh mountains. "The town of Dolgelley is the chief town in Merionethshire in the centre of the county," wrote George Lewis to the SPG's secretary in the early eighteenth century, "and hath in it many poor boys and girls, who for want of some charitable provision are forced to stroll and beg their living."[33] Dr. Joseph Jones, Dean of Bangor, also regretted that many children in his parish "must go forever and anon to beg for victuals: their being no poor rate settled in these parts, it is the constant method to relieve the poor at their doors, and the houses of several parishes being scattered about at a considerable distance from each other increases the difficulty poor children labor under."[34] Without many crafts locally, labor intensive arable farming, or many positions available in their own households, the gentry failed to support any system of parish apprenticeships. So the young beggars were not simply orphans and "bastards," but were also sons and daughters of respectable mountain yeomen and husbandmen. Telling of the problems of the new charity school in 1701, the Reverend Humphry Jones of Glassbury, Brecknockshire, noted that many parents "would be glad to have their children taught but they are not able to find them victuals or clothes, except they stay home and so do some work, or go out to beg."[35] Childhood begging was an unattractive solution to northwestern scarcity, but many farmers apparently avoided this solution by sending their children out of Wales.

Many northwestern men called themselves "husbandmen," "tradesmen," and even "yeomen," who rented acres of mountainside for their small herd of cows, cattle, and sheep. Their similarly situated neighbors would so honor them. But such men had much less wealth than "middling" people in southeastern England. As the Welsh historian David W. Howell noted, most Welsh farmers, "when compared with the substantial tenants of the large farms of the southeast and southern midlands of England . . . belonged to the laboring class."[36] Of course, Welsh and Cheshire farmers were not wage-earners and had little, if any, class consciousness. This assertion is helpful, however, for northwestern farmers and farmer-artisans lived a subsistence existence and most were unable to provide economic independence for themselves or their children. Their efforts therefore supported the wealth and power of the provincial gentry, or a larger kin group, rather than the autonomy of their own households.

MANY MIDDLING northwestern lineages, nevertheless, did survive without the means to form "little commonwealths" or compensatory formal institutions. Lacking alternatives, many northwest-

erners relied upon the family. They tended to emphasize familialism, as would the northwestern Quakers. In order to provide family
continuity and personal dignity in the face of scarcity and individual household poverty, however, many middling northwestern
households had learned to pool their meager resources among a
number of different people and households. These alliances did not
merely highlight the economic deficits of northwestern middling
households; they provided the sinews of northwestern society.
Northwestern Quakerism would develop as a radical, charismatic
version of northwestern farmers' traditional reliance on informal
human relations.

Many northwestern farmers preferred an "extended" commonwealth" to the "little commonwealth" of southeastern English and
New English fame. An impressive number of very poor middling
northwesterners left wills for just this reason. In a sample of 422
people between 1660 and 1688 in Cheshire, Radnorshire, and Merionethshire, 43 percent of those with personal estates under £100 left
wills; and in the counties supplying most early Pennsylvania emigrants—Merionethshire, Cheshire—53 percent of such people,
against those who died intestate, left a will. In Wales, will-writing
was inspired partly by English law. Welsh people were forced legally to translate their wills into English or Latin. Poor Welsh
people accepted this insult in order to avoid a worse indignity:
English intestate law which confined intestate distribution of
wealth to the nuclear family and thereby violated the way northwest
people had learned to preserve their own families and dignity.

Only the wealthiest households lived well without significant
sharing with extra-household kin and neighbors. Robert Lord Viscount Cholmoldely, owner of a gigantic estate including a 58-
hearth home in southern Cheshire, gave little in his will to the
church, servants, tenants, or extra-household relatives. He simply
gave £300 to his wife annually, £6,000 to his second son, £8,000 to
his unmarried daughter, and his vast lands to his eldest son.[37] They
could live well without the help of kin.

The wealthiest gentry in north Wales also seldom shared with
extra-household kin. They did develop dense networks of local
household dependencies through their bequests. Their wills often
described much of a Welsh village's social structure from the top to
bottom. In Towyn, Merionethshire, William Vaughan, Esq., gave
£2 to the Bangor Cathedral and £2 to repair the local parish church.
He also wanted "my wife and son Jenkin, heir-at-law, to be good

and charitable to, and take care of, Catherine David, my nurse: Rees
Jones, my servant; Lewis William, Evan John Thomas, John Ellis,
my old servants and decayed tenants.'' Mr. Vaughan also ''forgot''
the debts of two tenants; gave one servant £2, another ten shillings,
his main servant ''the messuage where he dwelleth for natural life'';
his dear nurse Catherine David £2 annually; and a Towyn lunatic
woman maintenance for life.[38] Mr. Vaughan merged many of Towyn's middling households' economies with his own.

A quarter of the men and women in Cheshire who had estates
over £300 did give, however, over 10 percent of their wealth to extra-
household kin and neighbors.[39] Because these were all yeomen, it is
possible to speculate that they may well have retained some wisdom
from the interdependent household economics of poorer Cheshire
middling people, for northwest men and women living on the better
side of poverty, estates of £100 to £198, did often share their substance with extra-household kin (see Appendix: Table 2, for a statis-
tical summary of bequests). A butcher in Sandbach, Cheshire, with
a personal estate of £138, Thomas Boult, left a wife, a shop, and a
young son. Having nobody to run his business to keep his family,
he gave his oldest nephew and apprentice John Boult all the shop,
its tools, and a chamber in his household for seven years. Though
sharing the shop's profits with Boult's wife and child, this nephew
was designated the interim breadwinner, head-of-household. Thomas Boult fastened this relationship by giving more than £3 to his
brother, the boy's father.[40] Similarly, a dairying yeoman in Allostock, Joseph Whisham, left a wife, two young sons, and three
daughters. He made his eldest son the heir of the fee-simple farm
and gave his remaining children a total of £100. Whisham split the
farm evenly during their lives, however, between his wife and his
mother-in-law, Alice Meesham.[41] His mother-in-law was clearly
being repaid for earlier financial and labor services.

In Wales, many middling farmers proudly adopted kin's claims
to their household's substance. Such sharing showed a healthy
defiance of southern English impositions by reverberating ancient
Welsh tribal loyalties. Although he left a pregnant wife and a young
daughter, Morgan ap David, a Merionethshire yeoman, gave almost
one-third of his estate to his siblings and their children. He proclaimed that the estate must be divided ''one half to pay legacies and
funeral expenses, one fourth to children, and one fourth to the wife,
according to the ancient and ordinance custom of North Wales.''

True to his honor, David gave money, livestock, and weaving equipment worth over £26 (24 percent of this £107 estate) to his sister, two brothers, nephew, and two nieces. His immediate family, no matter how it grew, got only the skimmings. If his pregnant wife's child survived, he or she was directed to get "£10 from my daughter Elizabeth's share."[42] The extra-household kin's share was clearly inviolable.

By including and involving extra-household people in their household economies, many Welsh and Cheshire middling people left behind stronger supportive networks than their households could create individually. In 1681, Joseph Buckley, Houghton, left a wife, two young sons, and a young daughter to share a tiny £23 estate. Instead of concentrating his estate on his children and wife, Buckley shrewdly built a network of supporting kin and neighbors. He gave £3 to his kinsmen John Wilson and Edward Massey and provided an endowment yielding nearly £1 a year to his sister, and after her death, to his niece. These kin got more than half his estate.[43] In many cases, such extended family ties erased all sign of a primary commitment to the nuclear household. In the summer of 1678, the widower Phillip John Phillip, Landack, spread his small estate nearly equally among his child, nephews, and nieces. The nephews got between ten shillings and £1 apiece, and Phillip's legitimate son got only ten shillings. Phillip also made his nephew, not his son, the sole executor of his estate.[44] Indeed, in the context of the Northwest's economy, those smallholders who left estates under £50 and who exclusively divided their estates among wife and children were not fighting for household autonomy. They surrendered, giving their children a few shillings, a cow, and some sheep, so they could make a deal with landlords or employers, whose needs and kindness the children would soon consult for their livings.[45]

Showing powerful kin and neighborly loyalties, married but childless men gave more money and land to their nieces and nephews than to their wives. In almost 90 percent of 35 cases, the wife got one-half or less of the estate; an equal or larger share went to sisters, brothers, and chiefly to nieces and nephews.[46] A large number of single people also left wills and gave the largest share of their estates to children. Hoping to win help for their households' survivors, many poor middling people also pushed gifts and honors on their landlords.[47] In context of northwest middling poverty, such sharing of proportionately significant wealth among extra-household kin, neighbors, and landlords was neither an insult nor loss to children, but a strategy to protect them by prudently investing in helpful people.

IN ANGLO-AMERICAN culture, poverty has long been regarded as a mark of moral failure. And in the middle of the seventeenth century Puritans and the newly arisen Quakers, experimenting with a new, purified sense of self, became disillusioned with the northwesterners' system.[48] Were these critics correct in sulfurously denouncing middling northwestern society as ethically brutish? Luckily, the drama and moral implications of these sharings in the Northwest inspired a native yeoman, Richard Gough, to record with almost exhaustive detail a seventeenth-century northwestern community's family life and ethics, his well-known *History of Myddle* (1701). His intimate descriptions do confirm that seventeenth-century northwestern middling households struggled with scarcity by living inextricably tied with kin, neighbors, and landlords. They do suggest why Quakers needed to revise northwestern family life. They also show, however, that northwestern tenant farmers had built a strong tradition of emotional liveliness and human caring upon which the Quakers might base their new, holy family ethic.

Myddle lay some nine miles north of Shrewsbury in Shropshire, a county bordered by Montgomeryshire to the west and Cheshire to the north. Living on 12 freeholds and 45 tenant farms, dispersed on hilly, clay soil, Myddle farmers made their rent money from the sale of livestock.[49] Myddle tenant farmers were more often motivated by fear of shame and by desire for honor than by personal guilt. Whatever its precise sources, guilt appears historically to be the special product of the tender, intense relations of privatized nuclear households, or some emotionally intense equivalent, where effective internal voices could be intimately implanted in young children's minds. Having porous and often eclipsed households, northwest middling people trusted the pillory and gossip more than tender mothers or fathers. They trusted effective moral sanction to public humiliation and the memorable recording of a family's misdeeds and mortifications in the locality's oral history. "If any man shall blame me for that I have declared the viciouse lives or actions of their ancestors," wrote Gough, "let him take care to avoid such evil courses that he leave not a blemish when he is dead."[50]

Even the well-educated, puritanical Richard Gough entrusted social order less to Christ's ministers than to shame and honor.

Myddle parish church was divided into forty-seven pews, each in possession of the residents of a farm or group of farms. Sitting in a pew symbolized moral behavior acceptable to the Anglican Church authorities, but, more importantly, an honorable position within the community. A seat in church gave every Myddle farmer and his family a stage and audience every Sunday to display and validate their position and identity before the eyes of the people with whom they shared their lives and children. The seating arrangement had great significance. Gough arranged his history by pews, constantly emphasized their importance, and judged pew placement a sacred mystery.[51] When the Puritan minister Mr. Joshua Robinson rearranged the communion table and altar during the Cromwellian period, "there happened a difference between John Downton of Alderton and William Formeston about the right of kneeling in the sixteenth pew on the south side of the north aisle, and John Downton putt a locke on the pew dorre, but William came on the Lord's day following, and giving the pew dorre a suddain plucke, broke off the lock." Men and women's fights for their rightful pews were fights for their personal and familial dignity. Tension increased when more Cromwellian redecoration advanced some cottagers' pews toward the front, "a thing unseemly and undecent," in Gough's view. A solemn parish meeting was convened (the ecclesiastical courts were in Cromwellian suspension) in order to restore the perceived social order. The subsequent consensus on pew placements, carefully recorded, quieted the village.[52]

Though placed toward the back of the church, tenant farmers, particularly those who boasted generations of ancestors in the parish, held much honor. They lost this honor, however, if they suffered rituals of public humiliation. So while often ignoring private vices, tenant farmers always made an effort to prevent overt mortifications. Worried middling parents sent their juvenile delinquents far from the surrounding countryside, not to rehabilitate them spiritually or even to save their skins, but to remove their likely and shameful jailings and hangings from the sight and recording of neighbors. A Myddle tavern-keeper, Thomas Jukes, exiled a larcenous son by placing him into apprenticeship with a roving juggler who happened to pass through the village.[53] Michael Braine, of a long-standing Myddle family, came to Myddle following the death of his brother and brother's wife in order to preserve the family's leasehold and also to raise his brother's son William. William robbed meat from several neighbors' houses. The Braine clan took the only possible action: "at last he was sent away," noted Gough, "I know not whither."[54]

Such ethics were well justified. Only Myddle's local elite could run households akin to "little commonwealths." These 36 families, just 30 percent of those Gough described, occupied the 12 freeholds at one time or another; sat in the front pews; called their farm houses "halls"; and added "Mr. and Mrs." to their names. Sixteen of these families had two or more sons and thirteen of these practiced primogeniture. Even their wealthy, younger sons, lacking opportunity locally, often traveled far from Myddle for their livings. After being bankrolled by parents through schooling or expensive apprenticeships, many entered, with their parents' capital, lucrative trades or professions in Shrewsbury, Bristol, London, and lesser market towns. Among the sons of Mr. William Watkins, for example, Francis, the eldest, got the Shropshire land, and George, Richard, and Thomas became independent goldsmiths and distillers in London.[55]

The great majority of Myddle's seventeenth-century households were life-leaseholders living on small farms providing them with too little income to finance their sons and daughters from childhood to adult independence. They had heavy responsibilities. They saw 2.7 children per household reach adulthood, according to Gough's knowledge, 132 sons and 90 daughters (the Myddle elite had 3.52 children reach adulthood, by Gough's memory). Because they found that one lifehold absorbed all their capital, most tenant farmers practiced primogeniture. While many of their sons became life-leaseholders, many (at least 46 sons, or 35 percent) were put out as servants or apprentices. Unlike the expensively entered, heavily financed, and lucratively pursued trades and professions of the freeholders' sons, however, their trades of blacksmithing, tailoring, and shoemaking required little capital to enter or pursue; and failed to earn enough income to support economically autonomous households.

The careers and households of these children depended as much on the kindness of friends, landlords, and kin as on the mutual supports or ethics of "little commonwealths." Seven younger sons became career soldiers and sailors. Army life required the pursuit of personal and group honor, the practice of deadly violence, and the taking of orders, not the intelligent and individualized accumulation and conservation of family land and capital.[56] Ten sons also enjoyed life-long careers as gentlemen's servants— cooks, grooms, valets, and dog-trainers. Francis Jones, the younger son of a butcher, "went to be a servant at Stanwardine Hall when he was but young, he continued there a menial servant about thirty years." Gough did not denounce such a career, though he knew that such positions diminished loyalty to wife and children. Jones did get married, but "after he was married he belonged to the family whilst he was able to do service, but his wife lived at Marton."[57]

Eldest sons who inherited life-leaseholds did seek their own profits and partly raised and placed their own children. Yet, their desire to see their children survive demanded that they expand their household economies and sympathies outward. Lifeholders re- newed their leases only at their landlords' pleasure, and placed their children successfully only with landlord and kin help. Francis Jones, the father of the dutiful servant, was a leaseholder of Mr. Corbert of Stanwardine Hall, where his son Francis got his living. Such lifeholders also needed kin to help their children overcome crises or just the normal problems of scarcity. Richard Cleaton, a tenant, married Anne Tyler. The couple soon argued among them- selves and "Richard Cleaton . . . out run his wife, and his wife bigge with child." The abandoned child "was brought up by Allen Chal- loner (the smith) of Myddle," for his "wife was related to William Tyler."[58] Another tenant farmer, Bartholomew Mansel "married one Nightengale of Leaton," who died soon after delivering their second daughter—a more typical crisis. Mansel married again, but his daughters by the first marriage were reared "by their kinde Uncle, John Dod, and by him preferred in marriage."[59] Kin gave or found livings for middling children in happier times. William Lloyd, the younger son of a life-leaseholder, was an "apprentice with his Uncle Jewkes, who gave him his house, shop, and lands in Shrewsbury."[60] Even poor kin could offer the needed link to a landlord's patronage. Gough often described dense mazes of inter- locking middling- and upper-class kinship and patronage networks that helped to provide comfortable survival, if rarely independence, for many Myddle sons and daughters. Typical was the complicated connections supporting Bartholomew Pierce, son of a Myddle tenant farmer and tailor. Bartholomew Pierce served with Oliver Cromwell in France. "Soon after" he came back to Myddle, and "by the assistance of his cousin, Thomas Formeston, then servant to Roger Kinaston, of Hordeley, Esquire, he was preferred in service to

Mr. Mytton of Hallson, who had married the daughter of Mr. Kinaston."[61]

Because middling parents needed help for their younger children from powerful households, they accepted the eclipse of their own parental influence by gentry paternalists. For instance, Roger Mould, a Myddle tenant, placed his two sons at early ages in life-long personal service with Mr. Baker of Sweeney: Thomas Mould became Mr. Baker's cook, and John Mould became Mr. Baker's groom.[62] Servants were often matched, wed, and sponsored in such households by the gentry. Mary Mathes, daughter of a Myddle cobbler, "was somewhile a servant to Mr. Manwaring of Sleape Hall, and there married her fellow-servant, John Foden, a Cheshire man." With Mr. Manwaring's help and horizontal kin connections, they "came to live in Mr. Lyster's chief farm in Broughton, where they kept a good stock of cows and a good team of horses with which he carried goods to London."[63] Many tenants' children also grew to prefer the religious creeds of their powerful masters to those of their poor parents. In one of several cases of country house conversion, "Thomas Lovett, Jr., was entertained (when he was very young) in the service of Mr. Gower of Chilleton in Staffordshire, a Papist, and leaving the religion wherein he was born and baptized, he betooke himself to his beads."[64]

Nevertheless, Myddle's tenant farmers were people partly undirected by the dictates of honor during early childhood and courtship. When Richard Gough's gossip about courtship in seventeenth-century Myddle is systematized, it suggests that love-matches were common; that the children of poorer tenant farmers were more likely than the children of gentry to both initiate their own marriages and to rebel if necessary against parents or kin; and that they were less likely to be placed into marriages by parents and relatives. Among the 33 marriages of gentry and wealthy freeholders that Gough carefully described, 75 percent were arranged by parents, 25 percent were initiated by children, and none was accomplished by children in the face of parental opposition. However, among the 66 marriages of tenant farmers, craftsmen, and cottagers that Gough carefully described, 65 percent were initiated by children, and 11 percent were accomplished in the face of parental opposition.[65]

There were, to be sure, plausible economic and political reasons for these differing patterns. Compared with middling parents, gentry parents like Mr. Robert Corbet of Stanwardine Hall had more to gain politically and economically from using their children as pawns in the marriage market. Such wealthy children had far more property and honor to lose if they objected to such arrangements or sought mates considered objectionable. However, the tiny estates and leases of middling children were vitally important to them also. A simple cost-analysis of courtship may obscure important interior influences and differences. Having grown in more intimate environments (smaller households) and having experienced later separation from mothers, the children of tenant farmers were better prepared emotionally to be more active in seeking intimacy and sexual pleasure in married life as adults.[66]

Most middling children had been nursed by their own mothers (some of whom also nursed the children of the local gentry) and they had been young children in small households. They knew briefly the pleasures of intimate attention from parents and siblings. At least, many clearly sought the adult equivalent in marriage. Especially after a few beers at one of the many local taverns, Myddle's tenant farmers were emotionally warm and sociable. On the other hand, even among the children of tenant farmers, marriage involved the transfer of important resources. The husband's family, including non-household kin, frequently transferred land (often a life in a three-lives-lease), and the wife's family provided a large monetary portion to capitalize the land. Marriage was also a public event affecting the reputation of clans, and a political event confirming or rearranging clan power. Parents and kin therefore expected marrying children, particularly the eldest children, to consult them, to accept their vetoes, and to often follow their dictates. As a result of the potential misfit between emotional preference and ethical demands, the conflict between private love and clan loyalties and honor was routine in seventeenth-century middling mate selection and marriage (Quakers would later spiritualize, discipline, and formalize these conflicts; they did not introduce human love or parent-child conflict).

The middling clans of the village of Myddle often suffered, as Gough recognized, when they coercively denied for the purpose of clan honor the emotional preferences of their children in mate selection. In Gough's own yeoman family, Ann Baker "was a lovely, handsome woman, and was marryed (more to please her father than her selfe) to a neighboring gentleman of good, (but of decaying) estate." Ann Baker accepted loyally, but, after having a son, she left her husband and "went away with a captain, who promised to take her over into Ireland, but he left her at Chester." The Gough clan tried to avoid scandal: "my great grandfather being then old and dark sighted, sent my grandfather to Sweeney, to make up the breach, which was done by giving a second portion." The bribe was ambiguously successful: "she returned again to her husband, but dyed not long after. . . ."[67] Sinister consequences also flowed from Richard Hussey's decision to marry his household ward, Elinor Butter, to his son. Hussey wanted to capture Butter's £100 portion for his clan. Elinor Butter reluctantly accepted the marriage, but "soon became too familiar with William Tyler, her next neighbor." Hussey left her. The final result of this mercenary and ambiguously incestuous mating, as Gough highlighted, was William Tyler's unambiguous commission of incest with his own daughter by Elinor Butter.[68]

Many middling children were more assertive and rebellious. Many pursued their loves with considerable financial sacrifice against parental and kin opposition. Conflict over courtship was a tradition in some Myddle lineages. "Michael, the eldest son of Michael Braine, displeased his father by marrying Jane, a bastard of one who went abroad spinning for neighbors, and was called Black Nell." His parents' marriage was similarly framed: his father Michael Braine had "marryed Susan, the daughter of Roger Lloyd, of Myddle, which soe displeased her father, that although he had but onely child, he gave her nothing."[69] The counterclaims of love and honor often split parents. Arthur Plungin, son of a Myddle farmer, "displeased his father by marrying the widow of Thomas Tyler of Balderton, who had many small children, so that he gave them little or nothing; but his mother was kind to him."[70] Romeo and Juliet were occasionally evoked, Myddle-style. When James Wicherly fell in love with his next neighbor, his father tried to stop the courtship. Unfortunately, when "this young James was endeavoring to come to his mistress, and passing through some out buildings that he might not be seene, he got a fall and broke his thigh and died."[71]

Though being routinely and often happily subverted by middling love, Myddle's regime of honor and shame was occasionally and less attractively tarnished by clan bullying, as the story of the Tyler clan shows. Richard Gough rightly believed William Tyler "of the most debauched morals of any in this parish." Tyler had fornicated with the estranged wife of Richard Hussey. He had a child by her. Tyler took this child, Nell Hussey, as his house-maid and he committed incest with her, producing a second "bastard".

Tyler also stole sheep and assaulted people. Some of his daughters were "lewd" women. However, the Tyler clan sat relatively undisturbed in their pews in Myddle Church and kept their honor unblemished.

Tyler and his clan simply stopped people from humiliating them publicly. When Tyler's nephew, Richard Challoner, "was bound over to appear at the Assizes for stealing a cow," William Tyler prevented the shameful hanging by telling the prosecutor "that this Challoner was his kinsman, and it would be a disgrace to me as well as to the rest of his friends to have him hanged, and that his friends would raise £5 among them to pay for the cow in case he would forbear the prosecution." Sympathizing with Tyler's interest, the prosecutor accepted the bribe and Challoner was freed. The Tyler clan defended their honor violently, if necessary. Hoping to jail Tyler for debt, Mr. Thomas Braddock "employed Rees Wenlock to serve William Tyler with a writ." Tyler persuaded Wenlock to stop on the way to court at Tyler's sister's house where Tyler's kin assaulted Wenlock and freed Tyler. Mr. Braddock then got a more muscular group of tenants to serve Tyler in church. Again, "many of Tyler's companions, and some women of his relations came to rescue Tyler." After a fight, "Tyler was set on horseback, and . . . went toward the goal." The Tyler clan was inconsolable, although they faced, particularly in relation to their greater sins, a relatively minor public humiliation, a temporary jailing for debt. "The consternation and lamentation of Tyler's friends," noted Gough, "especially the women, was such as I cannot easily demonstrate."

Because of their ethical priorities, even unrelated local people helped unwittingly to keep the sinister Tyler clan's banner riding high. Tyler in old age finally faced the gallows for stealing some sheep. Tyler's virtuous grandson, Thomas Tyler, was the chief witness against him. The jury refused to believe the youth, however. As Gough noted, "the jury conceived it malicious and blamed him for offering to hang his grandfather, and soe old Tyler was acquitted."[72] The northwestern jury raised kinship loyalty above property rights and above the choice to witness justly against a brutish life. Such ethical priorities were necessary, the jury implied, in order to live well in England with scarcity. The complex relationship of kin and gentry in household life, and the related ethic of honor and shame, allowed the tenants of Myddle to be warm, stable, and ethical.

NORTHWESTERN Quakers built upon this lively tradition. Middling northwesterners' promiscuous familial ethics and their ignorance of the Bible and Gospel preaching had long alarmed southern Puritans. But in the early 1640s northwesterners' distinctive society became an unavoidable issue. Soon after civil war erupted in 1642 between a Puritan dominated Parliament and Charles I, the King fled his Oxford base and headed toward Shrewsbury in northwestern England. Parliament was holding London and the wealthy and populous southeastern half of the country. Charles I could collect provender and a large army only from the more sparsely populated northwestern half of England. Dense and tight relations between northwestern middling kinship groups and their gentry landlords had long existed in northwestern England to overcome the region's scarcities. The King now used these patronage connections to raise an army of lusty northwestern tenants, who kept Parliament's forces at bay.[73]

A Puritan soldier of genius, Oliver Cromwell, emerged to lead Parliamentary forces to victory at Marston Moor in 1644 and Naseby in 1645. The Cromwellians carried off a military coup against Parliament, and on January 30, 1649 they executed the king of England. From 1649 to 1660 the army and Oliver Cromwell shakily ruled England as a Puritan republic. The pacification and conversion of northwesterners was high on Cromwell's agenda. He did not seek murderous revenge against these military foes as he did the Irish. He recognized them as Englishmen, respected their military prowess, and blamed their opposition upon former Anglican Church leaders' tolerance of the northwesterners' religious and ethical backwardness. He recognized that northwesterners' relative poverty and the dispersion of their settlements need dictate some revision of his own church ideal of small congregations with resident, university-trained Calvinist ministers. Accordingly, in February and March 1650, the Rump Parliament passed the acts for the Propagation of the Gospel in Wales and in the four Northern Counties. The Welsh Act established a regime of university-trained and lay itinerant ministers to travel over Wales and its border country. It was hoped that these holy men, with the support of occupying troops and the Holy Spirit, would dissolve the familial loyalties of northwestern farmers, and would establish the light of God's Word in "the dark corners of the realm."[74]

In the early 1650s the Puritans ruled northwestern England with sermon, Bible, and army. Itinerant Puritan ministers like

Walter Cradock, Vavasor Powell, and Morgan Llwyd eloquently led a Puritan awakening in Wales and its border country. A brave and sprawling Puritan community developed among a minority of northwestern farmers and artisans. Quaker prophets, derived from a Puritan background, soon appeared on the scene. Some northwest Puritan reformers like Judge Thomas Fell and Morgan Llwyd graciously accepted them as allies in their own difficult campaign to evangelize the "dark corners." The Quakers, however, revealed a significantly different method of conversion, and soon developed a crucial seedbed of popular support which often grew at the expense of the fledgling northwestern Puritan communities. Rejecting the authority of Anglican traditions and even the sole authority of the Bible, and therefore the teaching ministry and sermons, the Quakers believed that God's Word was born into every man and woman because of Christ's Resurrection and could be experienced in communal silent meetings for worship and in tender relations between Quakers, the "Light" answering the "Light." The essential features of their new, scattered communities in the Northwest were Quaker meetings for worship, idiosyncratic language customs, human relations based almost solely on love and tenderness, and the holy nurture of Quaker children. Although both groups spread news of the Holy Spirit zealously, neither group was totally successful. After the Restoration in 1660, the older Welsh gentry swept the Puritans and Quakers from power.

Puritan congregations, even when they shared itinerant ministers and used laymen in new ways, were too costly for northwestern middling people to maintain. Most northwesterners also felt insulted and threatened by the Quakers' radical purity, particularly by their denial of all rituals of honor and by their social exclusivity. Quakers worried fanatically about the corruption of their children's gift of the "Light" by "carnal talkers" and therefore tried to protect and control their relations with outsiders. Richard Gough praised Myddle's Cromwellian pastor, Joshua Richardson, for trying with sermon and Bible to make his parishioners deeper Christians within normal social networks. But Gough could not tolerate the Quakers' shunning of Myddle's interlocking networks of family and church life. "That phanatical, self-conceited sort of people," he huffily described the few Quakers in his parish.[75] Moreover, the Quakers' family ideal, particularly its emphasis on protecting children, proved excessively expensive.

Yet in certain backwood districts, the Quakers were effective interlocuters between southern Puritanism's emphasis on the Holy Spirit and northwesterners' emphasis upon human relations. Quakers' beliefs could seem better suited to local conditions and therefore to the wisdom of a merciful God than the Puritans' heavily institutionalized dispensation. Quaker meetings, like Puritan congregations, derived from religious ideas about the Holy Spirit imported into the northwestern region. Yet, Quaker doctrine and strategy were closer than Puritanism in spirit and form to the realities of indigenous northwestern middling life. Unlike the Puritan reformers, the Quakers relied exclusively on sanctifying human relations and domestic arrangements in households and meetings. The Quaker prophets claimed that the Holy Spirit was best transmitted spontaneously among friends and kin. In this way, Quakers set the sacred world in conformity with middling northwesterners' secular reliance on human relations. Quakerism became especially persuasive to northwestern Puritan laity in remote areas where Puritan congregations faced severe obstacles. For example, by 1663 almost every major Puritan lay leader and much of the less illustrious Puritan laity in Merionethshire had become Quakers. The Quakers also recruited well among Puritans in the enormous parishes of central Cheshire.

Because they were middling northwesterners, northwestern Quakers were fascinated by the potentialities of familial relations. Because they were sincere religious fanatics, they sought to change the ethics of northwestern British middling society at the most intimate level. Quakers came to disagree with most northwestern farmers over the farmers' emphasis upon clan honor and their willingness to merge their households and children promiscuously with their neighbors and landlords. These issues had deep cultural and social significance. Cross-cultural research by anthropologists has established that parents rarely teach their children to be self-defeatingly independent, if they themselves have long relied on relationships outside the household. Such parents teach their children to be wisely dependent. The "middling households" in Britain from which the Pennsylvania immigrants came had never been "little commonwealths," but were long beholden on outsiders for survival and the completion of essential tasks. They did not customarily teach or show their children the ways of independence.[76] Only a major spiritual cataclysm moved some in that uncharted direction.

BECAUSE Quakers by faith felt responsible for nurturing and protecting their children's gift of Grace, they set their households apart,
soon left the scarcities of northwestern England, and dissolved the
interdependent familial and social traditions of northwest Britain
in the powerful, self-contained, Quaker middling households of the
Delaware Valley, Pennsylvania. In light of middling society in
seventeenth-century northwestern England, the Quaker Pennsylvania settlers effected a radical transformation. Theirs was not a story
of middling continuity between old England and the New World.
Unlike southeastern English Puritan settlers of seventeenth-century
Massachusetts, Pennsylvania Quaker settlers from northwestern
Britain were undeniably familial as well as religious radicals in
context of their social origins.[77]

Yet, the first Quakers communities developed in northwestern
England and a large share of the early settlers to Pennsylvania were
northwestern middling people. Thus Quaker Pennsylvania middling society would contain many northwestern social definitions,
no matter how the Quakers transformed them. Most obviously, the
settlers continued to live in Pennsylvania on dispersed farmsteads,
the only type of agriculture they had known. The Quaker settlers
were also as clannish as most middling northwesterners. In their
religious thought, Quakers significantly replaced the genetic kin
with a spiritual kin—"the children of God." Yet their communities
tried to insure religious purity by erecting severe marriage disciplines to prevent Quaker children from marrying outsiders. In 1705
the Reverend George Rosse described the Quakers around Chester,
Pennsylvania with some justice as that "haughty tribe."[78] The
Quaker settlers were also as fascinated by honor, though they replaced clan honor with the Deity's honor as revealed in their lives—
"the honor of Truth." Their meetings would try to erase considera-
tions of honor within households by insisting that such households
uphold the honor of God's revelations. The settlers were as pugna-
cious, though they replaced violent clan feuds and lawsuits with a
spiritual feud against the "world"—the "Lamb's War."

But what the northwest British-Pennsylvania Quakers learned
most positively from their secular northwest British experience was
how to solve familial and spiritual problems through human relations instead of with expensive institutions, like southern-style Puritan congregations, which northwesterners could not afford. Thus
Quakers burdened households with unprecedented moral and spir-

itual responsibility; northwestern middling *mentalité* underlay the radical familial order of the Delaware Valley, Pennsylvania; and radical revisions of northwestern middling life, not southeastern English, led most swiftly and directly to an ideal of domesticity in America.

CHAPTER TWO

Spiritual Tribalism

In the late 1650s George Fox and Margaret Fell became preeminent among a large number of inspired Quaker preachers. Their leadership is wonderfully mysterious, but one distinctive strength is explainable. More than other early Quaker leaders, they respected the social resources of middling upland farmers and tradesmen. Beginning with new religious insights and an impoverished laity, they ended by forming a religious people distinguished by egalitarian, loving relationships and morally self-sufficient households. Their efforts took a lifetime. But they introduced a new family form in order to sustain Quakerism. They were the founders of Quaker organization and of Anglo-American domesticity.[1]

At Swarthmore Hall in the center of northwestern farmers' economic marginality and related clannishness, Fox and Fell first formed an exciting and workable model of female-centered domesticity from Quaker religious experiences. Fox then absorbed the primacy of uplanders' informal household and extra-household human relations in his vision that holy spiritual tribalism was to be the burgeoning religion's social form. In his view, Quakers were to be a great spiritual tribe, the "Royal Household of God." But another problem awaited them: separating Quaker relations from the carnal ties of embedded upland kinship and neighborly clusters from which their first converts originated, would resemble in their religious organization, and with whom they lived. To solve this

53

problem Fox and Fell erected a thoroughly spiritualized family discipline for Quaker households that raised love over honor in all relationships, and they reinforced this discipline by establishing men's and women's monthly meetings.

The itinerant Welsh ministers recruited by the Rump Parliament also de-emphasized the more expensive institutional features of southern Puritan ministers' doctrines. They created a brilliant religious rhetoric that accentuated northwesterner's emotional ties to family. But their warm, interior definition of salvation was undermined by the southern-style Puritan churches they hoped to erect.[2]

Their leader was Walter Cradock.[3] He defined justification, the infusion of regenerating Grace through faith in Christ, as the emotional acceptance of God as a fully trusted, holding parent. The true believer was like " . . . a child . . . there is exceeding boldness in a fond child to ask anything of his father . . . a child will sit in the lap of his mother, and snatch a thing out of her hand; so . . . one that is fond of God with a holy fondness, he knows he may leap into his father's lap at any time, and into his arms and ask anything without courting or compliment." Instead of urging comparisons between the sinful self and God's law, Cradock warned gently, "if thou call on God with fear and canst cry, abba, abba, that is as much as daddie, daddie, as our babes used to say . . . thou art spoiled and hurt."[4] Cradock lectured successfully in Cardiff in 1634, in Wrexham in 1635, and founded the first Independent Church in Wales at Llanfachas in 1639. He converted two great Puritan Welsh ministers Vavasor Powell and Morgan Llwyd.

Llwyd and Powell developed Cradock's affecting rhetoric with poetic eloquence. They refused to install southern English style church discipline, because they thought sainthood an interior relation with God that defied definition by behavior or belief. Powell wrote, "we love men more because they are of our opinion, than because they are saints, and friends of Jesus Christ. Hereupon we make opinion and not union with Jesus Christ the ground of communion and fellowship with one another."[5] Llwyd thought saving divine intimacy inconsistent with uniformity in either opinion or behavior: "men's faces, voices differ much/ saints are not all one size/ flowers in one garden vary too,/ lett none monopolize."[6]

Cradock's, Llwyd's, and Powell's promises of gentle intimacy between God and sinful humans differed from the rhetoric of southern Puritan ministers like William Perkins who demanded explicit behavioral changes and much anxiety as evidence of conversion. Richard Baxter thought Cradock an antinomian. Cradock, Llwyd, and Powell did ignore the terrible implications and inspiring anxieties of the sinner confronting God's law, the basis of much southern Puritan awareness. Whatever the Welsh ministers' orthodoxy, their rhetoric better answered the conditions of northwestern life. Perkin's system of intense Bible study and constant ministerial oversight of behavior was too expensive for hillside farmers who shared their parish ministers with households spread over five or six mountainous townships.

The Welsh ministers had a difficult time uniting their affecting rhetoric with Puritan church government. At Wrexham in 1651 Llwyd formed a separate congregation of saints. After preaching in the parish church, he prayed with his chosen brethren.[7] By 1653, lacking any criteria but his sensitive perceptions, Llwyd discerned his brethren's subtle separation from the Holy Spirit, "their souls are dryed up within/ for want of heavenly moisture/ their love grows cold because of sin/ that works an inward torture."[8] When help and money from London Cromwellians also dried up, he began to doubt that the preached Word of God and southern Puritan church organization, no matter how sensitively blended, could serve the Holy Spirit in the Welsh mountains. He sent in 1653 two prominent members of his chosen congregation to inspect the new teachings of George Fox, the young Leicestershire wool agent, known as a Quaker, who was earning a reputation in the North by spontaneously speaking from the Holy Spirit. Llwyd was still dissatisfied. Powell and Llwyd began praying for, and predicting, the timely arrival of the Second Coming. Such a decisive event would provide them with an adequate solution to their enormous problems.[9]

Meanwhile major Cheshire gentry sought to block these ministers' heated rhetoric from crossing the mountains. Members of Cheshire's major gentry sided with Parliament during the civil war for political reasons. Unlike the top Welsh gentry, they continued to exercise power in the 1650s. As J. S. Morrill has shown, these nominally Puritan gentlemen socialized more often with royalist gentry neighbors and kin than with the lesser Puritan gentry. Nevertheless, these county-families served on the Cromwellian commissions and filled church vacancies with moderate Puritan ministers like John Newcombe and Adam Martindale. They hoped to shield Cheshire from the social leveling of extreme religious experiments. Encouraged by Cromwellian military officers and aggressive lesser Cheshire gentry, the Welsh ministers' doctrines, and even more dangerous ones, did cross the Welsh border and found a Cheshire audience. In 1659 the major Puritan Cheshire gentry fomented an unsuccessful rebellion against the Cromwellian regime. The leading rebel Sir George Booth had been a supporter of Cromwell. But he lost all patience with the Cromwellians, when he noticed that the largest Quaker community in Cheshire was his tenantry at Pownall Fee.[10]

George Fox benefited from the success and failure of native Puritan reformers. Fox had an honorable, courageous character, especially impressive to upland men and women reared within the ethic of family honor. Indeed, if George Fox's *Journal* were not primarily a spiritual classic, it would live as a frontier classic. In its story, a young shepherd from Leicestershire with a divine call rides on horseback through the edges of England, restoring insane women to inner peace, frightening cosmopolitan ministers from their pulpits, piercing judges into anguish with his eyes, enduring repeated riots and stonings without recanting or even changing his facial expression. He invades the center of cosmopolitan life, London, where he earns the respect of the country's leader, Oliver Cromwell. The hero marries the most beautiful, gracious, gentlest woman in the wild Northwest. The journal is spiced with amazing tales, home remedies, egalitarian values, atrocious spelling, and a larger than life manly, gentle folk hero dressed in leather britches. Such elements not only impressed northwesterners but were later interwoven into the formula of American frontier literature, including those about a rural Pennsylvanian Quaker's son, Daniel Boone.[11]

The Quakers also appeared in context of the northwestern frontier refreshingly anti-institutional. Fox and many other early Quaker prophets earned their first followings and reputations by providing spiritual and physical cures to rural people lacking access to cosmopolitan and expensively produced remedies. While they highly valued the Bible, many early Quaker leaders also tried to learn as much as possible from the spiritual human body. In seventeenth-century British popular medicine, as Michael MacDonald has shown, the spiritual and physical human body were considered identical. MacDonald named George Fox the best practitioner of physical-spiritual healing of his day, a pioneer of the effective, non-coercive, talking treatment of mentally anguished people (the method was later employed in the 1790s at the model Quaker asylum, the York Retreat, which began the modern treatment of mental illness in England).[12] After his first major revelations, George Fox had been "at a stand in my mind whether I should practice physic for the good of mankind, seeing the nature and virtue of things were opened to me by the Lord."[13] By his own accounting, using his revelations and divine insights, Fox cured over seventy nearly hopeless patients. He carried around a clyster pipe (a seventeenth-century medical instrument) and later left medical paraphernalia to his family and friends.[14] In Philadelphia in 1690, the most socially prominent Welsh Quakers—Griffith Owen, Thomas Wynne, and Thomas Lloyd—were all physicians and surgeons, as well as religious and political leaders. They were vernacular healers, not formally trained physicians. Formerly a cooper's apprentice, Thomas Wynne taught himself surgery. A Quaker critic later charged that Wynne was better equipped "to mind his axes and saws" than surgical instruments or human observation. Only Thomas Lloyd spent time at a university, one year at Oxford. These unofficial physicians earned the trust of northwest Quakers by providing them with accessible intellectual, spiritual, and physical services.[15]

The Quakers' case against their rival reformers, the Puritans, turned on knowledge of the spiritual human body. George Fox always referred to Puritans as "professors," partly a jibe at their claim that Christian ethics and laws might be fully professed by converts but never fully lived or embodied in people. Fox thought their sense of limitation an unfortunate result of their idolization of the Biblical text. Instead of seeking within themselves for love, Christ, and the Light, he argued, they fashioned an idol from scriptural words and tried to fit themselves to what they knew only dimly in themselves. As William Smith told "the professors" in 1668, "the mystery of the kingdom is hid from your eyes, and you run into words with your carnal minds and earthly wisdom, and from what is written draw something to yourselves and form up a likeness in your conceivings, and bring that forth in the strength of your wills: and that is your foundation and the first principle of your religion."[16] Smith claimed that Puritan coldness and factionalism followed from their inner self-ignorance.

Quaker prophets valued authenticity of feeling and expression over mere book learning. They thought the Bible the Word of God and they tested all their revelations by its text, but they also limited truthful readings to those made by people who had already reached deep within themselves to become informed by the Holy Spirit. The central medium of Quaker worship was thus not the reception of a well-prepared sermon, as among the Puritans, but a silent meeting, a gathering where all social criticism or support was purposefully suspended to reveal and communicate the divine truths embedded in the spiritual human body. Such meetings were communal without the usual communal restraints. At least two people were needed to begin a meeting, as George Keith explained, because "the measure of life in one doth after a secret and unspeakable manner, reach unto the measure of life in the other, and flow forth whereby the one is raised and strengthened and enlarged by the other." As more silent worshippers were filled, "the life and light of God . . . spring up in them . . . uniting in one even as many small streams become a large river of life, which in wholeness and universality of it, hath its course, motion, and operation, in and through every member."[17]

Speaking occurred in meeting in the same spontaneous way. The speaker was passive, an instrument who had an "opening" to the Holy Spirit. As Richard Farnsworth noted in 1663, Quaker ministers "speak as they are moved by the Holy Ghost, and as the Spirit gives utterance." The referential content of the speaker's sentences was almost irrelevant, "for it is not so much speaking true things that doeth good, as speaking them from the pure, and conveying them to the pure . . . ."[18] Accordingly, meetings were designed, to be as free as possible from conventional etiquette. In 1650, for example, George Fox gave an insane woman free rein in three or four meetings in Nottinghamshire with the hope of curing her by the power. Fox admitted disadvantages, "there were many Friends almost overcome with the stink that came out of her, roaring and tumbling on the ground."[19] Through 1676 Fox continued to criticize overly polite Friends "that do judge such sighers, prayers, and such who make a joyful melody (from the word dwelling in their hearts), they who judge such, are not in the spirit that makes intercession."[20] Autistic rocking and regressive noises were also allowed. As Geoffrey Nuttal has noted, "the Quakers did not get their name for nothing."[21] Such meetings grew less surprising, but remained the mainstay of Quaker communities. Their liveliness was a constant topic of Quaker journals.

Instead of carefully scrutinized oral professions of faith, the Quakers' only measure and test of regeneration was what Quakers called an "honest" or "holy conversation." "Conversation" was defined in the seventeenth-century, according to the *Oxford English*

Dictionary, as the "manner of conducting oneself in the world or society." The Quakers' concept of "conversation" included the idea that it was reflective of a person's inner being and that it communicated meaning, as denoted in the King James and Genevan Bibles ("Only let your conversation be as becometh Gospel" (Phil. 1:27); "Be an example of believers in conversation in purity" (1 Tim. 1:2); "They may also be won by the conversation of their wives (1 Pet. 3:1)). Accordingly, they included within "conversation" not only speech but also gesture, conduct, and presence (what Quakers called "savour"). Thus, instead of relying on the close study of the Bible, expensively trained preachers, and intensively educated, small congregations, the Quakers could form much cheaper holy communities. Each Quaker was an embodiment of the Word and therefore preached inside or outside of meetings, with or without words, to other Quakers or "tender" people.

The Quakers combined their revelations, experience, and insights from the spiritual body into a folk theory of divine language. This theory could conveniently form the basis of a sacred speech community of the Holy Spirit for people used to aural communication, but who could not afford frequent access to southern-style preachers.[22] Rejecting all set forms of speech, including the prepared sermon, as willful and worldly, Quaker prophets believed that when the sinful, prideful, false self was quieted, God's Word (the Light, Seed, Holy Spirit, etc.) would be spontaneously voiced in people's hearts and minds. The Light would then condemn the old prideful man, reducing and then exalting the believer into God's child, who would then enjoy a fresh, loving, sinless relationship with the creation and other people. The prophets believed everyone was born with the instructing and redeeming Light, as sealed by Christ's crucifixion and resurrection. They thought most people willfully buried it with honor, pride, and lust, and became "carnal talkers" whose lives, speech, and presence were false and deadly. On the other hand, being led by an inner revelation equal to that the Apostles had received from the direct instruction of Christ, the true convert was an embodiment of the Word of God, a charismatically honest man or woman, whose very presence would preach truth to, and would often convert, "tender" people.

Quakers constantly preached to one another and to the "world" outside of worship meetings. The Quakers' peculiar language testimonies—the use of "thee" and "thou" instead of "you", their refusal to swear, their refusal to haggle over prices, their refusal to engage in hat honor, etc.—were all preaching "vocabulary" in "holy conversation." Quakers suspected every speech act of being most likely a prideful, worldly fabrication. They therefore tried to stop every idle word or unnecessary action. "In the evening," Joseph Pike would "call over my actions during the day, and when I saw I had spoken more than I ought, or used unnecessary words . . . my heart, being tender, Oh! how would I be bowed." Pike's model was his friend Samuel Randall, whom Pike never heard "speak an idle word, during the time of our intimate acquaintance, which was about forty years."[23] When they did speak, the Quakers were notoriously honest. They refused to swear oaths partly because swearing implied that their unsworn words were sometimes lies. Quaker merchants and shopkeepers introduced fixed prices into English commerce because they regarded the conventional overpricing of commodities in order to allow for haggling a form of lying. The famous "thee" and "thou" were also adopted for honesty's sake. Fox prescribed the faithful use of "thee" (usually reserved for lovers, children, and servants) instead of the respectful "you" as the pronoun referent for individuals. From his reading of the Bible, Fox decided "thee" and "thou" were the proper personal referents in the singular and "you" proper only in the plural. To call a person constantly "you" was thus saying he or she was two or more people, a pridefully false statement, leading to a false relationship.[24]

The early Quakers usually replaced the etiquette of honor with the etiquette of authenticity in their "vocabulary." They were abrupt and unceremonial when meeting strangers, yet physical when meeting and leaving people they knew well and liked. When meeting or leaving one another, as George Keith later reported, instead of doffing hats, curtseying, and muttering conventional face-saving epithets, even staid Quakers "not only take their Friends by the hand, but oft grip, and press hard with the hand, and some of them also press hard the wrist as well as the hand, to feel the life in the person whom they do grip."[25] In 1663 Benjamin Furly judged conventional bowing and curtseying as portrayals of false feeling. He argued that real honor and love were expressed, as by the Quakers, in "certain natural, lively actions, that are inseparable from it, and so consequently true and infallible, according as the indwelling honor leads, moves, guides, directs, and puts forth itself, either by giving the hand, falling on the neck, embracing, kissing."[26] Advertising such physicality, in a letter of 1681, Roger Haydock of Lancashire asked Phineas Pemberton, grocer, in the same

County, to convey his greeting to all Pemberton's large family and neighboring Quakers "with kisses of love our soul saluting them," though he allowed Pemberton to do it "severally" in order to save time.[27] Any reading of the large collection of Swarthmore letters among the earliest ministerial Friends uncovers the unabashedly honest and intimate expression of strong sentiment among early Friends.

Such a holy speech community was particularly persuasive within the social and economic context of northwestern Britain. The Puritan lay minister Richard Davies noted that in 1658, while preaching for Vavasor Powell in the Welsh mountains, he had often thought of Jeremiah, xxxi, 33, 34, a prophesy that God "will put my law in their inward parts, and write it in their hearts. . . . " As Davies huffed up another Welsh mountain, he "thought it would then be a happy day when God would be the teacher of his people himself: that we need not teach every man his neighbour or his brother, saying 'know ye the Lord.'"[28] Davies later discovered happily that the Quaker frontier doctors could use personal experience and knowledge, silent meetings, and authentic language, not an expensive public institutional infrastructure, to work their spiritual cures. Davies became the first native Quaker in Montgomeryshire.

IN THE LATE 1650s and early 1660s, the Quakers gained most of their most durable, communitarian recruits in Cheshire and Wales from clusters of kin and neighbors whose interest in the Holy Spirit had been heightened by the Cromwellian propagators' rhetoric. At least in the documentable cases, most northwestern farmers, especially among the groups who later emigrated to Pennsylvania, became Quakers not by hearing public Quaker rhetoric, but by having Quaker ideas and language injected into established relations among kin and neighbors who had been informed previously by radical Puritan ministers like the Welsh propagators. Cheshire and Welsh Quaker converts were less often individualistic listeners than members of listening groups, mostly clusters of kin and neighbors. Such people would be retained in Quakerism by Fox's ability to blend his language of the Holy Spirit with reformed, middling family life.

Early Quaker ministers did make individual converts in Cheshire and Wales, but disconnected individuals were rare and impotent in the Northwest. When ministers were too individualistic, they lost the people who persevered. All the invading Quaker ministers were heroically faithful, but some were insensitive to their clannish audience. Sensing the promise implicit in Llwyd's delegation to George Fox, two major Quaker ministers, John Lawson and Richard Hubberthorne, reached Wrexham in October 1653. Llwyd and the elders of the gathered church of Wrexham gently approached Lawson and Hubberthorne in order to reach spiritual agreement. However, the Quaker ministers ignored the established reform community and bullied their sympathetic preacher. As Lawson boastfully described it, Llwyd "was silent . . . Richard [Hubberthorne] laid more judgment on him, the priest sat sobbing." The Quaker ministers then held demonstration meetings which made so much noise, a critic reported, "as not only affrighted the spectators, but caused the dogs to bark, the swine to cry, and the cattle to run about." The Quaker ministers entered a town with people sympathetic to the Quaker message, but galloped from town without a single convert. Lawson had similarly dramatic and insensitive misadventures at Malpas, Cheshire.[29]

By March 1654, Thomas Holme, Elizabeth Leavans (who later married Holme), Elizabeth Fletcher and Jane Waugh had replaced Hubberthorne and Lawson in Cheshire. They operated chiefly from the city of Chester. Their spiritual dramatics gained attention for Quakerism: "many people came in" to their lively meetings "as they came from the steeple house, and looked upon them that were trembling and crying, and were astonished." Holme and his associates were soon in Chester prison, where he continued to astonish and entertain people with two successive nights of loud, spontaneous, Paul-like singing: "and about midnight, I was compelled to sing and the power was exceedingly great." After their release, Holme and his partners visited locally raised groups in Congleton, Frandley, and Northwich. They were arrested and returned to Chester prison. After being released, Holme went through Chester "naked as a sign," was sent back to prison, where he wrote a letter to Margaret Fell complaining about the lack of discipline among the Chester Quakers, a group of "filthy decrepit and contrary spirits" in his description. He failed to observe that his own individualistic, dramatic style had attracted like-minded people.[30]

The city of Chester never developed a sizable Quaker community, though it was the Quaker ministers' major focus of attention and drama. The theatrics of the original Quaker witness in the city, particularly the spiritual demonstrations of Thomas Holme and his followers, had made Quakerism into a religion of individualists, people unconnected to the city's familial linkages. Between 1655 and 1681 in the Quaker registers, there were only 12 Quaker households from the city of Chester, an unimpressive 4.5 percent of the Quaker households in the county. According to the Episcopal visitation of 1669, only one small Quaker meeting existed by that date in Chester's nine parishes—a meeting broken up at Edward Morgan's house in St. Peter's parish on August 1, 1669. The authorities counted only 22 people present from five Cheshire parishes. The geographical spread of the worshippers suggested that this was the main and probably only Quaker meeting in Chester. Only 17 of the attenders were from the city itself. Three of these 17 people had been converted to Quakerism by 1654. Thus, over a 15-year period (1654–1669) Quakerism in Chester had grown by only 14 people, a pitiful showing. As the Quaker historian, William Braithwaite, noted, "in Cheshire . . . the Quaker community that came into being suffered from the overwrought spiritual conditions under which it had been fostered." This insight was true for Chester, not Cheshire.[31]

Quakerism spread best in rural areas of Cheshire seldom visited by dramatic ministers. Some thirty miles northeast of Chester lay the spacious rural township and parish of Mobberley (over 10 square miles in area). By 1669 Mobberley and the adjoining township of Pownall Fee had the largest concentration of Quakers in Cheshire. By 1652, a group of families in Mobberley had "sat at the house of one Richard Yarwood . . . whose custom was when met together neither to preach nor pray vocally, but to read the scriptures and discourse of religion, expecting a farther manifestation." A recent convert Thomas Yarwood arrived in 1652 at this household, probably his kinsman's, and "asked Rich to let him have a meeting at his house the first day following, who readily condescended; where upon it was concluded to acquaint the aforesaid therewith, and most of them came together, with several others, which made a considerable assembly, and many of them were convinced and as with one mouth confessed that it was the truth which had been declared that day, being that which they had long waited for: and from that time a meeting was continued thereabout and is now called Morley Meeting." Yarwood spoke briefly. The people in Mobberley fondly remembered Thomas Yarwood as a man who "would speak but a few words, yet would reach to the seed of life." They clearly became Quakers, not as listening individuals, but as a group, as "with one mouth."[32]

Ties of affection and trust, over which the excitement of "holy conversation" could rapidly spread, had already existed. By 'an accounting of 1669, the 12 Quaker households of Mobberley were composed of neighbors and kin. The Yarwoods comprised three households—that of Richard Yarwood, freeholder; Jonathan Yarwood, blacksmith, and his wife; and widow Yarwood. Other family groups included the brothers William and Peter Key, schoolmasters, and Thomas Heald, carpenter, and his son William.[33]

Neighboring was also important to the spread of the Quakers' loving message. The influence of neighbor upon neighbor was powerful in these backwater parishes. On 13 February 1656, John Forshoe of Overwhitley (a town about ten miles from Mobberley) complained that his neighbor William Mosse, a Quaker tailor, had bewitched him with stories about black horses. Forshoe claimed that Mosse had threatened that if Forshoe continued "longer by Mr. Elcocke [the parish minister of great Budsworth], he would be led by the Devil; but wished this informant to follow their way, meaning the Quakers'; and he should be led by the spirit, which this informant utterly refused, and said he was in a good way already." Forshoe was so disturbed by these insinuations from his neighbor that only by accusing him of witchcraft could Forshoe internally erase his neighbor's influence and arguments. According to the 1664 hearth tax returns for Mobberley, Roger Bradbury and Randle Blackshaw were adjacent neighbors; and the households of William and Peter-Key, Thomas Heald, and John Finlow were nearly adjacent. Quakerism spread to the adjoining township of Pownall Fee probably along these kinship and neighborly associations. The Episcopal visitation of 1669 reported 11 Quaker households in Pownall Fee, where neighboring was also a feature of the emerging Quaker community. According to the 1664 hearth tax list, 14 of 17 Quaker households or 82 percent lived at one end of the township, or among the first 28 of the 56 Pownall Fee households inspected by the tax collector. Eight of the 17 Quaker households in the township lived clustered almost adjacently in one area.[34]

In North Wales, the Quaker message spread similarly: through conversations and subdued demonstration meetings among clusters of kin and intertwined landlords and tenants previously involved with the Welsh propagators, particularly Powell and Llwyd. In the late 1650s and early 1660s the Quaker message quietly converted most of the old Merionethshire and Montgomeryshire Puritan community. A Baptist minister reported of Merionethshire in 1675 (the county supplying almost a third of the Welsh Tract Pennsylvania settlers), "the few professing people that were heretofore in this country joined either to Wrexham Church, or else to Mr. Vavasor Powell's that met in Montgomeryshire . . . but since the change most of them turned quakers and so continue. . . ."[35] The Quakers gained few others in North Wales.

A former follower of Powell, Richard Davies began the Quaker ministry in Montgomeryshire in 1658 with a visit to "the Independent Meeting, and those people that I formerly belonged to, that were a separate people, gathered chiefly by Vavasor Powell." They met at Cloddiechachion, near Welshpool at the house of Davies' near kin. After Davies interrupted the main speaker, "a near relative of mine, that owned the house, took me in his arms, and led me out of the house through the fold, and through a gate that opened to the common, and shut the gate after me." Because the great majority of his kin and Powellian associates remained with their church, Davies retreated in 1659 to London's Quaker community. Davies got married and started his haberdashery business, useful preparations for another foray into Wales.[36]

Davies returned to Welshpool in 1660, the year of the Restoration. He found "those professors who had been and were in great power, began to be faint-hearted, because of the report of bringing in King Charles the Second; which in a little time was accomplished, and those that were in great pomp, were brought to prison themselves." Davies sought arrest himself in order to meet intimately with his former brethren. Family ties again moved events. A Royalist army officer, indebted to Davies' father, arrested the Quaker, but other kin tried to bail him out. Davies had to avoid a Royalist uncle, a new Justice of the Peace, "lest he should stop me from going to prison." Once in jail, although Davies had "little to say among them, but a sigh or a groan," he converted two inmates, Cadwallader Evans and Margaret Bowen. Cadwallader Evans gave Davies access to Evans's landlord, Mr. Charles Lloyd of Dolobran, a former Cromwellian Justice. After seeing preaching fail, Lloyd was seeking a new way to retain a reforming faith of the Holy Spirit in North Wales. After a few demonstration meetings at Evans's tenement, Charles Lloyd and many of his tenants and neighbors joined the Quaker movement. In 1662, Davies settled a Quaker meeting at Penllyn, near Bala, in Merionethshire among "some Friends and tender professors there." At Tyddyn-y-Gareg, near Dolgellau, Owen Lewis, "a man that had been in commission of the peace in Oliver's days," had already turned Quaker. He and Davies soon brought into the Quaker fold many other former Cromwellian officers and commissioners in Merionethshire, including Robert Owen of Dolserre, Owen Humphry of Llwyngrwritt, and his father and brothers.[37]

As a consensus formed among dissenters in North Wales to investigate Quakerism, native Quaker ministers de-emphasized public rhetoric. Llwyd's and Powell's unequal eloquence had failed them. Thomas Ellis, a former Cromwellian justice, deacon of Vasavor Powell's church, and recent Quaker convert, had been, noted Davies, "an eminent preacher among the independents" but after becoming a Quaker, he became quieter. As late as 1669, noted Davies, Ellis's "mouth was but very little as yet opened by way of testimony among Friends." Although one of the chief Quaker ministers in Montgomeryshire, Ellis saw no reason to speak "till he found a very weighty concern upon him." With the best preaching proven ineffective in the Welsh mountains, and with simple "sighs and groans" converting old Puritans, Ellis thought silence the best policy. After they saw their gifted ministers failing and then totally buried by the Restoration, many Welsh and Cheshire religious reformers reconstructed their gathered communities and households with "holy conversation," the Quakers' unorthodox concept of divine interpersonal communication.[38]

DESPITE such advantages, the early Quakers faced a major moral obstacle blocking them from penetrating and holding northwest kinship networks. At first, Quakers were too pure for the impulsive emotions, physicality, and conflicts of northwest middling households. Rather than confront the messy ambiguities and ambivalences of family life, many early Quaker leaders chose to run away from their wives and children.[39] "I wish to God I had married a drunkard," said Miles Halhead's pursuing wife. "I might have found him in the alehouse; but I cannot tell where to find my husband."[40] In this regard Swarthmore Hall was decisive. In 1652 Goerge Fox converted the Fell family of Swarthmore Hall. He gained not simply a safe-house protected by gentry patronage but also a compelling demonstration of how the Light could regenerate middling northwestern family life. By following, learning from, and using this experience, Fox grew to lead the Quaker movement.[41]

Swarthmore Hall housed an attractive cast for a great family drama of regeneration.[42] Perched in the desolate, rugged district of

Furness in northwestern Lancashire, Swarthmore Hall housed a proud Puritan gentry family. Among the household's major assets was Judge Fell's young wife, Margaret, a woman of beauty and intelligence.[43] Judge Fell had long been a powerful advocate of Northwest reform: in 1641 Justice of the Peace in Lancashire, attorney for the County Court of Westminster, attorney general of North Wales, and then in 1651 judge of the Assize for the Cheshire and North Wales district. Judge Thomas Fell was aware of the failures of Cromwellian reform campaigns in the Northwest. Although steady supporters of their parish minister, William Lampitt, the Fells remained open to new religious ideas.

The Fells ran their large household of eight children and twelve servants according to reformed Puritan principles. They mixed respect for traditional social honor with Christian love and legalism. They encouraged their only son, George, to ride, hunt, and shoot. They sent him to the best grammar schools in the area. They also provided him with a same-aged companion, William Caton, the relative of a nearby clergyman.

In late June 1652 the household's relations were deeply changed when Judge Fell's wife, Margaret, then 38 years old, heard George Fox, then 28 years old, tell the audience in nearby Ulverstone Church about the priority of internal spiritual revelation to the letter of the Scripture. Fox's interior focus so immediately impressed Margaret Fell that she, "sat down in my pew again, and cried bitterly: and I cried in my spirit to the Lord, 'we are all thieves; we are all thieves; we have taken the scriptures in words, and know nothing of them in ourselves.'"[44] Fox and his fellow Quaker ministers Richard Farnsworth and James Naylor joined Margaret Fell at the Hall and in the following days and weeks converted most of the large household. Judge Fell returned from his circuit three weeks later, and was told by the local leadership that "a great disaster was befallen amongst his family, and that they were witches . . ." (the Quakers' ability to persuade people through intimate relations, not public rhetoric, frequently provoked such accusations). Naylor and Farnsworth managed to quiet the "greatly offended" Judge, who was willing to entertain the Quakers as allies in his reform efforts.

He was less happy, however, about the radical changes in his household's conduct and leadership. Giving him a taste of her new spiritual and moral authority, while the hungry, tired Judge sat nervously fingering his dinner, Margaret Fell "sat down by him . . . and whilst I was sitting, the power of the Lord seized upon me, and he was struck with amazement, and knew not what to think; but was quiet and still. And the children were all quiet and still, and grown sober, and could not play on their musick that they were learning: all these things made him quiet and still." The next morning the local minister, William Lampitt, arrived to revive the Judge's orthodoxy. But Judge Fell remained strangely "quiet and still" and allowed the Quakers to meet at his house the next Sunday. And while they did, wrote Margaret Fell triumphantly, "my husband went that day to the steeple house [Ulverstone Church], and none with him but his clerk, and his groom that rid with him: and the priest and the people were all fearfully troubled; but praised be the Lord, they never got their will upon us to this day."[45] Judge Fell remained cooperative until his death in 1658, when Margaret Fell assumed total control of the household.

Margaret Fell's new revelations and new freedom from codes of honorable discourse increased her vitality and authority. Her vibrancy affected the whole household, servants included. She made the Hall into a familial analogue of a lively Quaker meeting. Private experience of the Truth led to new tenderness and sharing in the household. As people warmed to each other, the religious experiences grew deeper, which led to more tender sharing. George Fell's companion William Caton basked joyfully in the new familial order. "Oh! the love which in that day abounded among us, especially in that family! and the freshness of the power of the Lord God, which then was amongst us: and the zeal for him and his truth, the comfort and refreshment which we had from his presence—the nearness and dearness that were amongst us toward one another—the opening and revelations which we had!" "We were willing to sympathize and bear with one another," Caton continued, "and in true and tender love to watch over one another."[46] Other servants and blood relatives also discovered the magic of uniting "holy conversation" and family life, especially when that family life was charismatically guided by a comely and truly spiritual woman.

Like others at the Hall, Caton recognized Margaret Fell as the household's spiritual leader and his own spiritual mother, "who as a tender-hearted nursing mother cared for me, and was as tender of me, as if I had been one of her own children. Oh! the kindness, the respect, and friendship which she showed me, ought never to be forgotten by me."[47] Neither he nor any of the Swarthmorians forgot her. After Caton left Swarthmore for itinerant Quaker ministering, chiefly in the Netherlands, he, like most of the others, wrote to her frequently. He often wrote about her marvelous empathy, whose recall helped him in his lonely travels, "And when I thus behold thee in the invisible, if I be suffering, I am comforted, if weary and heavy laden I am eased and refreshed, seeing thy hand stretched forth to me, to draw me nigher and nigher unto thee, that thou mayest take part with me of sufferings." He enjoyed imagining her, he wrote, sitting "spinning flax most joyfully, being clothed with honour and beauty . . . arrayed like a lily of the field."[48] Margaret Fell's daughters seemed joyous replicas of their charismatic mother. Puritan patriarchy was never as lively or as emotionally authentic as this.

The remarkable familial revolution at Swarthmore Hall grew famous among Quakers. People at Swarthmore Hall got along so lovingly, noted Caton, that "came that worthy family to be re- nowned in the nation, the fame of which spread much among Friends: and the power and presence of the Lord being so much there with us, it was a means to induce many, even from afar, to come thither; so that at one time there would be Friends out of five or six counties."[49] A Durham Justice of the Peace, Anthony Pear- son, wrote in May 1653 that he learned more about religion from a few days at Swarthmore Hall than he had in a lifetime of sermon listening: "Oh! how gracious was the Lord to me in carrying me to Judge Fell's to see the wonders of his power and wisdom—a family walking in the fear of the Lord, conversing daily with him, crucified to the world, living only to God."[50] As the legend spread, some visitors imaginatively stage-managed Swarthmore Hall into the perfected, original Quaker family. George Fox took decent advan- tage of the Hall's spiritual excitement and lessons. He remained close to the Swarthmore family and learned much from them. He made Swarthmore the center of the Quakers' communication system. Margaret Fell became the chief correspondent with traveling Quaker ministers. Fox promoted her as the ideal Quaker woman, especially in place of Quaker viragos like Martha Simmonds.[51] He valued her opinion on family discipline. She became the spiritual mother of the spiritual Quaker tribe. In 1669, at the wedding of George Fox and Margaret Fell, Miriam Moss offered a testimony that "in the year 1657" she had sat in the Swarthmore Hall garden and had inwardly seen "that G.F. and M.F. were joined together in that one eternal spirit, and they should be joined together in the bond of love which could not be broken. . . ." Moss's testimony was indecent—Judge Fell did not die until 1658.[52] Nevertheless, the gossip and projections meant that Fox's visions had found a charming and exciting familial embodiment. Little Swarthmore Halls developed among the wealthier radical northwest families.

SWARTHMORE HALL and Fox's leadership helped make Quakerism attractive to northwest reformers. Yet these new spiritual clans of "holy conversation" needed more than a model and a spiritual language. They required a severe code and discipline to ensure their further spiritualization. By 1681, for example, the Quakers of Pownall Fee and Mobberley had formed a strong kinship group through Quaker marriages. The Burgis family of Pownall Fee had in that township intermarried with the Piersons (1671), Milners (1672), and Janneys (1672); and the Burgis daughters had crossed the township and parish line to Mobberley to intermarry with the Blackshaws (1661), the Hobsons (1676), and the Bradburys (1684). Quakers in these localities quickly found themselves related to one another not only by the Divine Seed but also by shared kin. Some of this kinship pre-dated Quakerism and promoted the transmission of the faith, just as the faith expanded and deepened kinship ties.[53] If Quakerism was not to degenerate rapidly into just another northwest tribe, (which it was in organization) exchanges within families and households had to be kept unusually pure, lively, loving.

Fox had already begun to define and execute the task. Fox wrote thousands of instructing letters. Almost five hundred of these apostolic letters, usually those written to groups of Quakers or meant to be general pronouncements on major issues, were published in 1698 by English Friends. Any classification of this collection by theme and date shows that Fox's interest in familial conduct came early in his prophetic career, not just as death and persecution thinned the Quakers' ministerial ranks, but just as the Quaker communities in the Northwest developed. Fifty-four percent of his letters on family life were written before the Restoration and the beginning of systematic persecution. In 1653, he wrote his first letter on household communication, directed to "all Friends everywhere that have wives, or that have husbands, or that have children, or that have servants; or servants that have masters; or children that have parents that are not Friends." It told them to rely on the power of Quakerly silence and "holy conversation" to manage or convert intimate unbelievers, for "your chaste conversation (ye walking in the Light which comes from the Word) may answer the Light in them which they hate and walk contrary to. . . ."[54] Fox wrote his first letter on marriage in 1653, followed by a detailed letter on the marriage procedure in 1654, and his first letter on childrearing in 1655. By 1657, Fox was regularly defining the Quakers as a holy, spiritualized tribe, "the family and household of God."[55]

From the standpoint of social strategy, as well as religious doctrine, George Fox felt compelled in these letters to advocate and design the radical spiritualization of all household emotions. Protestant reformers in southern England had ample resources to construct extra-household institutions, like Puritan congregations, which could provide Christian social discipline, while still allowing the play of some impulse to remain sanctioned within the household. Fox did not have such resources or institutions in northwestern Britain. He had to work with marriage, household childrearing, and kinship relations—and he had to inform these with "holy conversation" so that they could bear the weight of sustaining Quakerism among adults and nurturing the Truth among children. The idea that households and family relations could bear such massive moral weight was of course as revolutionary as the extreme spiritualization Fox advocated.

Fox began by defining marriage as a more disciplined relationship than Puritans had advised. Puritan ministers had innovatively advocated the spiritualization of household relations, but they strove for perfection in their churches, not households. They usually had allowed that even regenerate people, particularly women, retained some sin and that the Christian marriage was a place where some lust and impulse should be morally sanctioned and exercised. A puritanical advice-giver, Thomas Hilder, advised his readers in 1653, for example, to "'be very careful in thy choice to satisfie thine eye, both in the person and favour of such a one as thou wouldst enjoy as thy consort, both in bed, and at board (as we may say)," and noted, "he whose wife is not to him as a loving hinde and pleasant roe will be ravisht with a strange woman, and embrace the bosom of a stranger."[56] This was humane advice. Yet, having no other institutions available except household intimacies or intimacies erected in worship or business meetings, Fox would not accept even figurative "hindes" or "roes" in Quaker marriages. Fox humorlessly removed all lust from marriage. Since a Quaker marriage existed as if the Fall never occurred, women were to be spiritually equal to men in marriage, not "weaker vessels." And Fox

reserved holy marriages only to those who by full obedience to the
Light could "witness transgression finished," who were ready to
testify publicly and repeatedly about the legitimacy of their motives,
and who were willing to have their characters and intentions carefully examined by the whole Quaker community or its delegates, so
that "the pretence of the spirit's moving may not be a cloak or cover
for beastly lust."[57]

Although he inveighed against lust in marriage, Fox and his
allies were purposefully quiet about what form conjugal sexuality
might take. Misinterpreting his intent, some New England Quakers
lived together in the late 1650s literally above lust, celibately as man
and wife, one couple for over four years. As the dismay of Quakers
visiting from England showed, the New Englanders had missed the
point, which was not to avoid conjugal sex, but which was to
spiritualize it.[58] In the love letters of the Swarthmore group, for
example, the leadings of the Light and of the libido were welded
together into one tender, spiritualized expression of holy marital
union. In 1667 Thomas Lower wrote to his absent betrothed, Mary
Fell, "and now my dearest, unto whom my heart is perfectly united
(and that which first begot our union each unto another) inseparably knit, in that do I most heartily embrace thee in the arms of pure
affection and seal it unto thee with the lip of truth, with which I
solace myself in the sorrowful days of this our distant approaches,
until it please the Lord to make our union more entire and complete."[59] In 1681 Daniel Abraham wrote similarly to Rachel Fell
about his love for her, "which originally is excited by, and derived
from something which in itself is of an immutable being, and
therefore in its progress doth not allow of any mutability of waver-
ing," and which finds "a daily increase of true and ardent affection,
tending to and pressing much for the full enjoyment and accomplishment of that which at present may be but seen at a distance."[60]
Thanks to such divine sublimations, Quaker honeymoons became
holy visitations. After marrying Annecken Derricke in 1662, the
busy itinerant William Caton noted, "I continued several weeks
with my dear wife, and the Lord was pleased very much to comfort
and refresh us together with his infinite loving kindness which
abounded to us, and with his heavenly blessing which he caused to
descend upon us: for which our souls have cause for ever to praise
and magnify his name."[61] It was such an emotional elision of spirit
and sexuality which would fascinate, amuse, and horrify popular
London writers and their southern audience.

Whatever its contemporary outlandishness, Fox and Fell carefully constructed marriage discipline to achieve this spiritualization. No matter that a proposed union began with sexual attraction (as many Quaker critics and ex-Quakers insisted most did), the physical emotions of the union were often sublimated by the time the initially lusting partners had passed voluntarily through the spiritual obstacle course which the Quaker community placed in their way. As early as 1653 the procedure assured a considerable lapse of time between first commitment and final marriage. The partners had to testify in various meetings about the purity of their motives and spiritual leadings. After falling in love by their own inner witness (never by arrangement, much less coercion), the couple were to go privately to some older Friends for advice. If the elders approved the proposal, the couple could announce their intended marriage toward the end of their own locality's worship meeting. Their testimony of intention alerted local Friends to re-examine the proposed newlyweds and to bring objections to the surface. If they passed, the partners could then be married by their own words of the spirit at a worship meeting attended by at least twelve older Friends. Margaret Fell issued an epistle in 1656, endorsed by George Fox, amending this procedure. Even before privately informing Friends, the couple, she insisted, must pitilessly examine their own motives. At their marriage, they must speak "what the unlimited power and spirit gave utterance." They must receive a marriage certificate signed by witnesses, and take the certificate as soon as possible to a Justice of the Peace. This procedure took at least two months. It took much longer, however, if the couple lived in different meeting areas, if any parents or close relatives lived far away, or if any spiritual or romantic obstacle was uncovered. During this waiting period, the partners had to refrain from sexual relations. Puritans often forgave couples who fornicated between betrothal and marriage. The Quakers summarily disowned them as unworthy of the faith.[62]

The Quakers' lengthy, intense procedure did change the emotions of proposed marriages. In Frandley Monthly Meeting, Cheshire, John Shalcroft fell in love with Katherine Dunbabin before she became a Quaker. She began to attend meetings because of their love. Someone in the meeting discovered the worldly origins of their relationship and cautioned them. In the fourth month of 1689 John Shalcroft appeared at meeting and acknowledged his "weakness in proposing anything relating to marriage with Katherine Dunbabin." He claimed that "before she came amongst Friends and frequented their assemblies they both became concerned for their beginnings and proceedings on account of marriage and affirming they both judged the matter and made an end for a considerable time." To better prove their sincerity, they gave their relationship additional patient and intense scrutiny. They continued to see each other and stayed in love but they refrained from sexual relations, and then they proposed their intentions again to the Frandley Meeting one year and six months later—more than two years from their first romantic involvement.[63]

The Quaker marriage discipline also aimed to avoid the disorder and family conflicts which often surrounded middling youths' or their parents' marriage choices. By 1660 couples had to show evidence of parental assent before proposing their intentions to a meeting. If a relative objected for reasons of finance or honor, however, the couple could ask their monthly meeting to liberate them for marriage over kins' objections. If kin continued to interfer, they would be disciplined. At the Morley Men's Meeting, Cheshire, in 1681, for example, a prestigious committee which included many future Pennsylvania emigrants (John Simcock, Thomas Janney) overruled Joseph and Mary Endon's effort to stop the marriage of their daughter Margaret with John Walker. With "a living sense upon our spirits" the committee judged "that in the grounds and life of the matter in the young people, there was a sense of the hand of God with which our spirits had unity and what could be said against it by the said Joseph and Mary Endon was not in any weight in the Truth in the least to lessen or weaken our judgments." Joseph and Mary Endon accepted the marriage's holiness, but "old Mary Endon said if our judgment were according to what was in her mind etc. . . ."[64]

Giving priority to holy love was, however, a hopeless policy among poor husbandmen. Such priority stripped middling parents of their ability not merely to arrange marriages but also to veto them or even to delay their accomplishment. A hard-pressed northwestern husbandman could not run a disciplined, solvent household with his children coercing him with their divine loves. In order to restore parental morale and authority, yet not to formally deny the Word of God, the general position became by 1690 that young Quakers should make no "motion or procedure . . . upon account of marriage without first acquainting their parents or guardians therewith, and duly waiting upon them for their consent and agreement therewith."[65] Finding that some young people argued that their love was divine and therefore unstoppable, the Quakers later refined their position to prohibiting youth who had not yet received parental consent from "drawing out the affections of one another."[66] The weight of the meeting thus moved toward defending parental authority, but the priority of holy love was never denied, only awkwardly muzzled. As a result of such a procedure with contradictory messages, many Quaker youth in Cheshire, Wales, and later Pennsylvania married outside the Quaker discipline with an inspired, holy sense of self-righteous rebellion against spiritually jaded parents. Even such failures testified to the efforts and chances the Quakers were taking to make holy love the comprehensive principle of marriage.

Fox and his adherents did not stop at completely spiritualizing marriage. Lacking the resources to establish alternative institutions, they had to rely on the household for childrearing. They demanded that parents suppress all impulse in childrearing and accept it as a loving responsibility requiring full vigilance and total self-control. Fox wrote letters dealing partly with parental duties in 1653 and 1655, but his interest clearly peaked in the late 1660s, largely because he and other Quaker leaders felt that many Quaker parents were being too permissive. In the excitements of early enthusiasm, two Quaker writers in 1660 had recommended, with meeting approval, virtual parental passivity. Seeming to discourage all parental intervention, William Salt told parents to "be not rash or hasty toward them, but to labour to instruct them, and with love and meekness to gain them."[67] Humphry Smith believed little children were better appreciated than disciplined, "for behold, and look upon young children, and see how innocent and lamb-like they look: and consider if everything were as good as God made it; and how much more if they were brought forth in the covenant of God?" Smith recalled how his parents had almost destroyed his fresh relation to God. His father had made him kill farm animals just to place a backbone in the sensitive boy, and his mother "hath come to me, its like hundreds of times, both when I was a child and a man," when Smith had sat communing with God, "and in her pity hath laid hands on me, and bid me should not sit studying so, for surely I would make myself a fool, not knowing what my condition was." Even thinking Quaker parents were capable of such intrusions, Smith concluded, "therefore let the Lord God be the teacher of your children, who hath given them life and being: a better teacher you cannot provide for them, nor direct them unto, and that which may be known of God is manifest in them: and let that lead them, and guide them in his fear."[68] Parents were merely to enjoy and protect their children's spiritual growth. When Quaker parents actually labored only with "love and meekness" to gain their children, they apparently, and not surprisingly, raised many brats among the saints. As this became clear, Quaker leaders demanded by the late 1660s vigorous parental intervention.

While Puritans focused their discipline on children's natural sin, Quaker writers continued to focus their discipline upon parents—only now increasingly misinformed, indulgent, and passive parents. These Quakers were not adopting the puritanical view that children were basically unredeemed "natural men" who needed their parents to uproot, even violently, their corrupt natures as a preparation for receiving Grace. What made Quaker advice-givers so angry at permissive parents was that their children had received the gift of the Light, that these children were too young to be responsible for preserving it, and that these overly fond parents had allowed such children to squander their gifts before these children reached the age of discretion. Unlike bad Puritan parents, bad Quaker parents did not merely fail to help save their children, they were responsible for killing their children's God-given Grace.

Quaker advice-givers did note children's dual nature: the child possessed both the Seed and original sin. However, most advice-givers criticized not children but parents for their destructive over-fondness. "Oh, that there were not cause for me to break forth into a lamentation for the sake of poor children, who are hurt through their parents' extreme love, or foolish fondness over them," wrote John Field in 1688, "but oh! my soul hath and doth lament over them, saying, if there be any truth in the proverb (that it is possible to kill with kindness) I am sure (with grief do I mention it) that many tender children are like to be destroyed by this extreme fond-ness from their fond parents, except it be prevented by a timely moderation."[69] Seeing the Quaker childrearing problem similarly, John Banks noted in 1692, "some spoil their children in letting them have their wills so much, that they become disobedient and rebellious, and so give away the power so much to the will of the child and lessen their authority. . . ."[70] As a result, Quaker advice-givers reserved their harshest punishment, not for disobedient children, but for overly fond parents. Joseph Pike thought the old proverb "foolishness is bound up in the heart of a child, but the rod of correction shall drive it from him," less useful than his own version, "foolish fondness being bound up in the heart of those parents, the rod of church discipline should be used in order, if possible, to drive it away."[71]

Quaker parenting became so spiritualized that the advice-givers became contradictory. The crosscurrents of advice doubtlessly confused Quaker parents. Such contradictory advice meant also that Quaker parenting was a frightening responsibility which required access to, yet control of, all emotions and all situations—complete self-discipline combined with full insight. Although the most notable advocate of the doctrine that all children everywhere were born with the Seed, George Fox recommended by 1665 a vigorous hand, even physical punishment, when correcting children.[72] Other Quakers, almost as authoritative, were simultaneously advocating gentler interventions. In 1667 Isaac Pennington advised parents when finding sin "to put them in mind of any of these things, in the fear and wisdom of God, with tenderness and gentleness, that many may reach the witness; but to take heed of upbraiding them, or aggravating anything, lest they be thereby hardened, and the bad raised and strengthened in them."[73] In 1670 the noted Quaker minister Stephen Crisp instructed the women's meeting at Ipswich, "that all women in profession and having children, may bring them up in the fear of God; and that they use no uncomely, rash, or passionate words unto them, for that sows an evil seed in children, which may come up and dishonour God in the next generation."[74]

Nor was there any practical escape from total responsibility. If parents trained their children fully and carefully, noted John Banks, "what way or course in after time their children may take when they are from under their power, the parents may be clear of their children in the day of account."[75] Such projected acquittal was, however, more theoretical than real. Parents who set bad examples for their children, or who were overly indulgent, were responsible for their children's spiritual deaths. And even if parents were persistent and vigorous correctors, they were still guilty if they ever used passionate words or hit with primitive rage, and thereby provoked "their children to wrath" and hence destroyed their children's souls. Nor could Quaker parents avoid these challenges of self-control by convenient absence or non-involvement; "a child left to himself bringeth his mother to shame," noted George Fox.[76] Little wonder that a late seventeenth-century Quaker schoolmaster, John Richardson, praised his wife Anne, who "was an affectionate and tender mother to her children, yet corrected them when occasion required, without passion, or the least appearance of disorder of mind, and had them in great subjection, at which I often admired, and thought, surely she is come by the workings of the Holy Spirit to a greater dominion over her own spirit than many who appeared to be her equal."[77] The minimal virtues for good Quaker parenthood were constant attention, tenderness, objectivity, self-control, and insight.

In order to make such spiritual households workable, Fox required self-disciplined, rational women in every household. When establishing a nationwide system of monthly meetings in the mid-1660s, Fox decided to include women's meetings in each jurisdiction. The responsibility of such women's meetings included visiting the sick, caring for young orphans, caring for poor Friends, disciplining younger women, inspecting the characters of women who announced their intention to marry, and overseeing all aspects of life which men or mixed company could not decently observe or discuss. Fox's chief purpose was to ensure household discipline. Fox knew that women had always discussed sex, husbands, birth, and children among themselves, but he wanted these vital topics discussed and administered under holy discipline, and wished women's valid insights enforced with full church authority. Additionally, Fox noted, "that there is many things that is proper for women to look into, both in their families and concerning women, which is not so proper for the men, which modesty in women cannot so well speak of before men as they can amongst their own sex." He also thought no men "but ranters will desire to look into women's matters."[78] Following such logic, Fox effected his most radical, fateful accomplishment in reorganizing the Anglo-American family: the encouragement and empowerment of spiritualized mothers as institutionalized in holy women's meetings.

The promotion of holy childrearing was at the center of his thoughts. As Fox told women's meetings in 1676, "so the women in the time of the gospel, light, and grace, are to look into their own selves and families, and to look to the training up of their children, for they are oft-times more amongst them than the men, and may prevent many things that may fall out, and many times they make or mar their children in their educations." Fox also wanted the best Quaker mothers to have the authority and power to train younger women to be like themselves (here was the original premise, incidentally, for *Little Women*). "These aged women," noted Fox, "must teach the younger women: first, to be sober; secondly, to love their husbands; thirdly, to love their children; fourthly, to be discreet; fifthly, to be chaste, and keepers at home . . . that the word of God be not blasphemed."[79] Speaking of the emerging hierarchy in the women's meetings, Fox noted, "some are of a more large capacity and understanding than other women, and are above to inform, and instruct, and stir up others into diligence, virtue, and righteousness, and godliness, and, in the love and fear of God, to inform and reform their families, and to help them that be of a weaker capacity and understanding than other women."[80] Fox wanted to give "spiritual mothers" unprecedented power to reproduce themselves socially.

This meant granting women new authority. In every other community, including that of the Puritans', women's characters were formed to please fathers, male ministers, and husbands, for women and property passed from father to husband (married women could not generally own property). Mothers usually had only gossip and the informal power of personality to affect their daughters. But on Fox's rule every Quaker woman had to answer to her independent female superiors before she answered to her husband or her community's male leaders. Fox had stipulated by 1670 that all women who wished to marry as Quakers had to announce their intentions with their intended spouse to their local women's meeting, had to endure month-long inspections of their characters by a female committee, and had to return with their intended to hear the verdict and receive advice. And Quaker men, who wished to marry as Quakers, had not only to choose a bride who would be approved by female Quaker elders but had also to offer themselves in powerless postures twice before the female elders (once to propose and again to hear the verdict). As such subordinate posturing suggested, these men would then have to accept the female elders' continued intrusions into their marriages and households.

Many devout Quaker men squealed with pain. They hated the women's meetings, particularly their power over marriage, especially the requirement to appear powerlessly before them twice in the marriage procedure. Echoing the most nightmarish anti-Quaker penny-press literature, Richard Smith, a Cheshire Quaker, complained in 1677 that "setting up of women's meetings runs parallel with the bringers in of circumcision among believers."[81] Fox understood that women's meetings pained men, but he thought that they were an essential part of his familial scheme. Fox suffered through ten years of schism for this position (the Wilkinson-Story schism) and reported nightmares of bulls chasing him over northern British hedges.[82] His strongest allies were the women called to office. As Mary Elson warned, "the more opposition we have had against our women's meetings, the more we have increased in the power of the Lord, and He hath blessed our endeavors and service."[83] By 1674, men and women had moved to different sections in worship meeting in order to reinforce the establishment of separate spheres of influence and expertise.[84]

With full empowerment of spiritualized mothers in 1675, Fox largely completed his design for comprehending with love and "holy conversation" all honor, impulse, and conflict in regenerate British households. Fox's thorough spiritualization of household life followed logically, to be sure, from his doctrine of "holy conversation." If Quakers were nearly embodiments of God's Word, as expressed in their speech, presence, and conduct, they should have households of comparable purity. But Fox's unwillingness to compromise on any spiritual exaction, despite the protests of many Quakers, was also influenced by the traditional worldly tribalism of his earliest recruits and the implausibility of eclipsing in northwest Britain the household and kinship connections with any other, differently organized, institution.

THE EMOTIONAL demands of the Quakers' new spiritual tribalism were obvious in the programs of northwestern British Quaker monthly meetings. From 1670 the Cheshire monthly meetings worked hard and creatively to change regenerate northwestern householders from worldly to holy, spiritual tribesmen. Seeing every human relationship as bearing upon the general communication of the Light within the community, the meetings felt compelled to pry and revise such relations with little regard for privacy, male prerogatives, or kinship ties. The Cheshire meetings counseled and disciplined at least five battling couples between 1670 and 1693, and they also mediated arguments between kin over monetary support of orphaned children and aged parents.[85] The Cheshire men's monthly meetings thought nothing of telling families not merely how to live but also where to live. Worried about the influence his carnal brother-in-law was having on Peter Dix, the Frandley Monthly Meeting became alarmed in 1683 when they learned that Dix "hath taken a house in the same land near adjoining to his brother Nathan Maydoll." They appointed a committee to advise Dix "forthwith (if he can) to relinquish the contract for the said house and to take one elsewhere." When Dix demurred, they disowned him.[86] When in 1688 the Frandley Meeting thought a widow was living in quarters which had "considerably impaired her condition as to worldly matters," they made a complete review of her finances "so care may be taken how or whether to advise her removal."[87] When they found Abraham Merrick "who hath of late been much ensnared by evil company of which he hath frequently been admonished to shun yet they are prevalent to the grief of Friends," they told him to leave the county.[88]

Meeting instrusions were as creative as they were invasive. In Morley Monthly Meeting, covering Wilmslow, Mobberley, Congleton, and Stockport parishes, a form of compulsory family-group therapy began in 1696, and it lasted for at least two years. This was the first family-group therapy or therapeutic family-group worship in the British historical record. Some gloomy Cheshire farmers and their wives were apparently inhibiting the flow of spiritual excitement in their households (the general causes of this gloom will be discussed in the next chapter). On November 4, 1696, the Morley Men's Meeting noted that "for the preservation of the members of the body (of the Church of Christ) . . . tis thought fit that each particular meeting as an addition to their former care doth make a more particular inquiry . . . how things are with and amongst Friends in their families: and tis tenderly advised that care be taken in every family that nothing be encouraged or countenanced that may hurt or weaken any in appearing in a faithful testimony for the truth of God; and in order to it, we desire Friends may be free and open in expressing themselves upon this occasion in their aforesaid meetings as how they have been preserved from heaviness."[89] As in other of their views on authentic language, they believed that some suspension of normal social criticism, "free and open expression", was the way to uncover truth. Three months later, the Morley Men's Meeting happily announced that "most Friends freely expressed themselves in their preparative meetings signifying how things have been with them in their families to the comfort of this meeting, and where any refuse to answer the requests of Friends in this matter, those deputed for to take care for the month are desired to inquire of them the reason of their refusal and to signify to the monthly meetings."[90] Silence was not approved in this situation.

During one family session a Mobberley farmer, Jonathan Yarwood, raised objections about the intrusiveness of the procedure,
but shied away from further criticism when asked by the monthly
meeting to express fully his dissent.[91] Two years from the first
family therapy meeting, the Morley elders heard "a pleasing account how in several meetings Friends had expressed themselves
very cautiously . . . and there being benefited by it, and that those
that had been overtaken with heaviness were sorry for it and hope
for the future to be more careful."[92] Spiritualized domestic love was
no idle boast among these obscure northwest British farmers and
their wives. Among many other things, their meetings attempted to
enforce compulsory household happiness through the free and open
sharing of the emotional minutiae of household relations.

THE POLITICAL and social implications of Quaker familialism
caused southerners to review their opinions about Quakers. At first
London Grub-Street writers of penny pamphlets accused the new
northern Quakers of using talk of free grace to escape all civilized
restraint. The London writers associated Quakers with the Ranters,
a small group who argued that all things, including sexual promis-
cuity, were permitted to true possessors of the Holy Spirit. Thus, on
the woodcut frontispiece of *The Quaker's Dream* (London, 1655),
Quakers embraced over the rubric "free will" and the six naked
Quakeresses danced wildly above the rubric "above ordinances."[93]
Thus, the frequent stories of Quaker buggery with horses.[94] London
writers continued, as late as 1671, to picture Quakers as sexual
gourmands. In Mathew Stevenson's *The Quaker Wedding* (1671),
for example, "the libertine comes to the Levites' room, and is at
once both the parson and the groom, he babbles like a brute, and by
and by he takes the bride, and goes to multiplying."[95] By 1675 the
pamphlet writers recognized Quaker familial sublimations. The
frustration and temptation presented by the Quakers' conflations of
sex and the Holy Spirit was the only theme in four London anti-
Quaker pamphlets, published in 1675.[96] Tellingly, they attacked the
Quakers with more venom for spiritualizing conjugal relations
than they ever had for being reputedly unrestrained.

The underlying terror of this ugly literature was mother-son
incest, a fear and fascination elicited by the Quakers' thorough
spiritualization of marriage and married women. The writers were
accustomed to seeing themselves as rational and women as irra-

tional "weaker vessels". Such a view allowed them to imagine copulating or beating women with little guilt. But Quaker men were suddenly seen as being trapped into marriages with women too tender, authoritative, and spiritual for unpunished conjugal sex. In *The Quaker Turned Jew* (London, 1675), a Quaker did seduce a spiritualized Quaker matron, but he felt so unusually guilty afterwards that he mutilated himself. After he was detected "he resolved upon the following penance, for immediately he returned to his closet, drew forth the man of sin out of his breeches, and beholding it with an eye of indignation, 'thou based and filthy member (quoth he) whose standing hath occasioned my fall, I will now take vengeance upon thee,' saying which, with a sharp knife he circumcizes himself, and sending for a surgeon applyed remedies to the wound; resolving to expiate his offense by dissembling himself for the future, to perpetuate any such nefarious crimes." He simply completed his ruinous spiritualization and total isolation from British society by becoming a Jew.[97]

In the *The Secret Sinners* (London, 1675), a frustrated Quaker husband fornicated with his maid-servant, because, as he complained, his tender, older, ministerial wife was essentially forbidden, "by reason she hath kept all her light within, and held none forth till now of late, it has dryed her up, nay, burnt her to a charcoal; and again I say unto thee, she is stricken in years, and regardeth not the flesh . . . ."[98] On the story's logic, the husband could either remain celibate in marriage, commit adultery, or commit a worse, unnamed offense with his holy wife-mother. Such were the supposed problems awaiting men in new Quaker marriage.

The writers continued the formula of the Quaker husband's escape from an overly spiritualized and authoritative wife into adultery in the *Yeah and Nay Almanacks* of 1679 and 1680, allegedly prepared for Quaker customers, in the *The Quakers' Art of Courtship* (London, 1710) and in the ex-Quaker Elias Bockett's *Aminadad's Courtship* (London, 1717). In these pieces, the Quaker male was trapped by his religion into a marriage too spiritualized for conjugal sexual exercise. He usually used Quakerly language to seduce a forbidden woman, though less forbidden than his own wife.[99] Bockett's story was only slightly different. In his verse narrative, two naive Quaker youths believed their love was based on the spirit, not sex, but became disillusioned after a riotous, drunken, wedding night. Yet, it was the gallivanting male Quaker hypocrite who became the stock item. He walked on stage briefly, for example, in Thomas Walker's *The Quaker's Opera* (London, 1728) to seduce a prison-maid.[100] He appeared as Israel Pemberton in Pennsylvania in the 1760s in two political cartoons explicitly about Benjamin Franklin's use of the Quaker party to attack the Penns' proprietary interest. In the corner of both cartoons, the cartoonist placed the Quaker lecher gratuitously but conspicuously going about the usual business of seducing a forbidden woman, a bare-breasted Indian squaw.[101] In time the images of Quaker eroticism became more explicitly comic than venomous. They focused more and more on the sexual excitement and humorous double meanings inherent in tender, Quaker language of spirit love. Eventually popular Quaker images became stripped of all sinister erotic connotations. Nowadays Quaker images are exploited to sell not erotica but breakfast cereal.

POPULAR writers possibly aimed their rage at Quakers to express anxieties about upper class familial trends. By the late seventeenth century rich London merchants, southeastern aristocrats, and many wealthy gentry families were treating their wives and children more sensitively, more spiritually. They hoped to raise sons sufficiently self-composed and sociable to take advantage of the new careers in the consolidated English state or in its expanding national and international markets.[102] Sophisticated Puritan ministers also advocated spiritual reform of marriage. These men were more powerful than mere upland Quaker livestock farmers, but the Quakers were more radical. For all their documented changes, rich, cosmopolitan Englishmen never wanted to deny the moral importance of the Anglican Church or the boarding school. Even Puritan clergymen regarded women as "weaker vessels," receptacles of lust and irrationality who should not be allowed to speak in church (even radical Puritans like John Milton agreed whole-heartedly).[103] The Puritans insisted that churches based on educated rationality, not female prattle, needed to be retained to promote the Holy Spirit in England. Southerners could afford extra-household institutions, so they did not mind allowing some healthy irrationality in the household. Only the Foxian Quakers thought differently.

The ideal of domesticity emerged first, not in response to any new fracturings of familial relations caused by the activities of markets (though it might in other circumstances), but in the response of upland, middling, religious zealots to their reliance upon kinship clusters, household ties, and friends. Historians have searched for family change in England in gentry country houses near London, in bourgeois townhouses, and in Oxford and Cambridge educated clergymen's sermons. These are the most plausible places to look, for economic and political change in the seventeenth century was led by southeastern English people. The spectacular growth of London from a small city of some 40,000 people in 1500 to a colossal city of some 300,000 people by 1700—and its development as an international and national labor and economic market— marked great changes in English life. The consolidation of the English state and the internal expansion of a national market in land, agricultural produce, and textiles had an immense impact. Southeastern families did change. Yet only when such political, economic, and religious changes met the resistances of the old poverty and customs of upland smallholders did a significant group abandon all reliance upon formal institutions and begin advocating thorough domesticity.

Domesticity was an essential part of George Fox's and Margaret Fell's religious strategy, primarily to remain faithful to their revelations, secondarily to draw and keep northern and northwestern farmers within Quakerism. The Quakers wanted to base worship on nonverbal spiritual intimacy and even to spiritualize married women into authoritative and sexually threatening household and extra-household ministers. They wanted to make households totally spiritual and therefore morally self-sufficient. Upland Quakers created the most spiritualized household relations ever seen in England.[104]

CHAPTER THREE

A Family of Great Price

Whatever its advantages locally over the Puritans' reform program, northwestern British Quaker domesticity was still politically and economically implausible. Neither the Royalist nor Puritan state had use for a system which created conscience to the exclusion and disdain of a morally authoritative upper class or the profession of university-trained ministers of the Word of God. Not counting jail-time or tithe destraints, the Anglican authorities squeezed Cheshire and Welsh Quakers between 1660 and 1685 for at least £1,500 in persecutorial fines.[1] Quaker domesticity was also too expensive for a pre-industrial society of limited wealth, especially in one of that society's poorest regions. The Quakers' plain infrastructure of un-paid, spiritually educated ministers and modest meeting houses hid their households' need for more wealth than northwestern England could supply. Unusually costly was Quaker leaders' logical insis-tence that Quaker parents raise their children in environments of joyous "holy conversation" and that they place their children on livable land or in occupations exclusively among pious Quakers. Such Quaker households had to reject "worldly" northwest mid-dling households' prudent compromises with economic scarcity: their limited sense of responsibility for their own children's souls, and their reliance upon kin and gentry clusters. Not surprisingly, misfit, northwestern British Quaker households experienced a po-tentially fatal crisis between 1660 and 1700 in which they not only failed to gain many additional proselytes but also lost well over half their own children to the "world."

Yet, just because of its implausibility, northwestern British Quaker domesticity proved its durability and creativity between 1660 and 1700. The Quakers' struggle to pay the new familial costs during these years was partly responsible for the following creative developments: 1) their refined preoccupation with childrearing and spiritual, behavioral discipline; 2) their use of the monthly-quarterly-yearly meeting system to increase and maintain wealth and children within the Quaker community; 3) their cultivation of entreprenuership and economic prudence and the fostering and honoring of such entreprenuerial men and their qualities by the Quaker community; 4) their migrations within Great Britain to take advantage of the opportunities opened by Quaker entreprenuers and across the Atlantic to develop Pennsylvania land; 5) their development of a vision for America of a new type of landed society, especially fostering of Quaker domesticity. The northwest Quakers lost many members during this period, but they also created two small empires—a commercial-industrial empire centered in northern British towns, and a landed empire centered in Pennsylvania. If the material and political world of seventeenth-century Britain failed to accommodate the peculiarly demanding requirements of Quaker domesticity, these first practitioners of domesticity found the inner resources and the outer luck to make worlds in which their family system was plausible.

CONDITIONS in northwestern Britain were not entirely repressive. The Quaker's new discipline apparently improved middling Quaker households' health and fertility. Using only those family reconstructions in which the death of at least one spouse was documented, 126 Quaker Cheshire households and 57 Quaker South Welsh and Hereford couples formed between 1650 and 1690 had an average of 4.23 and 4.61 live births per marriage respectively, a fertility achievement surpassing the 3.75 live births per first marriage produced by 47 coeval non-Quaker Cheshire marriages. And, if Quaker and non-Quaker Cheshire burial registers can be compared, the children of the Quaker couples also enjoyed better health. Non-Quaker Cheshire households lost 1.41 children to death before the children reached 24 years; the 126 Cheshire Quaker households lost one child. The Cheshire Quakers did better than even the wealthier rural families of Terling, Essex.[2]

Quaker family discipline and faith can be credited with producing some of these benefits, if only because, by the late 1660s, the Quaker meetings were selective about who could get married in meeting and whose names appeared subsequently in the Quaker marriage and birth registers (British parish registers were not so exclusive). By meeting testing and certification, Quaker partners were loving and responding people. Quaker partners were more companionate than the average—at least, first Quaker marriages in Cheshire were made by couples whose ages were closer together than non-Quakers couples. In Cheshire, during this period, the Quaker men on average were only 3.6 years older than their female partners compared with six years for non-Quaker men. In 32 Cheshire Quaker marriages formed between 1658 and 1724 in which ages of both male and female were known, the men averaged 29.8 years at first marriage and the women 26.12. The women were older in seven of these marriages; the partners shared the same age in four marriages; the men were older in 21 marriages—two-thirds of the time seven years or less. Surveillence, voluntary marriage, spiritualized love, closeness in age led to higher fertility and better health.[3]

Though the Quaker partners produced an unusually large number of healthy children, they failed to convert many of them to Quakerism. The increase in Quaker marriages and births in Cheshire and Wales, expected from such a bumper crop of children, never occurred. Between 1650 and 1679, Cheshire Quaker couples had 503 births, but there were only 298 Cheshire Quaker brides and grooms between 1670 and 1699: 42 percent of those born were unaccounted for. In south Wales between 1650 and 1679, south Welsh Quaker couples had 343 births, but only 169 south Welsh Quakers married between 1670 and 1699: 49 percent of those born were unaccounted for (many of the marriages were second marriages).[4] Northwest Quaker children simply abandoned Quakerism, or at least the region, in large numbers. The problem was not the high standards of Quaker family life and discipline per se, but the Welsh mountains and other barriers erected by the limited northwest economy, worsened by Anglican persecution, against the fulfillment of exacting Quaker familial standards.

Few children married within their quarterly meeting districts, and many probably never married or married outside the Quaker community. Ninety-eight Cheshire Quaker couples who remained in Cheshire between 1650 and 1684 saw only 32 percent (86) of all their surviving children married in Quaker meetings in Cheshire and Staffordshire; and among the 21 rooted South Welsh couples only 15 of their surviving children, a pathetic 18 percent, married in meeting in South Wales or Hereford. A few of these children doubtless married as Quakers elsewhere in England, Ireland, or America. But most migrant children were probably lost to the "world." The northwestern quarterly meeting registers covered an extensive geographic area—for example, the Cheshire-Staffordshire register covered two counties and part of North Wales. Cheshire had a few economically strong Quaker centers like Frodsham and Congleton which might have attracted Welsh Quaker youth. Yet, the Cheshire registers show few outlying Quakers marrying natives within these counties. In a sample of 128 marriages between 1660 and 1710 registered in the Cheshire-Staffordshire Quaker records, almost 86 percent of the first marriages (103) were between people born in Cheshire or Staffordshire. Among the 25 marriages that included people from outside these counties, twelve of the outsiders were from Lancashire, just across the Cheshire County line.

As confirmed by an analysis of 19 Cheshire Quaker men who died before 1700 whose wills or probate inventories could be found, northwest middling households needed more wealth, as well as more spiritual discipline and charisma, to guide their children into the Quaker fold. The eleven men whose estates, including land, leases, and personal property, were worth over £150 found marriages for a small share of their children; but the eight Quaker men whose estates fell below £150 found marriages for none of their children. Eleven such Cheshire men who died before 1700, all having estates over £150, had 39 surviving children and among them 17 married Quakers in Cheshire and Staffordshire meetings, a retention rate of 43.5 percent. This rate was hardly reason for a celebration, but it was far better than that experienced by poor Cheshire Quakers, still the majority of the movement. John Tappiley married in 1674 and by the time he died in 1688, this Norley, Cheshire, husbandman had three sons, ages ten, nine, and seven. In 1685 he left an estate of £35—his most valuable possession being his two cows worth £10 collectively. None of his sons married among the Cheshire or Staffordshire Quakers, and this was the typical experience. Eight such men died before 1700, all having estates under £150; they left 24 surviving children and not one of them married among Quakers in the Cheshire and Staffordshire meetings.[5]

While weakening over-matched households, English persecution did not directly cause households' failures to marry their surviving children within the regional Quaker community. The households that experienced harsh persecution actually did slightly better producing married Quaker children than did those households that largely escaped fines and jailings. In Cheshire, 41 percent of 98 rooted households experienced at least one episode of severe persecution: 38 percent of these spent at least a month in jail, and paid out at least £815 collectively, or an average of £21 per household, which was nearly a solid middling farmer's annual income. Such losses of time and money certainly hurt households' ability to keep their children within the Quaker community. Nevertheless, forty of the most harshly persecuted Cheshire Quaker households had 114 surviving children of whom thirty-eight (33 percent) married as Quakers in Cheshire or Staffordshire: fifty-seven Cheshire Quaker households who experienced little financial loss from persecution had 155 surviving children of whom 48 (31 percent) married as Quakers in Cheshire. Both groups retained a paltry share of children within the regional Quaker community. Seven of the eleven wealthiest Quaker households examined did experience severe financial losses from persecution, losing between 1654 and 1689 £315 collectively. Anglican informers were wicked enough to go after wealthy targets from whose losses the informers skimmed a percentage. Yet analysis shows that in none of these cases were the financial losses from persecution decisive in preventing these households from marrying their children within the Quaker community. Among the nine poorer Quakers, only three men experienced major losses and these men lost just £22 collectively. While a considerable sum for poor farmers, its retention in their hands would not have given them enough to keep their children both in the county and in Quakerism, at least as married adults.[6]

In light of these figures, and the experiences of Anglican Cheshire and Welsh farmers during this period, there is really nothing surprising about the inability of most middling highland northwestern Quaker households to retain any more than a third of their children as married folk within the regional Quaker community. (The Quaker family system and their stubborn adherence to it is surprising.) It should be remembered that among 47 middling Anglican Cheshire households formed between 1656 and 1681 the parents had 110 children survive to 24 years and saw only 32 of their children married within their parishes, or 29 percent of all surviving children. Their experience was not greatly different from that of 98 Quaker households who retained 32 percent of their surviving chil-

dren in the regional Quaker community. Only the Quakers' radical
beliefs about children and childrearing made these dispersions hurt
so deeply. No matter how innovative spiritually and emotionally,
Quaker households by and large were being defeated by the same
old economic realities that plagued all middling Cheshire households and which prevented them from providing good livings
regionally for their children. Ninety-eight rooted Cheshire couples
had produced just 52 marriages in Cheshire and 21 South Welsh
couples had produced just 15 regionally marrying children—or at
most nine Quaker marriages. Within just one generation of their
religion's founding, 119 Quaker households that stayed in northwest
Britain had managed to produce only some 61 replacement couples,
the northwest Quaker community being thus reduced by 49 percent.
Such a reduction might have been an honorable badge of spiritual
martyrdom if the Quakers had belittled marriage and children. They
claimed, however, to have divinely designed a spiritually infectious
family system. They regarded every child lost to the "world" a
tragedy and they lost them by the bushel load. Thus, from a regional
perspective, the northwest Quaker community between 1660 and
1700 was facing its painful reduction and extinction.

IN ORDER to meet the costs of their family system, the northwest
farmers had to find new resources or perish. Not surprisingly, the
late seventeenth-century northwest Quaker communities generally
buzzed with desperate economic exertion and strategies, though
these local efforts were often inadequate.

The wills of seventeenth-century Cheshire Quakers show, for
example, considerable reform of customary inheritance patterns
toward increasing intra-household obligation, and increasing parental economic responsibility. Many farmers tried to make an
independent economic base (a freehold farm or a three-lives-leasehold) for more than one child. A few farmers even tried to make
their daughters independent (most northwestern farmers thought
the purchase of a life-leasehold for one son enough of a burden). For
example, William Crimes, a Quaker yeoman of Weverham, Cheshire, left in 1699 his real and personal estate to his wife, Elizabeth
Crimes, to rear his three children, all daughters. But upon his wife's
death he had directed the family freehold to his eldest daughter
Mary (born 1684). Just before his death, Crimes also bought additional land in Weverham, which he left to his second daughter,

Elizabeth (born 1687). Both elder daughters, Crimes insisted, were to pay his youngest daughter, Rebecca (born 1692), £100 collectively. Thus, two of Crimes's daughters got freehold estates encumbered with heavy household obligations.[7]

A similar pattern of effortful accumulation and intra-household obligation was followed by Joseph Endon, a husbandman in Bossely, Cheshire. Endon and his wife Mary had produced during a 36 year marriage seven surviving children (two sons and five daughters). In 1682, with help from the local monthly meeting's intervention against her parents' objections, the Endon's second daughter Martha married at age 28. After their mother's death in 1683, the eldest daughter Ellen and the third daughter Mary also married in Quaker meeting, while another daughter Sarah married a non-Quaker by 1688. Joseph Endon, the widower, died in 1688. He left the Bossely farm, held in three-lives-leasehold, to his eldest son, then 28 years old. Additionally, Endon had bought another three-lives-leasehold in Rode which he left to his second son, Jacob, who was then 25 years old. He treated both sons identically. From these sons' farms, Endon stipulated, the remaining, unmarried daughter, Hannah, then 19 years old, was to receive £120 at age 21 and £200 at age 22, a large portion. Endon also treated his Quaker sons-in-law well, giving them £40 apiece in addition to their previously received marriage portions. His disobedient daughter Sarah received only £5, however, being clearly penalized for her worldly choice and previous behavior (a number of other Quaker fathers similarly penalized, though they did not entirely disinherit, disobedient children). In this disciplined Quaker household, obedient children were treated alike according to gender role; intra-household obligations among siblings were increased; and there was a clear effort to expand the household's economic base to accommodate the Quakers' egalitarian, individualistic, and protective childrearing principles. Incidentally, even the hard-working, cautious Endons had problems: only four of their seven surviving children married in Cheshire and Staffordshire meetings. As the general statistics show, Cheshire and Welsh Quaker farmers could not stem the loss of their children simply by individual effort and care.[8]

Cheshire middling Quaker households continued to rely and intertwine with extra-household kin, if they were Quakers, but their role was increasingly eclipsed by the monthly meetings. Typically in transition was the wealthy Cheshire yeoman, William Gandy, who died in 1683 with both his daughters previously married, one to a non-Quaker. The Quaker daughter received £400; the non-Quaker daughter £50. After these exactions were paid from his real estate, the land was transferred to his Quaker brother, Edward Gandy. William Gandy also gave his other brothers and their children each £20 and gave the same amount to the Frandley Monthly Meeting.[9] Almost all the wealthy Quakers gave substantial amounts to their monthly and quarterly meetings. The money was most often earmarked for the support of poorer Quakers' children. From the eleven wealthy men's wills analyzed came £88 for such purposes.[10] The monthly meetings could superintend children with more moral concern than could "carnal talking" kin.

With such resources, the northwest Quaker monthly meetings tried, between 1660 and 1700, to solidify the economic base of Quaker households and, when that failed, to save and place orphaned or impoverished children among Quakers. Aside from constantly reminding Quaker farmers to make wills in order to avoid inefficient use and alienation of household resources, the monthly meetings provided constant oversight and compulsory advice to regional Quaker entreprenuers and tradesmen. In 1673, the Quarterly Meeting of North Wales decided to take "a more especial care and regard to the condition of such Friends that are in a declining state as to outward affairs amongst us" and appointed "unbiased and understanding men" to advise them.[11] A Quaker had best lay his books (and they best be neat and complete) before meeting experts at the first hint of financial difficulty, and he had best take their advice. If he failed to take such precautions and went bankrupt, he was often disowned. By 1695 the Morley Men's Meeting in Cheshire grew more intrusive: they appointed a committee to "inspect into the state and circumstances of all Friends that are traders or dealers, if possible through timely and seasonable advice, they may be prevented from making breeches in or upon our ancient testimony by involving themselves in debt they cannot seasonably and honestly discharge."[12] The committee swept through the market towns of north central Cheshire uncovering imprudent Quaker dealers and compelling them to sell tenements and commodities to make good. It was mainly because of the burdens of Quaker familialism that bankruptcy, although not mentioned in the Ten Commandments or the Sermon on the Mount, became a moral, disownable offense among the Quakers.

Following George Fox's advice, the meetings also tried to place and support young Quaker orphans in spiritually healthy and economically hopeful apprenticeships and service with sober, pious Friends, who would take care for these children's souls and later placement. Even before the formal establishment of monthly meetings in the late 1660s, northwest Quakers were informally taking care of poor children on the brink of falling into the economic webs of the destructive "world." While compiling a history of the sufferings of south Welsh Quakers, the Quarterly Meeting of South Wales also recorded "disbursements toward the relief of the poor and other exemplary uses belonging to the church," all events taking place before the formation of meetings for business. One typical series of incidents involved the death in 1665 of the indebted Morgan Eynon of Haverfordwest, "he left his wife with five children: William Bateman of the said town, weaver, took one; Lewis David of Llandewy took another child; part of his debt, vizt: twelve pounds or thereabout, was paid by Friends of the several meetings, the remainder his relect Jane Eynon satisfied and took care for the other three children, one of them being infirm in his eyesight."[13] After their formation, the monthly meetings absorbed responsibility for orphaned and poor Quaker children. Between 1670 and 1700, three Welsh meetings supported eleven apprenticeships and four Cheshire meetings supported twelve. Inasmuch as there were significant gaps in the extant meeting minutes and active meetings whose minutes were entirely lost, the actual number of meeting-supported apprenticeships was doubtless much larger. The Quaker meetings spent more money on such children during these years than on direct relief of sufferings from persecution.

Despite their smaller economic base and the payment of well over £1,500 to Anglican authorities and informers, these meetings also spent more money per child than did the comparable parish apprenticeship system of the regional Anglican church and state. The Quakers' superior commitment to children was obvious in North Wales—many Welsh parishes, as noted, had no parish apprenticeship system. Although the SPG in the late seventeenth century did begin to establish charity schools in the mountains, the SPG did not handle orphan placement directly.[14] Parish apprenticeships for orphans were common in Cheshire, but the Cheshire system was visibly less generous per child than that of the poorer Quakers. Between 1670 and 1700 in Audlem, Church Hulme, and Wybunberry parishes in Cheshire, 15 parish orphans were fostered out to local households for terms of an average of 7.5 years; the mean fee given by the parishes to the foster households with each child was £3. The Cheshire Quaker meetings fostered out at least seven orphans during these years to Quaker households for terms of an average of seven years; the mean fee given by the meetings with each child was much larger, however, £7.[15]

The Quaker meetings' efforts were occasionally outstanding. In 1674, the North Wales Quarterly Meeting discovered that an orphan, Mordecai Moore, dreamt of becoming a barber-surgeon. Charles and Thomas Lloyd, vernacular physicians themselves, combed Wales and discovered the Quaker publicist and frontier barber-surgeon Thomas Wynne. The Montgomeryshire, Shropshire, and Merionethshire meetings then raised over £10 to pay the clever boy's apprenticeship fee (the highest fee paid by Cheshire parishes was £5). Thirteen years later, in 1687, now a prosperous surgeon, Mordecai Moore gratefully paid back the £10 to the meetings.[16]

Female children commanded smaller fees than male orphans in both Anglican parish and Quaker meeting, and almost all girls were placed out as domestic servants, occasionally learning a specialized household skill like butter-making. The two communities' commitments, as reflected in the fees given, remained visibly different, however. For example, in Church Hulme parish in 1670, Ellen Leay was placed out as a butter-making domestic servant for seven years with a fee of 16 shillings and 4 pence; her master was to release her "in as good apparel as she now hath with her." In contrast, in 1700 the Morley Monthly Meeting placed out Martha Taylor as a servant for seven years with a fee of £6 (120 shillings) and demanded that her master release her in "handsome apparel."[17]

The northwestern British Quaker meetings failed to command adequate resources to find places regionally, however, for all needy Quaker children. As family reconstructions suggest, there were almost 300 surviving Quaker children born between 1650 and 1700 who might have benefited greatly from a financial supplement. Here is where persecution had hurt deeply. During these years, the Cheshire Quaker community paid out at least £1,189 and the South Wales' community lost at least £206, and such figures do not count the value of the work-time Quakers lost in prison or the losses from distraints following unpayment of tithes. Although the bulk of these losses were incurred by relatively wealthy Friends whose economic base in land and trade usually allowed them to support and place their own children adequately, the losses cut the capital available to the meetings to invest in regional apprenticeships for poorer Quakers' children. By 1712, the Quarterly Meeting of North Wales admitted that even its limited program covering a diminishing number of Quakers was causing severe financial strain; collections from the monthly meetings, they noted, "fall much too short to answer the said services," and they wrote a letter to wealthy Bristol Quakers "laying before them the circumstances of this meeting."[18]

Even if the money lost to persecution had been returned, too few lucrative positions existed in northwestern mountains and badlands for all needful Quaker children, a situation shared by all northwestern children, especially Welsh children. In 1703 the Quarterly Meeting of South Wales began to inquire, for example, "if any Friend may want a girl being about ten or eleven years of age for an apprentice and to give an account to the next Quarterly Meeting." A place had still not been found for her in the region by the next quarterly meeting. While the meeting continued to look for a "proper place for her," the meeting also began to ask her father "whether he is willing to let her go to Pennsylvania in case no other place be found for her in this country."[19] They thought it better that she risk the dangers and loneliness of the Atlantic crossing than the corruptions of non-Quaker economic networks. After persecution ended, northwestern British Quakers became interested in cheaper, collectivized schemes for educating children in protected environments. The Cheshire Quarterly Meeting in 1697 decided to support a school in dressmaking at Chester and in 1699 gave a Friends school at Middlewich the interest of £100. The Morley Monthly Meeting in 1698 "thought fit that Friends he reminded monthly to put their children-to school and to encourage the school at Chester by sending children to it."[20] The Frandley Men's Monthly Meeting in 1697 noted that they read with deep interest a London paper, doubtless from the Quaker social visionary John Bellars, "touching publick houses to be erected for employing youth."[21] The roots of the Quakers' long commitment and contributions to cheap, efficient, mass education, including the later Lancasterian system (1803), lay in these years of Quaker familial crisis. The efforts of rooted northwestern Quaker households to individually and collectively save themselves and their children, while heroic, were ultimately hopeless. There was simply too little wealth in middling pre-industrial northwestern British households for Quaker domesticity.

SOME LOCAL Quaker gentry tried to solve the problem by risking their estates in economic innovation. The northwestern Quakers' familial crisis, and probably similar crises in other economically unprivileged regions of England, first ignited famed Quaker entreprenuership, and then provided a compelling rationale for the Quaker community's continued encouragement of men of great wealth. By the middle of the eighteenth century, the English Quaker community was characterized by numerical decline, urbanization, and entreprenuerial achievement. "By the second half of the eighteenth century the English Quakers had established themselves as the founders and managers of great firms," noted David Brion Davis, "manufacturing porcelain, locks, instruments, drugs, and china: they were the leaders in mining, particularly of lead and in the production of brass, zinc, copper, and other metals."[22] The gallery of great, opulent Quaker entreprenuers included the succession of Abraham Darbys, who first used coke successfully in England to smelt iron ore and who founded the gigantic Coalbrookdale ironworks in Shropshire; the Hanbury family, who developed among other things South Welsh ironworking and metalworking, including the Melingriffith tin-plate works, the largest in the world by the end of the eighteenth century; the Barclay family of Scotland who used a mercantile fortune to lay the foundations of Barclays Bank International; and the list could go on. Some of them centered their operations initially in the northwest and north and often developed new technologies and new financial arrangements to extract new wealth from seemingly intractable northwestern resources.[23]

The Lloyds of Dolobran tried to save North Welsh Quakerism by such innovations, but failed (they did handsomely when they moved out of Wales, however). Charles Lloyd II, a former Cromwellian Justice of the Peace and then Quaker mainstay in Montgomeryshire, Wales, stayed in North Wales at Dolobran, Meifod parish, Montgomeryshire, while his brother Thomas Lloyd went to Pennsylvania and became a most influential politician in that colony between 1681 and 1694. The Lloyds' ancestral estate, Dolobran, was an affluent holding by highland Welsh standards: a small demesne farm, several tenant farms, a manor house, and a lesser house. Its profits alone could not bankroll the North Welsh Quaker community, however. In 1697, a year before Charles Lloyd II's death, the Montgomeryshire Quaker community had been reduced by migration to a mere handful of families. Charles Lloyd II's son Sampson and daughter Elizabeth Lloyd had themselves already left for more lucrative opportunities in Birmingham. Only Charles Lloyd III and his wife Sarah (Crowley) Lloyd stayed with the patriarch at the mountain home. Old Charles Lloyd II still hoped to save Quakerism in Montgomeryshire. "We be not clear of this place," he noted, "it lays hard upon us that the meeting be better settled, lest it be scattered." The dispersions of Quaker families and the decline of the Quaker neighborhood, he wrote, "will hasten my hoary head to the grave more than all my prisons, debts, and traveling."[24]

In 1697, six months before Charles Lloyd II went to convalesce and die at his daughter's house in Birmingham, Charles Lloyd III took on his father's burden and leased an iron forge at £40 a year at Mathrafal, just across the Vyrnwy River neighboring the Lloyd property. The forge took pig iron and further smelted it with charcoal and shaped it with hammers into bar iron, which would then be sold to ironmongers, including the Lloyds in Birmingham. The venture was initially a success. Aside from improving the main house at Dolobran, Charles Lloyd III used his new profits to shore up the local Quaker community. In 1699 he contributed over 40 percent of the funds for the building of the first Quaker meeting house in Montgomeryshire.[25] He largely funded the hiring in 1701 of the first Montgomeryshire Quaker schoolmaster, and within a few years the Quaker school grew to over twenty students.[26] Employing at its height over forty men, the iron forge also sustained many Quaker households in Meifod parish. At the top of this Quaker iron society, Amos Davies, clerk of the Dolobran Monthly Meeting, was also clerk of Lloyd's forge. John Kelsall, the first Quaker schoolmaster at Dolobran, lodged at Amos Davies's house, married his daughter, and later replaced Davies as clerk of the Dolobran Monthly Meeting and also of the iron forge.[27]

Childrearing was a major preoccupation of the revived Dolobran Quaker community. Reflecting his and other Quakers' concern about childrearing, John Kelsall kept a notebook from 1710 to 1712 in which he jotted down the names of visiting Quaker ministers who came to Dolobran meeting, and what, if anything, they had to say about children and youth. They kept him scribbling: among the 91 days in which visiting Friends were present at first day meeting, advice and exhortations about or directed to children figure predominantly on 32 days (35 percent of the total). On the 3rd month, 3rd day, 1703, Nicholas Locke "had a word of advice to parents and overseers of children to be careful over them for they were the heritage of the Lord"; on the 4th month, 6th day, 1708, Mary Ellerton of Yorkshire "had very good counsel and wholesome advice to children to mind the fear of the Lord in their youth, which would be the beginning of wisdom, and to learn to depart from iniquity, a good understanding"; and on 9th month, 3rd day, 1709, Charles Osborn "had good advice to parents desiring them to cry to the Lord for their children, etc., and to children that they might fear God, avoid lying, and every evil thing, telling them that though all men should combine to make one great and happy man, yet all that was not to be compared to the benefit and pleasure that abounds to such as fear the Lord etc. . . . ." Kelsall and the whole community responded with fear and sadness when any Quaker child went into the "world" to marry.[28]

In an effort to further enlarge the economic base of the Montgomeryshire Quaker community and his own paternalistic status, Charles Lloyd III built between 1717 and 1719 a new forge on his Dolobran estate and became half-owner of a coke-burning iron furnace at Bersham, near Wrexham, some thirty-five miles from Dolobran. At his apex Lloyd was a North Welsh Quaker iron czar, worth over £7,000, easily the greatest fortune of any Quaker family in North Wales and enough substance to keep the Montgomeryshire Quaker community afloat. The Bersham Furnace failed to repay Lloyd's and other Quakers' enormous investment, however, and by 1727 he was £16,000 in debt, and fled to France briefly to escape his creditors. Montgomeryshire Quakers understood that Lloyd had risked his fortune to renew their scattering community, and therefore the North Wales Quarterly Meeting refused to "join in condemnation or denial of him the said Charles Lloyd." Shropshire Friends, particularly Lloyd's creditors who received eight shillings back for every pound sterling they invested, were more willing to punish Lloyd. After the North Wales Meeting became deadlocked, the Yearly Meeting for Wales disowned the shamefaced iron baron in 1730. Charles Lloyd lived the rest of his life quietly in Birmingham, where in 1742 he was reinstated as a Friend, but the Dolobran Quaker community passed from the face of the earth.[29]

Fleeing the unpromising commercial prospects of the Welsh mountains, Charles Lloyd III's brother Sampson had earlier re-settled in Birmingham, where he became a successful ironmonger. His sons, Sampson and Charles, developed his interest into an iron empire and their sons moved into banking, intermarrying with the Hanbury and Barclay families. By the second half of the eighteenth century, the Lloyds owned a growing bank with London and Birmingham offices, the foundation of Lloyds Bank International

Ltd., still one of the world's most powerful banks. Following the inherited family wisdom, occasionally wheezed from deathbeds, "Never thou buy Dolobran," the Birmingham Lloyds overcame normal sentiment and refused to repurchase their ancestral estate and proven commercial sinkhold, Dolobran, until 1878, by which time they could safely buy almost anything in the world.[30] Avoiding both great business failure or success, Charles Lloyd III's uncle, Thomas Lloyd, had taken his large family of ten children in the 1680s to Pennsylvania, where he grew in religious and political responsibility and prestige, but never comparatively in capital. By 1710 each segment of this able family had made a characteristic response to the Welsh Quakers' familial crisis of the late seventeenth century, caused by the combustible mixing of a stingy economy with an expensive family doctrine.

QUAKER FAMILY doctrines and the Quaker households' crises also caused an abnormal number of northwestern British Quaker households to break their ties with kin and neighbors and to migrate unusually long distances. Among 146 Cheshire Quaker couples married between 1650 and 1684, 48 or 33 percent left Cheshire. Among 57 couples in South Wales who married during these same years, 36 or 63 percent left South Wales.[31] The percentage of Quaker households migrating such long distances was considerably higher than that of the general northwestern population of households and marked a significant break with northwestern custom.

Many British studies show, of course, high rates of geographical mobility among seventeenth-century middling people, but they also show that such mobility was largely confined to specific times in people's lives. Specifically, young unmarried people between the ages of 14 and 30 tended to move frequently, often long distances, but they stopped moving when married and burdened with children. As early as 1967 E. A. Wrigley noted, "there is a growing volume of evidence that in England in the seventeenth and eighteenth centuries mobility before marriage was very high but was reduced once marriage had taken place."[32] Subsequent research by Anne Kussmaul, R.A. Houston, Peter Souden, and others has confirmed this contrast.[33]

This tendency also obtained in relatively poor northwestern Britain. Although northwestern children often moved long distances to find livelihoods, they stuck, once married, to marginally profitable tenant farms. For example, in 1600, James Bankes wrote a lengthy memorandum for his son in which he evaluated the holdings and incomes of forty-three of the livestock-farming tenants on his Winstanley estate on the Lancashire plain. His tenants ranged from Lawrence Farclough, who had a holding of 50 acres yielding an annual income of £20, to Ann Clarkson, a cottager, who held less than an acre, which yielded her an annual income of 10 shillings. Eighty percent of Mr. Bankes's tenants had holdings under 20 acres and 86 percent of them had incomes from their tenements of under £15 annually. These northwestern British middling householders, nonetheless, showed immobility patterns similar to those found in southeastern England. In 1600 James Bankes mentioned fifty of his tenants and cottager-tenants, including the forty-three whose income he evaluated. Seventy-five years later, thirty-six of these tenants' surnames, or 72 percent of all the tenants of 1600, reappeared in this son's 1675 rent rolls. A succession of rent rolls for the Winstanley estate between 1669 and 1675 show that during this six-year period only twelve of the individuals mentioned in 1669 disappeared from the rent rolls. In seven of these 12 cases, the absentees' tenements were assumed by people with the same surname: for example, Widow Wethersby replaced Robert Wethersby, and Humphry Chadwick replaced Thomas Chadwick. Only five of the 66 families or just 7.5 percent present at Winstanley in 1669 had died out in the male line or had moved from the manor within a six-year period.[34]

Similar immobility amid poverty also marked the tenant farmers of Myddle, Shropshire, the pastoral community studied by Richard Gough and David Hey. Myddle's tenant farmers had acreages and incomes as paltry as those of Mr. Bankes' tenants at Winstanley and were as immobile. In an analysis of the Myddle Church parish registers from 1541 to 1700, David Hey discovered that in the periods from 1541–99, 1600–43, and 1647–1701 "old families"—those resident in Myddle for a generation or more—accounted for from 80 percent to 81 percent of all entries in the parish registers in each period. In each of these periods, these "old families" composed only from 39.4 percent to 41.8 percent of all families mentioned in the registers, but these other families, in most cases, were simply represented by a single laborer or servant, who happened to die or marry, while passing swiftly through Myddle. This mobile population of youth, servants, and laborers (all single) swirled around the virtually immobile married tenants. Each of the "old families" had an average number of from 7.36 to 12.28 entries per household in each period, while the new people averaged only 1.34 to 1.85 entries per surname. Hey concluded that in this 160-year period "the tenement-farmers [tenant farmers] in particular formed the core of the community, and their property only went out of their hands upon the death of the last male heir."[35]

As noted, seventeenth-century northwestern British middling households were rarely what has been called "little common-wealths," that is individual economic units who expected by their income and labor to pay for all their needs. To a greater or lesser extent, all conventional northwestern British households participated with neighbors, kin, and landlords in the sharing of household economies. This sharing was particularly helpful in the preferment of middling children, particularly those who were slated to travel long distances and to take great risks in their livelihoods. By staying in one locality for a long time, by accepting as a consequence low incomes and residential permanence, middling households not so much accumulated adequate financial capital to run economically autonomous households, which seemed an impossibility, as accumulated what might be called "human capital"—strong linkages to local kin, neighbors, and gentry—which could be "cashed in" at crucial times. Among these crucial times were certainly the times their surplus children required help finding livelihoods. Naturally, in this situation, many middling children moved, using the human capital which their parents, ancestors, and local kin had accumulated in a given area. Such children could either travel along these connections to their livelihoods or use them as security to engage in individualistic adventures, knowing the connections back home would serve them if they needed to return. Many young northwestern youth were, as a result, individualistic risk-takers and frequent movers, but upon marriage they tended to remain in a locality in order to begin accumulating the human capital which their children and grandchildren would need to establish their homes. Immobile parents and mobile youth—and mobile and immobile stages of life—were actually positively economically related in these provincial upland societies, and composed one coherent strategy of familial survival and child preferment.[36] Radical Quaker domesticity, on doctrine, largely reversed this wisdom, for the Quakers placed a premium upon retaining children and warned against promiscuous reliance upon neighbors, kin, or landlords.

The destinations of these many migrating northwestern Quaker households is difficult to assess. Unluckily, between 1670 and 1710, the extant Cheshire and Welsh meetings' records discussed the removals of only 23 households or single people: of these, 16 went to Pennsylvania, 4 to Ireland, 2 to London, and 1 to Bristol.[37] In seeking to fulfill Quaker family ideals, hard-pressed Quaker households who chose migration apparently had two major options: they could seek positions in the new empires created by Quaker entreprenuers in northern towns, or they could go to Pennsylvania. The choice they made obviously had a major impact on careers and the lives of these households.

Northwest Quaker domesticity was able to find or create adequate resources locally in northwestern and northern towns, most notably Birmingham, where Quaker entreprenuers established new wealth and patronage systems surrounding metalworking, retailing, and manufacturing. These new urban empires opened appreticeships and access to business and the professions to many Quaker youth. Yet, aside from the financial risks inherent in innovation, the Quakers' reliance on entreprenuers and entreprenuerial environments included the more elusive problems of the spiritual and moral price poor middling households had to pay. Some insight into the lives of middling northwest Quaker households that migrated to town to enjoy the paternalism and new economies of new British Quaker entreprenuers is provided by the journal of William Stout, a very wealthy northwestern Quaker ironmonger and grocer in Lancaster, Lancashire, who kept a journal from 1680 to 1742, detailing his economic rise and concomitant reformist involvement in the lives of at least forty Lancaster children and youth, none of whom was his own child.

As his dour portrait suggests, neither Stout nor the life he prescribed for Quaker and other youth was ideally charismatic. Second son and third child of a small yeoman farmer, Stout was born in 1665 in the country village of Boulton Holmes, Lancashire. He was apprenticed in 1680 to Henry Coward, a Quaker ironmonger in Lancaster. Absorbing the atmosphere and values of Coward's associates, Stout became a Quaker in 1685 and showed how it could become a way to wealth. Collecting £199 from his father's estate, and borrowing £10 from his sister Ellen, Stout set up his first shop in Lancaster in 1687. Cautiously and diligently (he often slept in his shop to catch early morning customers), he bought iron from the Darby and other works and tobacco from Virginia and sold it retail to customers and wholesale to shops in smaller market towns. By 1700, he was worth £1,399, by 1716 some £2,794, and £4,950 by 1726.

Though a kind, generous man, Stout rarely radiated Foxian joy or spontaneity. In 1702, at the age of 38, Stout fell in love with and courted Bethia Green, a young and lively Quakeress. But "I perceived that she was very averse to it in respect to my age and plaine appearance and retired way of living, and avoided all opportunity of my comeing into her company, although her father and mother would have encouraged me."[38] The other lively Quaker lasses of Lancaster were similarly repelled and Stout did not want to marry someone as dull as himself, "so that I contented myselfe with living with my sister Ellen, who was as careful and diligent to serve me as much or more than if I had been her own sone."[39] Aside from money-making, religious meetings, and long walks, Stout's major emotional outlet was superintending the educations of at least forty Lancaster children and youth: his nieces and nephews, his apprentices, his many wards by trusteeships to which Quakers' wills appointed him. Discussion of these children and youth consumed nearly half of his *Autobiography*. His financial contributions to youth consumed at least £1,200 of his estate. Stout's difficulties with his children unintentionally showed the depredations town and commercial life made on the enticement and joy of Quaker family life.

Stout believed human character, particularly if informed by the Light, could endure and even thrive in the demanding, competitive commercial world of Lancaster, but, as he repeatedly told his wards, almost any departure during life from "holy conversation," any surrendering involvement with "carnal talkers" or their style, led to spiritual, familial, and commercial ruin. Stout devoutly wished to warn the children and youth placed under his supervision of such dangers. Chilling, for example, was Stout's admonishing analysis of the Quaker grocer and draper, Thomas Green's household. Stout noted with approval that Green was "an industrious and reputable grocer and draper from his youth," that he married in 1664 Elizabeth Brinkall, "a good director in house keeping," and that he had four lively children. The Greens, however, allowed the "world" to intrude once into their household's innocence: "they had the imprudence of taking into their house two gentlemen and their wives to board whilst their children were young, intending for profit; but put them upon plentyfull provision and living, and their children

to partake of the same, and fashionable clothing and communication . . . they could not forget it when their borders were gone."
Once the pleasures of the "world" contaminated a household,
showed Stout, they inevitably sickened not only the soul but also
commercial prowess.

Once Thomas Green's wife was stricken she spread the evil
about: Elizabeth became "too easy, and entertained some flattering,
dissembling women, who were chargeable to them, and drew out
their children to excess in victuals, apparel, and vanity in conversation." Nevertheless, for many years, the eldest son, Richard seemed
untouched and stayed close to the shop, but ten years after he
assumed his father's business, "he fell into company of my man
Troughton [Stout's old apprentice], William Godsalve, and such
like, to sit drinking, and gradually to excess; and neglected his
father's business, and became sottish . . . at least to the excessive
drinking of brandy, a pint in a short time, which killed him. . . ."
He died at age 34. The symptoms were never so latent with the rest
of the children. The second son, Joseph Green, inherited £500 and
bought a millinery shop, "but soon become negligent and sottish
. . . and broke. . . ." The "worldly" contamination made Bethia
Green shun Stout's advances and marry "an Irish man of a facetious
and agreeable disposition . . . but of no substance," who opened a
chandler shop in London and soon "broke." The youngest daughter also opened a millinery shop, but "spent her time in treating and
being treated by fashionable people till she has spent all and became
an object of charity." Thomas Green died prematurely and, thought
Stout, agonizingly as the father helplessly watched his children
destroy his estate and hope.[40]

Stout consistently made a cogent case for the positive impact
Quaker family discipline and communication might have on developing commercial savvy. He left little room, however, in his person,
or in his advice for happiness, joy, or pleasure. Even in Stout's
pointed descriptions, there was ample evidence that more than
"carnal talkers" were destroying his charges. Among Stout's thirty-
eight wards, almost all of whom were set up in trades and marriages—often with Stout's help—18 or 42 percent literally went
broke and died penniless. Many of the others were constantly on the
borderline of financial ruin. The harsh, unremitting, competitive
world of provincial market towns literally drove some of Stout's
most diligent and promising wards crazy. For example, in 1704
Stout helped young Peter Wilson learn and become established in

the dry salter trade in London. "He was very exact in his accounts," noted Stout, "but in the year 1718 he became uncapable of his business, and became a lunatick, and would give his goods about him, so that his friends shut up his shop and confined [him]. . . ." Another diligent young tanner in 1705 "being of an easy credulous disposition, he was put upon and defrauded; which brought him into distraction and dispair, so as to be confined and bound, where he remained some years." Another ward simply gave up his trade and wandered through the countryside.[41]

Stout disapprovingly noted that many of his Lancaster brethren and sisters wanted a less demanding arena for domesticity. In 1698, "Robert Haydock of Liverpool freighted a ship for Phila-delphia . . . more than twenty persons, old and young of our meet-ing of Lancaster, tooke this opertunity, sold their estates, and tooke their families."[42] After suffering an epidemic at sea, this ship *Brittania* arrived in Philadelphia in 1699, with half of its passengers dead, "and many of them heads of families." Only "the misfortune of this ship," noted Stout, "discouraged from removing" many other Lancaster Quaker families, "disposed to sell their estates and goe to Pennsylvania to dwell."[43] Whatever Stout and other success-ful Quaker entreprenuers might hope and build, many Quaker households thought family life in late seventeenth-century provin-cial English commercial towns too joyless and dangerous a contrast to George Fox's promise of peace and inner happiness.

From nearer the bottom of the new Quaker northwest entrepre-nuerial patronage networks, John Kelsall's diary tells much the same story about a Quaker household that migrated within north-western Britain. Born in 1683 of a Quaker father, an innkeeper, who migrated from Cheshire to London by 1682, John Kelsall was brought to Lancashire, after his father died in 1683 and his mother died in 1687. His guardian was his mother's kindly Quaker brother, Timothy Cragg. In 1701, at the age of 18, Kelsall became the first Quaker schoolmaster at Dolobran, Montgomeryshire, and earned a salary of £15 a year. He lodged, as noted, for many years at the house of Amos Davies, clerk of Charles Lloyd III's Mathrafal forge, and married Amos Davies's daughter Susannah in 1711. Soon after, he moved to the cottage adjoining the Dolobran meetinghouse. Absorbing knowledge of the iron business from his busy surround-ings, Kelsall was hired in 1714 on a £25 annual salary by Abraham Darby as clerk of Darby's Dolgyn furnace near Dolgellau, Merio-nethshire. In 1720, for a slightly higher salary, Kelsall became the clerk of Charles Lloyd's new forge at Dolobran, to which he and his family returned. He also oversaw sales, material, and books for Lloyd's Bersham Furnace, near Wrexham. From 1714 to 1727 Kelsall extracted a good income from the Quaker entreprenuers. When Charles Lloyd's fledgling North Welsh iron empire collapsed in 1727, however, Kelsall's income declined with little interruption. He took a farm, stocked with two cows, near Dolobran; he made £6 annually. From 1729 until it shut down in 1733, Kelsall clerked the Dolgyn Furnace, a mile from Dolgellau, for Henry Payton of Dudley. In 1733, Kelsall attempted to run a Quaker school at Dolgellau, but the Merionethshire Quaker community was now too tiny to support the school adequately. In 1734 he went to Cork, Ireland, to establish a school, but failed to earn enough income to support his family. In 1736, he took his family to Chester, where he picked up various jobs bookkeeping and supervising the loading of iron onto ships. He died in 1743, age 60.[44]

Kelsall was an educated and devoted Quaker father. His wife Susannah Davies supplied him with a large family: ten births between 1711 and 1732 and nine children who survived past Kelsall's own death in 1743. In preparation for fatherhood, from 1701 until 1712, Kelsall absorbed into a notebook all the childrearing advice he heard from traveling Quaker ministers who visited Dolobran. In August 1723, as he rode from Dolobran to Hereford, "my mind earnestly concerned to beg of the Lord that my offspring might not know such smooth times as to make them unmindful to inquire after the Lord," he wrote, "and oh, me thought I could tenderly desire that they might live to see that ancient and noble prophecy take place wherein the truth should cover the earth as the waters cover the sea." Dismounting from his horse, and removing his hat, Kelsall prayed that "I and mine live to be of some service to the Lord's truth in our day." It was then back onto his horse and to the iron business, in which some of his prayers, at least his objection to "smooth times," would be visibly answered.[45]

Although Kelsall earned over £20 for 13 years (a fine income in North Wales) and was a literate, well-connected, experienced business clerk, he eventually could not prevent his growing household from scattering uncontrollably. During his lucrative iron-clerking years, one child moved away at 18 years, one at 14 years, two at 13 years, one at 11 years, one at 4 years. During his years of solid income, however, departure from home, even when the destination was far way, was not tantamount to emotional departure or certainly to liberty from Kelsall's oversight. Elizabeth, their fifth child, was sent from home at the age of four not only because of household overcrowding but also because Susannah Kelsall's childless sister and brother-in-law, the John Gilberts, requested it in 1724. In addition to being Quaker kin, they also lived in Birmingham, a town frequently on Kelsall's business itineraries and a town full of good commercial prospects. Indeed, The Kelsalls also sent John, Jr., then 14 years, to live with Betty and the Gilberts. He would gain his apprenticeship with John Gilbert's help in the burgeoning Quaker community of Birmingham. He would also keep his eye on Betty and would regularly write reports home.

During August 1725, John Kelsall spent a week in Birmingham, partly on business for the forge, until "the child was got a little acquainted with her Aunt and she parted with me pretty easily." Kelsall visited them again, after a two-day trip from town, and "was glad to find my daughter Betty well and hearty."[46] Back in Dolobran, Kelsall received a letter from John, Jr., two weeks later and "was glad to hear by it that he and his sister were well and contented there." Letters were frequently exchanged, but not all reports were positive. Kelsall returned to Birmingham in February, 1727, "not a little glad to find my dear daughter Betty well and also my son John whom I had not seen for almost a year and half." Kelsall failed to record, however, his usual happiness at seeing his brother and sister. Instead, he recorded, "had much talk this afternoon with sister about home reports: I heard of her being unkind to my daughter, but she would not own much.'" Before he left Birmingham, Kelsall received the Gilberts' promise to bring Betty to meet him at the approaching yearly meeting at Salop. When he met his daughter, he took her home to Dolobran for a month's visit. While allowing Betty to return to the Gilberts, Kelsall continued to keep a close eye on them through his son John and through his other connections in Birmingham. Thanks to Kelsall's constant pressure, household relations improved. When Kelsall visited Birmingham in February 1728 he was "glad to find them [the Gilberts] and daughter Betty in good health" and was particulary happy to find that his daughter "seemed well pleased and was made much of by them."[47]

The Kelsalls chose apprenticeships with similar care; for their long term profitability, Quakerly atmosphere, and proximity to points on Kelsall's business itineraries. For example, Kelsall apprenticed Amos at age 12, in 1725, with John Seddon, a Quaker clockmaker in Frodsham, Cheshire. Before the indentures were signed, Amos worked and lived with Seddon for two months on a trial basis. John Kelsall visited him twice during this period. After all appeared satisfied, the indentures were signed on the 8th month, 4th day, 1725. For £15 Seddon would keep Amos for eight years and would teach him to be a clockmaker and shopkeeper. Nor did Kelsall then forget his son. Kelsall visited Amos four times during the next year; wrote to him an average of three times a month; and twice met John Seddon at Chester fairs and discussed young Amos with his master over a pint of ale and dinner.[48]

Despite his exertions, John Kelsall began to lose control when Charles Lloyd's iron empire collapsed in 1727. Except for brief employment at Dolgyn furnace, Kelsall never again earned the £20 plus he had gotten with the Lloyds, but struggled as a migrating farmer, schoolteacher, and part-time bookkeeper until his death in 1743. The moral and financial settlement of his crowded household had only begun in 1727, however. John and Amos were out to apprenticeship and Betty had been recently fostered out, but in 1727 Benjamin (age 9), Thomas (age 8), Mary (age 3), and Timothy (age 1) were still at home and Susannah Kelsall would provide the household with two more robust children: Susannah in 1730 and Sarah in 1732. To make matters worse, John, Jr., returned home unexpectedly on March 24, 1728; his master Richard Ainges, a Quaker Birmingham brass-founder, had gone broke and had left with everything, including the £8 Kelsall had given him in 1725 as an apprenticeship fee. The day after hearing the bad news, Kelsall wrote to his entreprenurial Quaker network (John Gilbert, Sampson Lloyd II, Charles Lloyd IV, and John Fowler) in order to find an alternative place for his son. Kelsall got word two weeks later that indeed a Quaker brass-founder in Wolverhampton was willing to take his son apprentice. By May 24, 1728, seventeen-year-old John, Jr., was in Wolverhampton relaying back the information that Hewitt, the Quaker brass-founder, "expected £10 with him and six years service, which was what I did not expect." Kelsall could now hardly afford such a high fee; he had hoped that John, Jr., might find a position for only three or four years, and therefore his years and investment with Ainges would be not entirely lost. By June 11, 1728, Kelsall was in Wolverhampton himself haggling with William Hewitt, who made it clear that the price had been conscientiously and unalterably set by Quaker standards. Kelsall sadly rode to Birmingham and obtained an agreement by June 13 with John Dynason, a less profitable file-cutter, to take John, Jr., for six years for nothing. Kelsall then returned to Wolverhampton to persuade his son to accept the less lustrous Birmingham offer.[49]

By June 24, Kelsall well saw that acquaintance with Quaker entreprenuers could not relieve his parental powerlessness: "was this day under a weighty concern in the sense of affairs relating to myself and others as foreseeing little prospect of anything but exercises and troubles many ways."[50] By the time he died in Chester in 1743, except for the four children at home, his children were widely scattered in Quaker commercial networks. None had yet, to their father's knowledge, discarded their Quaker heritage and principles, yet their father had no reason for optimism: all were unmarried, unestablished, and undercapitalized. Like their father, they would understand the meaning of honest wages.

A DIFFERENT kind of entreprenuer increasingly active in northwestern Quakers' lives was William Penn. Penn was not as commercially or industrially oriented as William Stout or Abraham Darby. Son of a successful and politically acute sea admiral, who had been awarded estates by both Oliver Cromwell and Charles II, William Penn, the younger, was, aside from his religious radicalism, a member of the southeastern upper gentry, a man with personal ties at Court, and income largely from tenanted land. William Penn had experience with balancing books and assessing markets. He had managed after 1666 his father's Irish estates. Yet Penn saw no final solution for the crisis of Quaker familialism solely through banking, metalworking, or merchandising. An unabashed, somewhat sentimental, advocate of rural life (and a man whose wealth lay largely in land), Penn prescribed toleration and a landed empire in America, first as trustee in 1674 of West New Jersey, and then as sole proprietor of his own American province. Thanks to his personal connections at Court and Charles II's financial and personal debts to his father, on March 4, 1681, Penn was granted a charter by Charles II appointing him and his heirs "true and absolute Proprietaries" of a tract of land, called Pennsylvania, lying north of Maryland, south of New York, and extending five longitudinal degrees westward from the Delaware River. In addition to making profits from the sale of this new land, Penn wanted to provide a haven especially for desperate rural Quaker householders to practice Quaker familial discipline, intimate communication, and childrearing without being traditionally poor or without becoming excessively commercial. He certainly understood the importance of commerce, as his plan for Philadelphia as an Atlantic port showed. Yet, among other things, his "holy experiment" was clearly a matter of providing adequate land and adequately commercially profitable land (both for himself and his customers) for Quaker familialism.

Penn designed his promotional literature, his public relations, and his colony for an audience of desperate northwestern rural families and their leaders. Initially, Penn sold 5,000 acres for just £100 (only some two shillings and six pence per acre).[51] Penn exalted the retention of Quaker farming. He told Pennsylvanians to form townships of 5,000 acres with each farmer having lavish, contiguous holdings of 100 to 500 acres. He advertised that cheap land would permit a "more convenient bringing up of youth," and would end English parents' addiction "to put their children into Gentlemen's service or send them to towns to learn trades."[52] Penn understood that commerce was vital, but he planned his commercial town, Philadelphia, to be a "green countrie town" in which access to excessively large city lots were offered first to lavish buyers of rural land, and he gave a monopoly of trade to "Society of Traders" to which membership was again restricted to large rural land developers. He wanted to bring Pennsylvanians, not commercial severity, but ease, or as he wrote from Pennsylvania in 1683 to three northern English Quaker ministers, "here is enough for both poor and rich, not only for necessity but pleasure." And writing from Chester, he contrasted the character of his rustic colonists with commercial adepts, "our heads are dull . . . but our hearts are good and our hands are strong." In a subsequently famous 1682 letter of farewell to his wife and children, Penn told them, ". . . of citys and towns of concourse beware, the world is apt to stick close to those who have liv'd and got their wealth there. A country life and estate I like best for my children. . . ." Anticipating and then flattering his northwestern rural customers, Penn told Robert Turner in March, 1681, that he had wanted to call his colony "New-Wales." He renamed the first town he saw in Pennsylvania, the Swedish settlement of Upland, "Chester."[53]

Northwestern Quaker farmers were gladdened by the prospect of Penn's landed empire. From the early 1680s the Welsh and Cheshire meetings regularly used Pennsylvania to solve their members' family problems. It cost a meeting £7 on average to find a spiritually safe apprenticeship for an orphan in England, but meetings could send entire households to Pennsylvania for the cost of less than £10. In 1690, for example, the Quarterly Meeting of North Wales raised £9 to help "a poor friend called Robert Ellis with his wife and children towards Pennsylvania."[54] In at least three cases between 1683 and 1699, even the wealthier Cheshire meetings raised money to send entire households to the new colony.[55] Poor Quaker households learned quickly that cheap, fertile land might happily solve their childrearing predicaments. By the end of the century Welsh meetings had become so depopulated that they generally began to discourage Pennsylvania emigration. In 1698 the Yearly Meeting of Wales was "under a deep sense and consideration that some Friends by their irregular and disorderly and unsavory proceedings and runnings into Pennsylvania having been a cause of great weakening, if not total destroying of some meetings in this dominion of Wales . . . we therefore earnestly entreat Friends for the future to consult with Friends in the Quarterly and Monthly Meetings and to have their unity before they resolve to remove to Pennsylvania."[56] When Richard Lewis told the struggling Dolobran Meeting in 1713 that he wanted to take his wife and children to Pennsylvania, they asked him to "weigh the matter more duly and find a right clearness in himself and wife before he undertake such a journey." However, the next month they recorded sadly, "Friends are more willing that he might stay amongst us," but "he being not satisfied to do so, Friends do leave him and his family to their freedom."[57] The new policy of guilt-inducing exhortation seemed to have little impact on this popular migration.

The emigrants to Pennsylvania were, even within a religion of zealots, a comparatively pious lot. Superficially, the Quaker emigrants to Pennsylvania appear to be mere refugees from persecution, but they were in fact Quaker activists who worried about persecution and household dispersions. The households that emigrated to Pennsylvania experienced, especially in South Wales, more persecution (or more painful and expensive persecution) than those households that either stayed or migrated internally within Great Britain. The rooted households in South Wales, when persecuted, also paid half the money in fines and were jailed a quarter as often as the inflicted Pennsylvania emigrant households. Although no Quaker register exists for North Wales, a collation of Pennsylvania sources with records of Quaker sufferings suggests the same story: among 38 immigrant households in Pennsylvania, arriving between 1681 and 1695 from North Wales, 16 or 42 percent had experienced significant fines or jailings, 14 or 37 percent had been jailed, and these families paid out £6 on average.

The Restoration acts against Quakers were aimed directly at punishing activists and leaders. For example, the Second Coventicle Act of 1670 fined people for being at unauthorized religious meetings and aimed to break those most responsible for them. For harboring a conventicle or meeting, the fine was £20. For speaking and preaching at a conventicle, the fine was £20 for the first offense and £40 for the second offense. Other anti-Quaker acts were structured similarly. Only the enforcement of the Elizabethan recusancy act, which fined a person £20 a month for non-attendance at Anglican worship, covered passive Quakers, and this act was seemingly used most often to cripple Quaker ringleaders.[58] Many Pennsylvania emigrants had been repeatedly cited and punished by authorities for their stubborn refusal to curtail Quaker activities and voices. In 1676, for example, John Simcock was caught preaching for the second time at Ridley, Cheshire, and lost £41; he was caught preaching again in 1678 and lost £90; he was caught preaching at a Quaker funeral in 1679 and lost £100. Now well known as a Quaker ringleader, Simcock was cited in 1681 for absence from national worship and fined £40. He lost between 1676 and 1681 at least £271 for his persistently bold leadership. Among repeat offenders in Wales, who were also Pennsylvania emigrants, were Hugh Roberts, Robert Owen, Thomas Ellis, Thomas Lloyd, and Cadwallader Thomas.[59] Thus, when signing on with William Penn, such men may well have thought of cutting future losses. Even if they did, they stripped the Cheshire and Welsh Quaker communities of many of their most active, dedicated members (for tabular summary of entrenched and migrant households, see Appendix: Table 3).

Quaker activism, financial losses from persecution, and familial distress were mutually reinforcing. Active Quakers were not only most likely to suffer harsh financial losses from persecution but were also naturally most deeply disturbed by the scattering and corruption of their own and other Quaker households. The financial losses from persecution additionally deepened their gloom about the scarcities of the northwestern British economy. Persecution and scarcity, seen in the light of the unusual demands of Quaker familialism, created a compulsion for emigration to Pennsylvania among a core of faithful northwestern Quakers.

Indeed, the Quaker householders who remained in Wales appeared less combative about the poor retention rate of their children, and less inspired to Quaker activism by their relatively low rate of suffering. The scarcities of the Welsh economy and the expensiveness of Quaker domesticity dictated that by 1730 old Quaker meetings were scattered and dead, particularly in North Wales. John Kelsall, the clerk of Charles Lloyd's forges, traveled much and usually spent his time, when possible, with Quakers; but when he visited the Dolgellau, Merionethshire, Assizes in 1722, he spent the whole evening with George Lewis, the Anglican rector; and when he got to Bala—on his way back to Dolobran—he spent the night in an inn, but saw no Quakers.[60] These two towns in the 1660s had been the hotbeds of Merionethshire Quakerism.

In 1739, James Gough, an English Friend, visited Wales and found a lonely Quaker, John Goodwin, in the mountains near Shropshire. He told Gough that in the early 1680s most of the Quakers in his neighborhood left for Pennsylvania, including his own father, mother, and siblings, "but a higher power directed his stay in his native land, and to that he gave up father and mother and everything." A happy Quaker marriage comforted him, but life was admittedly lonely and difficult. As Gough related, "[Goodwin] lived and maintained his family on a farm of four pounds a year, but at length had purchased it and improved it, so that as the time he reckoned it worth six pounds a year" (this was not an anti-Welsh satire). Despite his minute income, with "most of the meeting being then gone to Pennsylvania," Goodwin became the most prominent Quaker in his neighborhood. Itinerant Quaker ministers en route from South Wales to Shropshire often stayed at his house where "he had but one bed, which he left to them, he and his wife taking up their lodging in the stable."[61] The last Quaker stronghold in North Wales, the Dolobran Meeting, succumbed after 1727 to Charles Lloyd's bankruptcy. John Kelsall noted several Quaker families leaving, and he left also.[62]

In Cheshire, where the economy was more hospitable to Quaker familial ambitions, rooted and Pennsylvania emigrant households experienced comparable persecutorial suffering. What primarily distinguished rooted and emigrant households were the number of children per household. The internally migrant households had 1.11 more children per household than rooted households, and the Pennsylvania emigrant households had 1.35 more children per household (see Appendix: Table 3). Because these figures were derived totally from Cheshire sources and because of the relative youth of the migrants, they understate the difference. Fifty-one percent of the 34 migrant families to Pennsylvania had been married for ten years or less and 21 percent had been married for five years or less. Many had additional children after they left Cheshire. Randal Malin of Netherton, Cheshire, married in 1676 and had two small children when in 1681 he bought 250 acres for £5 in Upper Providence township, Pennsylvania. In 1683 Randal and Elizabeth Malin settled there, and, while their two English-born children survived, they had another child. Elizabeth Malin died in 1687 and Randal married again in 1693 to Mary Hollingworth of Newcastle County. They had five more children, three of whom survived to 24 years. Experiences such as Malin's were common among the many young, economically pinched Quaker couples who came to seventeenth-century Pennsylvania.

Having or anticipating a houseful of children simply made persecution and northwestern poverty hurt more. In 1679 John Sharples lost nearly £10 in goods for being one month absent from his parish church. The Sharples household had seven spiritually vulnerable children (in 1679 ages 16, 13, 12, 8, 6, 3, and 1) to support in apprenticeships, farms, and marriages. Instead of gambling with his large brood's corruption, Sharples in 1681 bought 1000 acres in Chester County, Pennsylvania for £20 and soon after took his family there. Most likely John Sharples was not thinking of his own physical comfort and social promotion; when he emigrated he was 57 years old.[63] Jane Lownes paid out 12 shillings for being at a meeting in 1676 at Newton, Cheshire, a bad loss for the wife of a poor Northwich tradesmen. Jane Lownes had deeper worries. In 1680 her husband Hugh died and now this Quaker mother had four children (ages 20, 18, 15, and 12) to place safely in life from her husband's paltry estate. Instead of despairing or fostering her children out to kin, Widow Lownes used this estate in 1681 to buy 150 acres in Pennsylvania for £3 and she took her children there in 1683, first living in a cave. Whatever her discomfort, Widow Lownes laid the economic base in Pennsylvania for the marriages of her two sons at ages 27 and 33, a nice feat for a poor Quaker widow from central Cheshire.[64]

Not every middling northwestern emigrant household was involved in a tearful melodrama. Born in Castle Bith, Pembrokeshire, Wales, in 1645, Morris Llewellyn inherited the family life-leasehold. In 1673, at the age of 28, Llewellyn married Anne Young as a Quaker. He generally avoided persecution, though in 1677 he paid out almost £3 in tithe distraints: a lamb and over £2 in hay and corn.[65] Although Anglican authorities usually took more in such cases than a mere 10 percent of Quaker farmers' incomes, Llewellyn was seemingly making near £20 a year, a good middling Welsh farmer's income. Though he might hope in Wales to avoid major persecution and utter poverty, Llewellyn was not a rich man; and by 1682, he and Anne had two sons and a daughter (another daughter, an infant, died in 1679). Instead of trying to set these sons upon expensive and modestly yielding Welsh leases or breaking them to Quaker commercial life, Llewellyn in 1683 bought 250 acres in Pennsylvania for £5 and arrived in Haverford township, Pennsylvania, in 1686 with his wife, two sons, and daughter. Llewellyn was now 41 years old. In 1689 in Haverford a third son, Griffith, was born, while all the other children thrived. Thanks to fertile Pennsylvania land, good markets in the West Indies for Pennsylvania flour, and hard work, Morris Llewellyn was able eventually to purchase 1,000 additional acres in the Welsh Tract for his sons.[66]

While the majority of northwest British Pennsylvania emigrants had been in distressing familial economic situations similar to those of Lownes, Sharples, and Llewellyn, some relatively wealthy and seemingly invulnerable northwestern British Quaker households also perceived Pennsylvania as an irresistible childrearing garden. Such families were chiefly worried about the social corruption of their privileged children. Wealthy northwest Quaker families, while doing better than their poorer brethren and sisters, still lost many of their children, as statistics have shown, to the seductions of the "world." So reminded was John Bevan, a member of the minor Welsh gentry, an owner of three large farms in fertile Llantrissant, Glamorganshire. He was rarely persecuted, being the life-long friend of the parish rector. Nevertheless, his wife Barbara Bevan, a genteel "nursing mother" on the model of Margaret Fell, admonished him about the dangerous moral ambience of their Welsh neighborhood. "Some time before the year 1683," Bevan later wrote, "I had heard that our esteemed Friend William Penn had a patent from King Charles the Second for the Province in America called Pennsylvania, and my wife had a great inclination to go thither and thought it might be a good place to train up children amongst sober people and to prevent the corruption of them here by the loose behavior of youthes, and the bad example of too many of riper years." John Bevan loved Glamorganshire, "but, he noted, "I was sensible her aim was an upright one, on account of our children, I was willing to weigh the matter in a true balance." Under his wife's tenderly righteous pressure and with Penn's low land prices beckoning, Bevan found that he could keep his three Welsh farms and still buy 2,750 acres in Pennsylvania (Bevan was the only Welsh Tract settler, though not purchaser, not to sell his British property). After "we stayed there [Pennsylvania] many years, and had four of our children married with our consent, and they had several children, and the aim of my wife was in good measure answered," Bevan returned eagerly to Glamorganshire in 1704 with his wife and favorite daughter, a gifted Quaker minister.[67] Bevan thought Pennsylvania a wonderful place to rear and settle children, but apparently too much of a lowland nursery to waste his spiritually vigorous old age. Yet, most of the other Welsh Quaker leaders chose to die in Pennsylvania.

The North Welsh Quaker leadership, particularly the aging former Cromwellians, were great boosters of Pennsylvania. These aging reforming, religious radicals viewed Pennsylvania from a near lifetime of defeats. They had hoped in the 1650s that Llwyd and Powell with Cromwell's backing would bring the Holy Spirit to the Welsh mountains, but saw the propagators' churches split and their great spiritual leaders jailed, humiliated, or dead by 1660. They had turned to Quakerism in the late 1650s and early 1660s, seeing it as the proper avenue of religious reconstruction for Wales, but by 1675 they were seeing their new spiritual tribe of Children of the Light being scattered by persecution and especially by an economy unresponsive to voracious Quaker familial needs. Charles Lloyd III's iron empire aside, they knew that if Quakerism was to survive in England it would not be in North Wales. Approaching or well into middle age in the 1680s, these experienced social and religious radicals appeared the leaders of two collapsed reform movements, the pathetic twice-defeated. Pennsylvania, the Welsh Tract, was their last chance to see the Holy Spirit kept alive by men and women speaking Welsh.

They helped Penn recruit customers in Wales and then served as major politicians in Pennsylvania. They were experienced leaders. Many had served personally on county commissions during the Interregnum. For example, Robert Owen, the son of the attorney at the Court of Marches at Ludlow, had been a parliamentary military officer during the Civil War, in 1649 a member of the Welsh composition committee, from May 1651 a militia commissioner for Merionethshire, and a commissioner of the peace under the Barebones

Parliament and Protectorate. Owen had also led in 1659 a troop of Welsh Puritans into Cheshire against the Booth rebels and was formally thanked by the Council of State for his valor.[68] Thomas Ellis had been in judicial authority in the 1650s in Caernorvanshire, and as Richard Davies noted, "according to his place, somewhat sharp against offenders."[69] Many of them also had held central positions within the Welsh Puritan congregations. Thomas Ellis was the deacon and major lay minister of Powell's Montgomeryshire church; Richard Davies was also an active lay minister for Vavasor Powell. They negotiated in 1681 with Penn for the consolidation of Welsh holdings in Pennsylvania in a semi-autonomous Welsh Tract of 40,000 acres, in which Welsh would be spoken in Quaker meetings and legal proceedings. They then purchased over 30,000 acres and sold this land in smaller parcels to Welsh Quaker tenant farmers. Although middle-aged, Thomas Ellis, Robert Owen, John Humphry, Thomas Lloyd, Thomas Wynne, and Hugh Roberts all chose to emigrate to Pennsylvania where they provided the colony with much of its early political leadership. As they began to die in the 1690s, the survivors bought a book for the Radnor Monthly Meeting, Pennsylvania, and recorded loving testimonies about the trials and final triumph of each old Cromwellian.

HIS LIFE-LONG involvement in provincial social and spiritual reform also emboldened Thomas Ellis in a letter in 1685 to define for George Fox the reason for Pennsylvania: "I wish those that have estates of their own and to leave fullness in their posterity may not be offended at the Lord's opening a door of mercy to thousands in England, especially in Wales and other nations, who had no estates for themselves or children. And that all their industry could not afford them the meanest food and rainment that might properly be sayd to belong even to slaves or servants, nor any visible ground of hope for a better condition for children or children's children when they were gone hence."[70] The justification of Pennsylvania was, he knew, not the relief of persecutorial suffering, but the relief from the poverty that was defeating radical Quaker familialism in northwestern Britain and elsewhere. The years between 1660 and 1700 had taught reformers like Thomas Ellis much: they had gotten experience in administering a community of radical families, and they had sharpened their vision of what Quaker familialism needed to be workable. Armed with the organizational skill and detailed vision earned in these struggling years of familial crisis, Thomas Ellis wrote just after reaching Pennsylvania a short poem that clearly re-enunciated Quaker familial goals in a spirit long overdue for faithful upland reformers of the Holy Spirit, "A Song of Rejoicing."

PART TWO

Triumph of Quaker Domesticity

The Delaware Valley, Pennsylvania
1681–1750

If the fool would persist in his folly he would become wise
WILLIAM BLAKE

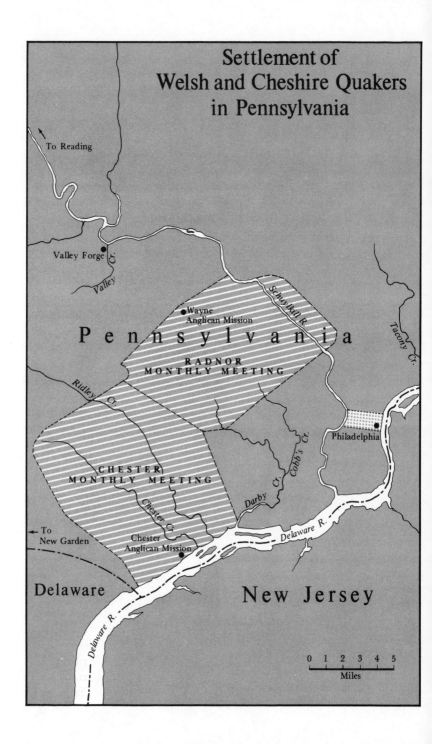

CHAPTER FOUR

Quaker Domesticity with the Grain

The first party of forty Welsh Quakers set sail to Pennsylvania in May 1682 from Liverpool aboard the *Lyon*. During their eleven week voyage, the passengers drank three pints of beer daily, ate cheese, and held silent meetings. Edward Jones, a barber-surgeon and their leader from Bala, oversaw the passengers spiritual and physical health. On August 13, 1682, the *Lyon* sailed onto the Delaware River and the passengers disembarked at Upland, the center of a small Swedish settlement. Jones counted noses and happily reported, "the passengers are all living, save one child yt died of a surfeit; let no Friends tell that they are either too old, or too young [to come over], for the Lord is sufficient to preserve both to the uttermost. Here is an old man about 80 years; he is rather better yn when he sett out. Likewise here are young babes doing very well, considering the sea diet." Jones now turned, with the aid of Providence and the new land, to help his passengers cure their child and community destroying poverty.

Inspection of the old residents, about 200 Swedish and Finnish farmers around Upland, discouraged Jones. Their log houses, mean dress, and untidy farms reminded him of the rural poverty his Welsh settlers had abandoned. He tried to convince himself that the land would yield better by observing that the old settlers "plow but bungerly." Jones waited impatiently at Upland for four or five days while their land, Merion township in the Welsh Tract, was surveyed. He then trekked along the Delaware, passed the intended town of Philadelphia (still forest), and inspected their site in the forests along the Schuylkill River above the projected city. "I hope it will please thee and the rest yt are concerned, for it hath most rare timber," he wrote happily to another Merionethshire leader, "I have not seen the like in all these parts, there is water enough besides."

The land was ample and favored to support the Quaker settlers' enormously expensive child nurturing and settling ambitions. The land north of New York City, including most of New England, had been robbed of its productive top-soil by glaciers. But glaciers had never visited the Delaware Valley. Southeastern Pennsylvania's fertile soil, composed of limestone, sand, and many minerals, was formed from the decayed eastern edge of the ancient Appalachian mountains. Pennsylvania had fewer navigable rivers than Penn's maps had promised. But the Delaware River was a good highway into the Atlantic, and the land was traversed by many creeks and rivulets. Jones was satisfied. Although a former dweller in pastoral mountains around Bala, Merionethshire, he had a kind of religious vision: where trees currently stood, he saw bountiful grain to feed his families. "And as for ye land," noted Jones, "we look upon it [as] good and fat soil generally producing twenty, thirty, and forty fold." He was so confident of grain surpluses that he told an expected settler, John ap Thomas, "thou must bring mill stones and ye irons that belong to it, for smiths are dear."[1]

Jones stayed alert. He wanted the poor Welsh families, largely composed of children, to begin working their land immediately. So, before the end of August, Jones and his party left the relatively comfortable billets of the unambitious Swedish farmers. They moved to the their forested land and lived meanly for several seasons. They just wanted to see the grain. They planted barley on some cleared Indian land, but the harvest season was rainy, "and it began to sprout rendering it unfit for bread." They bought venison and fowl from the Leni Lenape (Delaware Indians) and some cows from English settlers in the lower counties. They tied the cows with vines to trees or stakes driven into the ground. They dug caves into the precipices along the Schuylkill River for shelter and walled and extended them with wooden planks.[2]

Another Welsh party arrived in 1683 with the former Cromwellian Thomas Ellis in charge. They quickly settled Haverford township in The Welsh Tract. They were also anxious about poverty and prone to visions of wealth. In 1684 Ellis wrote some lyrics about the child-saving land he saw, his *Song of Rejoicing*:

> Pennsylvania an habitation
> with certain, sure and clear foundation
> where the dawning of the day,
> expels the thick, dark night away
>
> Lord, give us here a place to feed
> and pass my life among thy seed
> that in our bounds true love and peace
> from age to age may never cease.
>
> Then shall the trees and fields increase
> heaven and earth proclaim thy peace,
> that we and they—forever Lord
> shew forth thy praise, with one accord.[3]

His song prayed that the Quaker settlers, by adhering to their faith and responsibilities, would create peace and love. They would simultaneously increase orchards and fields. By feeding their children with the Holy Spirit and ample land and wheat, they could settle their children, their and God's seed, within the protection of "holy conversation." Assuming Quaker parents remained faithful, tender Friends, they would perpetuate their holy tribe in Pennsylvania forever. Ellis's expression and purposes were sacred, but his vision was down-to-earth.

More from design than accident, and as much from communal as individual desire, the settlers' grain began growing impressively within a few seasons. The Philadelphia merchants knew how and where to market the flour. As William Penn noted in 1685, "The earth by God's blessing, has more than answered our expectation: the poorest places in our judgment producing large crops of garden stuff and grain . . . some plantations have got twenty acres in corn, some forty, some fifty."[4] By 1685 the merchant Thomas Budd was accurately predicting that the sale of flour to the West Indies, where land was largely covered with slave-produced sugar cane, would be the Quaker farmers' major business: "Flour and bisket may be made in great quantities in a few years the wheat being very good, which seldom fails of finding a good market in Barbados, Jamaica, and the Carib Islands: great quantities are sent each year from London, and other places, which if they can make profit of it, we much more for the reasons already given."[5] By the next year, enough surplus flour was being produced to enter the West Indies trade in earnest (only four years from the first Quaker settlement). In 1686, Dr. Nicholas More noted, "Doctor Butler had bought two hundred bushels of wheat at three shillings six pence, to transport, and several others, so that some thousands of bushels are transported this season, and when this crop that now is gathered is threshed, it is supposed that it will be abundantly cheaper than now it is, for there has been abundance of corn this year in every plantation."[6] And as David Lloyd carefully reported on October 2, 1686, "I shall only add, that five ships are come in since our arrival, one from Bristol with 100 passengers, one from Hull with 160 passengers, one from New England for corn, and two from Barbados; all of them, and ours (of above 300 tun) had their loading there, ours from New England, and the rest for Barbados: and for all this, wheat (as good, I think, as any in England) is sold at three shillings ready money (which makes two shillings five pence English sterling) and if God continues his blessing to us, this province will certainly be the grainery of America."[7] Within a few years, formerly upland Quaker farmers helped begin North America's best established and most expansive wheat trade.

The farmers used Pennsylvania's fertile land and benefited from the Leni Lenape's clearing of many fields and burnings of forest underbrush. Quaker Philadelphia merchants knew the West Indies' markets. Yet, the upland settlers' desperate search for adequate profits to provide land and material to protect their children provided the underlying motive and principle of organization. Both Merionethshire and Cheshire immigrant farmers remained mixed farmers in Pennsylvania, but they quickly and nearly uniformly changed their agricultural priorities. Quaker farmers from the dairy lands of Cheshire kept cows in Pennsylvania, but they concentrated on grain cultivation, not cheese production. Merionethshire farmers gave up tending large herds of sheep, goats, and cattle for plowing their undulating Pennsylvania fields for grain, a form of agriculture many of these mountain farmers had never known (between 1670 and 1690 over 50 percent of husbandmen and yeomen in Merionethshire grew no grain whatsoever).[8] Typical was Robert Lloyd, a bachelor, who arrived in the Valley in 1683 from mountainous Llangower, Merionethshire. He married and had children soon after. Although he had rarely seen fields of wheat, he developed by 1714 a large Pennsylvania wheat farm with well over 50 acres in cultivation, producing annually at least 240 bushels of wheat, 20 bushels of barley, and 100 bushels of oats. Evaluated together at £62 in 1714, the grains easily exceeded in market value all of Lloyd's animals.[9]

Such crop conversions were not stimulated because wheat was a bumper crop, at least not like tobacco or sugar were. A number of decades earlier, these exotic plants had ignited "boom psychologies" in the Chesapeake and West Indies among British men desperate for gentlemanly status and wealth. In order to cash in quickly, settlers abused their white servants and then began buying slaves. They forgot their economic traditions and even much of their former civility.[10] Wheat did not make gentlemen, but only enough profit to allow the settlers to live decently and have enough surplus wealth to buy more land for their children. These settlers' faith and hard British experience had taught them to pursue such modest profits.

Pennsylvania land was sufficiently fertile and versatile to support many different types of farming, including the planting of tobacco. Only their near unanimity of concern for their children's futures, which Quaker faith, doctrine, and the settlers' underlying tribalism evoked, could so swiftly transform natural desires to make enormous profits, or to continue traditional patterns of agriculture, into innovative, decently lucrative, but communally safe, wheat farming. By shifting with remarkable uniformity and speed from previous livestock farming to growing grain for the West Indies' flour market (later this market would be extended to southern Europe), the northwestern British Quaker farmers in Pennsylvania spoke again "with one mouth," and showed how desires for economic advancement and the needs of "holy conversation" could be reconciled.

THE SETTLERS' interests were not entirely economic, materialistic, or even familial. Indeed, radical child-centeredness greatly helped the Quakers maintain a strong religious community. The Delaware Valley Quakers' sprawling townships composed of contiguous farmsteads looked uncommunal. Their settlement pattern, especially when set beside spacially tight and tidy seventeenth-century New England towns, could seem the onset of promiscuous commercialization, privatization, and individualism. In the settlers' real lives, however, the seemingly sprawling townships of the Welsh Tract and eastern Chester County closely connected like-minded people to their institutions. The Welsh and Cheshire settlers lived on dispersed farmsteads in Pennsylvania, because the uplanders had known no other type of agriculture. They were accustomed to keeping communities over considerable space. Just as the Morley Monthly Meeting in Cheshire organized household discipline over dispersed hillside farms, the Chester and Welsh Tract Monthly Meetings, whose committees moved about on long-legged horses, covered their more densely collected Pennsylvania membership with the "discipline of Truth." The undulating, often flat, southeastern Pennsylvania countryside did not intimidate mountain men and women. While voluminously documenting the existence of a strong religious community (some ten reels of microfilm), the Radnor (Welsh Tract) and Chester Monthly Meeting minutes from 1683 to 1765 failed to contain any arguments over the placement of schools or meetinghouses. These settlers were more comfortable communalizing the vastness of the American forests than were New England villagers from southeastern England.[11]

Children made piety and profit compatible. The settlers' private wealth did not destroy their communities, it made them possible. The northwestern British Quakers had known poverty and had consequently lost their children. In Pennsylvania, the Quakers prudently chose to stock their communities with wealthy households which could retain their children. Not only did these communities allow their members to pursue wealth for their children but they also gained their members' adherence and participation by helping them. The monthly meetings encouraged economic virtues and reinforced the settlers' natural desire to get decently rich. They also provided many forms of advice to help parents save their children.

Finally, by confining childhood socialization largely to private spaces, and making those private spaces increasingly wealthy and enticing, the transplanted Quakers did not need to establish legally any restrictions of public preaching. As noted, unlike other colonies, there was no established religion in Pennsylvania. Quakers made the transmission of the Holy Spirit an intimate matter, not a public matter of explicit catechisms, rituals, and doctrines. Because they thought public enunciations of doctrine ineffectual, they could and did maintain communities while tolerating a wide array of strangers, so long as the strangers did not loudly intrude into Friends' sacred intimacies. The Pennsylvania Quakers could simultaneously endorse pluralism and morality. Wealth, vast spaces, pluralism, and a religious-moral community could be plausibly reconciled in North America. People simply had to work tenderly and hard to nurture the Light in children.

In 1686, Thomas Ellis expressed much of this vision in a letter to George Fox. He reminded him how much poor Welsh tenants needed this Pennsylvania land for their children. He also told Fox they were developing the land in Haverford township with order and wealth, "about fifteen families of us have taken our land together and there are to be eight more that have yet come, who took [to begin] 30 acres apiece with which we build and do improve, and the other land we have to range for our cattle." Ellis reported a tight Quaker community, "we have our burying place where we intend our meeting house, as near as we can to the center, our men and women's meetings and other monthly meetings in both week dayes unto which four townships at least belongs. And precious do we find other opportunities that are given as free will offering unto the Lord in the evenings, some time which not intended but Friends coming simply to one another the Lord appears to his name be the glory." Ellis's single complaint was that "several young people continue to come over without certificates which is a trouble to Friends." These lusty youngsters, lacking proof of their "holy conversation," would have to delay their marriages.[12]

This term "conversation" was centrally mentioned in 95 percent of all the Welsh immigrant's British removal certificates available from 1681 to 1695 (65) and in 87 percent of all those fully recorded for Quakers within the jurisdiction of the Chester Monthly Meeting (22). The certificates described the spiritually sound presence of the immigrating farmers. In the 62 Welsh certificates received by the Radnor (Welsh Tract) Monthly Meeting between 1682 and 1690, 36 different adjectives or adjectival phrases described the adults in these 62 Welsh certificates. The adjectives used most often were "honest" (33), "blameless" (14), "loving" (13), "tender" (9), "civil" (8), "plain" (7), and "modest" (5). The adjectives related to Christ-like qualities, except two cases of "industrious" and one case of "punctual." Charismatic Christian and economic virtues could be melded.

The certificates were used to judge which immigrants were capable of Quaker intimacies and finally of Quaker parenthood. Without a certificate, a young Quaker arriving in the Delaware Valley could not get married in meeting for some years—until his or her true character could be judged. They were part of a larger scheme: the construction of an ideal speech community in southeastern Pennsylvania, where the Word "preached" in Quakerly gesture, language, love, and tenderness would be exchanged constantly in human relations, most intensively in meetings and households. In essence, the settlers divided human behavior into two "languages"—"holy conversation" (the speech and demeanor of a converted person) leading to self-denial, expression of "truth," and salvation; and "carnal talk" leading to corruption, pride, and death. These farmers carried a mandate purposefully to nurture and protect their children within relations of "holy conversation."

Many of these settlers' removal certificates dwelled upon children and parenthood. The settlers were composed of men like Griffith John, whose total "endeavor hath been to bring up his children in the fear of the Lord according to the order of Truth." The certificates also made plain the settlers' perception of the demanding relationship between parents' "holy conversation" and their children's spiritual development. Children were born with Adam's sin and Christ's redeeming Seed. Which developed as the major principle in their lives depended on the environment in which they grew. Particularly important was the character of their parents. The Merionethshire Meeting said of William Powell, for example: "His conversation since [his conversion] hath been honest and savory in so much that his wife came soon to be affected with the Truth, and became a good example to her children by which means they also became affected with truth, innocency, and an innocent conversation to this day." Virtually all young children were discussed in these optimistic terms. The meetings viewed only young bachelors and spinsters with some anxiety. None had reached social or religious maturity as bearers of the "truth," most were only "hopeful." The meetings consistently expressed confidence, however, that parents of self-denying, tender, "holy conversation" would ultimately raise children of similar character. Elizabeth Owens was "hopeful," for example, because "she came from good and honest parentage, and from her infancy she was educated and instructed in the doctrine and principle of truth from which she has not revolted, but according to her measure lived in profession to this very day." No explicit belief developed in these communities that children of church members, being part of Abraham's seed, were virtually assured justification. In reality, however, the Quaker parents and their meetings believed that they could help save most of their children. They need only work with emotional purity and economic productivity to keep them close.[13]

Whether at home or serving on committees of the Chester or the Radnor Monthly Meetings, good parents ably protected precious "holy conversation." Monthly meetings were composed of Friends in good standing from all the local worship meetings under their jurisdiction. In order to accommodate the distances caused by the settlers' sprawling farms, the monthly meetings traveled each month to a different township within their jurisdiction. For instance, the Radnor (Welsh Tract) Monthly Meeting convened in Radnor, Merion, and Haverford in successive months. Between the meeting's conventions, committees from both the men's and women's meetings roamed the countryside to visit families, conduct marriage inspections, and consult farmers and tradesmen in behavioral or financial difficulty. The men's and women's monthly meetings in Chester and the Welsh Tract, like those elsewhere, encouraged "holy conversation" by identifying and disowning "carnal talk" and by organizing life for the rule of the Word. Their aim was, as George Fox said, "that all order their conversation aright, that they may see the salvation of God: they may all see and know, possess, and partake of the government of Christ, of the increase of which there is no end."[14]

The Radnor and the Chester Meetings tightly enforced "holy conversation." Their communities were self-consciously holy speech communities. Although no settler was disciplined, much less disowned, for using "you" instead of "thee" and "thou" on occasion, he or she would be disciplined for conduct or language which sprang from the "worldly part" instead of the "Light." A Springfield overseer complained to the Chester Meeting because a farmer was often "using extravagant language."[15] Welsh Tract elders advised that some funerals were becoming "unsavory" because of "immoderately speaking," the survivors praising the departed's virtues excessively.[16] Speech and conduct were to preach the "Truth," answering the Light in others. Sins of language and conduct were melded. At a Chester meeting in 1700 a farmer "brought a paper to this Meeting wherein he condemned his taking too much liberty in drinking, riding, and unnecessary discourse."[17] The settlers' sought to make the material world around them express "holy conversation." Any unnecessary object or decoration was prideful. In 1695 the Welsh Tract Meeting charged "those Friends that are ordered to deal with those that walked disorderly should go into Friends' houses and inquire into . . . all such things as are superfluous, unnecessary, and inconsistent with Truth."[18]

Even apparel "preached" and thus was judged. The Chester men's meeting in 1719 made a typical entry: "A concern falling on Friends at this meeting as to what means might be taken to suppress the growing evil of superfluity in apparel, it is therefore thought needful that the parents and guardians who have any such under their care should be charged therewith."[19] "Holy conversation" was to be heard and seen in these communities, not lies, malice, or pride.

The primary procedural support of the settlers' social-religious design, through such business meetings, was their elaborate marriage discipline, which controlled the formation of new households and thereby the primary environments in which children grew. Most of the business that came before the Welsh Tract and the Chester (men's and women's) Monthly Meetings directly concerned marriage. In the Welsh Tract, in the men's monthly meetings (1683–1709), 46 percent of the business dealt with marriages: the next largest category of business, administrative concerns, like building burial grounds or arranging worship meetings, included only 17 percent of the itemized business. In the women's monthly meetings marriages took 54 percent of the business and charity 19 percent. In Chester, the men's and women's meetings sat together until 1705. Between 1681 and 1705, 53 percent of the business concerned marriages: the next largest category, discipline, accounted for 14 percent of the business. These figures do not account for the fact that marriage infractions composed the majority of discipline cases. In the Welsh Tract between 1684 and 1725, 82 percent of all condemnations involved young men and women and 78 percent marriage or fornication (fornications without marriage was rare, involving only 4 percent of the cases.)[20]

The Foxian marriage procedure was fully transplanted in the Welsh Tract and Chester, and remained time-consuming, thorough, intrusive, and delicate. Its non-coercive, voluntaristic flavor was particularly demanding on parents or guardians, who bore much of the blame for failure. As in England, prospective marriage partners had first to obtain permission for both courtship and then marriage from all the parents or close relatives involved. They then had to announce their intention of marriage before the men's and women's monthly meetings. After hearing the announcement, the meetings appointed two committees, each composed of two well-established Friends, in order to investigate the "clearness" from prior ties and particularly the "conversation" of the man and woman (two women investigated the woman, two men the man). The man and woman would appear at the next monthly meeting to hear the verdict, which, since the meetings warned off Friends with problems, was usually favorable. After the second visit to the monthly meetings, the marriage ceremony took place usually in the meetinghouse of the woman's family. The partners married directly before God, the guests and attendants served as witnesses, signing the marriage certificate. Soon after setting up their household, the young couple would be included among the households regularly visited by committees inspecting and urging "holy conversation" from the men's and women's monthly meetings.[21]

The marriage procedure addressed the latent conflicts in these settlers' tasks between personal spontaneity, sincerity, and inner discipline, and communal and parental authority. The settlers hoped to harmonize all these concerns happily and faithfully. Yet, though parents and meetings wanted to exercise keen oversight of marriage, Chester and Welsh Tract Quakers wanted partners to love one another before they wed in order to assure the spiritual aura and vitality of the household. Quaker ministers stressed this was to be a self-denying, virtuous, Christian love, not romantic lust. Ministers often told youth to make no final decision about marriage until they waited upon God in solitude. They would receive a spiritual assent or negative. They should then follow their convictions no matter what the obstacles.

Such emphasis on sincerity and non-coercion certainly complicated parental control. Reversing relatively progressive, spiritualized Puritan marriage procedures, in which children were allowed a veto over marriages arranged by their parents, Quaker parents retained a veto only over marriages initiated by their children. That veto was shaky. Given the authority the settlers placed in sincere love, this veto depended upon the optimistic expectation that young men and women permitted mobility would refrain from discussing marriage until they had obtained the consent of all parents involved. Young adults were to get acquainted only to the point of interest; they were then to stop short of irreversible involvement and enlist parental help and support. In order to deter premature promises, the meetings often sent oversight committees of elders to spy on youth during Chester or Philadelphia market days and fairs. Irrespective of such prying, children and parents most often followed the proper, delicate procedures, as illustrated by a surviving careful 1716 letter between the Chester County Mendenhalls and the Welsh Tract Roberts.[22] If parents remained hostile or indifferent, however, the couple could force the issue by informally involving an elder, by marrying out of discipline, or by threatening to do so. For example, in 1713, the Chester women asked, as a condition of approving their marriage, that Hannah Vernon "acknowledge the sin of speaking with (Caleb Harrison) about marriage before she had consulted her parents." She did so, with seemingly little embarrassment, and was wed.[23]

Knowing their options under the doctrine of sincerity, some Chester and Welsh Tract youth grew assertive and troublesome. To help their cases, young Welsh Tract women lobbied for their choices, filling the meetinghouse with supportive peers when they announced their intentions to marry. Such love politicking became so daunting that the Radnor Women's Monthly Meeting complained in 1725 that "this Meeting does not think it convenient that many young women accompanies any Friends when they go to propose their intentions of marriage to the Men's Meeting, and that it is desired for the future that none go but are allowed by the Meeting."[24] And though a young woman freely selected her spouse from the first to the final stages of courtship, if at the last minute her inner testimony demurred, she simply changed her mind, no matter the inconvenience to the monthly meetings, the banished groom, or the expectant parents. In 1705, after approving the marriage of John Martin and Jane Hent, the Chester Men's Meeting was surprised that the marriage had not taken place. They reported that "the abovesaid marriage not being accomplished, two women friends— Alice Simcock and Rebecca Faucit—spoke to Jane Hent to know the reason thereof, and her answer was that she could not love him well enough [for him] to be her husband . . . she also said that she was sorry that she had to proceed so far with him." This mild regret was the only apology that meeting would receive. There were several almost identical cases.[25] Some of the settlers' more troublesome children married non-Quakers or, by going to a Protestant minister or magistrate, married fellow Quakers outside the meeting discipline.

This delicate, non-coercive system generally worked in Pennsylvania, because parents supplied the material to make Quaker freedoms and responsibilities compelling. The related familial, moral, and economic strategies of 38 Welsh Tract and 34 Chester families—and how well they fit with Quaker communalism—was ascertained by collating the demographic evidence of these families' reconstitutions with their wills, probate inventories, reports on tax lists, and disciplinary and marriage references in the men's and women's monthly meetings of Chester, Radnor, and surrounding areas. Radical child-centeredness clearly persuaded the settlers to use their wheat profits quickly and extensively to develop and buy the Valley. The settlers almost uniformly saved their shillings to buy eventually enormous amounts of land in order to settle their children. By the late 1690s, according to a contemporary Pennsylvania Council's survey of Welsh Tract land transactions, the mean holding of 70 resident households in the Welsh Tract was 332 acres. In the towns comprising the Chester Monthly Meeting, according to the Chester County's treasurer's survey, the mean holding of 76 families was 337 acres.[26] Only six married men had holdings of under 100 acres, and 80 percent held over 150 acres. These Chester and Welsh settlers continued to buy land after 1699 as can be seen from a comparison of landholdings of 53 Cheshire and Welsh Quaker settlers in the late 1690s and the land which they distributed to their children by deed and will. In the 1690s these men had an average of 386 acres, about the same average as the general population of landowners.[27] As their deeds and wills show, however, they gave or sold to their children an average of 701 acres, an average increase of 315 acres from 1690. Seventy percent of the settlers gave 400 acres or more to their children.[28]

As their wills and deeds also show, these settlers bought, exchanged, and preserved land largely for their children. The 53 men gave away or sold a total of 160 parcels during their lives, a third of these to their children. Six men engaged in 46 percent of the sales, however. These men were land speculators, though this role combined with serving as middle men between William Penn and the first purchasers. The land speculators were often former Cromwellian magistrates like Thomas Ellis. From searches of deeds in Philadelphia and Chester County, the average farmer engaged in only two or three purely commercial land deals during his life. Land buying and selling was usually connected with family responsibilities. Hoping to settle all their sons on farms, and some grandchildren too, the settlers bought land as their households grew. A correlation existed between the number of sons a family had and the amount of land it held. Between the 1690s and the end of their lives, the three men without sons did not increase their acreage: those with one son increased their acreage an average of 135 acres; those with two sons increased their acreage an average of 242 acres; those with three sons an average of 309 acres; and those with four or more an average of 361 acres. Sons received over 200 acres on an average and daughters received somewhat less than the equivalent in Pennsylvania currency.

Thirty-nine of the forty-one wills existing for the 53 Welsh Tract and Chester settlers show large quantities of unused land which were later bequeathed to children. Joseph Baker, for example, besides his plantation in Edgemont, bequeathed a 200-acre tract in Thornberry to his son. Francis Yarnell bequeathed, besides his plantation in Willistown, a 120-acre tract in Springfield.[29] Only three men worked their additional land and only two men had tenants. A study of the inventories of these families also confirms the child-centered use of land. Of the 41 inventories, 27 of these men at the time of their death already portioned two of their children; seven of these men were nearly retired, though they still used their farms. The rest (14) had portioned only one child or none at the time of their death, so they were probably near the height of productivity. The average farmer had a small herd of animals (6 cows, 4 steers, 6 horses, 14 sheep, and 8 pigs) and was cultivating between 40 and 50 acres for wheat, barley, and corn. The rule of thumb in eighteenth-century farming was three acres for one cow (this was the practice in Cheshire), so the cows and steers would require at least 30 acres. The six horses would need about 6 acres and oats, and their 13 sheep about two acres a year. This gives a figure of at least 80 acres in use for the average farmer who had about 700 acres. The additional 620 acres awaited children.[30]

The child-centered land use pattern of Edmund Cartledge was typical, although he used more land than most. He had a personal estate of £377, including £63 worth of crops, mostly wheat, and £90 worth of livestock. In the "household chamber" and "in the barn" Cartledge had about 115 bushels of wheat, which was the harvest of about 10 to 15 acres. "In the field" he had 20 acres of wheat and rye (worth about £30) and 10 acres of summer corn, barley, and oats (£18). In total, he had at least 40 to 50 acres under cultivation. "In the yard" were a number of cows, pigs, and horses; and in the field a flock of sheep. According to the usual feed requirements, he used from 50 to 55 acres for these animals. For both livestock and crops, he used about 100 acres. His inventory described his farm as "250 acres of land, buildings, orchards, garden, fences, wood, and meadows," evaluated at £400. From 1690 to 1710, ten inventories show the evaluation of improved land was £2 per acre and unimproved land was 6 shillings per acre. A comparison of his evaluation with the general evaluations of improved and unimproved lands confirms that he used about one-half to two-thirds of his plantation. At his death, he also had 100 acres in Springfield and 1,107 acres in Plymouth at a low evaluation of £300, indicating that they were unimproved. Like the other Quaker farmers, Cartledge bought land to farm and more land to settle his children upon.[31]

These Quaker household accumulations were too large to fit the average needs or expectations of a conventional northwestern British middling, rural household devoted chiefly to the honorable preservation of the family line. Most of the settlers' sons got 200 or 300 acres of prime riverside or creek side land, often with a limestone house perched in the middle. Three hundred acres would seem to ensure to their children's households protection from "the world" and enough peace to enjoy and exemplify the "Truth." The Delaware Valley Quaker farmers were listening to the radically new familial obligations they thought dictated by "holy conversation" and responding vigorously to their previous inability to match such obligations in the Cheshire plains or the Welsh mountains. The Quaker farmers had found something to reconcile them to disciplined work in a lonely land. They worked hard with full communal approval to protect the Holy Spirit incarnated in the spiritual and physical bodies of their cherished children.

Some Quaker children caused problems, but they were usually tamed by kind parents and fetching farmland well integrated into an Atlantic market. An overwhelming majority of the settlers' children freely married other Quakers locally within the Quaker meeting discipline. Seventy-two Welsh Tract and Chester settlers' households had 361 children survive to twenty-one years of age. Of these 47 married out of discipline, 52 remained unmarried, and 262 married within the Quaker meeting. Thus, 72.5 percent of all children married within meeting. This was far better than the from 32 percent to 18 percent retention rate which Welsh and Cheshire Quaker households achieved in England. In the luxuriant farmlands of the Delaware Valley, radical northwestern British Quaker domesticity made a home for itself.

IN THEIR RUSH to develop Pennsylvania land for their children, Pennsylvania farmers did confront contradictions—some visible and solvable, and some latent and insidious. For example, wheat-farming required more work than the livestock farming that north-

western British settlers or their children were used to. Many Cheshire and Welsh Quaker households brought along servants, often the
children of neighbors in England. Yet, they and the settlers' own
children seemed an inadequate labor force to clear and plant the
land. In order to buy land and its furnishings to protect their
children, these farmers often felt compelled to take "strangers" into
their households as laborers. Indeed, the fertile but inexpensive land
of the Delaware Valley and the wheat boomlet allowed many settlers
to afford slaves.[32] The Delaware Valley Quaker's trading connections with the slave-infested West Indies provided them with an
accessible source of slaves. Maryland, a slave society, was nearby.
Many Quaker households in Pennsylvania, New Jersey, and Delaware did in fact buy many slaves. Yet, although slaves were not
absent from the Chester and Radnor households, the Chester and
Welsh Tract settlers had comparatively few. Of the 41 men who left
inventories, among those families that were reconstructed, only
nine recorded servants or slaves (25 percent) and four had slaves (5
percent) or about one in every 20 households. Relatively little use of
slaves was due to an explicit and unusually alert familial policy of
Welsh Tract and Chester Quaker leaders, and to the rapid and
pluralistic development of their economy.

Chester County elders' spiritual antennae pained to signals of
"carnal talk" or exotic people in their households. Robert Pyle, a
prosperous Concord farmer, writing in 1698, testified that he
bought a slave because of the scarcity of white domestic labor. Pyle,
however, felt the threat of contamination and had bad dreams, often
a warning sign for introspective Friends:

> I was myself and a Friend going on a road, and by the roadside
> I saw a black pot. I took it up, the Friends said give me part. I said
> not, I went a little further and I saw a great ladder standing exact
> upright, reaching up to heaven, up which I must go to heaven
> with the pot in my hand intending to carry the black pot with me,
> but the ladder standing so upright, and seeing no man holding of
> it, it seemed it would fall upon me; at which I stepped down laid
> the pot at the foot of the ladder, and said them that take it might,
> for I found work enough for both hands to take hold of this
> ladder.

Pyle concluded that "self must be left behind, and to let black
Negroes or pots alone."[33] To purify his household and himself, Pyle
manumitted his black slave. Cadwallader Morgan of the Welsh

Tract bought a Negro in 1698 so he could have more time to go to meetings and to serve the community. But Morgan soon felt that greed had been his real aim, that the slave symbolized the rule of self over the Word. Morgan also worried about the social and familial problems slavery might cause for Quaker households. "What," Morgan asked, "if I should have had a bad one of them, that must be corrected, or would run away, or when I went from home and leave him with a woman or maid, and he should desire to committ wickedness." Fearing many varieties of corruption, Morgan manumitted his slave and testified against slavery.[34]

Thanks to such influential local reformers, the Chester and Welsh Tract Quaker communities discouraged slaveholding locally, though less successfully within the Society of Friends generally. The Chester Quarterly and Monthly Meetings issued five letters or messages to the Philadelphia Yearly Meeting between 1690 and 1720, requesting a testimony against buying or importing slaves. The Chester Monthly Meeting in 1715 recorded that "it is the unanimous sense of this Meeting that Friends should not be concerned hereafter in the importation thereof nor buy any, and we request the concurrence of the Quarterly Meeting." In response, the Philadelphia Quarterly Meeting in 1715 chided Chester Friends for acting prejudicially against slaveowners in their Meeting by excluding them from positions of spiritual authority.[35] Nevertheless, the unusually low number of slaves among Chester County Quakers, in comparison with Quaker slaveholding elsewhere, suggests that the reformers' efforts continued to be locally effective. The rapid development of the Pennsylvania wheat economy was also significant in providing the Quaker farmers and tradesmen with an alternative labor supply. By 1720, this economy's prosperity and the Quakers' hospitality attracted thousands of immigrants, particularly Germans and Scots-Irish, many of whom were willing to serve as servants to pay for their passage. As the expert on Quaker slaveholding, Jean Soderlund, has shown, Quaker Chester County slaveholding was highest just after settlement, but declined rapidly after 1720 as European servants became available.[36]

Concern for "holy conversation" and for their children's souls, however, also brought farmers using white indentured servants worries. Friendly "conversation" conflicted with the economic desirability of beating the full labor value out of lazy indentured servants potentially helpful for getting land for children and prestige for parents. The Chester Meeting called one rich Quaker farmer before them in 1693 for whipping one of his male servants, as the man's striped back eloquently testified. The farmer condemned the act "for the reputation of truth" but said the lazy fellow was "worthless" and "deserved to be beaten."[37] By placing a slothful woman servant in a "noxious hole," another farmer thought he had devised the moral alternative to whipping and beating. The Chester Monthly Meeting thought his brainstorm unseemly, and he had to condemn it.[38] In 1700 the Welsh Tract Monthly Meeting established a "committee to maintain good order," which recommended "that Friends be watchful over their families and that they should be careful what persons they brought or admitted to their families, whether servants or others, lest they should be hurt by them." The committee devised techniques for disciplining servants without flogging them. When their terms expired, masters were to write "certificates . . . concerning their behavior according to their deserts." Given the Quakers' influence in the Pennsylvania countryside and the opportunities in the Pennsylvania economy available to reputable ex-servants, ex-servants need fear unhappy frustration unless they had good references. The meeting established a public committee to "deal hard with servants" and to hear their complaints about their masters.[39] No evidence exists as to what techniques the committee used to handle unruly servants, but they were probably non-violent. Because of their ideas about purified households and the strength of their neighborhoods and economy, these rural Quakers discouraged bringing Africans into the house and devised gentler ways of disciplining labor.

Some problems, however, were less easily seen or solved. While they methodically developed a liveable and affluent garden of radical domesticity under "holy conversation" in southeastern Pennsylvania, the settlers' communally approved pursuit of wealth for radical households did produce an insidious social contradiction which later limited the conscientious growth of Quakerism. The problem that most plagued these Quaker communities did not so much involve the treatment of strangers or the exploitation of lower classes, but the development of unjustifiably conflated spiritual and economic inequalities among Quaker neighbors.

Quaker domesticity produced in Pennsylvania a new kind of ruling American middle class which joined wealth, effective child-rearing, and spiritual innocence. The distribution of prestige in the Chester towns and the Welsh Tract confirmed and reinforced the pressure on parents to perform their interrelated economic and spiritual tasks successfully. But these pressures ultimately led to confusions between economic and spiritual competence. In these communities, the most successful parents tended to be wealthier than average. They received not only Quakerly children but also religious status and self-assurance. Participation in the monthly meetings was broad, but not all farmers and tradesmen participated equally. In the Welsh Tract (1683-89, 1693-95) twenty men and women shared a majority of the tasks of the monthly meetings. These Friends dominated virtually all the differing categories of tasks assigned to the meeting, including the arbitration of disputes, discipline, marriage investigations, and visiting families. The farmers described their leaders in terms of spiritual achievement: honorific terms included "elder," "ancient Friend," or they were familial: John and Barbara Bevan were a "nursing father and mother to some weak and young amongst us." The meetings expected leaders, more than others, to express "holy conversation." For example, an elder in Radnor in 1694 allowed his daughter to marry a first cousin, an act against discipline. It is a "scandal upon the Truth and Friends," the meeting decided, "that he being looked upon as an elder should set such a bad example." Such men and women were supposed to provide the same charismatic, loving authority for Quaker adults as Quaker parents provided for their children.

Among the men (see Chapter Six, below, for distributions of leadership among women) the leaders were successful fathers who were usually wealthy but who were not defined solely by wealth as leaders. Approximately 70 percent of the Welsh leaders came from nominally gentry families, but so did 18 percent of the less active, and 30 percent of the leaders were yeomen and artisans. Although some significant correlation existed between land and leadership, the high standard deviations show that wealth was not the sole or final determinant of leadership. Among the men in the 53 reconstructed families from Chester and the Welsh Tract, those who were leaders were more distinguished by their Quakerly children than by their wealth. Though above average in wealth, the leaders were not consistently the wealthiest men. On the other hand, their families were twice as well disciplined as remaining families.[40]

The religious standing of men in Chester and the Welsh Tract often hinged on rearing good children and providing good marriages for them. Those who could not control their own family had no claim to religious honor or trust. The Radnor and Chester

Meetings did not usually penalize a parent if only one child married out of discipline. Randal Malin, for example (as his ministerial career in Cheshire might have predicted), held ninety-eight positions in the Chester Meeting between 1681 and 1721, more than the other farmers studied. Yet, his daughter married out in 1717 (as did another in 1721, after Malin's death).[41] Richard Ormes, however, stumbled from leadership when his pregnant daughter got married in meeting in 1715 after fooling the female inspectors. This was an unusually bad infraction, involving lust and blatant deception. Ormes was a fully recognized minister, sent by the meeting on trips to Maryland, and an elder, holding about five meeting positions a year. Between 1693 and 1715, the Radnor Meeting sent him to the quarterly meeting five times. After his daughter's fall, however, this prestigious Friend did not serve his monthly meeting again until 1720, five years later.[42] Neither Ormes nor Malin openly cooperated with their wayward children. If a father did cooperate, he was disciplined and dropped from leadership instantly. Howell James held four positions between 1693 and 1697, but in the latter year, he went to his son's Keithian wedding. He acknowledged his mistake but never served the Meeting again.[43]

When more than one child married out, even if a father did not cooperate, the parents lost prestige and were often subjected to the criticism of the meeting. For example, Edward Kinneson held twenty-four Meeting positions in Chester and Goshen between 1709 and 1721, when his daughter Mary married out. He continued to be appointed at nearly the same rate until 1726, when his son Edward married out, and then he was dropped from leadership. Although he did nothing to encourage the marriage or cooperate with his son, the meeting decided that "the father has been more indulgent therein than is agreeable with the testimony of Truth." In 1733, James Kinneson, Edward's last son, married out. The Meeting treated Kinneson gently: "considering his age and weakness [we are] willing to pass by his infirmity." A major source of Kinneson's problem was his relative poverty. He has amassed only 200 acres of land. His children all married in their early twenties. They most likely would have had to wait to marry or might not have married at all, if they had confined themselves to the Quaker marriage market. Though he remained a Friend until he died in 1734, his wife Mary responded angrily to their humiliations. In 1741 the Goshen Meeting got word "that Mary Kinneson, widow of Edward, who some time since removed herself into the colony of Virginia hath forsaken our Society and joined herself to the Church of England."[44]

As this case suggests, given the competition for Quaker mates, poorer children who wished to participate fully in religious life had to control (or appear to control) their sexual and emotional impulses longer than wealthier children. Among the poorer families the mean marriage age was seven years older for men and almost six years older for women than for the children of the wealthier families. The children of Ellis Ellis, for example, a relatively poor Welsh Tract farmer, all married in the Radnor Meeting, but his two sons married at the ages of 49 and 34, and his three daughters at the ages of 29, 33, and 31. John Bevan's son Evan, on the other hand, inherited over 1,000 acres, and married at 19 years of age; John Bevan's three daughters married at the ages of 20, 20, and 18. Accordingly, poorer Friends married out more often. Only 15 percent of the children of the first generation Chester and the Welsh Tract married out of discipline, and virtually all of these came from the poorest families. The wealthiest families like the Simcocks, Bevans, Worrals, and Owens had only three children among 101 marry out of discipline, while the 30 poorest households had 36 delinquent children among 139. The richer Quaker households also produced fewer bachelors and spinsters. Nor did these Meetings treat rich and poor children identically; disobedient poor children were disowned at a much higher rate than disobedient wealthy children (see Appendix: Table 4).[45]

Poor and failing households suffered more religious stigma from fellow Quakers in the Delaware Valley than they had in Cheshire and Wales. Among the first generation of Welsh Quaker and Cheshire Quaker emigrants to Pennyslvania, the Quakers' tender, involving familialism and domesticity had been transformed from a formula for frustration relieved by group-therapy into an economically and socially successful family and community system. Troubled households were no longer the majority, but an annoying minority, a drag on general success in the Peaceable Kingdom. The 119 households who stayed in Cheshire and Wales, it might be remembered, produced only 51 Quaker marriages, a suicidal replacement-rate of 34 percent. Seventy Welsh and Cheshire households who emigrated to Pennsylvania produced locally 123 Quaker marriages a happy replacement-rate of 175 percent—and the grandchildren had good prospects. What made the Delaware farmers more successful was their ability and opportunity to exploit new resources and markets to provide land and social insulation for their offspring. The settlers were slowly changing, in effect, from despised, radical middling folk into a ruling American middle class defined by parental competence which included economic prowess, emotional self-discipline, and the possession of a quietly charismatic and sincere "holy" presence.

The Radnor and the Chester Monthly Meetings were run by effective Quaker parents who had mastered their spiritual and material tasks. Such leadership helped support the orderly, prosperous development of the Delaware Valley. On the other hand, since effective parenting depended partly on wealth, economic, parental, and spiritual competence silently became conflated. Even in the Delaware Valley some farmers and artisans failed to flourish. Set among a verdant scene of general economic and childrearing success, such men, their wives, and children suffered not only the disgrace of simply lacking the material goods and land of their neighbors, but also earned the visits of tenderly worried, wealthy elders, and the repeated shock of disownments. The people left economically behind felt cheated spiritually. As shall be seen, poor Quakers were the backbone of the Keithian schism, and the problem, so intertwined with the virtues of these communities, quietly grew worse.

IN COMPARISON with coeval middling families in the Chesapeake and New England, the radically child-centered northwestern British farmers in the Delaware Valley enjoyed, nonetheless, smoother and more harmonious economic, communal, familial, and religious development. The Chesapeake households were not easily comparable. They were largely formed from freed indentured servants. During most of the seventeenth century they suffered from malaria and other epidemics. The New Englanders largely came to America from southeastern England in household groups similar to those of the Cheshire and Welsh immigrants. Many came with more wealth and then enjoyed better health in North America. Yet most Puritan farmers, partly because they lacked good land and partly because of their conservative childrearing ideas, did not prosper as impressively as the Delaware Valley Quakers.

In the Puritan rural township of Andover, Massachusetts, in the seventeenth and eighteenth centuries, for example, parents had less fertile land, but far more responsible external institutions to accomplish equivalent tasks of Godly childrearing and household formation. Puritan parents shared responsibility with the local minister and church for their children's conversions. The church provided children with baptism and a vigorous intellectual regimen of catechism, Bible readings, and sermons. The Puritan towns by law provided schools. In accord with their community organization, the Puritans believed their children wholly unregenerated sinners, who required a mastery of the Bible before conversion, a belief which licensed hardy, sometimes insensitive, parental and communal interventions. Neither households nor spiritual intimacies were thought adequate to guide regeneration. Thorough domesticity was rejected.[46]

The households in the Chester and Radnor Quaker communities were surrounded by worship meeting and invaded by monthly meeting committees, but, insofar as people could affect them, childrearing and salvation of children were matters of holy human relations and intimacies primarily focused in carefully formed and overseen households of "holy conversation." In accord with their community organization, the Quaker settlers believed that children were indeed charged with Adam's sin, but also that they were born with the Light. Quaker children did not need as much book learning as Puritan children, but elicited more parental indulgence, nurture, and protection. They got much more land.

Because of their purposeful development of the wheat trade, their ethics, and their superior farmland, the formerly poor Cheshire and Welsh settlers were able to make their Delaware Valley households more independent and generous places for nurturing children than those of formerly economically advantaged southeastern English settlers and their descendants in Andover, Massachusetts. During the seventeenth and early eighteenth century in Andover, Massachusetts, as Philip Greven has shown, it was common for parents to allow sons to marry, live on their father's land, and yet not become landowners until their fathers died. According to Greven's description, "although the great majority of second generation sons were settled upon their father's land while their fathers were still alive, only about a quarter of them actually owned the land they lived upon until after their fathers' deaths." The proximity of the father to the households of his married sons reinforced a pattern in Andover of household economic interdependency and patriarchy. Seventy-five percent of the sons of the first generation settled in the closely packed township of Andover. Well into the middle of the eighteenth century, "many members of families lived within reasonably short distances of each other," as Greven described it, "with family groups often concentrated together in particular areas of the town."[47] This strong system of parental and grandparental power, as Greven argued, changed only slowly during the eighteenth century in the town. Such power was consistent with puritanical distrust of younger people. Indeed, although coming from putatively less tribalistic areas of England, the Andover settlers managed to produce, thanks to their relatively poor land and conservative child-rearing ideals, more interdependent households than did the initially more clannish transplanted Welsh and Cheshire farmers.

The Delaware Valley families were similar in demographic structure to those in Andover. Because Quaker birth and death records were poorly kept, it is possible only to estimate what health conditions were like in the seventeenth century along the Schuylkill and Delaware rivers. Twenty-five Quaker settlers, traced through the Quaker registers in England and America, had an average age of death of 67 years, with only four men dying in their forties. The survival rate of children also suggests healthy conditions. Based on a total of 72 reconstructed families in the first generation, the average number of children per family to reach twenty-one years of age was 4.73 in the Welsh Tract and 5.65 in Chester. In the Welsh Tract and Chester, based on 93 reconstructions of second-generation families, the average number of children to reach twenty-one was 5.53. These families were, nevertheless, smaller than those of 7.2 children to reach 21 which Greven found for remarkably robust early eighteenth-century Andover families whose children were born in the 1680s and 1690s.[48]

Andover began in a remote wilderness and its economically conservative farmers failed to produce a marketable staple; it took many years to develop a cash economy. Throughout much of the lives of the founding generation, as Greven noted, both grain and livestock were being used in lieu of cash in exchange for hard goods from Salem merchants. A lack of specie, cash, or credit is suggested by the fact that sons did not regularly purchase land from their fathers until after 1720, eighty years after settlement.[49] The fertile land of the Delaware Valley was more conducive to lucrative farming than the rocky soil of Andover. One thousand Finnish and Swedish farmers, who had been living mostly along the Delaware River for over fifty years, helped provide the settling Quakers with provisions. Quaker farmers were also quicker to exploit their opportunities. The Quaker settlers innovatively created the fast growing wheat market in Philadelphia under the control of able Quaker merchants with connections in the West Indies. Cash and credit rapidly appeared in Pennsylvania, as attested by the frequent and early purchasing of parental land by sons. As early as 1707, twenty-six years after settlement, Ralph Lewis sold over 100 acres to his son Abraham for £60, and after 1709 deeds of purchase were more frequently given than deeds of gift.[50] Naturally, being more profitably and child-centeredly involved in Atlantic markets, Delaware farmers consistently had more land for their children. Sixty-seven percent of the settling Andover settlers could only accumulate 200 acres or less for their sons, while 67 percent of the settling Quaker farmers accumulated 500 acres or more for their sons.[51]

Though the quality of differing soils and geographic conditions must be considered, differing ideas about childrearing also created differences in economic prowess, land transference, and household structure. It was no freak of nature that for young men and, indirectly, for young women the road to an independent household (independent from kin, not community) was smoother, shorter, and more luxurious in the Welsh Tract and Chester than it ever was in Andover. The Welsh Tract and Chester younger generation benefited, to be sure, from being members of smaller households. Their parents, however, had constructed the economy of the Delaware Valley to be far more comfortable for settling independent households than had Andover parents.

Quaker children worked and waited for their bounties, however. The late marriage ages of the Quakers strongly suggests that religious community played a major role in creating a different, richer pattern of independent household life in Pennsylvania. The settlers in the Welsh Tract and Chester carefully helped establish their children's new households by providing sufficient material wealth, even if it meant asking children to wait and labor a long time before marriage. Yet, in contrast to Andover, Quaker parents chose to make their children financially independent at marriage or soon after marriage. In pursuit of their household ideal of economic independence—reflected also in the peculiar Quaker marriage ceremony—they also set up their sons farther from home.

In Andover when a father gave a deed to a son he usually placed restrictions upon the gift. Most sons shared the frustrating experience of Stephen Barker, who received a deed of gift from his father

for a homestead and land, providing "that he carefully and faithfully manure and carry on my whole living yearly." His father
retained also the right to any part of his son's land "for my comfortable maintenance." Thomas Abbot of Andover sold his homestead,
land, and buildings to the eldest of his three sons in 1723 for £20, but
reserved for himself the right to improve half the land and to use
half the buildings during his lifetime.[52] Only one Welsh Tract or
Chester deed from the first to second generation contained a restrictive patriarchal clause, and no Quaker deeds from the second to
third generation contained such clauses. Nevertheless, fifty-four of
the Quaker settlers' sons received deeds in Chester and the Welsh
Tract: and 73 percent (40) received them before marriage or in one
year after marriage. Fifty-nine of the 84 sons who received land from
wills also received their land before marriage. Among all the second-generation sons in the Delaware Valley whose inheritance,
deeds of gift and purchase, and date of marriage can be known (139),
71 percent received land before, at, or within two years of marriage
without restrictions. Once established, three-quarters of the new
households in the Welsh Tract and Chester were economically
independent.[53]

Typical of the generous, yet disciplined, Quaker father was
Thomas Minshall, whose son Isaac married Rebecca Owen in 1707.
That same year, three months after the marriage, Thomas Minshall
"for natural love and affection" gave Isaac gratis the "380 acres in
Neither Providence where he now dwelleth." A younger son, Jacob,
married at the age of 21 in 1706 to Sarah Owen and that year
received gratis 500 acres of land and a stone dwelling house. The
Minshalls were among the wealthier families in Chester and Radnor Meetings; but poorer families also granted independence to
their married children.[54]

The mutual obligations in the Chester and Welsh households
meant discipline, though of a lovably involving kind. The case of a
family of comfortable means gives an idea of how independent
households in the Delaware Valley were created. In the household of
Philip Yarnell, almost all the sons received land for a price, and the
time between marriage and receiving a deed was a time for sons to
work hard, proving their vibrant manhood and paying off their
fathers. The purchase price would be returned to the family coffer in
order to help portion the other children. Among the Yarnells' nine
children, six sons and three daughters, their eldest son married at
the age of twenty-six in 1719 and completed purchase of the land in

The Quaker movement provoked anti-Quaker theological literature, but the cheaper, popular press, starting in 1675, focused on the fascination and terror of the Quakers' egalitarian, spiritualized marriages. This literature consistently projected the Quaker husband as adulterer, an image that reflected the darkest fears of Englishmen, not reality.

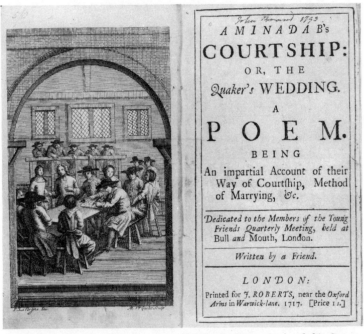

Title page and adjoining woodcut of Elias Bockett, *Aminadab's Courtship* (London, 1717), an anti-Quaker satire (*Courtesy of Houghton Library, Harvard University*)

THE
QUAKER
TURN'D
JEW.

BEING
A true Relation,

HOW

An eminent *QUAKER* in the Ifle of *ELY*, on Monday the 18th. of *April*. 1675. *Circumcifed* himfelf, out of *Zeal* for a Certain *Cafe of Confcience*, Renounced his Religion, and became a Profolited *JEW*.

With the Occafion, and Manner thereof, in all Circumftances.

LONDON,
Printed for *W. L*: 1675.

Title page of Anonymous, *The Quaker Turn'd Jew* (London, 1675), one of at least four ugly, anti-Quaker pamphlets which appeared in London in 1675. They focused on the impossibility of Quaker marriages. (*Courtesy of Houghton Library, Harvard University*)

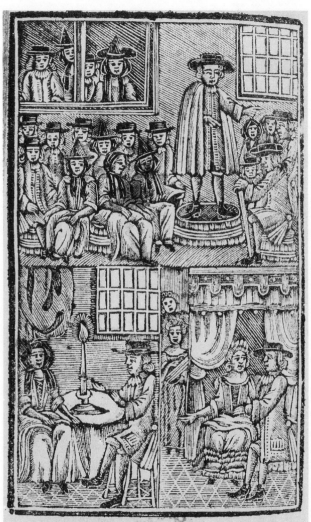

In Publick, fee, the Zealot feems a Saint,
Green-Apron'd Sifters whine, and Brothers pant;
But when retir'd, the Cafe is out of Doors,
He Courts in Cant, and Bully-like he Whores.

Wood cut from Anonymous, *The Quakers' Art of Courtship*
(London, 1710) (*Courtesy of Houghton Library, Harvard
University*)

will: Plumer

THE

QUAKER's

OPERA.

As it is Perform'd at

LEE's and HARPER's

Great Theatrical Booth

IN

BARTHOLOMEW-FAIR.

With the MUSICK *prefix'd to each* SONG.

LONDON:

Printed for *J. W.* And fold by *J. Roberts* in
Warwick-Lane; *A. Dodd,* at the *Peacock* without *Temple-Bar*; and *E. Nutt* and *E. Smith* at
the *Royal-Exchange.* 1728.   [*Price* 1 s.]

Title page of Thomas Walker, *The Quaker's Opera* (London, 1728), a musical featuring a Quaker adulterer (*Courtesy of Houghton Library, Harvard University*)

In this cartoon, *Franklin and the Quakers ca. 1764*, the stock Quaker adulterer appears in the left corner. (*Courtesy of The Historical Society of Pennsylvania*)

Edward Hicks (1780–1849) painted these farmscapes in the 1840s. Both depict Quaker farmsteads in Bucks County, Pennsylvania. The farmscape of David Twining's residence, Edward Hicks's foster home, was painted from memory as it appeared in 1785. Edward Hicks is the nurtured, five-year-old boy in the left corner. Both paintings highlight the domesticity, harmony, productivity, prosperity, and peacefulness of rural Quaker Pennsylvania life. Similar scenes in Chester County charmed Crèvecoeur and Brissot.

The Residence of David Twining (oil on canvas) by Edward Hicks (*Courtesy of Abbey Aldrich Rockefeller Folk Art Center, Williamsburg, Virginia*)

The Residence of Thomas Hillborn (oil on canvas) by Edward Hicks (*Courtesy of Abbey Aldrich Rockefeller Folk Art Center, Williamsburg, Virginia*)

John Singleton Copley (1738–1815) was a long-time resident of Boston and was early America's best artist. Copley clearly perceived a vital difference between the relationship of an elite Boston, Congregationalist couple, the Winslows, and that of an elite Pennsylvania, Quaker couple, the Mifflins. Both Mr. and Mrs. Winslow are formidable figures, but it is Mr. Winslow who looks directly at the viewer, while his wife, Jemina Debuke Winslow, looks off towards her spouse. The connotations of this conjugal portrait are patriarchal. In 1773, Mr. and Mrs. (Sarah Morris) Mifflin journeyed to Boston in order to communicate with Samuel Adams and other leaders of the revolutionary movement. Thomas Mifflin was a political radical and would be disowned by the Quaker meeting for his revolutionary activities, but his wife remained a Friend in good standing. In their conjugal portrait, Copley made Sarah Morris Mifflin the stronger of the two characters. Thomas Mifflin occupies the background and looks at his wife adoringly and somewhat sheepishly. Sarah Morris Mifflin occupies the foreground and, like Mr. Winslow, looks calmly and penetratingly through the viewer. The connotations of this conjugal portrait are matriarchal.

Mr. and Mrs. Isaac Winslow, 1774 (oil on canvas) by John Singleton Copley (*Courtesy of Museum of Fine Arts, Boston*)

Mr. and Mrs. Thomas Mifflin, 1773 (oil on canvas) by John Singleton
Copley (*Courtesy of The Historical Society of Pennsylvania*)

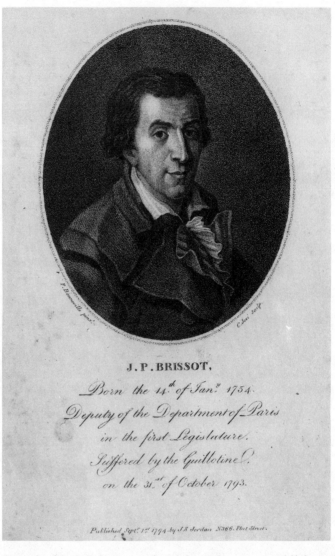

J. P. BRISSOT,

Born the 14th of Jany. 1754.

Deputy of the Department of Paris

in the first Legislature.

Suffered by the Guillotine

on the 31st of October 1793.

Published Sept. 1st 1794 by J.S. Jordan N.166. Fleet Street.

Portrait of J. P. Brissot, a major eighteenth-century publicist and champion of the Quaker family, from a 1794 edition of *New Travels in the United States, 1788.* After the Frenchman argued that Quaker life was essential to the development of American Republicanism, some Delaware Valley Quakers told Brissot that he resembled Anthony Benezet, the saintly Quaker reformer of French origins. (*Courtesy of the John Carter Brown Library at Brown University*)

1725, when he received 200 acres and a farm house for £60 Pennsylvania currency he paid to his father. Their second son also married in 1719 and bought his land from his father in 1724, a year earlier than his brother. He received a similar amount of land and also paid £60. The purchase price was about half the actual market value of the land. Yarnell's fifth son, Nathan, married in 1731 at the age of twenty-four and three years later received his land free in Philip Yarnell's will. Yarnell's third, unmarried son, Job, had a different role. In Philip's will he received "all my land in Ridley township," but had to pay £80 to daughter Mary Yarnell, half at eighteen and half at the age of twenty. Mary was only ten years old, so Job had eight years to raise the first payment. He never married. Though the Yarnells were one of the wealthier households in the Chester Meeting, they managed a vulnerable economic unit, particularly in view of the unique spiritual demands of Quaker parenthood. Their children tended to marry by inclination, not in rank order. When a son or daughter married, his or her work and the land given was lost to the other children. Like most Quaker parents, the Yarnells made the family into a revolving fund: new households became independent relatively soon after marriage, and with the money returned from children, the Yarnells bought more land for younger children and bonds for their retirement.[55]

This demanding, and involving, household system explains why the settlers' children married relatively late in life, despite the settlers' large landholdings. Although the Chester and Welsh Tract households had fewer children and over twice the farmland, their children married later than the Andover settlers' children and also later than the third generation in Andover, who married between 1705 and 1735, coeval to the second generation in Chester and the Welsh Tract. The marriage ages of Quaker men were older than those of men in Andover in both the second and third generation, and the marriage ages of Quaker women were older than those of Andover women in the second generation, though slightly lower than Andover women in the third generation. While bachelors and spinsters were rare in New England towns, at least 14.4 percent of the Chester and Welsh Tract youth did not marry (for comparative marriage age statistics, see Appendix: Table 5).[56]

Quaker domesticity was not a simple response to the land, but a carefully constructed social and religious system that shaped the land and its transference between generations. One of the ideals of these Quaker communities was clearly the economically independent household, focused upon and responsible for the nurturance and protection of its own children, a fitting reward for hardworking and honest Quaker young adults. Indeed, in contrast to the tight spatial proximity of powerful father and weak son in Andover, most second-generation Delaware Valley sons did not live in the same townships as their fathers. Forty-five percent of the sons (71) of the first generation Welsh Tract and Chester families settled in the same township as their fathers, but a majority 55 percent (88) did not. Most sons (65) lived in other townships because their fathers bought land for them there. Francis Yarnell of Willistown, for example, found land for five of his sons in Willistown (his own town), but also land in Springfield for one son, and land in Middletown for another. Andrew Job bought two of his sons land in Virginia. Indeed eleven of the second-generation Delaware Valley sons moved outside southeastern Pennsylvania to Maryland, Virginia, North Carolina, and Long Island onto land purchased by their fathers. John Bevan who returned to Wales apparently never saw his American sons again. Other Quaker fathers were not so distant, but they also willingly surrendered patriarchal power and land in exchange for "holy conversation" and their children's spiritual lives.

The tendency of Delaware Valley farmers to give land to their sons and money to their daughters, when they married, left many of these fathers bereft of a disciplining club. They took to exhortation and advice instead, some of which have survived. Edward Foulke, a rich farmer in Gwynedd, left an exhortation to his children written just before his death in 1741. He gave all four of his sons land near the time of their marriages. Evan Foulke, for example, received 250 acres in Gwynedd at his marriage in 1725.[57] But the generous, loving old man could still persuade effectively. He urged his children and grandchildren not to let business take priority over attending week-day meetings. He noted that business carried out at such a time "did not answer my expectation of it in the morning" (he implicitly expected his children to be deeply involved in business). By worrying about his childrearing practices, he guided their own: "it had been better for me, if I had been more careful, in sitting with my family at meals with a sober countenance because children, and servants, have their eyes and observations on those who have command and government over them." The perception of authority, he noted, as well as authority itself, "has a great influence on the life and manners of youth." He told them to be sincere: "Let me entreat of you dear children assume not the appearance of religion without a real possession of it in your hearts, your dear Savior compared such to a Sepulchre whited without but within full of dead men's bones. Yet I have a better hope of you. . . ." And far from distrustfully coercing services from his children to ease his old age, Foulke told them to worry only about themselves and their children, " . . . as for your father and mother, our time is almost come to a period, we have lived together above fifty years and now in our old age the Lord is as good and gracious as ever he was, he gives us a comfortable living now in the close of our days" (interest yielding bonds). Instead of fawning submission, he asked only for "your prayers for us in the most needful time, especially on a dying pillow and our time in this world come to an end, that we may have a gentle passage to eternal rest."[58] To instruct his children Foulke used love effectively within a persuasive atmosphere of wealth.

Not all Chester and Welsh fathers were so expertly sweet. Walter Faucit left in 1704 a less tender exhortation; he was dying and was genuinely alarmed by his wealthy, grown son's spiritual and economic dissipation, "if thou refuse to be obedient to God's teachings and do thy own will and not His then thou will be a fool and a vagabound."[59] Whatever his last worries, Faucit had already given his son ample property. Greven found no exhortations in Andover and most likely they did not exist. Stern seventeenth- and early eighteenth-century rural Puritan fathers left land, not advice, to obedient, married, middle-aged sons. Indeed, thanks to the realization of their radical domesticity, and the strategies they took to realize it, the Delaware Valley farmers, despite their stringent self-discipline, had more generous, bountiful, and less psychologically explosive household relations than many New England townspeople. No anxious children ignited a witchcraft craze in the Delaware Valley.[60]

THE QUAKERS' mixed-wheat farms doubtlessly damaged the ecology of the Delaware Valley, previously under the gentler control of the Leni Lenape. They also literally fed West Indian slavery by providing good and cheap food to the Islanders. Nonetheless, mixed-wheat farms tied into a lucrative Atlantic market constituted a relatively peaceful reconciliation between Europeans settlers' hopes, the forests, and Christian morality. These were the most economically successful family farmers yet seen in North America, capable of sustaining a vibrant regional economy, who grew abundantly a crop that did not require slave gangs or produce a "boom psychol-

ogy" during which European civility was almost totally forgotten.[61]
Of course, from the 1620s through the entire colonial period, the
modal economic unit in New England was a viable family farm—
quite successful indeed before the wheat blight of the 1660s. After
that date, however, New England farmers could not produce sufficient surpluses to hold foreign markets or sustain New England's
economy.[62] Similarly, New York also had successful family farms
from the 1650s, when New Netherland first began to attract migrating families on a fairly large scale. The Pennsylvania family farms
were far stronger, however. The Middle Atlantic region clearly
became the first to build a successful regional economy on the
agricultural surpluses generated by family farms, in which labor
was primarily supplied by family members, indentured servants,
and short-term hired labor. New York and New Jersey farmers,
many of them Quakers and many not, clearly also deserve credit for
producing this phenomenon. Nevertheless, within two decades of
the colony's founding, the Pennsylvania Quakers set the pace.

The Pennsylvania surplus wheat economy later spread into the
northern Chesapeake and into the Pennsylvania backcountry. It
attracted tens of thousands of immigrants and was largely responsible for the rapid development by 1760 of Philadelphia as early
North America's premier city. Though a majority of rural Quaker
settlers had arrived as British uplanders more comfortable and
skilled with pastoral than arable farming, the Pennsylvania Quakers established and guided this economy.

Quaker communalism and especially Quaker domesticity had
its uses in North America. By 1720 the Chester and Welsh Tract
Quakers and their co-religionists had established radical domesticity as a major, outwardly trouble-free vehicle of early North American social, economic, and political development. Combining acceptance of pluralism, disciplined privatism, child-centeredness, and
wealth, upland Quakers introduced a most enduring form of community into American culture. For later Americans, Quaker domesticity could meld with the North American landscape into Edward
Hicks's paintings of idyllic family farms, or Crèvecoeur's mythic
Pennsylvania farmer, the "new man."[63] The once failed social strategy of poor, clannish, northwestern British religious radicals,
Quaker domesticity, could emerge for many commentators of American life, particularly when stripped of its sectarian peculiarities, as
the best, most moral, almost natural, way to develop and tame the
lonely North American forests.

CHAPTER FIVE

Quakers on Top

Not every immigrant was charmed by the social and political arrangements dictated by the Quakers' familial tendernesses. In 1695, Mr. Robert Suder, an Anglican gentleman, arrived in Philadelphia from Jamaica. "I not having my health there, transported myself and estate here," he repined, "in hopes to find the same wholesome laws here as in other of his Majesty's plantations; and a quiet moderate people, but found quite contrary. . . ." He found the Quakers "in brawles among themselves and imprisoning one another for religion" (the Keithian schism); the Quakers describing the teachings of his Church of England as "the doctrine of devils"; the Quakers frustrating the defense of the colony; Quaker judges that "would sooner take a Negroe that is a heathen's word before a Church of England man's oath"; and Quaker magistrates who said that "the King has nothing more to do here than to receive a bear skin or two yearly. . . ." "As long as the government is in the hands of Quakers and Mr. Penn as they say has such interest [at Court]," projected Suder, "we that are his Majesty's subjects (which they are not nor never will be), we had better live in Turkey: there is good morality amongst them; there is none here." "They are establishing of a Free School for the growth of Quakerism and apostacy," concluded Mr. Suder, "which I pray God in His due time He may direct; and that we may live to enjoy the liberties of subjects of England, and not to governed by Dissenters and apostates that absolutely deny the Bible to be the Holy Writ, and Baptism and the Lord's Supper. . . .''[1] The idea in the late seventeenth century of founding a new society totally upon tender childrearing, not on an established church and the coercive injection of religion doctrine into children, was a radical project. Anglican gentlemen like Mr. Suder sincerely wanted to uproot the Quaker regime as soon as possible.

Many of Mr. Suder's complaints were justified. Well before 1720 the Pennsylvania Quakers had established a record of political and legal awkwardness. Pennsylvania politics were in constant crisis between 1683 and 1710, thanks largely, as Gary Nash has shown, to the Quakers' economic aggressiveness and political anti-authoritarianism.[2] Quaker courts were problematic. More Pennsylvania laws were disallowed by the English Privy Council than those of any other colony.[3] The Pennsylvania legal system had difficulty satisfying either the accused or the community. In a notorious case of 1715, an indebted millwright and his laborer, Hugh Pugh and Lazurus Thomas, gunned down Jonathan Hayes, a Quaker Chester County justice of the peace. Though many of the Quaker posse chosen to capture the two killers begged off as pacifists, the Chester County Court did capture and arraign Pugh and Thomas. However, Governor Charles Gookin decided that Quaker jurors, witnesses, and judges, who refused oaths and only gave affirmations, had no authority to try a capital case. He put the suspects on bail. They remained defiant free men for three years. Frightened by seeing one of their chief magistrates murdered with impunity, the Assembly in 1716 brought the matter before Gookin. He refused to bring the alleged murderers to trial.[4] The new governor Sir William Keith immediately gained popularity in 1718 by trying the culprits before a jury largely composed of Quakers. The trial attracted some 1,200 fearful onlookers. Pugh and Thomas were found guilty of murder and were condemned to hang on May 9, 1718. Nonetheless, the prisoners had "impudently to boast that they well knew it was not in the power of the government to try any capital crime according to the common and statute laws of England, which they would claim as their right." Before their appeal to the Privy Council was sent to England, they were hanged. The millwright and the laborer became dangling symbols of the strange expression of British law in Pennsylvania.[5]

The Quakers showed, nonetheless, little desire to share power with other groups. By 1726, Pennsylvania had a population of

40,000 people of whom only some 60 percent were English and Welsh settlers, some 23 percent Germans, some 12 percent Scots-Irish, and some 5 percent Finnish, Swedish, and Dutch. Between 1726 and 1755, about 40,000 Germans and 30,000 Scots-Irish arrived in Pennsylvania. The English, Irish, and Welsh Quakers shrank to a small ethnic and religious minority.[6] Yet far from sharing or opening power to new groups, the Quakers effectively tightened their control. In the 1730s the Quakers held 59 percent of the seats in the Assembly, dropping to a diplomatic 46 percent in 1736. However, following disputed elections in the early 1740s between themselves and a proprietary coalition eager to provide the vulnerable colony with a minimal defense during the War of Jenkins' Ear, they increased their share to 80 percent, rising to 83 percent in 1742, 1743, 1744, and 1745.[7]

Nor did they adopt an accommodating style. The Pennsylvania Assembly was less a club of politicians than a Quaker business meeting. While the separation of church and state was the dominant trend in Anglo-American society, the Quakers actually increased the conflation of Quaker church and Pennsylvania state during the eighteenth century. As Alan Tully noted, "of the thirty-six Quaker legislators who sat for Chester County between 1729 and 1755, twenty-five had represented their monthly meetings at the quarterly meeting level and fifteen had been authorized to attend the Philadelphia Yearly Meeting." Almost the same percentage of religious elders graced the legislative delegations from Bucks and Philadelphia counties.[8] The colony's major legislator during this period, John Kinsey, was speaker of the Assembly, trustee of the loan office, chief justice of the Supreme Court, and clerk of the Philadelphia Yearly Meeting, the holiest administrative post in colonial Quakerdom. Kinsey and the other elders ran the Assembly like a Quaker meeting, replete with prefatory silences, spiritually inspired speeches, declarations of the sense of the House, and few open votes. The minutes of the Assembly were terse, more like monthly meeting jottings than the record of a popular political body. Richard Peters, secretary to the proprietary, wrote that non-Quaker politicians need be "quakerized" to have any power, and Governor George Thomas observed that the Pennsylvania Assembly was "a conclave," not "a body of men who are accountable to their electors. . . ."[9] And far from providing poor immigrants with a kind of colonial "new deal," the Pennsylvania Assembly passed between 1726 and 1754 fewer than two acts per year on average, much less than any of the legislatures of New Hampshire, New Jersey, South Carolina, New York, Virginia, and Massachusetts. "England's addled Parliament of 1614, ridiculed for its failure to enact any laws or taxes," as Professor John Murrin has noted, "almost threatened to become a standard for emulation in Pennsylvania."[10]

Thus, Mr. Suder's prayer was not answered for nearly a century. The Quakers dominated the Pennsylvania Assembly from settlement to 1756 and from 1760 to 1776. From 1729 to 1755, the Quakers held 70 percent of all seats in the Assembly, a remarkable feat since by the 1740s by a simple count of church buildings they composed at the very most only 20 percent of Pennsylvania's religiously affiliated population. To make matters worse for men like Mr. Suder, the Assembly in Pennsylvania grabbed more power than any other colonial legislature and even more than the English Parliament. By the late 1720s the Pennsylvania Assembly had stripped the Council of all legislative and veto power; Assembly members had established their right to declare their own adjournments, and the Assembly had gained a sizable revenue from the annual interest payments of those who held mortgages from the provincial loan office (1723) and from an excise tax on alcoholic beverages. The Assembly appropriated this revenue by simple legislative vote. In no other colony did an Assembly raise and disburse money without executive interference.

Although eager to use patronage to develop an anti-Assembly, anti-Quaker, pro-proprietary interest in the province, even the second Proprietor, Thomas Penn, an Anglican, consistently selected Quakers for county clerkships and justices of the peace, even in the most diversely populated counties, where Quakers were a tiny minority. Thomas Penn thought only Quakers could lend legitimacy to governmental authority in the service of stability—and in the collection of his quitrents.[11] Indeed, Quakers were regularly elected in places where there were few Quakers. In Lancaster County, 53 percent of the assemblymen elected between 1729 and 1755 were Quakers.[12] In the inland city of Lancaster, a city in which Quakers were so few that no Quaker meetinghouse was built until 1760, "in fifteen of the twenty-one years between 1742 and 1763," according to the city's historian Jerome Wood, "at least one of the burgesses (two were chosen annually to run the town's government) was a Quaker; in 1761 both burgesses were Friends."[13] In backwoods York County, almost devoid of Quakers, 50 percent of the assemblymen between 1749 and 1755 were Quakers; and in German-dominated Berks

County, all three of the popularly selected assemblymen between 1752 and 1755 were Quakers.

Historians have celebrated Pennsylvania pluralism and tolerance without always recognizing or explaining why Pennsylvania maintained one of the most religiously exclusive regimes in eighteenth-century British North America. In no other colony was a religious minority, especially one with memorable radical origins and emphases, maintained as an elite status group almost exclusively privileged with providing the society with its political leadership. Much of the explanation of this bizarre phenomenon rests in politics itself, in the Quaker politicians' skill at building coalitions and exploiting issues. However, some of the answer also rests upon the success of Quaker domesticity.

Indeed, within a decade of Pennsylvania's founding, just because the Quaker fathers' chose gentle nurturance of children and therefore refused to acknowledge the absolute necessity of teaching the historical Christ to Quaker children, George Keith, one of the few *bona fide* Quaker intellectuals in Pennsylvania, decided that the Pennsylvania social order was in spiritual and moral disarray. Because of his prestige, his ability to probe weaknesses in the northwestern Quakers' radical social design, and his later alliance with prominent and wealthy Anglicans in Britain, Keith and his powerful Anglican allies presented the Quaker elite with a prolonged crisis of legitimacy. The ability of Quaker domesticity to not only inspire but also defeat such opponents showed the significant contribution Quaker domesticity made to maintaining Quaker political hegemony in Pennsylvania for nearly a century.

INITIALLY George Keith gave legitimacy to the northwestern Quakers' regime. Keith arguably dwarfed his northwestern British ministerial colleagues in Pennsylvania in recognized service to Quakerism, but he certainly surpassed them in intellectual cultivation and achievement. Among the some 29 Pennsylvania Quaker ministers principally involved in the schism, Keith alone had completed university training, receiving in 1658 an M.A. from Marischall College, University of Aberdeen. Keith alone was intellectually distinguished, a classmate and mathematical tutor of Gilbert Burnet (1643–1715), Bishop of Salisbury; conversant with Baron Christian Knorr von Rosenruth, a rabbinical and cabbalistic scholar, Franciscus van Helmont, a Continental scholar and author of the notion of the transmigration of souls, and Henry More, a major Cambridge Platonist. Aside from his mathematical and theological luster, Keith was an acknowledged leader of Scottish Quakerism. He suffered for over three years in Scottish and English prisons, he headed the Quakers' school at Edmonton, he was chosen in 1677 with William Penn, George Fox, and Robert Barclay to undertake a crucial missionary effort in Holland and Germany. The Scottish Quaker proprietors of New Jersey in 1684 made him surveyor-general of the colony. The Pennsylvania Quaker leaders in 1689 named Keith head of the Quaker school in Philadelphia on a salary of £50 annually, although he did little teaching. By 1690 Keith was gifted with 700 acres in Monmouth County, New Jersey; 300 acres in Middlesex County, New Jersey; 500 acres in Pennsylvania; and a mansion house in Amboy, New Jersey. The Delaware Valley Quakers duly and generously honored him as an intellectual in residence.[14]

Nevertheless, at least in retrospect, Keith's disaffection with the religious and social leadership of northwestern Quakers like Thomas Lloyd was unsurprising. Keith was only one of two Scottish first purchasers of Pennsylvania land and the only Scottish "public Friend" in Pennsylvania. Scotland was an even poorer agricultural society than northwestern Britain. Accustomed to rack-rents, not three-lives-leaseholds, and constant supervision by resident lairds, Scottish settlers in New Jersey, as Ned Landsman has shown, failed to endorse the social and spiritual necessity of Quakers' living on isolated family homesteads supplied by the profits from the wheat trade. Similarly, Scottish Quaker leaders tended to be sophisticated urbanites and had always preferred systematic doctrine and ritual to the total incorporation of the Holy Spirit in the social relations of an impoverished society. Two Scots, Robert Barclay and George Keith, were the early Quakers' most logical, programmatic thinkers. During their shared youth in Scotland, George Keith supplied Robert Barclay with concepts and criticisms for his *Apology* (1676), the major systematic treatise on Quaker beliefs. Keith had produced earlier *Immediate Revelation . . . Not Ceased* (1668) and *The Way to the City of God Described* (1679, but distributed in manuscript in 1667), the first systematic treatments of Quaker theology and the psychology of Quaker conversion. Keith's desire to have Pennsylvania "holy conversation" superintended by intellectual rigor and design was consistent with his intellectual and social background.[15]

While acknowledging that the Light in people derived from the incarnation, crucifixion, and resurrection of the historical Christ,

Thomas Lloyd and the northwestern Quaker leaders thought that in order to be saved children did not need to know anything about these events, until they were mature enough to understand them fully. The northwestern Quakers had not come to Pennsylvania to catechize their children like Presbyterians. The northwestern Quaker leaders believed in the sufficiency of "holy conversation" and based their social order upon it. Keith believed, on the other hand, that knowledge of the historical Christ was absolutely necessary for salvation and that infants who died before knowing the historical Christ could not be deemed justified. He thought that at best God might inform such infants before they died or might even choose to reincarnate them on earth in order to give them ample chances to hear and know God's Word. As an intellectual, Keith believed in the long-term importance of ideas and logic. Aware of the Ockham principle that "what can be explained by assuming fewer terms is vainly explained by assuming more," Keith thought that once knowledge of Christ was judged not absolutely necessary for salvation in every situation, the historical Christ would be ruinously neglected. If men and women could be saved without knowledge and faith in the historical Christ crucified, reasoned Keith, they would eventually bury all Bibles and simplify religious life to accord with the simplest route to heaven. For holding his qualifications about the spiritual effects of children's ignorance, Keith later called Thomas Lloyd a "devout heathen" and he grew certain that Pennsylvania Quakers' children would eventually be reared ignorant of the historical Christ, like "Deists, Turks, Jews." In short, Keith believed that excessive reliance on "holy conversation" in childrearing, particularly as a substitute for catechizing children as soon as possible, would destroy many children's souls and would eventually make Quaker Pennsylvania into a society, not of Christians, but of, at best, "virtuous heathens."[16]

Keith simply wanted operating Quaker doctrine to attain Christian respectability and definition. During his mission to New England in 1688, Keith confronted the familiar accusations from Congregationalists that Quakerism was not a Christian religion because the Quakers effectively slighted the historical Christ, the Trinity, and the Resurrection and, instead, idolized a disassociated Inner Light. In reply, Keith insisted that Quakers believed in all the Christian fundamentals, but only went deeper than other Protestants in recognizing and enjoying the "Holy Spirit." Although he was always careful to proclaim that Christ was a single human and divine substance, Keith often wrote, as a heuristic device, about an "inner Christ" and an "outer Christ." He argued that although Puritan ministers like Cotton Mather, Samuel Willard, and James Allen adequately presented the "outer Christ" (his incarnation, crucifixion, resurrection, and mediation), they scanted the "inner Christ," his Holy Spirit as it palpably dwelled in, regenerated, sanctified, and assured faithful Protestants. In reply, Keith's Puritan foes—Cotton Mather, Christian Lodowick, and Francis Makemie— ignored Keith's terms and argued that he misrepresented the opinions of most Quakers, who effectively denied the essential epistemological connections between the historical Christ and the Holy Spirit, as witnessed by their failure to produce an explicit creed, a confession of faith, or any systematic catechizing of youth. After being harshly criticized by Keith for writing a catechism which insufficiently explored the role of "Christ within" in spiritual regeneration, the Presbyterian missionary Francis Makemie retorted, "it is no strange thing to find Quakers quarelling our succinct way of composing our principles for young ones, because they are opposite to so early edification, which practice is very inconsistent with precepts, precedents of training children when young."[17] Such evasions infuriated Keith, especially because he worried himself about such "ranter" tendencies in Pennsylvania Quakerism.

Indeed, just before embarking on his mission to New England from Well-Spring, New Jersey, in May 1688, George Keith wrote a letter to English Quaker leaders carefully expressing his misgivings with Delaware Valley Quakerism. As usual, Keith wrote of the importance of not dividing Christ, of not talking only about the historical Christ to the neglect of the Holy Spirit in people, "nor as others have done, not Friends (God Forbid), but ranters and airy notionists, who teach and profess faith in Christ within, as *the Light* and *the Word*; but deny or slight his outward coming, and what he did and suffered for us in the flesh." Although he excused Delaware Valley Quakers from worshipping a disassociated Light, he not only described this heretical condition but proceeded to suggest that his Delaware Valley colleagues would degenerate in that unfortunate direction without his guidance. He expressed alarm about the poor educations being given "Friends' children and young people; for I have found a great want and defect in many, that they are but too little acquainted and known in the words of Holy Scripture; and a shame it is, if any in profession of truth, should be less skilled in the scripture-words and testimonies, than

Jews, or other professed Christians." Doubtlessly to improve Friends' children's poor educations, Keith promised to preach in scripture-words and "never be found to preach, write, or print any doctrine or doctrines of Christian faith and religion, that are not agreeable with the plain and express testimonies of the Holy Scriptures." Keith implied that other Pennsylvania Quaker ministers were not using scripture-words, were not emphasizing the historical Christ, and thus were not acquainting young Friends with proper Christian doctrine.[18]

After returning from New England, Keith began his campaign to settle Pennsylvania Quakerism upon sound Christian doctrine. Keith wrote and published in 1690 with the approval of the committee of the Philadelphia Quaker meeting, *A Plain Short Catechism for Children and Youth*, which described knowledge of the historical Christ, the bodily resurrection, the bodily presence of Christ in heaven, and the return of Christ as fundamental tenets of the faith. The catechism contained material obliquely hostile to the doctrine of the innocence of children. After confirming that access to the Holy Spirit was routed solely through knowledge of the historical Christ, Keith asked "is not knowledge and faith of this great mystery absolutely necessary to make a perfect Christian?" The answer was "yea." What then became of young children and infants, including the Quakers' children, unaware of the historical Christ? The souls of perfect Christians dwelled in heaven after death and received a heavenly body at the last judgment; but the fate of untutored children was unclear. Keith's catechism made only one ambiguous concession: "they who dye, not having had Christ outwardly preached unto them, but are sons or children of the first covenant, and retain their uprightness and faithfulness, can they perish in that state?" The answer was "nay."[19] This dispensation referred explicitly, however, to pre-Christian Jews who believed in the future coming of the Messiah, not to Friends' children. Keith said nothing else.

Although uncomfortable with such innuendos, Thomas Lloyd and the bulk of the Pennsylvania ministers initially supported Keith. They recognized him as an illustrious Quaker intellectual and were doubtless sympathetic towards his aim of providing Pennsylvania Quakerism with intellectual respectability. They thus approved publication of his attack on New England theology in 1689, of his short catechism for children in 1690, and even of his reply to Cotton Mather in 1692, during the schism itself. The ministers gagged, however, when Keith proposed in 1690 publication and adoption of a document, "Gospel Order and Discipline Improved." Though not extant, "Gospel Order and Discipline Improved" is from meeting-minute descriptions similar, if not identical, to "Gospel Order and Discipline," which Keith had distributed in 1692 among his followers. The main thrust of Keith's organizational reform was to insist on a confession of faith, "a pure and holy confession unto Truth in the most principle and necessary doctrines of ye Truth commonly and generally received by Friends." In a large meeting, new members were to "give a faithful account of the same [to] Friends," a relation of the work of the Light within themselves and also evidence of their knowledge of the historical Christ. Tongue-tied or shy proselytes, who "have not utterance fully and sufficiently to declare their convincement and what God hath wrought in them," could simply "answer to some few plain and easy questions, proposed unto them by some faithful Friends concerning ye most common and necessary principles of doctrine received by Friends, by answering to each question yea or nay, according to the nature of the question." Such professions would ensure that Quakers witnessed to the essential connection between knowledge of the historical Christ and regeneration.

The trouble was that the Quaker settlers' children were to be treated no differently than any other proselytes; they too would have to give a confession of faith before being received into full Quaker membership. Keith proposed that a separate book be kept by each monthly meeting to record not only the birth of each Friend's child, as customary, but also the "spiritual birth" of those Friends' children received into membership after a confession of faith. Keith did not spell out the spiritual status of Quakers' children between their births and the time they offered a confession of faith, "before they own as fellow members of Christ's body," but the implications were dire enough. A young child who died ignorant of the historical Christ and other Christian fundamentals, even if a tenderly nurtured child of a Friend, was not a member of "Christ's Body" (the Church) and therefore did not clearly partake of Christ's resurrection. The eternal fate of such children was uncertain at best.[20]

Keith denied the spiritual justification of Friends' children who died in infancy and the spiritual sufficiency of "holy conversation" in childrearing, the Light answering the Light in parent-child relations. By implication, Keith was insisting that Quaker parents, like their Puritan counterparts, race their children's frequent early deaths by precociously inculcating in their small children the Christian fundamentals with obsessive catechizing, no matter what such harsh education did to the tissue of tenderness between parent and child. By making young children's church membership and regeneration depend upon a confession of faith, Keith had now essentially adopted Makemie's stern Presbyterian position on early childhood literacy and catechizing.

Cheshire and Welsh farmers had generally come to Pennsylvania to develop child-protecting wheat farms and tender households of "holy conversation" as alternatives to the intellectualization of their children. Though no scholars, and still confused about Keith's larger purposes, the Pennsylvania ministers were sharp enough to see within "Gospel Discipline Improved . . . divers things new and strange to us." They refused to print it, much less adopt it. Thomas Lloyd and the ministers appeasingly offered to suspend judgment on it and "that it should be sent to England, to have the sense of Friends there upon it." According to the ministers, Keith then withdrew his reform proposals because he thought it "beneath us" to submit Pennsylvania deliberations to English Quaker review.[21]

As their differences over childhood education became clearer, relations between Keith and the leading northwestern British, Pennsylvania Quaker ministers cooled. According to the ministers' 1692 account, Keith took "great offense" when his reform proposal was tabled and "from this time he grew more industrious to gather up what he could against Friends and craftily to examine the faith of some, and if through weakness anything slipped from them, he would not fail to improve it to our reproach in publick meetings."[22] Keith began to see heresy, not just intellectual sloppiness, in the Pennsylvania ministry, and some ministers began to regard Keith as a heretic, not just an obnoxiously aggressive intellectual.

They began to find alarming discussions of children in his work. For example, Keith's 1689 tract *The Presbyterian and Independent Visible Churches in New England and Elsewhere Brought to the Test* contained disturbing, if still ambiguous, discussions of children's spiritual status. In accord with the views of most Chester County farmers, Keith denied that infants were "reprobate" or that "any infant dying in infancy go to Hell and perish eternally, only for Adam's sin. . . ." Since no scripture said infants were reprobate, since "sin is not imputed where there is no law," and since "children are not capable of any law," Keith reasoned that infants were not condemned by a just and merciful God. Keith argued, however, that ignorance was no guarantee of eternal bliss. Since dead infants had never known about the historical Christ, Keith reasoned, they had never received a full measure of Grace. What happened to them was uncertain: "and as for the general state of infants, and how they are particularly disposed of immediately after death, who dye in infancy, seemeth a great mystery, and is best known unto the Lord: for it is generally granted, that God hath his way to reach infants, and deal with them, both in the womb, and upon their mother's breasts; and therefore let us leave secret things unto God, until he reveal them, and be satisfied with what he hath revealed."[23]

Unluckily for the reception of Keith's reform campaign in the Pennsylvania countryside, Keith was himself not satisfied with such ambiguity. He had recently tried to solve, or at least speculate about, this riddle. Thomas Lloyd's son-in-law, John Delavel, had supported Keith's campaign for Christian knowledge until he learned about these speculations. Delavel learned from Keith—and told— that in 1684 Keith had translated, edited, and prepared for the press Franciscus Mercurius van Helmont's *Two Hundred Queries Concerning the Revolution of Humane Souls*, a speculative treatise based on a learned and ingenious exegesis of scriptural text which aimed to suggest answers to seeming contradictions between God's evident mercy, love, and justice and his apparent condemnation to eternal torment of literally millions of people who had never heard or read about Christ.[24] The treatise argued that every soul lived on earth as a human being twelve times, if necessary, coinciding with the twelve hours mentioned in Scripture. At least during one of these "revolutions," each soul read or heard enough about Christ to be saved, if faithful, or damned, if not. The treatise contained much surmise about the spiritual state of infants which Chester County farmers thought alarming.[25] The book itself, and more tales about it, spread throughout the Quaker countryside. Naturally, Chester County farmers and their wives did not like being told by public Friends that their children were reincarnated strangers from another time, place, or race; they did not like speculating during their infants' funerals that their infants' souls might be enroute to Boston. Nor did they like hearing by implication that swift and harsh catechizing was mandatory, and that reliance on "holy conversation" mere folly. Many Pennsylvania Quakers concluded that Keith's "manner of preaching the faith of Christ crucified and raised again, in being necessary to make men Christians and sons of God of that free woman, and children of the new-covenant, doth infer [Keith's] holding of the revolutions, to wit, that all poor gentiles, dying without all hearing Christ crucified and raised again preached to them, must of necessity live again in a mortal body, in order to hear that doctrine outwardly preached to them, or then be damned."[26] Most Quaker farmers were too tender and too tribalistic to want any part of a reform campaign which condemned their innocent infants to possibly twelve reincarnations. Keith's reputation with most farmers was ruined.

Keith's 1691 reply to the rumors, "Truth and Innocency Defended against Calumny and Defamation . . . ," merely confirmed most farmers' horror. Keith noted that he was not the sole author of the work, but that he only "put into writing" much of the book. He noted that the hypothesis in that book was only his rational opinion, not a fundamental belief as a Christian (these derived from Holy Scripture as confirmed by the Holy Spirit). He did not demand that fellow Christians believe in the revolution of souls. In fact, he thought it an abstruse and difficult doctrine, and "I have been very shy and backward, either to lend or recommend the said book." He showed more intellectual honesty than political savvy, however, when he continued to argue, "that the necessity of the faith and the Gospel of Christ crucified and raised, etc., in order to perfect salvation, must need infer the necessity of the doctrine of revolutions, at least after some sort," and that "it is more tolerable to admit the consequent [the doctrine of revolutions] than to deny the antecedant [the necessity of faith in the Gospel of Christ crucified and raised to effect justification and salvation]." Keith warned Quaker parents not to allow their emotional distaste at the doctrine of revolutions to mislead them into denying the necessity of knowledge of the historical Christ to salvation. Such a rejection, Keith warned, not his speculations, would destroy the Quakers' children. "And if God in his infinite mercy," argued Keith, "in these American parts, (where we have but few Bibles, and very few other books perused by many among us, that teach the necessity of this faith) had not raised a Godly zeal in some to revive and raise up this most precious and necessary doctrine concerning the faith in Christ, both within us, and without us, the faith and remembrance of it would have been (in probability) lost, in many families, in a little time, especially it being rarely preached by many high pretenders to the Light within, but rather as occasional, as other historical things of the scripture. . . ." Such "high pretenders"' erroneous and neglectful policies, warned Keith, would "bring our posterity to be Indians or heathens."[27] Keith made an honest and strong reply. It was hardly, however, what most Chester County parents of "holy conversation" wanted to hear about their children or parenting.

Also helping to separate Keith from the Pennsylvania Quaker mainstream was the unexpected emergence of a frontier intellectual, the midnight-candle-burning Chester miller, Caleb Pusey. Born in Berkshire, England, then a London last-maker, Pusey was manager and part owner of a grist mill on Chester Creek. He was an assemblyman, councilor, and man of moderate wealth, but not a recognized Quaker minister. Needless to say, he lacked Keith's command of Latin, Greek, Hebrew, or formal logic. His only published work previous to the schism was an obscure, anti-Baptist rant written in England many years earlier. With some justice, Keith dubbed him the "miller-philosopher" with a "dull stone." Nevertheless, when the Pennsylvania public ministers still seemed confused about Keith's larger purposes and direction, Pusey began in 1691 to collect all available published work by Keith, read this work carefully, and developed a plausible interpretation of Keith's intellectual, spiritual development and direction. Pusey's views later became endorsed by the Pennsylvania ministers. Pusey rose from obscurity to be the primary anti-Keithian pamphleteer, sanctioned by the Philadelphia Yearly Meeting.[28]

Pusey read Keith's work before and after the *Two Hundred Queries*, and argued that the arguments of the *Two Hundred Queries* had changed Keith's mind about the necessity of teaching the historical Christ to infants and young children. He believed that he discovered that Keith "in his former books laid down for doctrine that men lived faithful to what by the Light of Grace and Spirit of God was made known to them though they had not the matters of Christ's outward birth, death, resurrection, and ascension revealed or made known to them, yet living faithful to what God by his Light or Holy Spirit had made known to them they should be saved. . . ." This was the doctrine of most Chester County farmers. Pusey concluded that Keith changed his mind about the epistemology of Christian conversion because he "imbibed some conceited notions," namely, the doctrine of the revolution of human souls, and "not finding the desired acceptance of these and other notions, he grew very hot and angry."[29] Although certainly arguable, Pusey produced a plausible version of Keith's intellectual development, one that helped Pusey's Pennsylvania colleagues see that Keith was not just trying to enhance Pennsylvania Quaker childrearing and discipline but was trying essentially to change them, and one also that opened Keith to the charge of placing intellectual arrogance above the palpable enjoyment of the Holy Spirit.[30]

Publicly exposed as an enemy of the innocence of Quaker children and a harsh critic of parenting on principles of "holy conversation," Keith became more of a liability than asset to the Pennsylvania public ministry. Thomas Lloyd could not prevent some country ministers, whom Keith had humiliated with his sharp tongue, from attacking the Delaware Valley's vulnerable intellectual. At the Philadelphia Yearly Meeting in September 1691, Thomas Stockdale, a recognized public minister, formally accused Keith of preaching two Christs, and four months later another public minister, Thomas Fitzwater, accused Keith of "denying the sufficiency of the Light within." Thomas Lloyd still wanted peace. He and other ministerial leaders tried to contain the budding schism by treating these affrays as unpleasant personal bickerings among Keith, Fitzwater, and Stockdale. Keith insisted, however, on using these opportunities to clarify the serious doctrinal issues at stake in Pennsylvania society by persistently demanding that Stockdale and Fitzwater be themselves barred from the ministry for denying the necessity of knowledge and faith in Christ crucified for perfect salvation. Thus, the Stockdale affair consumed six separate meetings, and the Fitzwater affair two prolonged meetings.[31]

During these discussions, Keith recorded a list of doctrinal absurdities uttered by his opponents, confirming his view that the Pennsylvania ministry was denying the importance of the historicity of Christ. For example, Thomas Fitzwater supposedly prayed, "O God, that dyed in us, and laid down thy life in us, and took it up again." and Robert Young, "that he did not find Christ without in all the Scripture. . . ."[32] When Thomas Lloyd and other leading ministers failed to condemn any of these men or their doctrines, Keith concluded that they had come to Pennsylvania "to cloak heresy and deceit," and "that there were more damnable errors and doctrine of the devils amongst the [Pennsylvania] Quakers than any other Protestant profession."[33] After Keith published his accusations against individual ministers and the ministerial leadership, his ministry in 1692 was disowned by the meeting of ministers. Soon after, they engineered his disownment from Pennsylvania Quakerism on the basis of his unChristian behavior.[34]

As the theological dispute surrounding children's spiritual status gained definition and heat in 1692, non-theological issues were added by both sides.[35] All of these issues and events confirmed and worsened the schism, but it was fundamentally a disagreement over the spiritual status and education of Quaker children. Because he was occasionally abstruse and usually cautious about offending the minds of the uneducated farmers he was trying to reform, the Delaware Valley's intellectual often mystified the farmers. Indeed the debates of the Keithian schism ran so abstrusely to discussions of the "inner" and "outer" Christ and to the physical details of Christ's resurrection that many historians have concluded that the theological content of the schism went over the heads of Pennsylvania farmers and was the occasion, not the cause, of the emotional, though seldom violent, schism. Actually, the main issue presented by Keith was simple and explosive enough in early Pennsylvania: what did children need to know about the historical Christ in order to gain unambiguous salvation.

To the Pennsylvania Quaker establishment, the theological issue in dispute was a narrow epistemological point. As Samuel Jennings noted in 1694, "the question was not, whether faith in Christ without, as he died for our sins, and rose again, was not necessary to our salvation. But whether that faith was indispensably necessary to all mankind, and that none could be saved without it, though they had not the means, opportunity, or capacity to know or receive it?" This necessarily ignorant group, Jennings noted, included "a great part of mankind, as namely all those, that have not the use of the Holy Scriptures, nor the advantage of hearing it preached to them, which will affect many great nations, as also *infants, deaf* and *dumb* persons, and etc. . . . ." Keith's severe insistence that faith in the historical Christ was indispensably and absolutely necessary to salvation, Jennings noted, "carries with it a very *harsh* and *uncharitable judgment* upon all that part of mankind before mentioned; which I know not what can palliate, but the strange notion of the *Revolution of Humane Souls* which make it more than probable that they shall have the opportunity, one time or other, before the end of the world of hearing this *faith* and *doctrine* preached, and may receive it, though now they die without it." The notion of revolving souls, Jennings knew, frightened Quaker parents. Quaker parents were not even "ripe" for discussing it, noted Jennings, "yet how far [Keith] hath countenanced it, is known to many."[36] Keith's qualified endorsement of the revolution hypothesis in 1691, his "Truth and Innocency Defended . . . ," was the first publication of the controversy and the cause of his alienation from the mainstream of Pennsylvania Quaker opinion. Of course, Indians and mentally handicapped people, as well as children, were directly affected by the epistemological results of the dispute. Neither Keith nor the Lloyd group, however, ever showed much interest in converting the Leni Lenape Amerindians; they had come to Pennsylvania in order to save their own children.

This is not to say that the fate of the settlers' children, narrowly defined, was the main issue of the schism. Childrearing doctrine, as noted, impacted profoundly on the social positions and religious roles of parents and adults. By 1690 northwestern Quaker domesticity was no longer a dream frustrated, but an increasingly encompassing social reality which determined the Pennsylvania social order and adults' roles and status within this radical society. British Quakers who had wanted to see Quaker familialism realized now had to, as fortunate revolutionaries do, confront their program as reality. The Keithian schism involved matters of faith which transcended their social origin. There was, nonetheless, a clear tendency for Keith's supporters to come from those Quakers socially penalized and religiously subordinated by the unprecedentedly full and uncompromising realization of northwestern Quaker domesticity on the doctrine of "holy conversation."

Who were the Keithians and why were they attracted to George Keith? Historians have given different answers, according to the group of Keithians they have studied most closely. In his Philadelphia studies, Gary Nash has shown they were Quaker men shunted aside or angered by the rise of Thomas Lloyd's exclusionist faction in the early 1690s: 82 percent (71) of the known (male) Keithians in Philadelphia opposed a Council-sponsored tax in 1692 whose purpose was partly to provide a salary for Thomas Lloyd, and only 6 percent (12 of 207) of the later anti-Keithians in Philadelphia signed the tax protest.[37] It might be added that Lloyd of Montgomeryshire was the chief representative of northwestern British Quakerism in the colony. Taking a close look at over 60 Chester County Keithians from 1693 to 1702, Jon Butler found them to be "poor and modest settlers," many were "landless," some had been spiritually bullied by local magistrate-ministers.[38] For example, among 17 Keithians from the Welsh Tract, only eight appeared on any tax records; of these, only two were in the top 50 percent of the tax assessment, only three in the top 70 percent, and only four in the top 90 percent. Most likely the remainder were servants or had recently been servants. From other evidence, William David and Alexander Edward can be identified as such, although the latter was free and married by 1692 (Edward's wife also joined Keith). The Keithians were obscure in Welsh Tract Quaker community affairs; only two Keithians had appointed jobs in the Welsh Tract Monthly Meeting before 1692. All the other Keithians never took part in the monthly meeting, though two men were mentioned negatively as debtors and all were recorded in the birth, death, and marriage records.[39] Another substantial group of Keithians has been identified by Professor Ned Landsman: these were Scottish Quaker settlers in New Jersey, men and women chiefly from northeast Scotland, where, according to Landsman, there were only about five landowners per parish, where the tenantry suffered short-term leases, the constant supervision of lairds, and a turnover rate for tenants of almost 90 percent per decade in the latter part of the seventeenth century. This Scottish Quaker tenantry, almost to a man and woman, followed their countryman, George Keith, out of northwestern British, Pennsylvania-style Quakerism.[40]

What was common among these seemingly widely disparate groups of Keithians—Philadelphia artisans and small merchants, Chester County small farmers and ex-servants, and New Jersey Scottish tenants? All lacked the property, the appropriate type of property, or the traditions of property-holding most supporting of successfully running housholds of "holy conversation." Among the 64 Philadelphia Keithians of known occupation, 44 (71 percent) were artisans—brewers, bakers, butchers, carpenters, cardwainers, brickmakers, and coopers. Keith's positions attracted 56 percent of all the Quaker artisans in the city; this being the only occupational group in Pennsylvania within which Keith carried a majority.[41] Whatever their prosperity, urban artisans owned types of property and skills not easily transferable to all their children. By their very occupations and the exigencies of their businesses, urban artisans had to place out some of their sons at early ages to apprenticeship and they could not easily protect their children from "carnal talkers" in the city. On the other hand, being more literate, urban artisans could more easily transfer explicit knowledge to their children. In the Chester County countryside, Keithians tended to be tenants or freeholders of relatively small holdings. They had some land to give their sons and some cash for their daughters, but comparatively insufficient amounts to allow their children to compete well in the Quaker marriage markets. The transplanted Scottish tenantry of New Jersey faced restrictive land policies, as Ned

Landsman has shown, from socially conservative Scottish proprietors and thus remained even more deeply loyal than northwestern
Britons, who knew life-leaseholds and then generous American land
policies, to cultural traditions which subordinated the development
of personal and familial landholding to maintaining kinship and
communal ties. All of these disparate groups were socially and
culturally disadvantaged when trying to form or reproduce households of tender "holy conversation" on the northwestern Quaker
model. The family discipline of "holy conversation" was most
appropriate for large landholders in the countryside, and these
households composed the backbone of Keith's opponents and
Lloyd's supporters.

Some of these groups did display economic and political grievances against the rising Lloyd faction before the Keithian schism, but
such secular grievances were not easily separated from spiritual concerns in early Pennsylvania. Like other Quaker settlers from the
fringes of England, they had come to Pennsylvania for political,
economic, familial advancement within the context of spiritual fulfillment. Whatever secular advances they made, these men and
women found themselves at the bottom of the dominant Pennsylvania Quakers' spiritual and social hierarchies, because these urban
artisans, poor British farmers, and Scottish farmers lacked the property, types of property, or deeply held cultural traditions about property to approximate the childrearing and accompanying land distribution policies which northwestern British Quakers promoted and
defended. As was seen previously, advancement within the meeting
hierarchy required well-behaved children; well-behaved children
depended upon wealth which protected them from "carnal talkers"
and secured them strong positions within the Quaker marriage
market. Such a social system tended to conflate spiritual goodness,
religious leadership, social leadership, familial effectiveness, and
economic success. Poorer Quakers, who had difficulty running well-
behaved families simply for economic reasons, were punished by
subordination within monthly meeting hierarchies and inflicted with
self-doubt about the quantity and quality of their measure of the
"Holy Spirit." Richer Quakers, who ran well-behaved families
largely for economic reasons, were rewarded by social leadership and
socially promoted spiritual self-assurance about the impressive quantity and quality of their measure of the "Holy Spirit."

George Keith rallied many of the spiritually disinherited Quakers not simply because he opposed the Quaker religious, social, and

political leadership, nor simply because he raised a loud noise, but
also because his theological "hair-splitting" spoke directly to, and
evoked, poor and concerned Quakers' spiritual dissatisfaction. By
insisting on the self-recognized centrality of the historical Christ in
any person's regeneration, Keith attacked the uncompromisingly mo-
nopolistic emphasis on "holy conversation" and its economic, social,
and political supports, as a spiritual fraud, a version of idolatry. He
exposed the dominant Quaker leadership as people who had absolut-
ized the contingencies of human arrangements, including their own
social virtues, and who had consequently neglected Christ. The well-
ordered wheat farms, the holy, loving, convivial households in limestone farmhouses, and the domesticated elders and ministers were not
Christianity realized, Keith argued, but "a cloak for heresy and deceit," tools for heathenizing future generations in Penn's counterfeit
childrearing garden. The worms and slugs in the garden, the poor
Keithians, the guardians of the necessity of knowledge of Christ's
historicity, were the true *Christ*ians. The socio-economic distribution
of Keithians and non-Keithians in Pennsylvania and New Jersey
confirms the idea that Keith's position on the necessity of catechismal
education of young children stirred up opposition against, and rallied
support for, the northwestern British, Lloydian regime of Quaker
minister-magistrates. Such an analysis also shows how childrearing
issues in early Pennsylvania were inextricably tied to, and clearly
emblematic of, issues of adults' social and religious status, and of
wealth and political legitimacy, in a radically new society.[42]

IN ENGLAND, the Quakers' old northwestern Anglican opponents
celebrated the Keithian schism and tried to deepen the crisis. George
Keith left Pennsylvania in 1693 in order to prove his orthodoxy to
his Quaker brethren in England. Because Keith continued in England to seek vindication among Friends for his doctrinal and educational reforms, the London yearly Meeting in 1695 disowned him.
Keith sought allies among previously separated Quaker groups like
the Harp Lane Meeting in London, but found himself sought after
by the Anglican Church's top officialdom. Keith annually lectured
on Quaker errors at Turner's Hall in London. Few Quakers attended, but on one occasion four Anglican clergymen, with the
encouragement of the Bishop of London, were present. Francis
Compton, Bishop of London, had previously arranged to have
Keith's American writings freed from the custom house and pub-

lished and sold elegantly by Brabason Alymer and John Dunton, publishers of Archbishop Tillotson's works. A renewedly militant Anglican Church, under the leadership of Compton, William Lloyd, and Thomas Bray, sought in the late seventeenth century to win England's frontier lands, particularly the American colonies, for the mother church. Many of the leaders of this movement shared Keith's passion for educational reform, particularly the catechismal education of children and youth. Many were also old and experienced foes of the northwestern Quakers. They were eager to uproot the now vulnerable, radical regime of "holy conversation" developing in the Delaware Valley.[43]

On the first Sunday in February 1700, London Anglicans had real reason for encouragement: George Keith—the great Quaker intellectual recently alienated from his sect—was kneeling in St. George's Church, St. Botolph's Lane, and taking his first Anglican communion. Militant Anglicans had wooed him successfully. The Society for the Propagation of Christian Knowledge (SPCK), at its very first meeting on March 8, 1698, as item one, discussed George Keith: "resolved that Col. Colchester and Dr. Bray go and discourse George Keith in order to be satisfied what progress he has hitherto made towards the instruction and conversion of the Quakers, and to know what he designs to further to attempt. . . . " Two days later the SPCK resolved that its first sponsored publications would be three works by Keith. Two months later, Francis Compton, Bishop of London, invested Keith with an Anglican deaconship. On March, 1702, Keith was priested in Whitehall Chapel by the grand foe of northwestern Quakerism, William Lloyd, Bishop of Worcester, formerly of St. Asaph. Soon after, Keith was on board ship, the first Society for The Propagation of the Gospel. (SPG) missionary to America, on a salary of £200 annually.[44]

The SPCK, the SPG, and George Keith were all founded or recruited, and funded with thousands of pounds sterling, to fight a fateful battle for frontier children's souls—and consequently for adults' religious and social roles. Bray, Lloyd, and Keith appreciated the power of American Quakerism. In their view, the course of Anglo-American Christendom hinged on the resolution of issues of childrearing and early education which the Quakers provoked. These men worried that in the new age of Whiggish toleration knowledge of Christ was being lost in British society, particularly on its growing frontier. They thought the major agent of such corruption was Quakerism. These Godly men had often confronted ignorance of Christ, but it usually was shame-faced, stemming from slovenliness, poverty, and sin. The Quakers, in contrast, were proudly recommending that catechisms, hard knowledge of religious doctrine, and truly educated men be excluded from the family and communal circle in order to promote authentic Christianity within children. And to make matters worse, the Quakers were actually establishing avowedly Christian societies based on nothing more than supposedly charismatic household and communal relations not only in small backward areas of Great Britain but also, and especially, in vast areas of British North America. Bray knew the Quakers had a powerful interest in Maryland (where he had just recently battled the Quakers over establishing the Church of England), North Carolina, and Rhode Island and were already hegemonic in Pennsylvania and New Jersey.[45] Being mostly northwestern Britons themselves, these men knew that the Quaker heresy was peculiarly contagious in areas of dispersion and institutional weakness, like North America. Thomas Bray was the son of an obscure farmer from Marton, Shropshire, a villiage adjacent to Richard Gough's Myddle, an area of active Quakerism. In the 1670s, William Lloyd, then Bishop of St. Asaph, had alternatively fined, jailed, and debated the Montgomeryshire Quakers, Richard Davies and Charles Lloyd, whose descendants were currently among the leaders of the Pennsylvania Quaker regime. Soon after, Bishop Lloyd directed the St. Asaph notitiae, a census of Montgomeryshire children which became the informational basis for the SPCK's charity school movement in Wales, the Anglicans' answer to Welsh poverty and the Quakers' tendernesses. Unless Quaker "tenderness" was quickly curbed by well supplied catechismal ministers, the "dark corners" of the British Isles would be a tiny stain of sin compared with the "dark vastnesses" of eighteenth-century North America, where pretended Christians cultivated themselves as examples, not inculcators of sound doctrine, and self-righteously fed their children nothing more than false tenderness and ignorance.

These men did not use the term, "domesticity," but they knew the ways of the Quakers' alternative family system and its disturbing implications. When the Reverend George Rosse reported from the Chester, Pennsylvania, mission that "that this fatal weed of Quakerism" was "cultivated with the utmost skill and tenderness," they needed no elaborations.[46] Keith had headed two Quaker schools. From 1689 to 1693, he had campaigned in the Delaware Valley to get Quaker parents and ministers to accept, particularly in regard to their own children, the absolute necessity of knowledge in the historical Christ for perfect regeneration and salvation. His well-meant efforts to make the Quakers into Christians only angered the provincials and ended in frustration and angry schism. Soon after his Anglican conversion, Keith wrote the first Anglican account of the power of "holy conversation" which realistically acknowledged its efficacy, while explaining this phenomenon in materialistic,not spiritual, terms (effluvium and effluvia, excitement-producing, atom-like material was exchanged, argued Keith, in Quaker meetings and households through sighs and glances). Aside from founding the SPG and SPCK, Bray was the Anglican Church's leading authority on young children and the uses of catechisms, the author of *Catechistical Lectures on the Preliminary Questions and Answers of the Church Catechism in Four Volumes*. This book, dedicated to Bray's life-long friend, Bishop William Lloyd, told how effectively to teach children Christian doctrine in three stages—from birth to nine, from nine to thirteen, and from thirteen through adulthood. Although they differed with the Quakers about children's basic spiritual needs and adults' responsibilities, these men had as much experience with, and concern for, children's souls as any Quaker elder.[47]

With the support of Bishop Compton, Bishop Lloyd, and many Anglican gentlemen, Bray sought to supply militant Anglican clergymen to England's frontiers. Following Bray's methods, these clergymen would sensitively and expertly catechize children and youth, producing in the backcountry a knowledgeable and pious younger Anglican generation whose ardent psalm-singing would awaken their elders. Bray's, Compton's, and the SPG's strategy was boldly to attack everywhere Quakerism's false Christianity. In Rhode Island, New Jersey, and particularly Pennsylvania, the SPG would attack the primary sites of willful Quaker ignorance with George Keith, SPG selected and supported clergymen, and libraries featuring the anti-Quaker tracts of Keith, Charles Leslie, and Francis Bugg. The Anglican leadership felt confident that, with the Pennsylvania Quakers fractured by the Keithian schism, knowledge of Christ would be now welcomed among the Pennsylvania population. Such an injection of Christian truth, they hoped, would reverse Quaker domesticity's ruinous drive toward political, social, and moral dominance.[48]

The London SPG targeted the countryside of the Delaware Valley as its major theater of spiritual, ideological, and catechismal warfare. During his two-year (1702–4) tour of North America, Keith followed this strategy and spent approximately three months in New England (Bray regarded the New England Puritans as flawed, but dedicated Christians, and he gave books to Harvard library), five months in the Chesapeake, and fifteen months in New Jersey and Pennsylvania. Keith failed to convert any regular Quakers in the Delaware Valley, but he brought large numbers of former Keithians into the Anglican Church. In 1695, some Philadelphia Keithians had already founded Christ Church in Philadelphia. Keith was largely responsible for inspiring the beginnings of many churches in the countryside. With SPG backing, Chester County Anglicans had founded by 1707 two missions and built two handsome churches in Chester and the Welsh Tract, St. David's at Radnor and St. Paul's at Chester, and they developed satellite congregations in the backcountry at Concord, Marlborough, and Chichester. By 1710, the Chester County Anglican community grew to at least sixty families. The failure of the northwestern Quakers' regime of "holy conversation" to satisfactorily encompass the spiritual needs of all the Quaker settlers had now developed into an ominous, well-backed, religious, social, and political opposition to their new-fangled childrearing and consequential social radicalisms.[49]

BANKROLLED by English gentry money, furnished with dedicated ministers, and filled with parishioners desperate to establish a religious identity against the Quaker majority, these country congregations posed by 1710 a real threat to the social dominance of the recently fractured Quaker farmers. The social-spiritual desperation of the former Keithians originally gave these congregations unusual vitality. The former Keithians viewed the success of the Anglican Church as the only alternative to painful spiritual and social resubmergence and resubordination within the Quakers' radical familial order of "holy conversation." In 1704 "The Vestry of Chester, Alias Uplands, in Pennsylvania" petitioned the SPG for a schoolmaster "to instruct our children and youth" so they would not be corrupted with the base principles "they must need suck from Quaker masters and mistresses."[50] In 1706 the Vestry praised their Reverend Mr. Nichols for his "industry and pious care to reduce the people here from Quakerism's errors and heresys to embrace true Christian principles," and in the same year the vestrymen proclaimed, "we are in love with this Church."[51] When their minister left in 1709, they begged the SPG "to supply us with another missionary otherwise this poor church, seated in the very center of the Quakers, will quickly decay and become the object of derision to that people."[52] The SPG readily obliged: they poured before 1750 over £4,000 into these two missions, primarily in the form of salaries to twelve ministers (ten of whom had spotless records) and also into libraries. Early SPG ministers were animated and militant. Assigned to the Chester mission in 1711, the Reverend George Rosse struggled to defend the Anglican Church and English morality against the sway of the "mischievious brood of Quakers here."[53] Inspired and then exhausted by the task, he preached in one town after another to contain the spread of the "seeds of apostasy". John Humphry, Rosse's successor, was equally dedicated. Although sorely tempted in 1719 by an offer that "the worthy Governor of Maryland made me of a parish, worth in these good times in that province, not less than two hundred and fifty pounds per annum," the Reverend Mr. Humphry continued to live in the tiny town of Chester on a salary of only £50 a year. "I could not prevail upon myself to leave this miserable people to the spirit which actuates the Quakers," he proclaimed.[54]

Settlers from before the Quaker immigration and recent arrivals complemented Keithian energy with wealth and leadership. A quarter of the Anglicans arrived in Pennsylvania before 1690 and over two-thirds before 1700. A number of them, such as John Test, Walter Martin, and Jonas Sandelands, had been in Pennsylvania before 1683. Such experienced men provided a talented core of vestrymen. Jonas Sandelands, a small merchant in Chester, donated the ground for St. Paul's and was buried beneath the chancel; Jeremy Collet, a farmer, ran one of the first mills in Chester County; and Jasper Yeates purchased mills at Naeman Creek and served as burgess of Chester, Pennsylvania assemblyman, and as provincial councilor. In ability and experience, they matched Quaker leaders like Andrew Job, John Sharples, and Hugh Roberts.[55]

In the 1690s the Welsh Tract and Chester Quakers and Anglicans had almost equal access to the Valley's resources. Anglicans and Quakers carried on similar occupations; approximately 78 percent of the Quakers and 81 percent of the Anglicans were farmers. The rest were blacksmiths, innkeepers, cordwainers, and small shopkeepers and merchants. In the 1690s, the Quakers and the Anglicans also matched each other in wealth and land. An incomplete list of landowners in Chester County prepared in the early

1690s under the direction of Governor Blackwell, shows ten Anglican families with an average holding of 475 acres and sixteen Quaker families with an average holding of 450 acres. A sampling from a partial tax list of 1693 shows eleven Anglican families with an average assessment of 5s 6d, and thirty-six Quaker families with an average assessment of 3s 9d. But this roughly equal distribution of power and wealth among religious groups would not last long. Their family systems were far too different in form and purpose to support identical social and economic development.[56]

Indeed, in the ensuing and telling struggle for hegemony over this early American garden, the comparative doctrinal, ecclesiastical, and educational elegance and validity of Anglicans' and Quakers' arguments were sadly irrelevant. The telling issue was which family system— catechismal or charismatic—would work more productively in the Delaware Valley's cleared forests.

The Anglicans appeared the better advantaged both by contemporary expectations and by modern historians' assumptions about how the pre-modern Anglo-American middling family operated. Conventional historical wisdom holds that the Quakers' family system would flounder in a pre-modern setting, as it largely had in northwestern Britain, where the family's primary responsibility was the production of wealth, not the provision of expert socialization of children and emotional support. Quaker emphasis on motherhood, on this logic, would overburden women with too many jobs; Quaker willingness to bankroll children's marriages would squander limited resources; and Quaker emphasis on non-coercive schemes of childrearing would produce a feeble and unruly labor force. Nevertheless, analysis of 72 Welsh Tract and Chester Quaker families—their wills, inventories, tax assessments, deeds, and related court records—shows that middling Quakers by seeking to protect their children from the "world" and by maintaining nurturing familial love and peace effectively accumulated wealth. Quaker parents bought vast amounts of land, built large and comfortable houses, and distributed their wealth carefully and seemingly shrewdly to their children.

A similar study of 55 Welsh Tract and Chester Anglican families shows that middling Anglican parents, unburdened by concern for delicate nurturance and protecting environments, were actually less economically aggressive and able. They accumulated less land, built smaller houses, and distributed their wealth carelessly and unwisely, occasionally in efforts to establish gentlemanly lines in

Chester County. Tender, quasi-tribalistic strategies—Quaker domesticity—apparently had their palpable use in an unusual premodern setting such as Pennsylvania.[57]

The Quakers used the Valley's chief economic resource land, with more skill than did the Anglican families. For the protection of future generations and as a balm for family relations, Quaker settlers seized William Penn's generous terms for land. They bought, as seen, an average of over 300 acres per family before 1690 and then continued to buy more land after prices began to rise. Quaker farmers purchased over 300 acres apiece, on average, after 1700 (45 percent of all their land purchases occurred after 1690). The typical Quaker immigrant father in the Welsh Tract and Chester collected over 700 acres by the time of his death.

Quaker land use was consistent with Quaker religious goals. As seen, Friends did not plant much of their land. The Quaker farmers allowed most of their land to stand fallow for children. This policy seemed economically wasteful. They seemed to allow thousands of good acres to go unused. Nevertheless, the Delaware Valley's most profitable crop, wheat, was hardly profitable enough to support large gangs of slaves or servants on a Chesapeake-type scale. In this context, the Quakers developed their surplus acres relatively swiftly by generously giving them to their children or allowing their children to use land to earn enough money to buy it and to marry. For example, Ralph Lewis, who emigrated to Pennsylvania in 1683 as a servant to John Bevan, accumulated over 700 acres and sold or gave this land to his sons, not in order of their births, but when they wanted to marry. When Lewis could not afford to give land to a son (usually when a son wanted to marry at an early age) he was willing to make a deal which profited the son, the whole family, and the Delaware Valley. Beginning in 1705, Lewis gave a 300-acre tract in Edgemont to his third-born son, Evan, who married that year. Next, in 1707, Lewis sold a house and land in Haverford to his second-born son, Abraham, who also married the year he received the land. Finally, in 1709, Lewis sold a house and large farm to his fourth son, Samuel, for the heavy sum of £300. After three years of hard work on the land, Samuel paid his father, received the deed, and married Phebe Taylor.[58] Such flexible and productive familial strategies were common. Love, land grants, and planting could be simultaneously and profitably exercised within tender and generous corporate household economies in the Delaware Valley.

The Anglican farmers and artisans had a less auspiciously

involving relationship to land. Although they bought more land than they might have in England and Wales, Anglican parents saw no need to bankroll every son's love story, to ensure them all dignified and protected situations, or to protect them from migration to the city. Children were given baptisms, catechisms, not lifelong familial involvements. Scattered returns have shown that the Quakers' and Anglicans' desire for land appeared similar in the early 1690s. However, by the end of this settling generation, the Quakers accumulated almost three times the land per family that the local Anglicans did. Accurate assessment of total land holdings could be documented for 21 of 52 Anglican families analyzed. The others left Chester County or were tenants. Among these 73 families, 77 percent of the Quaker fathers accumulated 500 or more acres for their sons; only 10 percent of the Anglicans accumulated 500 acres or more.[59]

Differences in capital holdings did not determine much of this difference between Anglicans and Quakers. Anglicans and Quakers had similar wealth in the 1690s. More important, Anglican farmers and artisans who had as many sons and twice the cash and goods as an equivalent set of Quaker neighbors bought far less land. In other words, Anglican farmers and artisans who easily could have afforded land for their children did not buy it. To take an extreme example, the Wade family, converts to the Anglican Church, sold most of their valuable real estate in Chester borough, though they had three sons.[60] Some Anglican families who arrived after 1690 may have been discouraged by rising land prices, but these rising costs hardly slowed the Quakers, who bought land avidly after 1690. William Martin, an Anglican, had a personal estate of £273 and had three sons; he bought only 170 acres. In comparison, James Pugh, a Quaker, had a personal estate of only £111 and he also had three sons; he bought over 600 acres. Six Anglican households had a mean personal estate of £242, 2.3 sons on average, and bought an average of 269 acres. Seven comparable Quaker households had a mean personal estate of £129, 3.1 sons on average, and bought an average of 631 acres.[61]

Although they held less land per family than the Quakers, the Anglicans also used their smaller holdings less efficiently. Following customary British rules, they held their land until death or distributed it earlier in dynastic fashion. Reflecting an indifference to providing comfortable places for all their children, only slightly more than half the Anglican settlers wrote wills. Of 53 Anglican families studied, 20 either did not leave a will or left the area, 15 clearly died intestate, and only 18 left wills. Of 71 Quaker families studied, 11 either did not leave a will or left the area, 11 clearly died intestate, and 49 left a will. Five of the 11 Quakers who died intestate were old men who had already settled all their children; only 2 of the 15 Anglicans who died intestate were similarly situated. Nor were the Anglican intestate fathers poverty-stricken, they averaged £165 in personal estate and 192 acres.[62]

The Anglican men who did leave wills tended to invest in the family line rather than in individual children. Thus even the most able and purposeful Anglican fathers chose just the wrong policies for a colony rich in soil but lacking cheap labor, docile tenants, or a bonanza crop. Thomas Dawson, cordwainer and farmer of West Caln, tried unsuccessfully to establish a gentlemenly line in Chester County by heaping all his land upon one son. He had three sons and three daughters, and by the early 1740s he had accumulated over 500 acres and held £219 in bonds. In 1741 Thomas Dawson deeded all his 551 acres, *post mortem*, to his eldest son Abraham "for the advancement," he wrote, "of the heirs male of the body of the said Abraham Dawson lawfully begotten or to be begotten."[63] Dawson clearly did not want his estate dissipated among all his sons. In fact, fearing that his estate might fall into the hands of another line, he used his second son as a substitute heir. "If Abraham have no male heirs living," he wrote, "it shall go to my son Isaac's male heirs, and if there be no male heirs living, it shall go to my son Abraham's heirs or children or at pleasure to do as he thinks fitting."[64] Abraham, Dawson's privileged son, died in 1760, a moderately wealthy wheat farmer with a tenant on part of his vast land and two slaves helping him work the rest. Most of his land was not being used, however. Abraham left no male heirs and gave his land to his cousin and his brothers and the tenant's parcel to the poor of West Caln. Abraham also gave ten pounds to the local Anglican church.[65] Despite such grand gestures, he never rose to be a real gentleman. It was difficult to make a great fortune by concentrating land, English-style, in Pennsylvania.[66]

Dawson's thinking was nevertheless common among Anglicans who left wills. Most Anglican fathers, who held 259 acres on average, favored one or two sons, and sent the rest, as in England, to town. Considering the will-leaving churchmen who had more than one son, two divided their land equally, eight gave it all to one son, and four determined that the land be sold and the cash be divided among all their children. Less than a third of the sons mentioned in these Anglicans' wills received land. Even counting gifts of cash from the sale of land as division of the estate, only six of fourteen of the will-leaving Anglican fathers with more than one son practiced partible inheritance.

Policies of impartibility made sense in England and Wales, but they made rather less sense in the Delaware Valley. There, to a degree that traditionalist farmers could not conceive, the tender, egalitarian relations of the child-centered family provided a fine way of organizing work and land in a near-wilderness. The Quakers' superior economic rationality simply emerged as a byproduct of their radical familial ideas.

And in this setting, the Quakers' family system filled time more productively than did the catechismal family. The Anglican settlers, like some later tourists, found the Delaware Valley furnished drearily with land, trees, and Quakers. For their amusement, sociability, and sanity, they supported expensive public sport and games without the usual patronage of a gentry. The Quaker meetings frequently and disapprovingly mentioned such events, doubtlessly organized by their more festive Anglican neighbors. In 1730, for example, the Gwynedd Meeting spoke of "being sorrowfully affected with the prevalence of undue liberties such as shooting matches, singing, and dancing, and the like disorders."[67] Some Quakers got caught sipping excessively and riotously in taverns owned by Anglicans.[68] Though a number of Quaker youth and adults succumbed to these temptations occasionally, most found the approved alternative generally satisfying. They were to dissolve boredom and find company by making the trivia, responsibilities, and relations of private life fascinating, profound, and sacred.

Most visibly and mundanely, the Quaker settlers' unusual interest in the environments of their children's spiritual growth was reflected in concern for the setting and equipment of the home: ample chairs, tables, feather beds, and large, comfortable stone houses. Building very few impressive public buildings, the Quakers used the Delaware Valley's resources to make family households warm, convivial, dignified scences of the drama of life and spiritual growth. The houses of publicly oriented Anglicans reflected less domestic involvement.

The first generation's probate inventories show clearly that among families of similar wealth, the Quakers spent proportionately more money on furniture, particularly bedding, than did the

Anglicans (these differences grew in the second generation). And a more detailed look at expenditures on bedding, when collated with the number of children in each household, shows that Quakers had entirely different standards of middling domestic living than did the neighboring churchmen.[69]

Middling Anglicans' living arrangements were crowded by almost any standard, while Quaker living arrangements were more pleasant. The churchman Peter Eliot, for example, had a large personal estate of £281. His household consisted of three children, his wife, and three servants, a total of eight people. His house had five rooms and only three beds. In the Eliot household there were almost two people to a bed, even if the servants went bedless.[70] The Quaker Morris Llewellyn had a smaller personal estate £235 and also a household of nine people—himself, his wife and four children, and three servants. He owned a house with six rooms, and he owned twice as many beds—six to Eliot's three.[71] This meant only one person in a bed, if the servants slept on straw mattresses on the floor. Most significantly, all of the surviving houses from this period in Chester County—the Brinton House, the Pusey House, the Pratt House, the Sharples House, and the Collins House—were built between 1681 and 1730 by Quakers.[72] Almost all are large, built with stone, and suitable for modern families (Philadelphia suburbanites, making current historical investigation difficult, still live in a number of these houses). Not one Anglican left such a domestic artifact. The middling Anglicans did leave their handsome country churches, particularly St. David's and St. Paul's, monuments to their attempt to erect a public world. But in the Delaware Valley it was more profitable to dwell upon your own house.

The Quakers also kept mentally occupied and alert managing the money needed to buy enormous quantities of land and large houses for themselves and their children. Although some Quakers did go broke, most Quaker farmers and artisans were able money managers who gracefully handled the financial burdens of their expensive family system. Perhaps lured by horse races, shooting matches, cockfights, and taverns, and certainly less disciplined and directed by special communal institutions and ethics, the Anglicans showed less financial discipline.

Quaker men were expected to internalize the values of thrift and financial shrewdness that Benjamin Franklin, knowing many Quakers, would later secularize for the Anglican masses. As in Cheshire and Wales, financially troubled Quaker men received cautionary community attention. Fathers were expected to consult the monthly meetings for advice and aid at the first sign of dangerous indebtedness. When the Radnor Monthly Meeting discovered that Rowland P. was falling behind in his payments to various local Friends, for example, they called him to meeting "to speak with him and advise him to satisfy his creditors."[73] In such cases the meeting appointed a committee of successful men to help him balance his books.

The Chester Court of Common Pleas records and the Chester and the Radnor Monthly Meeting minutes show how well or poorly individual families did in staying out of serious debt. Quaker doctrine demanded that Quakers not sue one another in court unless the meeting had first been consulted and permission been given to sue. Both the meeting minutes and the court records must therefore be used to assess the Quakers' economic performance. From 1714 to 1735, the success of tender, fond-fostering households is clear: only 25 percent of the Quaker families ran into debt compared with almost 50 percent of the Anglican families.[74]

The remaining dispositions and executions also suggest the Quakers' care for their children's financial protection and the Anglicans' indifference. In over two decades only one Quaker family, the Simcocks, suffered a drastic fall from affluence because of debts, and only one poor Welsh Quaker had a lien placed on his land.[75] The other cases against Quaker families were less serious: they amounted to less than £50 and did not lead to the forced sale of land.[76] By contrast, debts ruined more Anglican families. During the 1730s Samuel Bishop was sued nine times for debts amounting to over £150.[77] Enoch Enochson, who left an estate of less than £150, was sued for a total of £204.[78] The land of John Wade was forcibly sold in 1731 in order to pay a £200 debt.[79] Charles Conner, a father of four children, was ordered to serve three years as a servant to his creditors.[80] The middling Anglicans' habits risked their children and the economic development of the Delaware Valley. The Quakers' fascination and reliance upon private arrangements fostered both.[81]

The general wealth of the two communities can be compared by averaging tax assessments for each family from 1715 to 1735. Four to six assessments based on land and livestock were collected for each family and translated into Pennsylvania currency assessments according to the appropriate rate of each year. These assessments were then averaged for each family. Also, the personal estates (capital, livestock, and furnishings) were compared from probate accounts for 67 families. Thirty-six percent of the Quakers were assessed more than £40, compared with only seven percent of the forty Anglicans. Fifty percent of the Quakers died with personal estates of over £200, compared with 41 percent of the Anglicans. The Quaker community had also many fewer poor families and many more affluent families. Though both Chester and Welsh Tract groups began with almost the same amount of resources, the Quaker families gathered significantly more wealth than did the Anglican families. Middling Quakers not only bought much more land but also gathered more taxable wealth and larger personal estates. By 1730, the tender-hearted Quakers had developed a community of flourishing households.[82]

THE VOCAL disgust authentically British families initially displayed at the Quakers' radical style and support of childhood ignorance began to fade. Anglican missionaries came to lose their popularity and role as saviors of a realizable reconstruction of British life. Anglican missionaries, it should be remembered, were initially optimistic about their church's place in the campaign to fight Christian ignorance and revive a recognizable British familial order in the Pennsylvania countryside. Before 1720, unchurched English and Swedes long resident in Chester, Anglican Welsh and English immigrants, and Quaker refugees from the Keithian schism had filled Anglican benches and coffers. In 1704 the Reverend Mr. Nichols had reported from Chester that "I do not want a considerable congregation every Lord's day, not withstanding my being seated in the very middle of the Quakers."[83] In 1707 the Reverend Mr. Evan Evans had reported that "in Chester, twenty miles from Philadelphia, upon Delaware River, they had a good church built . . . I preached the middle of December last in that Church to a congregation consisting of about 150."[84] This building, St. Paul's (the local Anglicans' major architectual accomplishment), had been completed by local Anglicans in 1714, outfitted with royal and aristocratic presents, and described by its vestry in a boastful report as being "one of the neatest on this continent."[85] Missionaries had cheered as satellite congregations grew in the 1720s at Radnor, Chichester, Concord, and Marlborough. In 1723 "The Clergy of Pennsylvania" had reported to the Secretary of the SPG that "the Church at Chester with those congregations that depend upon it are in a flourishing condition as appears to us from numerous and regular auditory that were present at our convention sermon in this place."[86]

But even skillful and optimistic Anglican ministers could not sustain this enthusiasm in the face of the Quaker success story. As early as 1712, the Reverend Mr. George Rosse despaired that "Quakerism has number and interest on its side and the true religion is crushed as unfashionable and impoverishing."[87] "This novelty [Quakerism] is so fashionable and prevailing in this place," he observed in 1712, "that some of those who own themselves Church people are strangely bewitched and lull'd into an indifferency about the baptism of their infants . . . I baptized last quarter of a year but two adults, formerly Quakers," he wrote, "and eight infants."[88] Increasingly the local Anglicans' identification with their church diminished into nominal loyalty and idle curiosity. Farmers and artisans would come to hear a sermon and watch the ceremonies on Sunday, but would do little else for or in the church. "I must beg leave to acquaint the Society," reported the Reverend Mr. Currey in 1760 from St. David's, "that although my hearers are many in number . . . I cannot get them to meet on an Easter Monday to choose a Vestry." There were also maddeningly few communicants.[89] While the Quakers' discussions about the morality of slavery displayed their deepening loyalty to their sect, an angry Reverend Thompson reported from St. Paul's in 1752 that "when I entered the mission of Chester a twelve month ago, I found no Church wardens or vestry, only some who had been Church officers ten years ago; the Church ready to fall into ruin; the surplice that was a Royal present rotting under the reading desk, and a considerable part of the missionary's library spoil'd or lost."[90] Thompson's successor, the Reverend Mr. Craig, told the same story in 1760: "In this village which is built on the River Delaware, wherein there are about thirty-odd families, there are not three who can properly be said to be decent members of our church, and of them, if the husband comes to divine service, the wife perhaps and children go elsewhere." He suggested the mission be closed.[91] Though its death knells were rung later, the militant English Church, somewhere around 1740, or earlier, had died in the countryside. The middling Anglican household and inculcations of Christian knowledge simply did not work as well in the Delaware Valley as the preoccupations of their radical neighbors.

Anglicanism flourished in Philadelphia, an environment much less friendly to Quaker familialism and also the destination of many rural Anglicans.[92] The Anglican Church in 1750 was also dominant in the Chesapeake and growing in New England, where the dominant Congregational church also emphasized the fostering of Christian knowledge in young children.[93] The Anglican churches had died prematurely only in the Pennsylvania countryside, where catechismal reform had initially looked the most exciting and refreshing. The career of Anglicanism in Chester and the Welsh Tract was tied clearly to the popular response to local Quakerism. Anglicanism owed much of its early liveliness in the Delaware Valley to the rejection of the Quakers' social radicalism and its passage to the growing respect for, or at least acceptance of, successful Quaker familial radicalism.

Just as the Anglican Church began to falter in the countryside, Pennsylvania became the destination of thousands of European immigrants. In the early 1750s, Gottlieb Mittelberger found deteriorations, similar to those among English churchmen, among immigrant, rural German churchmen. "Even the most exemplary preachers," he noted, "especially in rural districts, are often reviled, laughed at, and mocked by young and old, like Jews." "In Pennsylvania's rural districts," he continued, ". . . others, who are themselves baptized, nevertheless do not have their children baptized. When one asks them why, they answer: they neither see nor feel any difference between baptized and unbaptized young people."[94] The church's emphasis on honor, public display, and catechism became devalued increasingly by farmers and artisans watching privatism, denial of traditional rank, child-centeredness in the household, and de-emphasis upon explicit religious inculcation make the local Quakers rich.

The Quakers' unique linking of mixed-wheat farming, domestic retentiveness, inter-generational generosity, family labor (supplemented by servants and slaves), and tender socialization may or may not have produced authentic Christian youth, the central issue of the Keithian schism and the Anglican challenge. This familial formula, however, produced striking economic and social development and opportunity. The Quaker mixed-wheat farms' flour found ready markets in the sugar covered lands of the West Indies and then later in southern Europe. Thanks largely to this trade, Philadelphia cleared over 30,000 tons of goods in 1760 from its port (Boston, for example, had some 15,000 tons and New York 12,000 tons). Natural increase and immigration (mostly non-sectarian Germans and Scots-Irish) during the first half of the eighteenth century also helped make Philadelphia early America's boom town. Seventy years after its founding, all of New England contained 93,000 people and imported about one pound sterling *per capita* annually from England. Seventy years after its founding, the Quaker wheat area of New Jersey, Pennsylvania, and Delaware contained 220,000 people and imported from England about two pounds sterling *per capita*. Between 1714 and 1751, Philadelphia's population grew from 8,000 to 14,000 and its taxables from 1,420 to 2,075 (Boston's population remained at around 16,000 and lost almost a thousand taxables). Around 1757, the population of Philadelphia jogged past Boston's and ran ahead so quickly that by 1765 Philadelphia was the largest North American city (the population of Pennsylvania surpassed that of Massachusetts in about 1768). Meanwhile, the Quaker initiated wheat trade grew from its small garden in the Delaware Valley to envelop most family farmers from the Connecticut Valley to Maryland's eastern shore. By 1770, bread and flour became the second most valuable commodity (tobacco was first) exported to the world from the British North American colonies.[95]

The moral use of family labor and generous, equitable distributions of property distinguished the radical Quaker family system not only from those of transplanted and converted Delaware Valley Anglicans but also from those of New England farmers and Chesapeake planters. In a society without cities and with a labor system based on black slavery, Chesapeake farmers tended to give all their sons land too—unlike Delaware Valley Anglicans, they had no other place to send them for a livelihood. But whenever possible, southern planters used slave rather than family labor and encouraged habits of leisure and command, not convivial industry, in their children. They certainly never tried to sanctify household relations as the focus of spiritual and moral development in children as the northwestern English and Welsh Quakers did. Colonial New England farmers almost exclusively relied on family labor and were also committed to using household relations to promote personal conscience and religious Grace. But generally lacking good soil and convinced of the social and religious necessity of patriarchal dominance and control, New England farmers generally paid their sons and daughters less and later than Delaware Valley farmers.[96]

From the observation of such differing trends, Benjamin Franklin, Richard Jackson, J. Hector St. John de Crèvecoeur, and J.P. Brissot de Warville created the plausible legend of the Quaker or Quakerized family farm as the backbone of the development of a unique republican social order in North America. Using as their touchstone Pennsylvania's and Philadelphia's spectacular economic and social growth, they argued that Quakerized farmers alone could produce both virtuous and industrious children and significant wealth on the expanding frontier without expensive and corrupting European institutions. These men were practitioners of the new eighteenth-century art of political and moral economy that united the collection and study of social and demographic statistics, the study of "manners," and the study of trade and economic production for the purpose of assessing and predicting the development of standing societies. Their formulations probably expressed, albeit in far more sophisticated form, some important reasons thousands of non-Quaker, non-sectarian immigrants had for supporting or accepting minority Quaker hegemony decade after decade, year after year, even in Pennsylvania districts where no Quaker lived.[97]

Skillfully handled coalition politics certainly had much to do with creating Quaker hegemony, but Quaker domesticity also clearly played a role. The implausible radical, revelation-inspired reorderings of northwest provincial society—Quaker domesticity— became in North America a vehicle which helped a minority sectarian group unprecedentedly maintain political hegemony for nearly one hundred years in one of early America's wealthiest, most pluralistic, urbanized, populous, and dynamic colonies. Though the Quakers would pay later for ignoring Keith's critique, they frustrated their powerful opponents for many decades. Clearly, if they could sell Quaker magistrates like hot cakes to church people, ideologies and demonstrations of domesticity, whatever their deeper flaws, had taken root in North America.

PART THREE

Maintenance and Cooptation

From Quaker to American Domesticity
1750–1790

CHAPTER SIX

Wives—Ministers—Mothers

The Welsh Tract and Chester Quaker communities' use of intimate relations to convey the Holy Spirit, instead of the formal relations of extra-household institutions, had another major consequence: the creation of a tightly focused, characterologically consistent, social role for women.[1] The Quakers melded women's sexuality, spirituality, and maternal authority into a novel feminine mystique that later became the model for New England advocates of domesticity.

The initial set of Welsh removal certificates did not express fully George Fox's and Margaret Fell's opinion that women should occupy a powerful place in the Society of Friends. They wanted women to be spiritually equal with men, to have nearly a co-equal role in ruling the Society, to speak in worship meeting as recognized ministers, to exercise authority over men and women through their monthly meetings, and to hold full authority over "women's matters." Among these items, the Welsh meetings only recognized episodically the importance of women's maternal influence.

The 62 Welsh Tract removal certificates, recorded between 1682 and 1695, mentioned 57 men and 60 women (30 of the women were married, 4 widows, 11 spinsters, 14 children). The Welsh meetings gave some married women attention as mothers. Sina Pugh was noted as a "good, careful, industrious woman . . . in things relating to her poor small children wise, discreet, and circumspect. . . ."[2] In the few cases where a meeting described a public role for women, they used maternal terms. Barbara Bevan, for example, was described as "a nursing mother to some weak and poor among us."[3] In recognition of the maternal role, the wife's and the children's characters were usually discussed together, as in the removal certificate of Evan ap Powell and Gwen Powell, where the human path of truth flowed from husband to wife to children. The meetings also described the childrearing efforts of widowers cautiously. A Welsh meeting commended the widower Griffith John who had three children because "all his endeavor hath been to bring up his children in the fear of the Lord. . .," but neglected to mention his success.[4] Another meeting said Hugh Griffith was "a poor honest-hearted man" who "hath been a widower for these many years and has kept his motherless children not being very troublesome to Friends or others."[5] His children were somewhat troublesome by implication. The Glamorgan Meeting implicitly endorsed Barbara Bevan's maternal insight and authority by noting approvingly that the Bevans "would by no means be withheld of bringing their small weakly family along with them, to that very end, to have them brought up in the pure dread and fear of their God which they greatly feared would be wanting in their absence."[6] The meetings also spent as many words on spinsters as they did on bachelors, presumably because a nurturing Quaker household demanded a Quaker wife with spiritual qualifications equivalent to her husband's.

The Welsh monthly meetings mentioned, nonetheless, the names of only 18 of the 30 married women. When describing "our dear, beloved Friend, William Lewis, his wife, and family," the Treverig Meeting wrote much about William Lewis ("we and all faithful Friends had unity with him in the blessed truth, whose innocent life and unblameable conversation, and also the sense of his service . . . is fresh in our memory. . . .") but failed to mention Lewis's wife's name or to say a word about her.[7] The Pennlyn Meeting's discussion of "Cadwallader Morgan and family" spent forty words describing Cadwallader Morgan, but said only of his nameless wife that she was "likeminded."[8] Wives got names in eighteen of the certificates, but in eight of these the women's character got only one or two adjectives.

Such denials continued. Upon settlement, the Cheshire Quakers thought it convenient for the women to meet with the men in business meetings until 1705. From 1682 until 1705, the women had no autonomy or role in formal Chester Monthly Meeting Quaker

discipline, except inspecting marriages or talking to female offenders of the discipline under male supervision. Strengthened by self-
confident, vivid, female settlers like Barbara Bevan, Gainor Roberts,
and Martha Awbrey, the Welsh Tract's women's meeting was established almost upon settlement in 1683, but until 1693 it did not
conduct sufficient business to justify detailed minutes. In northwestern Britain, Quaker men apparently had too little property to
allow their wives' roles as spiritual mothers to flourish. The Quakers' economic crisis in northwestern Britain demanded creation of
new wealth to retain their children. Such a crisis supported over-
weening masculine leadership.

As lucrative wheat harvests became routine in Pennsylvania,
however, the selfless, meek, but authoritative Quaker female role
grew steadily. By 1693 the Welsh Tract women were finally filling
their meeting minute book with nearly as many entries as the men.
And in 1705 the Chester women were finally separated in business
meetings from the men and began their own women's meeting.
Swiftly growing into an independent, self-confident entity, the
Chester Women's Meeting boldly sent three members in 1711 to
"look into the men's old books to see what properly belongs to them
before they had this meeting, so far as the men think fitt. . . ."
While maintaining a polite posture, the women found, as expected,
nothing worthy of reappropriation, and thereby firmly informed
the men of a new day and of the moral illegitimacy of the days when
the wisdom of female elders was squelched in "the men's old
books."[9]

The rise of the women's monthly meetings did not mean,
however, that Pennsylvania was, as the German traveler Gottleib
Mittelberger insisted in 1754, "a paradise for women. . . ."[10] The
Quaker female sphere provided more responsibility than means to
poor Quaker women. The women's meetings in the Welsh Tract
and Chester increased women's spiritual prestige and spiritual-
maternal authority, not their economic prowess. Poorer Quaker
women often had to wait to marry, failed to marry at all, or had to
marry poorer men. They often failed as mothers (and therefore as
Quaker women) simply because their husbands lacked the property
to secure their children decent places in the marriage market. Poor
Quaker men might work themselves into prosperity or might leave
the Quaker community, but poor Quaker women found such solutions more difficult. Leading Chester and Welsh Tract men and
women so appreciated feminine spiritual talent, however, that the

exceptional poor woman, if gifted as a divine vessel of Truth in meeting, rose by her own talents to the top of rural Pennsylvania society. She joined there a group of materially privileged, socially responsible, and socially authoritative women who exercised a responsibility and influence over their worlds unprecedented in Anglo-American society. These godly wealthy women constituted an eighteenth-century American female spiritual "aristocracy," who by example and by vigorously exercised authority morally anchored the rapidly developing society of the Delaware Valley, one of the richest in North America.

The Puritans' exclusion of women from any authoritative role in the church had led not simply to the maintenance of the ideology of female irrationality and moral weakness, but, as Laurel Thatcher Ulrich has most artfully shown for northern New England women between 1650 and 1750, to the creation for women of a rich variety of often discordant social roles from passionate Eve, to virago, to witch, to church saint. A New England woman could possibly be identified at one time or another in all of these and more during her life. Women's experience was certainly as various in Quaker communities of the Delaware Valley, but the doctrine of "holy conversation," and particularly its social and institutional embodiments, unambiguously informed Quaker women's roles with but a single set of character traits. Women were to be exemplary wives, mothers, and ministers, as formally and informally defined, supervised and rewarded by families, powerful men, and, most significantly of all, the women's meetings themselves.[11] Whether dealing with children, husbands, or an audience of listeners, the good Quaker woman was supposed to sanctify and harness her sexuality to the purposes of "Truth" by becoming an embodiment of "holy conversation" who tenderly answered the Light in others. Each role had a different primary audience, but all demanded the same selfless, charismatic character traits. Many Delaware Valley women harmonized the roles of wife, minister, and mother into an influential feminine mystique.

Even after the settlers became materially secure and the women's meetings in Chester and the Welsh Tract began to exert real authority, the male settlers and their descendants remembered their impoverished past. Largely out of concern for children's well-being and economic protection, they insulated women from having any central economic authority or role. Probate inventories of seventeenth- and eighteenth-century Chester and Welsh Tract

Quaker households showed, to be sure, as much evidence of female home manufacturing and processing as coeval probates from settled Puritan villages in Essex County, Massachusetts.[12] While their husbands lived, however, Delaware Valley women, like Essex County matrons, rarely handled the money their commodities earned. And, after their husbands died, a higher percentage of Delaware Valley widows than Essex County widows continued to be economically fettered in their Quaker husbands' wills and in the countryside's Quaker-dominated, intrusively child-centered, orphan courts.

Orphan court accounts suggest that Chester County women rarely participated directly in the marketplace. Orphan court accounts consistently dwelled upon transactions involving food and clothing, commodities usually produced or prepared by women. The Chester County accounts seldom featured female traders, however. For example, from 1704 to 1713, Matthew Roberts oversaw the rearing of his deceased brother's three children—Rebecca age 12, John age 9, and Matthew age 6. Their father had been John Roberts, a Merion miller, who died in 1704, leaving a personal estate of £250, a moderate sized farm, and a grist mill. By running the mill and by sometimes renting it, and by selling selected assets, Matthew Roberts increased their personal estate by 1713 to £464. He also spent £428 on the children and their property. The greatest expense was the construction of a new mill in 1713.

He spent £179 during this nine-year period chiefly on the children's diet and clothes. During 1713, for example, Matthew Roberts spent the children's money on two quires of paper, 5.5 yards of linen, 3.5 yards of shallon, 14 mohair buttons, a coat, shoes, and a waistcoat. The Roberts' children were lightly educated (a total cost of £8) but impressively dressed. Most of the fabric was domestically produced by women and most of the food was provided by women. However, from the £60.75 spent on textiles and tailoring, women received only £1.82 or 3 percent. Of the £24.4 spent on diet, women got only £2.74 or 11 percent. Of the total £428 Matthew Roberts spent during this period on children, about half on commodities produced by women, he paid female producers or traders a paltry £5 6s 7d or 1.2 percent of all expenditures.[13] The same principle of gender distribution was clear in other orphan accounts.[14]

Women handled money seemingly only when no alternative existed, and in such cases, spinsters handled it more often than married women. In 1706, Rebecca Roberts became sick, probably with symptoms relating to the onset of her menstrual cycle. She was

14 years old. A female attendant, not a male doctor, supervised her. She and her female guests were festively hungry and thirsty. The accounts show that Rebecca and guests consumed "during her sickness" one bottle of wine, two nutmegs, one pound of sugar, one quart of liquor, and half a barrel of cider. She and her attendants apparently marked her transition into adult womanhood by swilling a bottle of wine and a gallon of punch. Aside, however, from the 7s paid "to a woman at Darby for attending Rebecca at the time of her sickness," all the money went to male caterers, including 9s paid Philip Price for "½ barrel of cider," although cider was processed almost exclusively by women.[15]

The near exclusion of married women from notable market transactions may have been universal in eighteenth-century Anglo-American society. Nevertheless, the Quaker fathers' preoccupation with saving children peculiarly removed their widows from the marketplace. The Quaker settlers' child-protecting inheritance strategies often curtailed Chester County widows' economic discretion.[16] According to a sample of wills, widows in north Wales were usually made unsupervised sole executrixes of their husbands' minuscule estates. Widows in Cheshire had more male supervision, but frequent freedom. In Chester and the Welsh Tract Quakers' wills, widows' economic activities were almost always explicitly circumscribed by male co-executors and male overseers.[17] In only three of 83 Welsh Tract or Chester Quaker wills (1681–1745) was a widow formally given unimpeded economic discretion. Even when Quaker husbands designated their wives sole executrixes without an explicit overseeing board, they still explicitly denied them economic freedom. In 1714, James Swaffer, a Quaker carpenter and farmer of Caln township, allowed "my dear and loving wife Elizabeth all singular lands and goods . . . to be disposed of at her pleasure," but stipulated "with the advice and consent of my brother William Swaffer of Neither Providence and my friend John Bezer of Chichester, yeoman, whose advice and consent I desire she shall take in all concerns of moment."[18] In 1722, Andrew Job also freed his wife from co-executors or formal boards of overseers, but "with this restriction that she doth nothing of moment without the consent or approbation of the preparative meeting of Nottingham."[19] These fathers worried that inexperienced but spiritually talented females might waste property the men had newly and carefully amassed for their children.

The Quaker farmers putatively held their potentially ministerial wives in greater spiritual esteem than the Puritan farmers, tradesmen, and mariners of Essex County, Massachusetts, did their wives, who were not allowed to speak in church. Yet the Welsh Tract and Chester farmers trusted their wives less in the sinful world with their farms and gave them less economic discretion in their wills. The Essex County farmers, artisans, and mariners were much like the north Welsh in so frequently naming their wives as sole executrixes (twice the rate of the Pennsylvania Quaker farmers), but were much like the Delaware Valley farmers in naming overseers, guardians, and trustees to overlook and guide their widows' work.[20] Nevertheless, the Essex County farmers and artisans gave their wives full economic freedom more often. In 44 cases in Essex County, Massachusetts, 1668–74, in which men left their wives sole executrixes, 17 men named no trustees to oversee the widow's activities (as shall be seen, the Essex County orphan court rarely named overseers themselves in such cases, while the Chester County courts often did). Of the 80 Essex County widows, then, 17 or 21.2 percent were given total economic freedom. For example, Ralph Elinwood in 1673, a farmer of Beverly, Massachusetts, with a total estate of £352 made "Helen my wife my lawful executrix and to make use of all my estate to bring up our children in the fear of the Lord."[21] No overseers were named. In 21 cases in the Delaware Valley where men left their widows' sole executrixes, 19 men also named trustees or the equivalent to oversee the widows' economic decisions. Of the 83 Quaker widows, then, only two or 2.4 percent were given full economic discretion.

When handling the estates of orphans whose fathers died intestate, the Essex County and the Chester County orphan courts treated the widows differently. The Chester County farmer-judges tended to distrust widows, while the Essex County magistrates tended to trust them. In a typical late seventeenth-century procedure in Essex County, the administration of the estate was given to the widow and, after she returned a valid inventory of her ex-husband's estate, the court proceeded to award precise monetary legacies prospectively to the minors to be paid by the widow when the children reached the age of 21 or marriage. The widow did not usually have to post bond for these legacies unless she remarried. In a typical case, the Essex Quarterly Court on March 26, 1672, granted the administration of the estate of John Chaney of Newbury, intestate, to Mary, his wife. An inventory amounting to £97 12s 4d was presented and notice taken that three minor children survived, John, Mary, and Martha. The court ordered "to the son £20 at the age of twenty-one, and to the daughters £10, each at the age or marriage with their mother's consent, the estate to remain in the mother's hand till they come to age, provided that if she married, security be given for the children's portions." The court apportioned the estate roughly according to the rules of intestate division operating in many other Anglo-American societies: the widow received a third, the eldest son a double portion, and the remaining children equal portions. In this case, however, the court gave the children only 41 percent of the estate and the widow 59 percent. The 26 percent beyond the widow's third was to be spent presumably on maintaining and educating the children; yet it was entirely at the widow's discretion how much she spent on such cares. The widow also enjoyed the profits of the estate and the accrued interest of the children's portions during the time they were set and the time they were paid. Thus, if Martha was three years old at the time of her father's death and married at age 18, her portion at just 4 percent annual interest would have grown to £16. Her mother was obliged to pay Martha, however, only £10 at marriage. Even omitting other profits of the estate, the mother could pocket £6 or 37.5 percent of Martha's rightful portion. Such procedures were usual in estates up to about £400.[22]

The Essex County court treated great accumulations of wealth differently. They sought to help widows and explicitly to protect minors' rights. In 1680 a Salem merchant, Mr. John Turner, died intestate, his estate amounting at £6,788, including two houses, several farms, five ketches, and interest in a number of sloops. He left a widow, Mrs. Elizabeth Turner, and five minor children. The judges did not apportion legacies prospectively in this case or allow the widow full discretion in paying them. The court did award the administration to the widow and "ordered that the estate remain in the widow's hands for bringing up of the children until they come of age." However, while immediately allowing the widow £1,500 (only 22 percent of the estate), they ordered that "the rest of the estate is to be divided equally between the children, only the son to have a double portion, to be paid when they are of age unless by the court's allowance they shall choose guardians, who may require their respective portions, and then the administratrix shall be discharged of any further charge for their education." The Essex judges did not neglect the posting of bond, as was usual, but ordered that "the houses and lands to stand as security, and if the administratrix should marry, other security to be given for payment of the legacies, otherwise the whole estate except the widow's portion shall be in the court's hands to take order for the security thereof." Finally, although the court did not appoint guardians for the minor children, they hinted that such might be appropriate. They also gave Mrs. Elizabeth Turner expert male assistance by ordering that "Captain William Brown, Mr. John Hawthorne, Captain John Price, and Mr. Thomas Gardner, Jr. are desired to advise the administratrix in the management of the estate."[23] Such concern for female frailty and orphan interest only accompanied very large estates of public impact. Except for such large estates, Essex judges trusted middling widows and thought overseeing them too carefully a waste of time. The great majority of intestate Essex County widows left the court with significant financial discretion.

Chester County farmer-judges showed greater care in protecting minor orphans from the possible dishonesty, weakness, and mistakes of even the poorest and most saintly widows. The Chester County court commonly awarded administrations to widows, but they almost never determined monetary portions until the oldest child came of age or until guardians were appointed. No estate was too small for such time-consuming and community involving procedures to apply. Also, at the point of distributing the estate among the children or their guardians, and the widow, the widow-administratrix had to file not only a complete inventory but also a complete account with vouchers for every shilling she spent on the maintenance and education of the minor children. Few intestate Chester County widows controlled discretionary capital. And intrusive almost air-tight court procedures doubtlessly dissuaded many Chester County widows from becoming greatly involved in the marketplace.

When Chester County widows tried to take their children's financial affairs into their own hands, they often provoked a challenge. Sarah Casey had to show her accounts of expense in 1732 for her child. Immediately, "William Rawson and Andrew Rawson, guardians of the said Gartree Rawson objected against an account of three pounds nineteen shillings and nine pence charged by the administratrix paid to Andrew Erickson—also against some part of ye funeral expenses and for maintenance of the child eight months, three weeks, and four days at 5 shillings per week amounting to eight pounds, seventeen shillings, and ten pence to cloathing ye child and paying the Doctor." Petty complaints, but they added up in time and money. Unable to determine the issues, the court postponed the case for two months, and when they took it up again found the "account remained unsettled." The court finally referred determination to "John Crosby, Caleb Cowpland, Thomas Cummins, and George Aston," all respectable Chester County yeomen. The issues, which probably amounted to the adjustment of a few pounds or shillings, involved seven farmers, a widow, two court sessions, and six months. The cause of this activity, Gartree Rawson, was described as an "infant."[24]

The Quaker dominated Chester County court consistently favored the "defenseless" minors. For example, when Lettice Chamberlain, a mother of six children and widow of John Chamberlain, married Thomas Vernon in 1734, the aroused court immediately appointed guardians to protect the interests of the minor children. About five years later, the guardians demanded Lettice Vernon's accounts and then showed contempt for her work. Lettice had charged £30 for the maintenance of Mary from nine years to fifteen years, but the court laid this charge "aside as unreasonable and not fit to be allowed because it appears by credible persons of ye neighborhood that at the decease of her father she was well worth her maintenance." It did not matter whether or not Mary had actually worked to her potential. The court revised the labor value of the other children similarly and recognized that Lettice had "the interest to this time of the shares of the personal estate belonging to the children," but her accounts failed to include such increments. The court reduced her claims accordingly. Lettice Vernon had claimed £236 for the maintenance and education of her six children; the court allowed her just £97, only 41 percent of her original claim.[25]

Most intestate widows in Essex County, Massachusetts, could freely use, reinvest, and profit from their deceased husbands' real property until their minor sons reached adulthood, though they could not sell real estate without court permission. In Chester County, where the apportioning and distribution of the estate was almost always determined when the children reached adulthood, intestate widows with minor children could neither freely profit from the use or rent of the land, nor sell it without court permission and careful oversight. In order to sell land, the Chester widows had to convince the court that their husbands' personal estate and the rent or use of their plantations were insufficient to pay outstanding debts and to maintain and educate their children. If they did so, they could only sell so much land as necessary to meet approved expenses. For example, in 1717, after carefully studying her accounts, the Chester court allowed Ann Blunston to sell a bolting mill and a small piece of adjoining land. In order to sell an additional farm, she then had to petition the court again, showing that the sale of this mill and land "was not sufficient to pay ye descendant's debts and bring up his children, as the law directs." She could not sell the land to whom she pleased; instead, the court ordered a sheriff sale of the property. Public notice of the sale had to be made in 12 different places; the sheriff oversaw the sale; and the court reserved the power to declare the sale null, if the price paid was thought too low. The money from such sales was credited to the deceased's estate and its use monitored on behalf of the minor children by the court and guardians.[26] A Chester County widow with minor children who yearned to sell her land and move elsewhere with her children was unfortunate. Just to get her share of the real estate she would have to have guardians appointed for all her minor children and would have to distribute two-thirds of the sale to these guardians. If any guardian objected to the sale and distribution of the land, the court would probably disallow the sale. Not only did her children's estates soak up virtually all the profit a shrewd Chester County widow might make from her deceased husband's resources, her children also tied her to the soil like a Russian serf.

Given the court's procedures, a high percentage of minor children in Chester County chose or received guardians, and a very high percentage of these guardians were men. "Guardians" were legal entities, both more and less than custodians of children, more money-managers than nannies. Their main job was to protect the property interests of minor orphans in court; a minor had no legal standing or any property, in law, without a guardian. Until a child reached age fourteen, the court could appoint guardians at anyone's petition. At the age of fourteen, children could appear in court and choose their own. In most cases, the guardians posted bond and assumed management of the minor's property, though in many cases the property was allowed to dwell with the widow who retained physical custody of the children and was overseen by the guardians. Pre-determination of the children's legacies in Essex County made the appointment of guardians uncommon. The usual determination of children's legacies when they came of age in Chester County made the appointment of guardians common. Also, if a

Chester County widow remarried or did anything economically assertive, someone—an uncle, a Quaker meeting, neighbors, even a suspicious registrar of documents—seemed to petition the court to have guardians named to protect the minor children from the possible errors of the widow.

When they did name guardians, the Essex and Suffolk county courts in Massachusetts often named women—at least far more frequently than did the Chester County court. For example, in Essex County, Massachusetts from 1665 to 1681, women composed 23 percent of the guardians chosen by the county court; they composed only 4 percent of the guardians so chosen in Chester County from 1716 to 1730. Such differing policies made common sense. Having been given the freedom and capital to make crucial economic decisions for themselves and their children, Essex County widows were often economically tested and experienced. Chester County widows had learned how to fill out vouchers and keep accounts under their court's oversight, but they were not encouraged to make crucial economic decisions. Neither prudent children nor the court wanted such sheltered people as their financial managers. This reluctance to name female guardians in Chester County increased over time. Between 1747 and 1764 the Chester County court chose 302 guardians (21 guardians a year) and of these a mere four or 1.3 percent were women.[27]

Radical Protestant insight, "holy conversation," a fear of scarcity carried from the past into prosperity, and the development of a child-centered wheat economy had fashioned an unusually economically constrained female role in Chester County, Pennsylvania. Among men who left wills, Essex County farmers were over twice as likely as Chester County Quaker farmers to give their wives full discretion over their estates. Unless their husbands were very wealthy, Essex County intestate widows were given almost full discretion over their husbands' estates. After being told what legacies they would have to pay when their children reached age, the court and neighbors left them alone to invest their dead husband's farms and businesses. Child-centered Chester County judges and men helped and circumscribed such widows and gave them as little economic discretion as possible. When choosing financial guardians for minor children, the Essex and Suffolk county courts often chose women, while the Chester County court and its clients avoided them.

Such differences probably had more to do with differing perceptions of minor children's spiritual needs for property than with differing male views of the role of women. Not accustomed to coddling children, and emphasizing knowledge more than nurturing environments, Essex County judges gave widows more economic discretion not only because they thought women financially able but also because they thought worrying excessively about orphans' environments and widows' errors was a waste of time. On the other hand, Chester County monthly meetings stressed nurturing environments and often praised male elders in memorials for their arduous service to orphans. The most spiritually respected farmers often appeared as guardians in the court records (William Stout provided such service in Lancaster, England). Remembering vividly how the dispersal of propertyless children had destroyed so many "tender plants" and nearly whole Quaker communities in Cheshire and Wales, Chester and Welsh Tract men gave their wives so little economic discretion probably less because they thought them inherently incompetent than because they were especially keen on their children's economic security and protection. Widows' discretion in Essex County reflected New England males' childrearing ideas; widows in Chester County succumbed to Quaker males' differing religiously sensitized interest in children and youth. An economically stifled Boston youth, Benjamin Franklin, though not technically an orphan, emigrated to the Delaware Valley in 1723 and, unlike Chester County widows, positively experienced this difference.[28]

Yet, the growing prosperity of Pennsylvania Quaker households led not only to discernible curtailments of women's traditional economic authority but also to the realization and enhancement of women's new formal religious role as the authoritative mothers of "spiritual Israel." As economic problems of childrearing were solved, the spiritual problems of childrearing became more apparent. And as wealth, economic opportunities, and non-Quaker immigrants accumulated in the colony, some alluring anchor was needed to prevent Quaker men and women from straying into secularization. Fulfilling the maternal authority Fox promised women seemed to help solve all of these problems.

Quaker men were never indifferent to young children, as the correspondence of the Pennsylvania male Quaker elite shows. Yet their chatter about children in its fondness, pretentiousness, and pontifications, reflects both their love of children and their need for more involved, realistic, expert help. In 1707 a Philadelphia merchant and officeholder, Isaac Norris, wrote to Joseph Pike, an Irish Quaker merchant-banker, "your little fellow is lusty and lively—a welcome stranger here—and I hope will be no discredit to this country." Pike was an influential and strict Irish elder; his parental trust in Pennsylvania as a school for Quaker virtue flattered Norris. To keep that trust, Isaac Norris put on the mantle of a nursery scientist and proclaimed to Pike that his tiny offspring was "backward in his tongue, but quick in his little signals and thinkings."[29] Norris announced to Jeffrey Pinnell in 1701 that William Penn's American-born son, John, was "a comely, lovely babe, and has much of his father's grace and air, and hope he will not want of a good portion of his mother's sweetness."[30] This was, in reality, making a bit much of a three-month-old baby's presence, or too little of William Penn's aging baby-face.

While racing back to London to save his colony from royal appropriation, William Penn kept up the insubstantial male banter about this infant. On the ocean voyage, "Johne, after the first five days, hearty and well, and Johne exceedingly cheerful all the way . . ." Penn told James Logan, his provincial secretary, a bachelor.[31] As John approached two years, Penn told Logan that the toddler "was perpetually busy in building or play otherwise," behavior reported to the busy Proprietor in his wife's letters.[32] In the Welsh Tract in 1704, Rees Thomas, a relative by marriage to Penn, described his American-born children to his Welsh father-in-law more credibly: the youngest, three-month-old Awbrey was "ye first Awbrey in Pennsylvania and a stout boy he is of his age, being now a quarter." The Merion farmer presumed knowledge of the common weight of such three-month-old infants. Nearly two years old, the eldest, Rees, Jr., "was a brave, bold boy," and "he remembers his love to his granfather, and also to his nanty Anne, he doth speak very liberally, but 'uncle' is a hard word."[33] The least credible male nursery-scientist was Gabriel Thomas, who in a promotional pamphlet of 1698, claimed that "the Christian children born here are generally well favored, and beautiful to behold; I never knew any come into the world with the least blemish on any part of its body; being in general observed to be better natured, milder, and more tender-hearted than those born in England."[34] Perhaps it was while listening to such tales in "expert" and fond male banter that George Fox decided that "women's matters" best be left to women and that they required a meeting of their own to lend a hierarchy of instruction, social reproduction, and communal authority to experienced female wisdom.

As THE Chester and the Radnor Women's Monthly Meetings emerged in the early 1700s in authority and self-confidence, they engaged in important charitable work, but chiefly sought to morally anchor their swiftly developing communities by overseeing the world of women, particularly by maintaining spiritual and moral discipline among women in all their spiritual-physical intimacies with children and men. In 1705 and 1706, for example, the Welsh Tract women's meeting did collect £17 and made 14 separate payments "to the poor," identifying need and proper assistance in each case. This charitable work was eclipsed, however, by even more time-consuming and involving efforts to mold the characters of women, mostly younger women. In 1705 and 1706, the Welsh Tract Women's Meeting inspected 20 women for 20 marriages, conducted nine discipline cases (all women), and had their own committees roving in the townships visiting families in order to encourage "holy conversation" and to identify infractions.[35]

The hierarchy of the Chester and the Welsh Tract Women's Meetings was as domestically determined as the men's. Spinsters had no power role in the Welsh Tract Women's Meeting. The spinster, Elizabeth Roberts, never served the Welsh Tract Women's Meeting, although she was the daughter of Gainor Roberts and lived with her powerful brother, Robert Roberts, at Pencoyd. Sidney Roberts, Robert Roberts's wife, was a very active member, however. Inspecting marriages, talking to young women about their sexual offences, and "women's matters" generally required women of genuine sexual, childbearing, and household experience. Indeed, what chiefly linked husband's and wife's communal and spiritual careers was the growth and behavior of their "tender plants." Children held both their mother's and father's communal prestige hostage. In a study of 29 married women living in the Welsh Tract, 24 played some role in the Radnor Women's Monthly Meeting between 1695 and 1730. However, during these 35 years just five women held 58 percent of all the jobs on committees and 63 percent of the appointments to the overseeing quarterly meetings. While these leading mothers were alive, not one of their children ever caused the least difficulty in the community. On the other hand, by 1705, Margaret

Jarman was clearly on the road to becoming an honored vessel of holy discipline, but then her daughter married out. Elinor Bevan and Ann Lewis visited Margaret Jarman, who acknowledged her sorrow, though not her responsibility, that "the child which she bore should be the cause" of "trouble to Friends. . . . "[36] She did not serve the Welsh Tract Women's Meeting again for three years. Given the nature of the marriage market, the status of women was dependent on their husband's wealth in the running of disciplined households and the accomplishment of holy marriages for their children. Female elders tended to be the wealthiest women in the community. Because of Quaker inheritance patterns, these prominently meek women did not inherit the earth, but they did control many of its assets to promote Quaker domesticity within a powerful religious community in which they shared leadership (see Appendix: Table 6).

Although their status often indirectly depended on their men (and Quaker men's ultimately depended on skillful wife-mothers), the women finally determined each other's spiritual and communal status. Gainor Roberts was not a mere reflection of her husband. She had emigrated as a 35-year-old spinster and was the only single woman among the first Welsh purchasers. She had already begun to clear and plant her 156 Pennsylvania acres, when in 1684 she married John Roberts. The newlyweds eventually amassed 1100 acres and built a splendid mansion, Pencoyd (their descendant, George Brooke Roberts, president of the Pennsylvania Railroad 1880–97, was born at Pencoyd in 1833).[37] Their men did often lead the men's monthly meeting; Rees Thomas, the husband of the most active woman, Martha Awbrey Thomas, was the most active man in the Welsh Tract Men's Meeting between 1693 and 1720. A strong possibility exists, however, that the Welsh Tract men were attempting to maintain Rees Thomas's status as equivalent to his wife's. Martha Awbrey Thomas had the best pedigree of anyone in the Welsh Tract. She was the daughter of Mr. William Awbrey of Llanelyw, who was connected by marriage to the Herberts of Montgomeryshire Castle. Martha Awbrey Thomas's brother William had married William Penn's daughter Laetitia and Martha Awbrey Thomas's second son, Awbrey (the stout infant previously described by his fond father), married William Penn, Jr.'s only daughter, Gulielma. The Penn connection was clearly through the maternal line. Martha Awbrey Thomas's husband, Rees, was so comparably déclassé that he had to argue with his Welsh father-in-law about

giving his children the surname "Thomas" instead of "Awbrey."[38]
The men failed to help Samuel Miles, however. Margaret Miles was
quite active in the women's meeting (see Appendix: Table 6) and
was also a minister certified to travel. Her husband, Samuel Miles,
was a sympathizer with George Keith and after 1698 a Baptist who
had himself dipped in Ridley Creek.[39] Samuel Miles was unable to
"corrupt" his daughters, however, so Margaret Miles's Quakerly
prestige remained intact.

Although economically privileged, the female leadership
worked hard. Aside from nursing and rearing her own children and
running her own household, for example, Martha Awbrey Thomas
inspected 33 separate women for marriage between 1695 and 1727,
the year she died. This job required a head for genealogy, a nose for
gossip, and spiritually discerning eyes. In each case, Thomas had to
determine whether or not an intended bride was too closely related
by blood to her intended, whether or not she had previous entan-
gling alliances, and, most of all, the nature of her spiritual character. The women's meeting gave Martha Thomas and a helper a
month for each inspection. The women's meetings took marriage
inspection seriously. The top female elders continued to do marriage inspections regularly even after graduating to being customary appointees to the quarterly meetings. Martha Thomas did three
inspections the year before she died.

The impact of these inspections counterbalanced the enormous
freedom young women otherwise enjoyed in marriage choice. In the
rural Puritan town of Hingham, Massachusetts, from 1710 to 1750,
as Daniel Scott Smith has shown, 138 daughters married usually in
birth order, the oldest first and so on, probably to prevent any
passed-over daughter from being insulted and stigmatized, a tight
system which implied a strong parental role in the timing of choices
of women's marriages. Excluding spinsters, only 11.6 percent of the
daughters married out of birth order. At their most spontaneously
fickle, between 1821 and 1880, only 18.4 percent of Hingham's
daughters married out of birth order. From 1710 to 1750 in the
Welsh Tract and Chester meetings, excluding spinsters, but including only daughters, 26 percent of 182 daughters married out of birth
order, a much higher percentage than any cohort of daughters in
Hingham, Massachusetts between 1651 and 1880.[40] In the Welsh
Tract household of Rowland Richards, for example, the first
daughter, Margaret, married first, in 1711, but the next to marry was
the third daughter, Elizabeth, in 1717; the second-born daughter did

not wed until 1721. Rowland Richards who died in 1724 consented to and provided the portions for such female freedom. Similarly, the three daughters of Meredith Meredith married exactly opposite to their birth order. As religious faithfulness might suggest, daughters tended to marry at the inspiration of their inner divinities, not parental or sororal convenience.

Early eighteenth-century parents and committees usually saw daughters married within meeting. The poorest daughters were an annoying exception. Weaklings in the marriage market, they often faced unpleasant choices: sinful men, parental objection, or celibacy. The first and second generation women's marrying pattern was similar to the men's. The poorest daughters married non-Quakers or Quakers in churches or magistrates' parlors far more frequently than the well-to-do daughters. Indeed, 12 of the 14 settlers' daughters who married out had marriage portions of £19 or less, the most paltry endowments. Thanks to a fine information network, the female elders often arrived at the scene of a marriage error before it became accomplished sin; but their timely arrivals and persuasive words seldom changed minds. The poor daughters were stubborn. One young woman in 1711 "would give little or no answer but expected nothing but sorrow"; another said "she did not expect she could be married among Friends with that man"; another in 1709 said, "that she received Friends' love and that she would not leave the man."[41] The elders took such rebuffs and losses sadly. In 1721, the Welsh Tract women sent a report to the quarterly meeting that "Friends are generally in love but that this meeting has been under some exercise from some time concerning some who would not take the advice of Friends, particularly some younger women, children of Friends."[42] The top of the female hierarchy often failed to convince poor women. But such talk about the nature of female sin and female social choices exclusively among women, some empowered with formal communal and religious authority, was itself very unusual in early America.

Using the same marriage inspection skills, Martha Thomas inspected seven migrating women and wrote their removal certificates. Aside from these forty inspections, she visited all the Quakers households in Radnor township on two occasions, and all the Quaker households in Merion on one occasion (non-Quaker households were often included). Each occasion took four months to complete. In each visit, she led a family devotion, discreetly advised the household members, and gathered information for possible disciplinary action. The Chester and Welsh Tract women's disciplinary and visiting committees were constantly abroad. In 1700, it was reported, for example, that "Gainor Roberts and Sarah Evans have visited Friends and found things well and better than when they first went about. . . . " In 1704 Ellen Foulke and Ellen Evans reported "that they visited Friends' families at North Wales and they have nothing to report."[43] By 1720, the Welsh Tract Monthly Meeting had grown so populous that "preparative meetings" were held in each township a little before each monthly meeting. Each of these meetings had one or two overseers to collect or receive information on discipline problems, to correct them locally if possible, and to report intractable cases to the monthly meeting. From 1720, Martha Thomas was named overseer at Radnor township "to inspect conversation." The Radnor Monthly Meeting also asked Martha Thomas on seven occasions to counsel personally younger and older women with severe problems in "conversation." In 1712, for example, she and Margaret Ellis were asked to "advise a young woman" about the bad company she was keeping.[44] In all of these situations, Martha Thomas had to be a good mother, often a good spontaneous minister, and often had to draw on her knowledge and experience as an exemplary wife. She always had to be a tender, female embodiment of "holy conversation."

Many mothers asked women like Martha Thomas for specific advice about difficult childrearing cases. For example, in 1724 the Radnor women reported that "Hannah J. desired Friends of this meeting's advice in relation to her daughter Mary, and it seems to be the opinion of several Friends in this meeting that her mother should encourage her to come and settle somewhere among Friends where she might be under their care and instruction, hoping thereby she might be reclaimed and reconciled to Friends again." Having given this advice, which expressed implicit confidence in the spiritual and ministerial effectiveness of the Quaker community of women, the women followed through by sending "Lowry Evans to go along with Katherine Griffith to speak to Mary . . . concerning her outgoing and to encourage her not to absent herself from meetings, although it were a cross to her, but to take it up and to despise the shame. . . . "[45] A disciplinary system which asked wrongdoers to "despise the shame" was unusual. In most early American communities, discipline usually rested on rituals of shame or humbling authoritarian violence, often a blend of the two. However, the Chester and Radnor matrons thought tars and feathers, or their various sartorial equivalents like white sheets and wands, superfluous apparel. Instead, they tried to appeal to the Light in disobedient women, and the men did also with men.

The women's meeting's elders required no invitation to help mothers with problem daughters. In 1721 the Welsh Tract Women's Meeting sent Katherine Jones and Sarah Evans "to talk to Sarah . . . concerning her daughter's conversation." The committee reported that Sarah" . . . seemed tender and loving and said she was sorry that she gave way to anything that was a dishonour to truth or gave trouble to Friends. . . . "[46] If a mother or her daughter showed loving contrition, the women's meeting would visit a sinner for months, occasionally years, without recommending disownment. Though the committees talked only officially to the daughters, such gentle committees even invaded widower's households, if they housed daughters in spiritual danger. Katherine Jones and Sarah Evans, peccant daughter specialists, were sent in 1720 to "advise Rowland's daughters concerning their misbehaviors."[47] Rowland was tenderly eclipsed, not nagged, scolded, or excessively respected.

The women's meetings also carefully oversaw the courtship behavior of young women. They made clear to women that they must never lessen their spiritual dignity by ever distorting their behavior or bodies to comply with the sinful demands or temptations of men. Although the elders spoke to young women chiefly about "the honor of truth" and the universal standards of "holy conversation," they mentioned occasionally the status of women within Quakerism. In 1750, for example, the Chester women complained about one young woman "for keeping idle, dissolute company to the scandal of her sex."[48] The elders wanted to erase the worldly notion that regenerate women were more likely to sin than regenerate men. The female elders were the autonomous guardians over the social network of Quaker women and they wanted that network to retain its spiritual status and effectiveness. Thus they condemned cheapened female postures no matter how innocent the circumstances. In 1713, for example, "Alice Pennell spoke with the young woman concerning the report that was made of the uncivil carriage which fell out at the time of her marriage, after she went home, in taking off her garters, which is a practice not allowed by Friends. . . . "[49] The female elders issued no licenses at harvest time. The Chester women helped disown an unrepentant young woman in 1720 "who was overtaken with strong drink last harvest and was seen dancing with a man's jacket on."[50] The standards of spiritual womanhood in the Welsh Tract and Chester were tightly defined and universally enforced.

On 18 occasions the Welsh Tract Women's Meeting sent Martha Thomas to the quarterly women's meeting, where the top wives and mothers discussed Quaker family policies and problems. In her last report in June 1726, as she, Mary Jones, and Ann Jones rode to the women's quarterly meeting, they summarized their yearly accomplishments and goals: "both first day and week day meetings pretty well attended, the poor are taken care of, and in the general things are indifferent easy; and a remnant is concerned that love and charity may abound and our discipline more fully to be put to practice to delivery that truth may prevail and prosper with love."[51] The maternal metaphor—the delivery, survival, and prospering of truth with love—was appropriate; these women had borne and bred 21 children between them. Also appropriate was their assumption that their responsibility included, not just women, but the whole community. If a Quaker gent wished to remain part of Quakerism, he had to marry a woman who was, usually from infancy, under the guidance of the women's monthly meeting, and whose character was then carefully considered, inspected, and approved by the leading female elders before marriage. After marriage, the gent would have to understand that his wife's behavior would continue to be overseen by the women's monthly meeting whose committees would frequently visit their household.

Over a period of thirty-three years, Martha Thomas was to be seen perched side-saddle on the finest horse Chester County could provide, traveling on committee assignment over the Pennsylvania flatlands to identify, uproot, and dissuade "carnal talk," and few other women in colonial America had more domestic authority or more wide-ranging domestic knowledge than she and her associates. As a testimony to Martha Thomas and their own spiritual importance and self-confidence, soon after she died in 1721, the Welsh Tract women collected a book of elegies about her character and ample career, and had it published in Philadelphia.[52] In the title of this work, they noted that Martha Thomas was a wife, mother, and elder, roles that might be kept discrete elsewhere but which were conflated into one ministering Christian presence in her person and career.

LEADING Welsh Tract and Chester Quaker men actively encouraged holy wife-minister-mothers by providing such social reproductions with love, money, and prestige. Though poor and single women could not rise in the female monthly meeting hierarchies and would have a difficult time in the male controlled Delaware Valley economy, they could become ministers, Once they did, they usually attracted wealthy men. Crudely put, wealthy men pursued them, at least one across the Atlantic Ocean, with flattery, love, and money. For Chester and Philadelphia County Quaker farmers, a wife's ministerial gift promised delightfully effective spiritual mothering of themselves and their children; and prestigious, joyful spiritual companionship. The richest Quaker farmers thus eagerly sought such "talented vessels," who brought marriage portions more valuable than gold.

The female ministers most active from 1690 to 1765 in Chester County and the Welsh Tract were Elizabeth Ashbridge, Margaret Ellis, Jane Hoskens, Grace Lloyd, Margaret Miles, Rebecca Minshall, Susanna Lightfoot, Elizabeth Levis, Alice Pennell, Elizabeth Richards, Mary Smedley, and Sarah Worrall. Aside from being "talented vessels of truth," they lived on the best farms with the wealthiest husbands, and maintained the most deeply convivial and disciplined households. These fourteen ministerial women's husbands were ranked fifth of 46 ratepayers on average in their respective townships. Seven of these women's husbands were the wealthiest or second wealthiest in their towns. In Edgemont, the wealthiest, second wealthiest, and third wealthiest men all had ministerial wives.[53]

The Delaware Valley female ministry, nonetheless, did not compose a closed order of rural Quaker plutocrats into which only the daughters or wives of the richest farmers might enter. Indeed, three of the top twelve ministers began as déclassé household servants and then, after cultivating themselves as spiritual vessels, married the Delaware Valley's wealthiest farmers on terms apparently dictated by these women themselves. Excluded by their gender role from the worldly marketplace, Quaker women found the ministry, intentionally or not, the major vehicle of upward social and economic mobility. Through advantageous marriages, female ministers' talents became well integrated into the combinations of wealth, religious prestige, and elegant domestic control which ordered eighteenth-century Philadelphia's rich near hinterlands.

Three upwardly mobile women, Elizabeth Sampson, Susanna Hudson, and Jane Fenn, lived the reality, however exceptional, from which Chester County females' Quaker dreams and roles were made. During their own day, their stories became legends which instructed women about their proper roles in Delaware Valley society. Whether the rewards were control of material wealth, social prestige, or eternal salvation, Quaker women in Chester and the Welsh Tract were taught by such women's success to seek to rise only with the spirit.

Cinderella: Susanna Hudson was born in 1720 in northern Ireland to a penniless Quaker household. She spent her youth in hard laboring domestic service. She became a minister at the age of seventeen. In 1741 Hudson married a poor linen weaver, Joseph Hatton. They opened a huckster's shop in Lisburn, Ireland, but her husband carelessly went bankrupt when she was nursing their first birth, twins. Another Irish Friend, hoping to keep her affecting ministry active, found the Hattons a small farm in nearby Lurgan on a three-year lease for an affordable rent. During these years, a witness noted, "her husband kept two looms going and she kept two cows, and they saved a little money. . . . " After discovering, as their lease ran out, that the other local tenant farms were prohibitively expensive, they decided to move to Pennsylvania. "Divers Friends were so affected with the thought of her leaving them, that they contributed their cares and endeavors to get them resettled among them." Irish Quakers paid the apprenticeship fees for all of her sons. Soon after her husband died in 1759, Hatton traveled on a religious visit to America, bankrolled by £15 annually left to her by another Irish Friend.

Her ministry impressed Chester County farmers, especially Thomas Lightfoot. He traveled in 1765 to Ireland in order to court and marry her. He took her to Pikeland, Chester County, where he was the township's second wealthiest farmer and the owner of a sawmill (his brother owned the local gristmill). Just before she died, Susanna Lightfoot said, "this I would have my Friends to know in the land of my nativity, as some there (though very few) said I should grow proud, if ever I grew rich; therefore, I would have them to know (not for my sake but for the precious testimony's sake) that the southern breezes have not yet soothed so as to make me forget myself; it is true, this has been a pleasant spot to live in, with an agreeable companion, and I believe it was nothing short of the good Hand which so provided for me, but my heart has not been in it." Susanna Lightfoot was certainly no less innocent for being recruited into the Chester County elite, but was hardly less a member of that elite for being so charismatically an innocent wife-minister-mother.[54]

Pygmalion: Jane Fenn was born in London in 1694 to modest Anglican parents. She was an intelligent girl, interested in theology, and "of a cheerful disposition, and having a turn for music and singing" (the "Holy Spirit" often chose women who could sing well like Fenn and Ashbridge). She became sick at the age of sixteen and decided to give her life to God, if it was prolonged. There were few religious careers open to young poor Protestant women in London, so an inner voice told her, she wrote, "If I restore thee, go to Pennsylvania."[55] Against her parents' advice (her father shrewdly suspected she wanted to become a Quaker), she emigrated in 1712 by borrowing £12 from a Welsh neighbor, Robert Davis, who was on his way to Philadelphia with his wife and family. Fenn's inner counsel also wisely told her to reserve the sale of her labor. As a result, Davis had to "wait till I could earn the money, on the other side of the water; for which, he accepted of my promise, without note or bond, or by being bound to indenture, in the usual manner."[56] Fenn worked in an Anglican Philadelphia household, but she disliked their nagging requests for a pleasant song. Because she refused an indenture from Davis to serve in another family she disliked, Fenn went to jail. Some of her friends soon paid Davis, released her from jail, and persuaded her to accept a three year position as a schoolmistress in a wealthy Quaker household in rural Plymouth township. Fenn converted to Quakerism soon after and received her first inner instruction to become a minister, at which her "outer tabernacle shook."[57]

    In order to become a Quaker minister, a young woman without any family tradition in the ministry, especially an Anglican by birth, had to pay her dues internally and externally. Fenn wisely refused to speak in meeting. For months she was in a dramatic state of spiritual agitation, often seeming to rise and speak in meeting, but swallowing her words and sitting down, making herself an object of pity and interest. Fearing her inner demand to speak, she often conspicuously absented herself from meetings and then explained her inner turmoil to concerned, sympathetic elders. When she finally did say a few words in meeting, her audience was probably relieved. Her lilting voice and inspired intelligence, moved by the Light, also affected the whole meeting.[58] Fenn's economic options widened once her ministerial potential became known. She moved to Haverford, where she hired herself out on a monthly basis as a housekeeper and where she also spoke occasionally a few words in meeting. She waited on her inner divinity to tell her where to settle permanently. At one Welsh Tract Meeting, David and Grace Lloyd, the richest people in the countryside, visited from Chester. Fenn's wise inner voice told her to settle with them. A few years before, the politically defeated speaker of the Assembly had moved from Philadelphia to Chester, partly in order to re-establish his political clout by cultivating rural Friends. In 1719 Lloyd was assessed in Chester at over three times the tax assessment of the second highest rate-payer, Benjamin Head. Grooming a young female minister in their household could recommend the Lloyds to pious country people and God. An inner voice told the Lloyds at this meeting to take Fenn "under their care, and nurse [her] for the Lord's service, with a promise that his blessing should attend them."59 Unaware of the Lloyds' inspired eagerness to have her, Fenn agreed to serve nearby in the household of Benjamin Head, the second richest man in Chester. After Fenn's first attendance at the Chester Meeting, Grace Lloyd asked her home. After mingling well with the local Quaker dignitaries and some visiting ministers (an informal job interview), Fenn was asked by the Lloyds to join their household. They made her their head housekeeper, gave her the keys to the silver, linen, and pewter chests, presented her proudly to their guests, and sat her at their dinner table, not with the lower servants. She became a confidante of Grace Lloyd, who was closer in age to Fenn than to her husband. Although she did some managing and account-keeping, and by so doing gained knowledge of the inner workings of an exemplary Quaker household, Fenn essentially held a sinecure.

With the Lloyds' backing, Fenn now spoke often and lengthily in Chester meetings, developing as a female "city-upon-a-hill" as she put it.60 Her meteoric rise naturally earned her envious "outward enemies, who waited for my halting; but, blessed by the mighty arm of power, that supported me through all, and preserved my feet from falling into the snares which were laid for me."61 Well supported by Lloyd money, Fenn began in 1722, at the age of twenty-eight, eight years of nearly uninterrupted ministerial work, traveling and speaking in Maryland, Virginia, North Carolina, Barbados, Rhode Island, Nantucket, Massachusetts, Long Island, New Jersey, Delaware, England, and Ireland. She returned to Chester in 1730 a celebrated minister. David Lloyd had died and had left her an income. She lived with Grace Lloyd at Porter House—a stately Chester mansion with a full staff of servants. In 1738, Jane Fenn married Joseph Hoskens, an upcoming Chester merchant and, inasmuch as she had no children, she apparently dictated the terms of the relationship. Hoskens moved into the mansion, assumed ownership under contract from Grace Lloyd, and managed the grand dames' money. Jane (Fenn) Hoskens returned to ministerial work in 1744 by divine direction and on her own money. During the rest of her life she also spent much time with her rich husband among the orchards of her splendid and fragrant Chester County home. Having started as a household servant in debt, Fenn had risen after only seven years in Pennsylvania, by the age of twenty-five, to near the top of Chester County society, and culminated her career only ten years later. This self-made (or God-made) woman was Chester County Quakerdom's spiritualized, rags-to-riches female equivalent of Quaker Philadelphia's secularized Benjamin Franklin.[62]

Beauty and the Beast: Elizabeth Sampson was born in Middlewich, Cheshire, in 1713. Sampson eloped at the age of fifteen with a stocking weaver, who died five months later. Her mother shipped her off to Quaker relations in Dublin. The lively young woman, who had a flair for dancing and singing, hated the strict discipline imposed by her Quaker uncle (Irish Quakers had earned a reputation for severity in discipline). Therefore, Sampson bound herself to serve in America, and landed in 1732 with sixty other Irish servants in New York City. She became the object of her master's sexual advances. Because she fended him off, she was badly treated and then slandered. She almost joined a traveling theatrical troupe, but, instead, impulsively married a poor Anglican schoolteacher who, as Sampson later noted, "fell in love with me for my dancing; a poor motive for a man to choose a wife, or a woman a husband." As was her habit, she followed impulse with conscientious self-discovery and realized she was trapped. She decided to follow her husband's rule, having no alternative, while exploring God through Bible study and observing various religious groups.[63]

After her husband moved them to Long Island, New York, Elizabeth's religious conscience began to torment her. Elizabeth had maternal relatives in Pennsylvania and she went to visit them; she found they were Quakers (they lived within the Chester Monthly Meeting) and found them cheerful, kind, and agreeable. She began attending meetings and loved them. She found a school-teaching job for herself and one for her husband in Chester. She sent for him, though she did not tell him about her Quakerly surroundings and commitments. When he finally arrived, Elizabeth Sampson noted, "I got up and met him, saying 'dear, I'm glad to see thee.' At this, he flew into a rage, exclaiming, 'the devil thee, thee; don't thee me.' "[64] The war was on.

The schoolmaster won the early battles. He arranged for them to live at the house of a local Anglican churchwarden, and on the advice of the local Anglican minister, the schoolmaster decided to remove her from this Quaker dominated area, and headed south. On the way, they entered a tavern in Wilmington, Delaware, and her husband entertained "the company with my story, in which he told them that I had been a good dancer, but now he could get me neither to dance nor sing." Sympathizing with the wronged husband, one of the company fetched his fiddle. Her husband started to dance with her, but this time Sampson passively resisted. He "pulled me round the room, till the tears fell from my eyes, at the sight of which the musician stopt, and said, 'I'll play no more: let your wife alone.' " Elizabeth Sampson had turned a ritual of communal suppression against herself, against her husband. She had engaged in her first act of conjugal passive resistance and had won by answering the Light in her male lynchers. She was exhilarated, "my soul was again set at liberty, and I could praise him."[65]

The couple found jobs in Freehold, New Jersey, another Quaker stronghold. With this considerable advantage, and with a growing sense of her own self-confidence and her husband's emotional dependence, Elizabeth Sampson grew determined, whatever the fuming of the outer man, to appeal directly to his inner susceptibilities. "I had now put my hand to the plough," she noted, "and resolved not to draw back." Though he beat her and threatened her with a pen-knife, she told her husband she was going to go to meetings and she went. He got the local Anglican minister to promise to engage her in debate; she smiled at the news, and the minister missed his appointment. The schoolmaster stopped going to Anglican services. He grew resigned, and one sabbath, lying on his bed, thought, "Lord, where shall I fly to shun thee?" and went docilely to pick up his wife at meeting. He began to attend meetings, though he left as soon as his wife rose to speak. Finally he stayed. Now only his male friends had to be defeated, "they used to come to our house, and provoke him to sit up and drink with them, sometimes till near day, while I have been sorrowing in a stable." Elizabeth Sampson had made passive aggression into an art; she could have less dramatically arranged, on stag night, to visit a friend or confronted him openly. Seeing her quietly suffering, he dispersed his friends and told her, "come in, my dear; God has given thee a deal of patience: I'll put an end to this practice," and he did. He "frequently in a broken and affectionate manner . . . condemned his ill usage of me." She was triumphant and relatively content, "the only desires I had were for my preservation, and to be blessed with the reformation of my husband."[66]

The schoolmaster became addicted to drinking. Sampson "murmured not; nor do I recollect that I ever uttered any harsh expressions, except on one occasion." When her drunk husband returned one evening, "and finding me at work by a candle, he put it out, fetching me, at the same time, a box on the ear, and saying, 'you don't earn your light.'" Sampson "at this unkind usage, which I had not been used to for the last two years . . . was somewhat angry, and said, 'thou art a vile man.'" He hit her again, but soon "went on in a distracted-like manner, uttering such expressions of despair, as that he believed he was destined to damnation, and he did not care how soon God struck him dead." Elizabeth Sampson: "in the bitterness of my soul, I broke out into these expressions, 'Lord, look down on my afflictions, and deliver me by some means or other.'" Now feeling especially unloved and hopeless, the school-master ran to Burlington, got very drunk indeed, and enlisted to go as a common soldier to Cuba in 1740. He soon missed his wife and her principles among the bellicose male society in the tropics. He refused to fight on pacifist Quaker principles at the scene of battle. His officers beat him, denied him decent food; he got sick, and died at Chelsea Hospital, in London. Elizabeth Sampson felt guilty about her dramatic words, "a thousand times I blamed myself for making such a request," she noted. Her primary commitment was to Truth, however. Beneath her meek, sweet, cheerful exterior was spiritual iron: "I have since had cause to believe that he was bene-fited by his rash act, as, in the army, he did what he could not do at home:—he suffered for the testimony of Truth."[67]

Her dramatic and failed marriage did not bring her censure; she had meekly crushed her husband's sin, and she earned her earthly reward. Quaker communities needed strong, meek, talented wife-ministers like Elizabeth Sampson, who could lead even intractable husbands to surrender to Truth. After her husband left and died (and it took some years to determine that he was, in fact, dead), she remained a minister in New Jersey, confined by poverty (he left her £80 in debt) to her locality. In 1746 she married Aaron Ashbridge, a pious Quaker and the second wealthiest farmer in Goshen township, Chester County. Being brought up by a pious Quaker mother, Ashbridge was used to living with female spiritual authority, and they found that "the company of each other was dear and delightful." Again she or the community's needs dictated the terms of the marriage. His money, emotional support, and appreciation allowed her to expand her ministerial range. She became a traveling minister and died on a mission to Ireland in 1755. She was memorialized as one of the most spiritually acute females in Chester County, Pennsylvania.[68]

RESPONSIBLE male Delaware Valley country Quaker leaders did not pursue, reward, and celebrate such talented women so handsomely from pious gallantry or pity, or entirely from emotional dependencies, but also from emotional knowledge that their religious familial and social order would collapse without the full development of such women's charismatic talents. Just as the relatively non-coercive Quaker social order needed adequate property to retain and tame children, it needed expert, hard-working female vessels of seemingly meek purity to embody and communicate "holy conversation" in intimate and public relations. Whether pedigreed or recruited, the female spiritual aristocracy was paid well and served well. If ministers, they spoke constantly in local and distant meetings. If elders, they informed mothers, disciplined daughters, repeatedly visited and gave spiritual performances in every household, and kept the marriage discipline. Authorized as "mothers of spiritual Israel", women indirectly but intimately affected every Quaker male. No other early American social order defined women so sharply or so effectively. In other colonies poor female servants might survive or be crushed by flaunting their sexuality, but perhaps only in the Delaware Valley could they rise to the top of society by sanctifying it.

SAMPSON, Hudson, and Fenn were not the only talented or known Delaware Valley women. The rural Quaker communities in the Delaware Valley were clear exceptions by 1730 to the rule that eighteenth-century middling women were among those who were "hidden from history," contributing people who were buried anonymously in patriarchal corporate family economies. In the Delaware Valley, the fame of middling women was contemporaneously exposed. Rural Delaware Valley monthly meetings, husbands, children, preserved letters, diaries, dying words, and memorials offer hundreds of private revelations to display these women as exemplary wives, mothers, female elders and ministers. In 439 pages, in a compilation of contemporary monthly meeting memorials dealing exclusively with early and middle eighteenth-century Delaware Valley Friends, *A Collection of Memorials Concerning Divers Deceased Ministers and Others of the People Called Quakers* (Philadelphia, 1787), women attracted 50 of the 162 entries or 31 percent. Not quite sexual equality among the religious elite, but still over 200 pages about charismatic women. The eleven volumes of John and Isaac Comly's *Friends Miscellany: Being a Collection of Essays and Fragments: Biographical, Religious, Epistolary, Narrative, and Historical* (Byberry, Pennsylvania, 1833–39) presented nearly five volumes of lovingly preserved contemporary minutiae about eighteenth-century rural Quaker women from Philadelphia, Bucks, and Chester counties and from scattered sites in New Jersey. No similar body of literature exists for any other colonial women, none is nearly comparable.

This literature simultaneously celebrated women, "holy conversation," and intimacy. According to this literature, much of these female ministers' and elders' spiritual authority was revealed chiefly in charismatic, intimate relations. Delaware Valley Quakers believed in a single, authentic, human expression: "holy conversation," and therefore conflated public and private domains easily. But even such religious doctrine cannot entirely explain why children and husbands so frequently preserved information about even the facial expressions of women. Clearly the sexual and emotional power of women had been shaped and used in new ways.

By penetrating her houshold routines and marriage, the Gwynedd Monthly Meeting, for example, explained their esteem for Ellen Evans, a Welsh immigrant in the 1690s, the wife of a minister John Evans, and a Welsh Tract elder in her own right. According to them, she was an infectiously energetic, happy, faithful matron, who liked to rise "early in the morning and encouraging others so to do, often observing that those who lay late, lost the youthful beauty of the day, and wasted the most precious part of their time: that the sun was the candle of the world, which called upon us to arise and apply to our several duties." After morning chores, she walked, except on meeting days, into her chamber "with a Bible or some religious book; where a portion of her time was spent alone; from which retirement she often returned with evident tokens that her eyes had been bathed in tears." She loved to read about early Friends and tried "to cultivate the same disposition in her family. . . ." As a wife, mother, and elder, she was zealous, but "she thought it safest rather to incline to the merciful side; firmly believing that the grace of God which bringeth salvation, had appeared unto all men. . . ." She was a tender and loving wife, who supported her husband's ministerial career and was particularly "a great support and comfort to him under his spiritual conflicts about the time of his appearing first in a public testimony." The whole community seemed to know that her husband and children, encased in her love and energy, simply obeyed her.[69]

Other female elders and ministers also held regular Bible readings and silent devotions in their households, and, like public ministers, shared the deep pleasure of their immediate revelations with their children. After a prolonged period of feeling God only at a distance, Alice Griffith of Gwynedd (c.1740), "one morning, after calling her two daughters, said, 'put by your work my children, for I have to tell you of a glorious visitation the Lord has pleased to favour me with.'"[70] Except during such trials of faith, many intimates testified that most of the great mothers were irrepressibly cheerful. The Middletown Monthly Meeting said of Grace Croasland (1703–69), "being married young, she early entered into the cares of a family; and being religiously inclined, and of a cheerful active disposition, approved herself well qualified for such a charge."[71] All the other elders were also gifted with cheer and serenity. David Cooper described his wife Sybil (Matlack) Cooper (d. 1759) as "a most kind and affectionate wife, a loving and tender mother . . . a graceful person, favoured with many precious endownments,—of a sweet natural disposition, a courteous and engaging deportment, being remarkably calm and steady."[72] Abraham Farrington converted swiftly to Quakerism after he joined the amiable household of Benjamin Clark in the 1730s, "I thought [says he] they were the best people in the world, careful in their words, yet cheerful and pleasant, so I thought I must be a Quaker."[73] He yearned for a Quaker wife and home of his own.

According to a host of witnesses, such joy and serenity were even present at death. Dying was the final spontaneous, public

performance of female elders' intimate ministry. Children, husband, and many Friends gathered around the dying woman's bed
and scribbled down her final words. Few female elders failed to use
the occasion to justify edifyingly their lives by expressing their
serene faithfulness. In 1708, dying Eleanor Smith of Darby told her
family, "I can freely give up husband and children and all this
world, to be with the Lord, whose presence I feel flowing as a river
into my soul."[74] "My husband is gone," Mary Haig said on her
death bed in 1718, "but I shall not long be a sorrowful widow; yet
not my will but thine be done; my speech fails apace; sweet Lord
Jesus, thou hath loved me from a child, and I have loved thee ever
since I knew thee, and my case is no doubtful case." She felt
confident that the Lord had "kept me sweet and clean all along
since I knew the truth."[75] Immediately before she died in 1750,
Lydia Dean, daughter of Joseph Gilpin of Birmingham township,
said, "it was the joyfullest day she ever had."[76] If more poignant
than usual, the best women's death-houses remained cheerfully and
convivially intimate, the medium of their families' moral educations.

In order to implant truth deeply within their children, female
elders relied primarily on faith in "holy conversation" and example, not in the artifices of explicit instruction and punishment. As a
Mount Holly, New Jersey female elder told her daughters, "strive to
turn their attention to that eye which ever beholds them, and sees
their secret thoughts—and this will consequently produce an awe
upon their minds that will more safely preserve them from sin, than
all the formal rules and restraints you can lay them under." She
argued that if a mother was a true vessel of "holy conversation" she
could control her children with little art: "your countenance will be
an awe upon the family, as well as your example to them; then
disorder and confusion will not find room therein."[77] Many female
elders apparently approached this standard, if their husbands are
any guide. James Moore of Sadsbury, Chester County, praised his
second wife as "no brawler, nor lifted up with pride; but one that
ruled well her own house, having her children and household in
subjection with gravity."[78] Elders and ministers thought deep affection was the best conduit through which "holy conversation"
flowed to husbands' and children's hearts. Working as a country
schoolmistress in 1713, Jane Fenn kept full control over the young
children with love, "my love to them was great,—and theirs equally
so to me, so that all my counsels were obeyed with pleasure." Love

never left a residue of fear, anger, or insincerity, thought Fenn, "and afterwards, when we met," she noted, "we could tell one another of it, with sincere regard and affection. They proved sober men and women."[79]

Not all of the finest rural mothers had the sustained charisma, nor their children the adequate attention-span, to make simple faith and maternal success synonymous (on doctrine, the best mother could have evil children). Thus, the memorial literature shows that even the best mothers held in reserve a repertoire of artful skills: restraining, admonishing, praying, advising, reproving, and occasionally lashing. The best mothers were stubborn, if gentle, authoritarians, not indulgent wafflers. Tough, mild, instrusive, plaintive moral endurance was often exemplified. Her monthly meeting praised Dinah James (1699-1766) as "an example of plainness herself, and careful prudently to suppress the contrary in her children, as long as they remained under her care, meekly dissuading in a moving manner, against any appearance of corruption in conversation, as well as the world's vain fashions and superfluity in dress, firmly maintaining parental authority in this steady resolution which she never departed from, that while her children were cloathed at her expense, they should submit to have their cloathes fashioned agreeable to her mind."[80] Phebe Smith was also known for being a tough but meek maternal minister. Born in Bucks County in 1737, her son Samuel Smith noted, "I was favored to have a mother who labored in much love not only to counsel, but to restrain from evil." When her advice failed to reorganize his sinful core, noted Smith, she suddenly and conspicuously became "engaged in fervent prayer that her counsel might be as bread cast upon waters, that might be found after many days."[81]

Praying over the child or husband was a frequent tactic, and other mothers often told their children about the prayers they could not hear. In 1765 cheerful Grace Croasland introduced her letter to her children, as "a few lines to you, my dear children, whom I have often mourned and prayed for; that the Lord might preserve you from falling into many snares of Satan; and my concern still remaineth for your preservation and steady watch against any appearance of evil."[82] By this time her children were well grown; she had been conspicuously praying and mourning over her children for 35 years. Especially visible and dramatic in suffering for her children was Ann Whitall of Red Bank, New Jersey. Her libertine Quaker husband took their sons fishing during the summers, sometimes on meeting day. "It is one of the greatest troubles I meet with," she noted in 1760, "I go with a heavy heart if my children don't go to meeting nor their father. But I must drink bitters. Oh, the bitters that I have to drink. Oh, the wormwood and the gall, and overwhelmed in sorrow every day I live." Her diary apparently often received what her husband and children would soon hear upon their return," . . . and I don't expect to see another summer, I am hardly able to go about the house, but my chief concern is about my children. Oh, if they may be preserved out of wickedness. . . . " She lived another 37 years from the day of this entry.[83]

The best maternal ministers also chose their last words carefully and heroically to hammer inward the advice they had continuously given their children. In 1766, five weeks before she died from consumption, Mary Moore wrote the following crafted letter to her grown, eldest son, Thomas Atkinson:

> My dearly beloved child: I am now in a poor state of health, not knowing that I may ever see thee again, but I am willing to let thee know my mind concerning thee. I cannot write much, but let it sink the deeper in thy mind. My prayers have been put up, days and nights, to Almighty God, for thy preservation, and my advice to thee hath been frequent, as thou knowest. I think I may say, I have done all that I can. I have discharged my duty, and am clear on thy account.[84]

After getting this curt, final notice, Atkinson sped to her bedside, and again "she told him in a very affecting manner, that she had said all she could say, and had done all she could do for him; and also expressed her clearness in regard of her duty on his account." She treated young neighbors more indulgently. A young woman who approached Moore's bed was told, "I am glad to see thee, for I have often thought of thee, I see something good in thy countenance, and I want thee to improve it."[85] On the other hand, Anna Webster of Plain Field, New Jersey, who died in 1762 at the age of 36 with young children, sweetly told her eldest son (still a child), "my dear child, let it never be said of thee, 'the foxes have holes, and the birds of the air have nests, but the son of man hath not whereon to lay his head.'" She also asked attending Friends to "notice her husband and children in their distress, and watch over and advise her children, not sparing to tell them their faults."[86] The best maternal ministers adjusted their words to the situation. Webster's children were still too young for the total impact of maternal silence.

The best mothers could wield the rod. A Chester County minister who raised her children in the 1710s, Elizabeth Levis told her matured children, "speaking of my own experiences . . . a tender, natural parent, that is truly concerned for the welfare of his children, when pleasant things will not do is under a necessity to use the rod, or more severe measures." On the other hand, the emotional context was important and also the use of compensatory rewards, "but when the child submits, such a parent rejoices; and administers that which is good to his child, according to his ability." Then, in a starkly reductionist passage, Levis likened God to a parent like herself, who manipulated emotional dependence to teach virtue, who "may see in his wisdom, at seasons, to hide his face a little, as behind a curtain, for the trial of our faith and love,—yet he will appear again; and when he appears, his reward is with him. . . ." Levis then apologized for being absent on ministerial travel.[87] However, the voluminous literature did not make much of lashing. A monthly meeting, for example, praised Betty Caldwell who "after the death of her husband in 1720 . . . had the care of the family upon herself, remaining in a state of widowhood upwards of 37 years, in which station she behaved with such prudence and circumspection, that her conduct, in bringing up her children *without much correction*, is worthy of imitation."[88]

Reforming husbands also elicited the rural women's most refined skills. In such cases corporal punishment and restraint had to be eliminated from their repertoire. In most other ways, however, reforming husbands and children drew on the same cultivations in women. No other group of coeval colonial women were better skilled at this art nor treated with such respect and gratitude by their charges. Many eighteenth-century Delaware Valley men praised their wives more warmly than their wives ever praised them. They particularly praised the almost maternal spiritual and emotional support and instruction they received. James Moore was particularly fond of cheerful, pious women; he wrote a lengthy memorial, "concerning his four deceased wives," praising each highly. His first wife, Ann Starr (d. 1761) was supportive, "a dutiful and loving wife, tenderly sympathizing with me in times of probation, affliction, or distress, either inwardly or outwardly, often giving me a word of comfort in the needful time." His second wife, Mary Atkinson (d. 1766), was his spiritual friend and authority, "thou that I much preferred to myself in piety and virtue . . . thou that was often concerned for my everlasting peace, and wast my chief delight in the world."[89] Edward Bradways noted of his wife Elizabeth, whom he married in 1761, "I can freely acknowledge, that in our first out in the world, she far exceeded me in a religious care, in attendance of meetings for worship, both on first and other days of the week." By constantly prodding him and being his example, she helped him toward obedience and he judged it "a great favor from the Almighty."[90]

Some men regarded submission to pious women as antecedent to their religious salvations. Born in 1731 in West New Jersey, Joshua Evans "was much under the care of my mother; and being her eldest, she kept me to wait on her until I was nine or ten years of age." He liked to ride "on the same horse with her to Evesham Meeting, of which [we] were members." He appeared destined at the age of fourteen, however, to join the world of men as a bricklayer's apprentice. On the way to service, he met an inquisitive old man who advised him, "be sure to be kind to your mistress, and keep in favour with the women." Evans accepted this advice and never refused to "go at the command of my mistress" and felt sorry for "apprentice boys whose trade exposed them to ramble through the country, and occasions them, at times, to be with vicious company," meaning male company. Nevertheless, after gaining his freedom, Evans joined "airy young company," and even acquired some worldly habits. However, after he married Priscilla Collins in 1753, he "was more easily weaned from my old associates than I had expected." He and his wife made his full reformation a joint project, "sometimes my wife sat with me in silence, shedding our tears together, when no words were spoken, and pouring out our prayers to a gracious God, in secret." They succeeded: Evans became one of the most observant ministers in the Delaware Valley.[91]

Even the most powerful men thought wife-reformed men manly and lucky. Samuel Fothergill, the youngest brother of the famous Quaker London physician Dr. John Fothergill, was a young reprobate by Quaker standards and was on the verge of being disowned by his pious father. Samuel Fothergill fell in love with, and in 1738 married, Susanna Croudson, a Quaker minister, fifteen years his senior. She reformed him to the delight of all. In 1739, Dr. John Fothergill wrote to his new sister-in-law commending her for the fine work in "restoring us a brother, and in part making him what he is." "I doubt not," noted Dr. Fothergill, "but his affection will engage him to regard whatever thou shalt think he ought to do;

for I cannot but believe that his quick and steady progress has been, and yet will be, greatly promoted by thy watchful, affectionate concern for him." Samuel Fothergill was twenty-three and his wife was thirty-eight.[92] When Samuel Fothergill grew up religiously, he became a major Quaker minister, who among other deeds traveled through Chester County between 1754 and 1756 calling for the reformation and purification of Quakerism. Was Susanna Croudson the wife, mother, or minister of Samuel Fothergill? The question is really unfair: she was clearly all three simultaneously.

ACCORDING to this eighteenth-century literature, many rural Delaware Valley women had by 1750 finely honed their characters to instruct both husbands and children. This literature, celebrating the exercise of female moral authority through selfless love within intimate circumstances, appears anachronistic in view of current scholarly understandings. It was not New England or the nineteenth century. Seemingly, "Marmee' and the March girls from *Little Women* had left their impoverished nineteenth-century Concord home in a time machine to save males' and children's souls among bountiful fields of grain in eighteenth-century Pennsylvania. Insofar as it was recollective, this literature may have revised past realities. Late eighteenth-century monthly meetings' and Quaker descendants' reminiscences of their Quaker mothers and grandmothers did gush. Yet virtually all of this literature was published in the late eighteenth century, many decades before the cult of domesticity arose among innovative New Englanders. Much of it is contemporary. Furthermore, early and mid-eighteenth-century evidence largely corroborates the stories and character portraits produced by these women's husbands, meetings, and descendants, and so does the social structure of the Chester and Welsh Tract communities. It is the modern historians who have created the impression of anachronism, and some confusion, with their arguments that New England Puritanism under the pressure of modernization (the American Revolution, textile mills, etc.) originated selfless, loving, domestically authoritative women. Though the domesticated female role of "true womanhood" or "truth womanhood" did evolve during the colonial period in the Delaware Valley and in New England, it clearly first reached full and unambiguous reality by 1750 in the Delaware Valley among the wealthiest and hegemonic rural women of one of early America's richest urban hinterlands. New England women would later use literary and economic talents developed in a society with a more variegated social role for women to create the fiction to nationalize, sadly or not, the Quakers' more constrained and focused female role.

CHAPTER SEVEN

Saints and Republicans

By 1750 the Welsh Tract and Chester Quaker communities reached their apex of exemplary communal development, reconciling wealth, productivity, tenderness, and holiness like no other people had in North America. By this time they were already attracting the attention of the French philosophes and continued to be the darlings of Pennsylvania voters. The province they ruled was luring more European immigrants than any other, and their city Philadelphia was growing faster than any other North American city. They had clearly made Quaker domesticity a force to contend with. Between 1750 and 1790 the Pennsylvania Quakers did little to discredit the system of domesticity that they had created. The secular growth of Pennsylvania continued unabated. And the Quakers made the spread of domesticity more likely by essentially surrendering their patent rights. During this period the Quakers decided that the holiness of their households were more important than the power they might accumulate by winking at the problems domesticity presented to a religious people. The Quakers conscientiously limited their growth, increased their distinctiveness from people of the "world," and resigned from political power. By 1790 the Quakers were an innocuous sect, and domesticity was open to exploitation by less sensitive consciences, including those of republican reformers eager to build a powerful, expanding nation.[1]

The second generation's problems reached definition in the middle of the eighteenth century; they provoked a group of exacting American and English Quaker reformers who blamed second-generation parents for corrupting the next Quaker generation with wealth. The reformers confirmed their view by noting that local meeting elders often refused to disown children for marrying outside of meeting. Such a policy, they argued, was increasingly polluting the Quaker household, the fountain of nurturing "holy conversation." Reformers became disgusted at the "mottled" composition of Quaker disciplinary meetings which included Friends married to non-Friends or the children of such suspect unions. In 1754 the reformer Mary Peisley demanded that, if reform was to proceed, half-breed Quakers must depart meetings for discipline, "otherwise we believe it will be building [the walls] up with the rubbish, which will never stand to the honour of God and the good of his people."[2] This spiritually tribalistic reform movement ended Quaker expansion, contributed to the loss of the Quakers' political power in Pennsylvania, and stigmatized second-generation Delaware Valley Quakers as spiritually unworthy of their fathers and mothers.

The reformers held the elders, including the aging, wealthy, ruling patriarchs and matriarchs of Chester and Philadelphia County, largely responsible for the spiritual emasculation of the Quaker household. Describing the second generation as "settled in ease and affluence," Samuel Fothergill noted that "a people who had thus beat their swords into plowshares, and the bent of their spirits to this world, could not instruct their offspring to those statutes they had themselves forgotten." The reformers wanted to save the rising generation from the evil of their fathers and mothers. "As every like begets its like," noted Fothergill, "a generation was likely to succeed formed upon other maxims, if the everlasting father had not mercifully extended a visitation, to supply the deficiency of their natural parents." "As it is hard to lift up a hand against grey hairs," recognized Fothergill, "my progress has been more difficult and afflicting than I can express."[3]

Fothergill used the rod, however. Writing in 1755 from East Nottingham, Chester County, Samuel Fothergill savaged the reigning Quaker eldership as being "not only dry, but very dry." "Many are the painful steps amongst the dead and dying I have tread," he continued, "the heritage seems in some places almost laid waste, through the negligence of those who call themselves watchmen, who appear to me the very tail of the flock, and it seems as if, whilst the people have made the outward wilderness as a fruitful field, the plantation and garden of God have been made as a neglected desert and barren wilderness."[4] Fothergill sent the same bitter news to his wife in 1755, "the greater part of the more advanced in years are rather obstructions than helps in the way, and must be removed before the family will be rightly replenished and strengthened from the living fountain."[5] Writing to Susanna Fothergill in 1755, William Logan repeated this ugly view of Chester County meeting leaders and elders: "Truth is at a low ebb in those parts, especially amongst elders and those of advanced years, great deadness and barrenness appearing amongst them in most places, which has caused some hard, affecting service to thy good husband."[6] John Churchman, a middle-aged Chester County minister, also flayed his aging contemporaries: "In many places there is a young generation coming up who will take the burden willingly upon them, not of constraint but of a ready mind, and the work will prosper in their hands, though at present they may be reproached by such souls who . . . know the anointing is upon the young . . . though departed from themselves, because of disobedience—and who are more jealous and spiteful than such at times are?"[7]

While spiritually demanding, these reformers' attacks were unfair to well-meaning and confused Chester County parents and leaders. Aside from being more forgiving of irregular marriages and enjoying more material comfort, the second-generation Welsh Tract and Chester elders were no more materialistic than their parents had been. George Smedley, Jr.'s house did contain comforts by 1765 that were typical of many second-generation households: many feather beds, walnut tables of various sizes, 22 chairs of various kinds, some 20 books, a desk, a tea table, a large mirror, a couch, and especially a large clock (costing £5 by itself).[8] His father, George Smedley, Senior, an original Quaker settler of Willistown, Chester County, had lived far more simply the year he died in 1723. His clothes were stored in two old chests. He owned only one long table and only three chairs. He ate with pewter spoons and without a table cloth or napkins. His inventory failed to mention any books. Probably because all of his children were portioned, he owned but one bed and sparingly farmed his 200-acre plantation. Yet, George Smedley had been an acquisitive frontiersman. He had purchased 250 acres in 1684, had owned 350 acres by the end of the 1690s, and had distributed 600 acres by deed and will to his five children.[9] Reformers regarded such mammoth real-estate acquisitions as a righteous escape from poverty, but they thought the second generation's walnut encased clocks only chimed the end of Quaker innocence.

Second-generation Chester and Welsh Tract Quakers did lose more children to the "world" than their parents had. About a quarter of their children married outside the Quaker discipline (109 of 465 surviving children) compared with 13 percent of their parents' surviving children. Of all the second generation's children who married, 28 percent married outside the Quaker discipline compared with 14 percent of their parents' marrying children. In their parents' generation, 59 percent of the households (41 of 69) experienced no discipline problems, but only 39 percent of the second-generation households were unblemished by a wayward child. Of course, such losses were collectively minor from most secular and most religious perspectives: after all, 72 percent of their children who married, married within meeting, and the major problem with wayward children was only marrying non-Quakers or marrying other Quakers without going through meeting procedures. Inasmuch as Quakerism was their religion, however, not their social strategy, they had to protect the meeting and the household as interrelated sacred institutions. They made sincere and holy conduct, particularly familial conduct, serve as a replacement for the rituals of formal observance, sacraments, and professions of faith that preoccupied other religious groups. They placed full responsibility for the nurturance of "holy conversation" upon intimate relations, particularly those within the home. They could only perilously trivialize, evade, or tolerate even slight deteriorations in their households' educational effectiveness and purity. In the face of Quaker parents' love for their children and the community's stringent requirements of Quaker familial purity, the question of whether or not to disown children who merely married irregularly became a disturbing and ultimately crippling religious, and even political, issue of love and conscience.

Second-generation Chester and Welsh Tract meetings did everything they could to get parents to control their children. Meetings denounced unsupervised youthful gatherings. In 1730 the Gwynedd Meeting typically noted: "This meeting being sorrowfully affected with the prevalence of undue liberties such as shooting matches, singing, and dancing, and the like disorders which too many youth fall into; we can do no less than recommend it that all parents, masters, and mistresses, overseers, and other faithful Friends to discourage and crush the growth of such disorders as

much as in them lies."[10] In the Radnor Meeting a delinquent youth
was cited in 1759 for being "disguised with spirituous liquors,"
"frequenting shooting matches," and as a consequence of "consum-
mating his marriage before a priest."[11] The meetings harshly disciplined brothers and friends who conspired with marriage delinquents. In 1749, Uwchlan Meeting complained of "M.M. for
marriage by a Priest to one not a member of our society without his
parents' consent, and of his brother George for accompanying
him."[12] Jacob V. was denied a certificate to West River and later
disowned, because an investigation uncovered: "That he acknowledged going with F.H. to Philadelphia and told Robert Charles that
Thomas Minshall was willing and had given consent for the said H.
to marry his daughter and so obtained a license, and when that was
done went with them to the priest, and when he came home denied
that he had any hand in assisting them."[13] When such efforts failed,
the meetings took to arguing and pleading with youth. A best-
selling book in Chester and Philadelphia counties was Moses West's
small book arguing the case against marriages between Quakers and
non-Quakers. In 1738 the Chester Men's Monthly Meeting ordered
"a hundred and twenty of Moses West's books respecting mix'd
marriages" and distributed them among the young men and women
of their communities.[14]

Second-generation parents usually supported the discipline
against their children. Only three parents were disciplined between
1730 and 1765 for conspiring with their children to evade the marriage discipline. Five sets of parents in Chester, Goshen, Gwynedd,
and Radnor meetings did ask for delays and reconsiderations. The
case of Josiah L. who cohabited with Sarah A. was extended four
months on the request of his father Samuel, but Josiah was eventually disowned.[15] Only a few parents left Quakerism with their children. Goshen Meeting reported that in 1747 that they received "a
paper from Thomas and Mary D. wherein she together with her
husband, because of a disgust they have taken at the Men's Meeting
for disowning their son J . . . , request to be no longer deemed as
members in unity with us."[16] Such requests and desertions may have
persuaded the Radnor and Chester meetings to become slightly
more lenient. In the first generation, 70 percent of those children
among the reconstructed families who married irregularly or committed related sexual infractions were disowned in the Radnor and
Chester meetings; among the second generation's offspring in 93
second-generation Welsh Tract and Chester reconstructed families,

only 57.1 percent of those who committed related infractions were disowned.[17]

The real problem was that domesticity was visibly unsuited—at least by the uncompromising standards of purity and conscience which the Quakers had to keep—to the growing inequalities and commercialization which Quaker domesticity had promoted in the Pennsylvania economy. Unlike their parents, second-generation Radnor and Chester leaders and their communities faced an unheroically treacherous economic and social environment for Quaker domesticity. Despite general prosperity, growing inequalities of land and personal wealth within the Quaker communities increased differing opportunities in the Quaker marriage market for wealthy Quaker children and poorer Quaker children. The increasing commercialization and articulation of the mid-eighteenth-century rural Pennsylvania economy freed youth from prolonged dependency upon their parents and thereby encouraged many Quaker youth, particularly many poorer Quakers, to select the liberal promises of Quaker family ideology and of the Pennsylvania economy. While accumulating their own wealth, they defied their parents and the community by marrying non-Quakers and Quakers outside of meeting discipline. Another reason elders came to accept the acknowledgments of irregularly marrying Quaker children more readily was probably that an overwhelming majority of erring Quaker youth were relatively poor.

ANALYSIS of 93 reconstructed second-generation Welsh Tract and Chester Quaker households shows a prosperous community unable to protect an increasing number of their children from either the lures or deficits of a vibrant, but complicated, economy.

The second, wholly American, Quaker Radnor and Chester generation did enjoy health and stability. Chester County household heads continued to live to ripe old ages. The mean age of death of 43 of 93 second-generation Chester and Welsh Tract household heads studied (those which could be known) was 63.2 years. Only 18 percent died in their thirties or forties, and almost 40 percent lived to be seventy or older. Seventy-five of the 93 families studied maintained a residence in one place from the date of formation to the death of the father. A slight majority (52 percent) remained within the jurisdiction of the parents' monthly meeting, living in Merion, Haverford, and Radnor, or Springfield, Middletown, Edgemont, and Chester. Five families, all of Welsh extraction, moved into Darby, and the remainder lived in towns west of their parents' homesteads, mostly on land their parents had bought for them in townships like Goshen, Willistown, Bradford, and Tredyffrin. Of the few families who did not maintain one residence, two became city-dwellers in Philadelphia, two moved out of Pennsylvania (one to Virginia and one to North Carolina) and the remaining 14 households moved their homes within rural Pennsylvania. Based on 93 reconstructions of second-generation Welsh Tract and Chester families, the average number of children to reach twenty-one years in second-generation families was 5.53 compared with 5.11 in the first generation.

A comparison of the probate inventories of 80 Welsh Tract and Chester Quaker households before 1730 with those of 69 Welsh Tract and Chester Quaker households between 1731 and 1776 shows the material enhancement, though not gentrification, of "holy conversation." Although well supplied with land, Quaker households before 1730 tended to live, like George Smedley, rustically. They slept on nice beds, but stored their goods in trunks, boxes, and chests. They ate on pewter plates with spoons and hands, rarely with knives and forks. After 1730, the average personal estate rose from £192 to £331. Although rarely luxurious, "holy conversation" at home was dignified by helpful equipment: 70 percent more rural Quaker households after 1730 owned a chest-of-drawers, 30 percent more owned desks, 37 percent more owned clocks, 45 percent more owned large looking glasses, 20 percent more owned books, 430 percent more owned teapots and tea sets, 24 percent more owned table linen, and 33 percent more owned knives and forks. Before 1730 the average rural Quaker household had three chairs but after 1730 the average household owned almost ten chairs. Quaker households not only enjoyed on average an additional bed, but stored their goods in chests-of-drawers and cupboards. They increasingly used table linen and ate with knives and forks and kept their food piping hot in chafing dishes. They more frequently enjoyed teatime with china cups.[18]

Compared with those of their parents, second-generation Quaker households tended to give or sell less land to their children. The settlers had handed over an average of 701 acres to their children, but the children gave only 400 acres to theirs. Second-generation Welsh Tract and Chester Quaker farmers had begun with as much land as their parents had, but failed during their lifetimes to increase their holdings half as much as their parents had. The settlers had given 72 percent of their sons an average of 278.3 acres, the second generation gave 64.7 percent of their sons an average of only 151 acres. Most of the second generation's sons got less than 200 acres and over 60 percent got less than 100 acres or no land whatsoever. The land the second-generation farmers gave was, however, more valuable per acre. The settlers' children had received vast tracts of fertile, unimproved, inexpensive land which they were responsible for clearing and improving. Ninety percent of the land second-generation parents gave was largely cleared and had a house and barns upon it, and often contained profitable capital additions. For example, in 1735 Daniel Humphry gave his son Edward only 60 acres, but the land was furnished with a limestone dwelling house and a fulling mill.[19] Close to 10 percent of the land handed out included major capital additions: mills, mineral works, two or more tenants. With an increasing provincial population making more tenants available and increasing the market for food and consumer goods, few Welsh Tract and Chester children had to worry about poverty. The increasingly commercial nature of bequests and gifts subtly altered, nevertheless, sensitive relations between Quaker parents and their children.

Second-generation households necessarily injected more commerce into their children's lives. Only with great difficulty could second-generation Quaker rural businessmen convert the production of their farms into land supplies similar to those their parents had accumulated. Though the price of land and the price of wheat, the major crop of Philadelphia and Chester counties, both rose from 1685 to 1770, the price of land rose at a much faster rate. Between 1689 and 1770, the price of wheat rose 40 percent per bushel, but the price of unimproved land in Philadelphia and Chester counties rose 377 percent per acre.[20]

A few Chester County farmers did expand their agricultural operations with servants, slaves, and hired laborers. Some Quaker plantations dwarfed anything seen in the settlers' lives. Ellis Davis of Goshen, who died in 1774, had listed in his inventory "two fields of wheat about 70 acres," valued at £46. He also had £35 worth of previously harvested wheat which according to average yields would have been the product of some 53 additional acres. He used at least 60 more acres to feed his large herds of cows, sheep, and horses. He used at least 183 acres annually for a yearly income of over £100.[21] Similarly Thomas Pennell of Middletown earned £201 annually from crops and livestock, the produce of at least 200 acres of fully cultivated land.[22] The wheat barons, Pennell and Davis, stayed abreast of rising land prices by dramatically expanding their farming operations.

Most Quaker farmers planted much as their parents had. Second-generation middling Quaker households produced on average £22.4 worth of wheat, while first-generation middling Quaker households produced on average only £15.8 worth of wheat. Richer Quaker households increased their production less dramatically, however. As their probate inventories show, second-generation farmers used on average from 52 to 75 acres annually compared with the settlers' average use of 60 to 80 acres annually—little difference. The unit and total value of second-generations farmers' produce rose. Considering, however, that commodity prices doubled between 1720 and 1760 and that the price of land quadrupled, the small increase in the value of second-generation produce simply illustrates the failure of second-generation farmers to compensate successfully for the inflation of land prices by increasing agricultural production.[23]

Not surprisingly, compared with their parents, the second-generation experienced somewhat greater inequalities in landholding and markedly greater inequalities in personal wealth.[24] No matter what the differences in their landholdings, the settlers had lived in similarly rustic material surroundings. The articulation of the Pennsylvania markets and economy allowed their children to develop visibly different ways of life according to wealth. By 1760, John Carter, an Aston blacksmith, had no other furniture but two beds, a couch, a desk, a small table, and a few chairs. He had 249 acres to distribute to his four sons and daughter.[25] In nearby Chester, in 1757, William Pennell's household was more lavishly run. Pennell owned 4 beds, 2 chests-of-drawers, 3 tables, 3 couches, 18 black and blue chairs, a large mirror, a green carpet, a large clock, a silver watch, a clothes press, and tea furniture. His family went to meeting in a handsome riding chair (£15). He had 525 acres and £412 in bonds to distribute to his four sons and two daughters.[26] His wife, Mary Pennell, was a recognized Quaker minister. Interestingly, all six of William Pennell's children married inside the Quaker meeting, while only one of John Carter's five children did.

Poorer Quakers, an increasing percentage of the Chester and the Radnor meetings, could not afford the price of labor to increase their profits and landholdings. Of the 66 second-generation Chester and Welsh Tract inventories analyzed, 18 farmers or 27.2 percent owned servants or slaves, only a slight increase from the 24.4 percent of the settling farmers who owned servants or slaves (6 percent of the second-generation farmers owned slaves compared with 5.2 percent of the first generation). Expense was an issue. Among the richest families (first quartile) that had younger children (all children under 21 years when the father died), four of six had servants or slaves listed in their inventories. Among upper middling families with younger children, five out of twelve had servants or slaves; among middling families with younger children, four out of nine had servants or slaves; and among lower middling families with younger children, none of seven held servants or slaves.[27]

The list of imported servants into Goshen township suggests that only about half the Quaker rural population thought servants affordable. The list covered servants imported into Pennsylvania who were purchased in Goshen township (the list does not include servants born in Pennsylvania) between 1736 and 1772. Seventy-five rate payers lived in Goshen in 1753; only seventeen had purchased servants. Though a few ratepayers in the bottom 30 percent of the tax list purchased servants, the richest households in the town accounted for the purchase of over half. Ten men whose tax assessment was over five shillings bought twenty-six of them or 57 percent. Yet, over this 36-year period, fifty-eight (or 77%) of the farmers did not buy any.[28]

Some poorer Quakers chose to migrate to places where land prices were lower. The causes of Quaker migration might be illustrated by a relatively famous case of Chester County childrearing failure and emigration, Benjamin Franklin's first business partner, Hugh Meredith, a Welsh Tract farm boy. Simon Meredith had placed his son in Keimer's Philadelphia print shop, where Benjamin Franklin, the recent Boston emigrant, was also working. The abstemious and persuasive young Franklin helped Hugh Meredith curb his severe drinking problem. With gratitude and parental shrewdness, Hugh Meredith's father offered to invest £200 in a printing partnership of Hugh Meredith and Franklin with the tacit understanding that Franklin would benefit his son morally. When Simon Meredith failed to raise £100 of the promised money, other likely Quaker investors refused to bankroll Franklin when they heard reports of Hugh Meredith again "drunk in the streets, and playing low games at alehouses." In 1730 Hugh Meredith resigned the partnership, freeing Franklin to attract investment, and he told

Franklin, "I was bred a farmer, and it was folly in me to come to town and put myself . . . an apprentice to learn a new trade. Many of our Welsh people are going to settle in North Carolina, where land is cheap. I am inclin'd to go with them, and following old employment." He concluded that his father "has really been disappointed." Franklin in 1731 printed in his *Pennsylvania Gazette* two articles by Hugh Meredith describing first-hand the geography of the Cape Fear region of North Carolina.[29] Spiritual and personal problems, like those of Hugh and Simon Meredith, attending the new economic articulations in southeastern Pennsylvania stimulated Quaker migration to the southern backcountry and Quaker reformers' efforts of purification and redefinition.

Migration was pursued more often by the second generation's children than by the second generation itself. As Larry Dale Gragg has thoroughly shown, between 1711 and 1800, 1,260 southeastern Pennsylvania Quakers moved down the Great Philadelphia Wagon Road, past Lancaster and York, across the Potomac River, and into northern Virginia, settling mainly between Winchester, Virginia, and the James River in the Piedmont region. This land rivaled that of southeastern Pennsylvania in fertility and was much cheaper. In 1774, for example, land in Frederick County, Virginia, sold for 30 shillings per acre while land in southeastern Pennsylvania sold for over 3 pounds an acre. The great Quaker migration down the Great Wagon Road failed to lure, however, many second generation Welsh Tract and Chester fathers and mothers. During the 1750s, when Pennsylvania land prices were dear, only 93 southeastern Quaker Pennsylvanians moved to northern Virginia. Fifty-seven percent of these migrants were single people, some of them children of the second generation. The migration accelerated dramatically in the 1760s, when 291 Quakers moved south, and in the 1760s 60 percent of the northern Virginia immigrants were married people and most had children. Gragg argued that shrinking economic opportunities in Chester and Bucks counties primarily spurred this movement. Inasmuch as economic opportunities, when commercial options are included, were not declining, Gragg's formulation needs refining. Chester County families (no more than 5 percent at most) began moving south when they began experiencing or fearing childrearing "failures" due to the newly diversified, consumer-oriented economy.[30]

Most second-generation Quaker households, in order to compensate for higher land prices, chose to remain near Philadelphia and to diversify their economic operations in the cause of protecting their children. Second-generation families bought more bonds, had more investments, rented more land, and followed more occupations than their parents had. The settlers had also been commercially oriented: 45.5 percent had owned bonds. According to their inventories, however, 51 percent of the second generation owned bonds in increasing amounts: Thomas Pennell owned £1,468 worth and William Trego £404.[31] First-generation investments were confined to land and loans, but second-generation farmers found additional opportunities: a farmer John Davis owned an interest in a Wilmington bank, Jacob Vernon an interest in the Thornbury schoolhouse, and Thomas Pennell one-eighth of a Wilmington brig.[32] Only two first-generation men (5%) got income from renting land, but 20 percent of their children received such income. Morris Llewellyn, Jr., got £12 annually from his tenant John Enoch; Jonathan Davies, a tavern-keeper, rented a farm for £15 a year; and Peter Worrall owned two lots in Chester Borough and received £1 annually for their lease.[33] Slightly more men pursued two occupations. The frequency of men with more than one occupation increased from 44.5 percent of the first-generation households to 51.5 percent, a majority, of 66 second-generation Quaker households in the Chester and the Welsh Tract meetings (female occupations were not counted in these figures). Mid-eighteenth century rural Quaker men were tradesmen as often as only farmers. The most common rural second occupation was blacksmithing, five households being involved, a carry-over from the first generation. However, new occupations appeared that reflected the rising "consumer" society in Pennsylvania: more innkeepers, clock-makers, gunsmiths, furniture-makers. Maintaining a consumer trade, as well as a farm, clearly helped many households protect their children. The average personal estate of men with two occupations was £402 compared with a mean of £264 for those with one occupation. Diversification was not a foolproof strategy, however, due to increasing competition. Despite carrying on a shoemaker's trade as well as a farm, Thomas Yarnell of Edgemont died in 1767, leaving a paltry personal estate of £70 for eight children, all in their teens and twenties.[34]

When parents gave their children capital instead of land, they also had to let their children build upon these gifts economically in order to have them enter successfully the Quaker or even provincial marriage markets. They had to ask their children to grow clever, gregarious, and self-disciplined in a Franklinesque fashion. Children "on the make" had to be increasingly freed from the dense web of economic and familial obligations that characterized the settlers' households. Quaker familial emphasis on tenderness, autonomy, and generosity under these new conditions produced numerous mildly delinquent children.

In order to see the effect of the new economic order on the Quaker family a number of families have been studied in detail. Seventy-two families have been arranged according to their average tax assessment, corrections being made for bankruptcies and men with occupations in which wealth would not be reflected accurately in the taxable categories of wealth: land, crops, and livestock. The average tax assessment was arrived at by averaging five tax assessments of the families and counting the highest assessment twice. The arrangement, needless to say, is a tool of analysis and the categories have no meaning beyond that.

The well-to-do remained the moral backbone of the Quaker community. The nineteen wealthiest Chester County Quaker second-generation families virtually replicated the form and effectiveness of the family system which a majority of Chester and Welsh Tract settlers enjoyed. These families gave 230 acres apiece on average to 90 percent of their sons. They gave their daughters an average of £75 as marriage portions, and 18 percent of their daughters also received land (almost no daughters received land in the first generation; this change was a sign that land now had a clear market value and was not merely a cheap raw material that required the owners' personal labor to make profitable).[35]

Though having less land to disburse than even middling Quaker households of the settlers' day, the household of wealthy yeoman Isaac Minshall of Providence nonetheless reproduced the economic relations of his father's household. Isaac and Rebecca Minshall lived in a pleasant house in Providence township on a large 408-acre plantation which Isaac had inherited from his father, Thomas Minshall. Before Isaac died in 1731, he had bought an additional 200 acres in Goshen from the profits of his farming and three-loom weaving business. He left seven sons and a daughter, ages seven, ten, thirteen, seventeen, nineteen, twenty-one, and twenty-three. In 1731 Isaac gave his sons, Aaron and Griffith, the 200-acre tract in Goshen to divide; Aaron also got the looms and Griffith some horses. His daughter Rebecca received £40, £20 from each of her older brothers, Aaron and Griffith. Isaac gave the 400-

acre plantation in Providence to his wife in trust for the four younger sons. After maturity, the four younger sons were to look after the financial and emotional welfare of their mother. With attractive land and capital, the Minshalls spun a web of obligations and generosity which was so typical of the settlers' families. They were rewarded; the only discipline problem occurred when Griffith Minshall, Isaac's son, married his first cousin. The meeting denied marriages among such close kin, and it took Griffith and his wife five years—from 1737 to 1742—to get the Chester Monthly Meeting to accept their profusive acknowledgments of sin. Despite Isaac's early death and the new economic complexity, the Minshalls largely remained in meeting, thanks to industry, mutual dependence, good planning, and wealth.[36]

By distributing capital goods as frequently as land to their children, wealthy families wisely adjusted to economic change. Daniel Humphry, miller of Haverford, gave one son, Samuel, 240 acres soon after Samuel's marriage for the discounted price of £60. The other sons got much less land: Joshua Humphry got 45 acres and one-half a grist mill; Solomon Humphry got 30 acres, a negro, and £30. Daniel Humphry owned five slaves and he gave a slave apiece to his daughters, Martha and Hannah. They also got £25 legacies paid by their brothers. The Humphrys were all obedient Friends, thanks as much to slaves and mills, as to land.[37] When there were no sons, as in the household of Jacob Edge, the daughters got productive goods: Abigail, Jane, and Hannah each received £53 and one-third of a grist mill. Two of three of these daughters married, both in meeting.[38]

The wealthy Chester County Quakers' family system was managed carefully: the average marriage age of the men was 26.6 and the women 25.4. Probably to help portion all children adequately, rich second-generation parents tended to hold their land longer than their parents had. Only nine of forty-two sons were given land by deed, another twenty were under age when their fathers died, so they received land at twenty-one. The land that sons received was all in Chester County, Philadelphia County, and in case of the two merchants, in Philadelphia. The township location of 17 gifts to sons can be known from wills: twelve of these gifts were in the same township as the father's plantation and the other five gifts were in nearby townships. For example, Thomas Smedley of Willistown was able to provide land for all four of his sons in Willistown: Thomas 250 acres; George 155 acres and bolting mills; John 400

acres; and Francis 233 acres.[39] It was more common for first-generation parents to give land in areas some distance from their home
plantations. After receiving land, twenty wealthy sons had some
obligations to pay off, usually to their sisters. The wealthiest second-generation Welsh Tract and Chester households were profitably as intertwined and mutually dependent as their parents had ever
been. These families were successful by Quaker communal standards. Eighty-three percent of the daughters and 84 percent of the
sons married, and they caused few discipline problems. Only 11
percent of the sons married irregularly and only 4 percent of the
daughters. Only five of nineteen families had any problems whatsoever. Of these peccant families two were led by Philadelphia
merchants, Robert Owen and Owen Roberts; they both had two
children marry irregularly. The other three families were led by
yeomen and each household had over seven children, and in each
household only one child married irregularly.

The next economic echelon of households (average assessments
from 6s to 9.5s) were less successful replicating the mutual dependencies of their parents' households and had more problems with
the monthly meetings. Being neither unendowed nor stingy, these
eighteen households gave an average of 144 acres to 81 percent of
their sons. They gave their daughters on average £47 as marriage
portions, and 20 percent of their daughters also received small
parcels of land.[40]

George Smedley, Jr., ran his upper-middling household of a
wife, six sons, and two daughters well. George Smedley had begun
with 265 acres from his father and accumulated a total of 567 acres
by the time he died in 1765 at the age of sixty-five. Smedley was a
prudent manager of his family's interrelated economic and religious
fortunes, though he suffered some setbacks. His sons, Joshua, William, and Caleb were portioned before George Smedley's death.
George Smedley gave his 29-year-old Caleb a deed for 91 acres in
1761 in Willistown for which Caleb had to pay only five shillings.
Working a farm too small to support obligations to his siblings and
father's household, Caleb lived as a bachelor for two years, prepar-
ing a marriage stake; he then married Elizabeth Blue, a non-Quaker,
and was disowned. Joshua was apparently given cash, not land,
when he appeared in 1753 as a "freeman" at the age of thirty in his
father's hometown, Middletown. He never married. William also
received a cash settlement by 1753 and he chose to marry a Quaker
woman, Elizabeth Taylor. The two daughters, Jane and Sarah, were

apparently portioned before 1760; both married in meeting. In 1760 the two remaining sons, Ambrose and Thomas, ages eighteen and fifteen, were at home. When George Smedley died in 1766 he gave Ambrose the 190-acre plantation with the condition that he pay his brother Thomas £50 in two years and maintain his mother at £10 a year. Thomas was an artisan: he received ten acres in Middletown, half a lot in Philadelphia, and £100. Ambrose married in meeting at the age of twenty-three, and Thomas married in meeting at the age of thirty-seven. This was a household operation very much like those of the settlers, though obviously run much less on land and much more on capital. George Smedley was able to keep his older sons at home until they were thirty because he had something to give them, and he did not begin portioning them until four years after his last child was born.[41]

The familial and "spiritual" consequences of new, compensatory capital bequests took its toll, however. Disciplinary success was ambiguous. Thirty-two percent of their sons (17 of 53) married irregularly and half of these failed to acknowledge convincingly. Such was true also for 24 percent of their daughters. Most households had a problem. Sixty-six percent (12 of 18 households) had at least one child marry or behave irregularly, and 27.7 percent had two or more delinquent children. At least no upper-middling household was a total failure.

Households with average assessments between 4s and 6s predominated in the second generation, there being twenty-eight such households in the sample. Half the sons in this bracket received an average of 102 acres. Other sons received cash gifts—on average £35. Only 2 percent of eighty daughters got land and landless daughters got on average only £30.[42]

Their children had to incur the economic and spiritual dangers of boosting their fathers' modest gifts into respectable stakes. Although J. M. was rated above the middle in Goshen township, he apparently gave his children too little substance to compete adequately. He had seven sons and a daughter; all the sons lived irregularly, only the daughter married as a Quaker. J. M. gave no land to his sons. Three of his sons never married, but were disowned for fornication, bastardy, and for going to war (probably for wages) in 1756 against the French and their Indian allies. Hugh Pugh's sons received £30 apiece and no land; none of them ever married. Benjamin Ellis gave his three sons 60 acres, 29 acres, and 30 acres respectively in Easttown. Not building well on these gifts, none of them ever married, and one son was disowned for debts. Benjamin Ellis's two daughters got £20 apiece and one, after moving to Wilmington, got married in meeting. Whatever his economic problems, Ellis was no pauper; he was assessed in 1747 at 3 shillings in Easttown, in the top half of the ratepayers. J. S. of Aston, a middling blacksmith, gave by deed his two adult sons 116 acres and 98 acres respectively; he asked each son to pay him £50. One son married out of meeting and the other son became a drunk and debtor. He gave his daughter Hannah £20; she married irregularly and was disowned.[43]

When T. E. of Gwynedd died in 1750 his eight surviving children were all twenty years or older. T. E. gave one son, Thomas, the 150-acre plantation; Thomas married at the age of thirty-two in meeting. The other sons had earlier received, in order: £30; £40 and a horse; £50; and £10 and livestock. Two of these sons remained life-long bachelors, one of whom was disowned for fornication. The remaining son married irregularly and was disowned.[44] Finally, Benjamin H. had four daughters: two married in meeting at the ages of thirty-one and thirty-four, and two remained spinsters. Among his four sons, he gave Daniel £2, but Daniel returned to Wales. Two enterprising sons, Joseph and David, received only four horses and £20 respectively; each was able to parlay these modest gifts into marriage stakes, and in their mid-thirties they both married in meeting. The last son John H. received when forty-three years old the 150-acre Merion plantation. He had married irregularly at the age of thirty-five, but had acknowledged his sin successfully. However, he was disciplined again in 1749 for denying a maintenance to his mother. Even members of this relatively successful middling household struggled to remain Quakers.[45]

Modest middling parental gifts clearly led to the deterioration in their children's obedience to Quakerly discipline. Seventy-two percent of the sons married, but 45.1 percent married irregularly: almost half. Daughters behaved better: 79 percent married and of these only 21 percent married irregularly. Nineteen or 67.8 percent of these families had at least one discipline problem, however, one-third had two children marry irregularly, and almost 20 percent had three or more errant children. These households were far from being poor, yet many were too modest to maintain involving obligations that would also give most of their children advantageous positions in the Quaker marriage market.

The eight poorest families had little success.[46] Sublimus Ellis's household was on relief; the other seven were self-supporting, though in the lower half of the tax lists. They were not objectively poor: a good percentage of their children married, 87 percent of the men and 89 percent of the women; but half the men and half the women married irregularly, and half these households saw three children or more marry irregularly. M. M. had eight children, three sons and five daughters, and M. M. lived to see them all disciplined. M. M., Jr., married irregularly at the age of thirty-three, but later acknowledged successfully. George M. married irregularly in 1747, later acknowledged successfully, and then was disowned two years later for helping a brother elope. Among the sons only John M. married in meeting. The daughters behaved worse. Hannah M. married irregularly at the age of seventeen; Mary M. was disowned for having a bastard; Margaret M. never married; and Rachel M. married her first cousin and was disowned. Finally, Susannah M. married irregularly in 1754, successfully acknowledged, and emigrated to Hopewell Meeting, Virginia.[47] These people were neither abjectly poor, economically unproductive, nor civilly evil: they were simply poor and sinful by the demanding standards of Quaker marital conduct and by the implicit economic standards of achievement enforced by the Quaker marriage market.

In summary, second-generation wealthy and upper-middling Chester Quaker households remained religiously respectable, though they had more problems than their seventeenth-century counterparts. Middling and poor families lost nearly half their children to the "world"; their difficulties signaled the excessively expensive standards of Quaker familialism even for Quakers living on nice farms in the middle of ample economic opportunities in their self-created garden spot, the Delaware Valley, Pennsylvania.

ONE SOCIAL curse for the Quaker discipline and for Quaker households in virtually every wealth stratum was the rise of the number of "freemen" or economically independent bachelors over twenty-one years in Welsh Tract and Chester towns.[48] The Pennsylvania Assembly had defined a tax category known as "freemen" in order to discourage stubborn bachelors, who were set aside to be taxed at a discriminatingly high rate. To qualify for this prejudicial position, a man had to be a bachelor, over twenty-one years, and had to be working for himself, not for his father, mother, or siblings. Among the Quakers, they were usually sons whose parents chose to let them live financially uninvolved in order to allow them freedom to earn their way into the Quaker marriage market. They became a major source of marriage delinquents and parental headaches.

In the seventeenth and even early eighteenth century, few "freemen" lived in these Quaker rural towns where youth was under exquisitively tender control. Goshen had two "freemen"in 1718 and four "freemen" in 1734; in 1753, however, the Goshen tax list showed 18 "freemen." Edgemont had 3 "freemen" in 1717, 1 in 1720, but 14 in 1734 and 13 in 1753. The jump in the number of "freemen" hit all the towns, but at different times. Ridley, for example, had only 6 "freemen" as late as 1734 and 13 in 1753. Tredyffrin had only 2 "freemen" in 1739 but 12 in 1753. Willistown went from having 6 "freemen" in 1748 to 14 in 1753. In 1715, the towns of Edgemont, Springfield, Upper Providence, Goshen, Ridley, Haverford, Radnor, Aston, and Middletown contained 29 "freemen;" in 1753 these nine towns had 105 "freemen." The population of households in these towns had doubled from 202 households to 408 households, but the number of "freemen" had almost quadrupled, a worrisome development for the Quaker guardians of gospel discipline and gentle control.

Nor can the increase of "freemen" be attributed simply to the libertine habits of non-Quakers who moved into these towns in greater numbers. It would be nearly impossible to know the religious affiliation of every "freeman" listed in the tax lists; men with the same surname were so common in Pennsylvania that such an analysis would require the reconstruction of virtually every family. However, by comparing the children of the sampled first- and second-generation Quaker families, the increasing frequency of "freemen" among Quakers is confirmed. Only 12.5 percent of the sons of the Quaker settlers appeared as "freemen" at least once. Among the sons of the second generation living in Chester County, 41 of 180 Quaker males (23%) were once classified as "freemen" during their lives. "Freemanship" happened most often in poorer families: 7 percent of the wealthiest households' sons, 20 percent of the upper-middling households' sons, 32 percent of the middling households' sons, and 35 percent of the poorest households' sons were once "freemen" in Chester County. At some point, many poorer parents had to give their sons freedom to earn their way into Quaker adulthood and marriage on their own effort.

"Freemen" were as a group more rebellious than the sons of any particular wealth stratum. Of all the Quaker "freemen" who married, 54.2 percent married out of Quaker discipline. Among the 4s to 6s middling wealth group, for example, there were 26 "freemen," most of whom had received only enough property or capital to begin to accumulate a marriage stake. Ten of them married in meeting; 10 married out of meeting; and 6 remained bachelors. Most struggled economically: they married at an average age of 31 years (75% of them in their thirties) compared to an average age of 28 years for all the sons in this wealth category. In 1753, Thomas Massey, Sr., released his 28-year-old son Thomas, Jr., with a little property and Thomas, Jr., became a "freeman." Thanks to hard work, Thomas, Jr., was able in 1774, at the age of thirty-nine, to marry within meeting. Many enterprising and unenterprising "freemen" did not wait on the Quaker marriage market, however. Peter Taylor died in 1740 and left each son £15. The sons became "freemen": John in Upper Providence in 1748 and Joseph in Caln in 1756. John Taylor never married and Joseph Taylor married out of meeting. In 1756, Joseph C., son of John C. of Aston, also became a "freeman" in Caln. Three years later he bought a 116-acre plantation from his father for £100. Three years later, in 1763, Joseph was disowned by the meeting for excessive drinking and debts. When he died in 1753, Benjamin E. of Easttown left 60 acres to his son Ellis. Ellis took up the plantation seven years later and became a "freeman" of Easttown. He was disciplined by the meeting in 1763 for fisticuffs and in 1765 for excessive debts, but was not disowned. In 1772, Ellis moved to Deer Creek in western Pennsylvania; he was 33-years-old and still unmarried. In 1756 Lewis J. became a "freeman" of Radnor; he owned a 42-acre farm and was 24-years-old. He was disowned for marrying a non-Quaker thirteen years later and for excessive drinking. In 1756, Thomas E. released his son Griffith, age 29 to become a "freeman" in Radnor. Thomas died four years later and left £50 to Griffith. Two years later Griffith married irregularly and left Pennsylvania. The liberal American idyll of the young male on the make spelled trouble for Quaker communities: "freemen" married late in life frequently married out of meeting and often never married at all.

"Freemanship" was, of course, more a symptom of relative poverty than a free-standing social institution. A collation of discipline and the portions given to 200 of the second generation's children shows indeed that more than mere freedom from familial obligations, the sons and daughters' economic situations were most decisive in determining which families and children would give headaches to parents, meetings, and the expectations of Quaker communities. Rich male children were three times better formal Quakers than their poorer brethren; rich women made obedient Quakeresses twice as often as poorer females (see Appendix: Table 7). The institution of "freemanship" had some independent impact, however. Sons were a greater discipline problem than daughters, and there were no "freewomen" in the Delaware Valley, no evidence that Chester County parents were prepared to give their daughters some property and freedom with the hope that they would earn portions to lure wealthy Quaker husbands. Whatever the correct admixture of poverty and freedom in the brew that poisoned so many well meaning, tender Chester County Quaker households, the Pennsylvania economic system failed to provide adequately for the Quakers' formal ethics and the household and meeting system that produced them. The irony was that the near hinterlands of Philadelphia remained one of the most prosperous and opportunity-rich areas in eighteenth-century Anglo-American society.

THIS SOCIALLY engendered childrearing crisis lay at the core of a far-reaching reform movement within eighteenth century Anglo-American Quakerism. Jack Marietta asked the essential question: "How did the reformers who numbered only a score or so before 1755 manage by 1775 to more than decimate the membership of the Society and to enlist most of the remainder in the struggle for reformation?"[49] The reformers were not alien beings, but simply the settlers' most spiritually and ethically talented children and grandchildren: John Churchman, John Griffith, Samuel Fothergill, William Brown, John Pemberton, Israel Pemberton, Sophia Hume, Elizabeth Wilkinson, Joshua Evans, George Churchman, Mary Peisley, Benjamin Ferris, William Logan, Anthony Benezet, and John Woolman, to name a few saints. They were certainly full of energy and insight. George Churchman between 1760 and 1763 recorded 124 journeys to visit worship meetings other than his own. Daniel Stanton and John Pemberton decided in 1757 to visit all the Quaker families in Philadelphia and vicinity, and they had visited by 1760 more than 500 households. Between 1755 and 1775, more than 34 English Quaker ministers, most of them reformers, visited the Pennsylvania Quaker heartland; they converted to the reform cause some formerly "libertine" Quaker leaders, particularly the powerful Pemberton clan: Israel Pemberton, clerk of the Philadelphia Yearly Meeting: John Pemberton, clerk of the Philadelphia Yearly Meeting for Ministers and Elders; and James Pemberton, clerk of the Philadelphia Yearly Meeting for Sufferings. The reformers gained control of the higher strata of the Society's disciplinary apparatus with such conversions and they used their power effectively.[50]

In September 1755, a Philadelphia Yearly Meeting committee of fourteen, including John Churchman, Samuel Fothergill, and John Woolman revised the disciplinary code. The Yearly Meeting also appointed a committee of thirty-one to inspect quarterly and monthly meetings' responses in order to ensure that the "corrupted" monthly meetings carried out the new code faithfully. For the same purpose, the Philadelphia Yearly Meeting ordered that at least once every three months every single meeting read a list of queries about the behavior of Friends, and report their answers to their quarterly meetings which in turn reported to the yearly meeting. To further jog the disciplinary system, the yearly meeting ordered that each monthly meeting appoint a select meeting of ministers and elders to be answerable to the quarterly meeting of ministers and elders. Jack Marietta has fully recorded and documented the dramatic results. In 1756, the "disciplinarians of the Society discovered 64.1 percent more violations of discipline than they had in 1755." While the number of violations increased significantly, the percentage of those pardoned after 1756 remained relatively constant, meaning simply that more and more Friends were disowned. The yearly meeting adopted in 1761 the additional draconian policy that in case of "irregular marriages" monthly meetings should no longer tenderly solicit acknowledgments but should proceed quickly to disowning, allowing the delinquents to seek pardon on their own initiative. Thus, between 1756 and 1760, only 52.7 percent of marriage delinquents were disowned, while the percentage of disownments of an increasing number of delinquents rose to 67.3 percent in 1761-5. The reformers' efforts emphatically retired older Quaker leaders' plans of building an expanding Society of Friends in Pennsylvania which could retain political and social hegemony. Between 1755 and 1776, the Pennsylvania meetings disowned 3,157 Quakers, some 21.7 percent of its 1760 membership. Between 1761 and 1776, 1,426 Quakers were disowned for irregular marriages alone, some 11 percent of its 1760 membership. The Society also lost the children of these newlywed ex-Quakers, so the impact of these disownments on the Society's population was much greater than even the net figures.

Retired was the notion that Quakerism could ever be a universalistic, instead of select, movement.

The reformers also added new testimonies and revitalized older ones. Introduced by female Quakers like Elizabeth Levis in the early 1750s, the reformers moved against the production, distribution, and the use of alcoholic beverages made from grain. Meetings had previously disciplined drunk Quakers while not mentioning the alcohol. However, in 1777 at the request of reformers from the Philadelphia Monthly Meeting and the Western Quarterly Meeting, the Philadelphia Yearly Meeting ordered that Quakers could not produce or sell liquor. Quakers involved in such businesses had to leave them, and Quakers could not drink liquor or sell grain to distillers. The Society also slowly accepted the keen ethical perception of John Woolman and other reformers that slavery was a hideous institution and that immediate abolition was the only Christian response. Chester County Quakers had long been suspicious of slavery, but had been frustrated in the their polite efforts to restrict it in the first half of the eighteenth century. In 1758, however, the reform influenced Philadelphia Yearly Meeting ordered that any Friend who purchased or sold a slave could not participate in the business of the Society, including discipline, unless he or she showed satisfactory and sincere repentance. Finally, in 1774, the Philadelphia Yearly Meeting decided to disown any Friend who bought, sold, or transferred slaves. On the pain of being excluded from any role in the Society's business, all Quaker slaveholders had to prepare their slaves for freedom with religious and secular education and they could hold them no longer than white indentured servants were typically held. The reformers made the Quakers the first religious group in Western society to advocate and practice thorough abolition.[51]

The Society of Friends' adoption of abolition as a policy and their crisis of childrearing and discipline were significantly related. As J. William Frost and Jean R. Soderlund have pointed out, eighteenth-century Quaker reformers active in the Delaware Valley can be divided roughly into two overlapping groups: those like John Churchman, the Pembertons, Samuel Fothergill, Catherine Payton, Sophia Hume, John Griffiths, and Mary Peisley who were primarily interested in restrengthening the marriage discipline, and those like John Woolman, Anthony Benezet, and David Ferris who were primarily interested in issues of humanitarian conscience like slavery and poverty.[50] By closely reviewing the whole history from

1681 to 1780 of Quaker anti-slavery thought and activity in the Delaware Valley, Jean R. Soderlund has shown exactly why anti-slavery Quaker humanitarians like Woolman politically required the support of the "tribalistic" reformers to finally get much of their abolitionist platform adopted by the Society of Friends. Analysis of the childrearing problems of Chester County Quaker households suggests why the "tribalistic" reformers had conscientiously and politically to adopt abolitionism. As Soderlund's careful analysis of Chester County slaveholding shows, wealthier settlers bought slaves in the early eighteenth century to clear their fields but, alarmed at the implications, testified through the Chester Monthly and Quarterly Meetings against the slave trade. During the eighteenth century, slaveholding slowly dwindled among Chester County Quakers. When the German and Scots-Irish servant immigration was curtailed by the wars in the 1750s, however, wealthy Chester County Quakers began again to purchase slaves. By the mid 1750s many Chester County meeting leaders were again slaveholders.[53]

During this period, the "tribalistic" reformers were essentially demanding that poorer Quaker parents, who could not afford slaves, accept the disowning of their working children by meeting elders whose more leisured children almost invariably married inside of meeting. Such children were often visibly benefited by land and money supplied them by the labor of their wealthy parents' slaves. Once the issue was raised by men like Woolman, the Society could hardly morally or politically justify an ugly process of holy slaveholders disowning the sinful children of poorer Quakers. The Society painfully worked through a type of conscientious exchange: for the sake of Quaker purity wealthy Quakers would surrender all their slaves, and poorer Quakers would surrender many of their children.

The reformers also contributed greatly to the dismantling of Quaker rule in Pennsylvania by making life miserable for Quaker officeholders. The reformers could not tolerate the ethical ambiguities arising from the old elision of political power and religious authority that had kept the "Quaker party" united, that had allowed the Quaker government to promote policies conducive to Quaker familial expansion, and that had prevented the development of a military establishment in Pennsylvania. The first major confrontation occurred during the Assembly's preparation and execution of the French and Indian War, efforts complicated by the Quaker Assembly's belief that Thomas Penn and his British and provincial allies would use the occasion to cripple the Quaker party's power in Pennsylvania. The Quaker Assembly had long assumed the ethical right to disburse money for the "King's use" at times of war without compromising their pacifist testimony. Everybody knew of course that the money was going to be used to arm, feed, and pay soldiers whose job was to kill people. However, when the first demand for military preparations against the French and their Indian allies came in 1754 from the English government, the Quaker Assembly wished to use the occasion to ensure their right to appropriate money without executive or proprietary oversight (an issue long in dispute with Thomas Penn). They appropriated some of the "defense money" to the "King" and some to be distributed by their own commissioners. They expected that Penn would have to accept the money bill and therefore the underlying precedent for the Assembly's power of appropriation. This innovation violated even their own previously qualified pacifist position.

The issue grew more complicated in the aftermath of General Braddock's crushing defeat in western Pennsylvania in July, 1755. Thomas Penn and his allies heightened efforts to disqualify Friends from the Pennsylvania Assembly. The Quaker Assembly passed a bill to raise £50,000 from taxes to be used by their own commissioners to defend Pennsylvania. The reform ministers of the Philadelphia Yearly Meeting had asked the Quaker assemblymen to withdraw from government even before this act, and in the face of this act many of the reformers refused to pay the tax and issued "An Epistle of Tender Love and Caution to Friends in Pennsylvania," which urged conscientious Quakers to disobey the Quaker Assembly. Thomas Penn and his allies gleefully used the "Epistle" to show the Board of Trade that the Pennsylvania Assembly was the creature of an irresponsibly pacifist faction in the Philadelphia Yearly Meeting. Despite the Assembly's agent's counter-arguments, the Board of Trade promised to seek legislation from Parliament barring Quakers from legislative service. Only the powerful London Quaker lobby's influence with Lord Granville, president of the Privy Council, gained a compromise with the English government: Pennsylvania Quakers would voluntarily leave the Assembly during wartime in lieu of being permanently disqualified from office. Only a few Quakers ran for the legislature in 1756, and of these only a few did not then resign their seats. This painful breach between reformers and politicians outlasted the French and Indian War and continued until the thorough ouster of Quakers at the time of the American Revolution.[54]

Until the 1750s, whatever their corruption or innocence, the regime of wealthy elders and Assembly politicians, united through the Quaker hierarchy of meetings, thrived, kept a good conscience, and stayed confident. Their efforts and examples were signally helping to keep an overwhelming majority of Quaker children in Quakerism, and were maintaining thereby the purity of the Quaker household. In the second half of the eighteenth century, established leaders and reformers faced a problem more perplexing than merely compromised leadership: the visible failure of Quaker childrearing. As Jack Marietta's excellent figures show, after 1720, Quaker marriage infractions in Pennsylvania rose well ahead of the Quaker population increase. For a time, eighteenth-century elders and parents adequately handled these discipline problems. The highest rate of disownments of marriage delinquents after 1720 occurred in the period 1741–45 (76.5%) under the regime of the "corrupted" elders (the highest rate of such disownments after the reformation of discipline was 75.2% in 1771–75).[55] Only when monthly meetings became flooded with marriage delinquents after 1746, mostly poorer Quakers, did the disownment rate drop, though never under 50 percent. Although marriage delinquency clearly increased after 1755 as a consequence of more rigorous enforcement, the post-1755 increase was truly part of a discipline and household crisis that owed more to economic and familial change in southeastern Pennsylvania than to parental corruption. Whether or not the Quaker party would have survived in some form without the childrearing crisis and the consequent breach between politicians and reformers, or would have lost anyway to the growing, militant, non-Quaker Whig majority, is arguable. Whatever the case, the childrearing and discipline crisis and the breach between the second-generation leadership and the reformers crippled Quaker politicians' ability to handle the political crises of the 1750s, 1760s, and 1770s. Unable to command the respect of their own co-religionists, Quaker politicians could hardly expect to command a whole province through years of war and crisis.

FORTUNATELY, some reformers avoided sulfurous denunciations of their elders, looked beyond individual complicity, and provided a sophisticated and still disturbing ethical critique of the connections between domesticity and unfettered American commercialism. John Woolman tried to understand the familial and economic dynamics that had led to the visible corruption of well intentioned men and women. Historians have celebrated Woolman as a saint, but have ignored him as an insightful, if eccentric, political and moral economist. Of all the reformers, and perhaps of subsequent historians, Woolman analyzed best how the history of the Delaware Valley Quakers and their family system slowly led to the corruption of "holy conversation."

Recognizing that the Delaware Valley and New Jersey Quakers had begun as poor British farmers and tradesmen, Woolman exposed their original sin as their seemingly innocent desire to protect their children from spiritually oppressive poverty, a desire good in itself, though disastrously consuming of spiritual liveliness. "There is an inclination in the minds of most people," noted Woolman, "to prepare at least so much treasure for their children, that they with care and moderate industry may live free from these hardships which the poor pass through." From such worthy love of their own children, though less good than the final motive of the authentic Christian, "people may grow expert in business, wise in the wisdom of the world, retain a fair reputation amongst men, and yet being strangers to the voice of Christ, the safe leader of His Flock, the treasures thus gotten, may be like snares to the feet of their posterity."[56] Such heedless child-centeredness was the historic curse, Woolman thought, of middle colony Quakerism.

The immediate evidence of corruption was luxury, the desire or achievement, chiefly for children, of more land, freedom from labor, comfort, and social honor than was absolutely necessary for life. Woolman argued that luxury or superfluity was not simply a violation of charismatic "holy conversation" but was the root of social and economic disharmony. Woolman's merchandising background and understanding of the Pennsylvania and New Jersey economy emerge clearly in his discussion of how luxury lurked beneath virtually every social ill. "We cannot go into superfluities," argued Woolman, "or grasp after wealth in a way contrary to his wisdom, without having connection with some degree of oppression, and with that spirit which leads to self-exaltation and strife, and which frequently brings calamities on countries by parties contending about their claims."[57] Quaker householders worried, for example, about the increasing abuse of alcohol in their communities. According to Woolman, they need only look at their own wardrobes, limestone houses, and solid furniture for an explanation:

> In time of trading, I had an opportunity of seeing that the too liberal use of spirituous liquors, and the custom of wearing too costly apparel, led some people into great inconveniences; and these two things appear to be often connected with universal righteousness; there is an increase of labor which extends beyond what our heavenly father intends for us; and by great labor, and often by much sweating, there is, even among such who are not drunkards, a craving of some liquours to revive the spirits; that partly by the luxurious drinking of some, and partly by the drinking of others, (led to it through immoderate labour) very great quantities of rum are every year expended in our colonies; the greater part of which we should have no need of, did we steadily attend to pure wisdom.[58]

Laborers and poor farmers were especially prone to excessive drinking, Woolman argued, because they had to labor immoderately to contend with the low wages and high rents imposed upon them by seemingly innocent Quaker farmers.

Similarly, southeastern Pennsylvania farmers might sneer self-righteously at Scots-Irish frontiersmen who sold rum to Indians, bilked drunk natives of their land, and thereby made the Native Americans furious and warlike; but, Woolman asserted, the eastern Quaker farmers in their pleasant houses were accomplices. "I remembered," noted Woolman, "that the people on the frontiers, among whom this evil is too common, are often poor; who venture to the outside of a colony, that they might live more independent of such who are wealthy who often set high rents on their land: being renewedly confirmed in a belief, that if all our inhabitants lived according to found wisdom, labouring to promote universal love and righteousness, and ceased from every inordinate desire after wealth, and from all customs which are tinctured with luxury, the way would be easy for our inhabitants, though much more numerous than at present, to live comfortably on honest employments, without having that temptation they are often under of being drawn into schemes to make settlements on land which have not been purchased of the Indians, or of applying to that wicked practice of selling rum to them."[59]

The worst sin and oppression which arose from the seemingly innocent desire to lessen the labor of children and to secure them from poverty was, of course, slavery, including the sin of man-stealing, promoting wars in Africa, destroying the souls of slaves by endless provocations, and murdering thousands of people during the middle passage from the African interior across the Atlantic. Small luxuries, noted Woolman, underlay this mountain of oppression. "Through departing from the truth as it is in Jesus, through introducing ways of life attended with unnecessary expenses, many wants have arisen," noted Woolman, "the minds of people have been employed in studying to get wealth, and in the pursuit, some departing from equity, have retained a profession of religion; others have looked at their example, and thereby been strengthened to proceed further in the same way: thus many have encouraged the trade of taking men from Africa, and selling them as slaves."[60]

Woolman did not believe that the corruption of luxury or its sad social consequences could be blamed on any group of leaders, or even upon a whole generation; instead, the corruption grew silently and insidiously until both the religious and surrounding secular society became infected. "Though the change from day to night, is by a motion so gradual as scarcely to be perceived," noted Woolman, "yet when night is come we behold it very different from the day, and thus as people become wise in their own eyes, and prudent in their own sight, customs rise up from the spirit of this world and spread by little and little, till a departure from the simplicity that there is in Christ becomes as distinguishable as light from darkness, to such who are crucified to the world."[61] In the beginning, just a few seemingly pious households, hoping to secure their children's futures, noted Woolman, acquired a little more land or a little more furniture than was necessary. Their example then spread; the people "by looking on these examples, and desiring to support their families in a way pleasant to the natural mind, there may be a danger of the worldly wisdom gaining strength in them, and of their departure from that pure feeling of truth. . . ."[62] Once luxury-prone households became tolerated and even admired by Quakers, even if their luxury was less than that of other groups, both the psychology of luxury and its oppression spread.

The ways of luxury once established as customs, Woolman argued, masqueraded as moral imperatives, and became almost impossible to eradicate: "so powerful are bad customs when they become general that people growing bold thro the examples one of another, have often been unmoved at the most serious warnings."[63] To make matters worse, corruption did not simply flow undiminished from one generation to another, Woolman argued, but increased during the mysterious intimacies of childrearing, "so that they exceed in wickedness those who lived before them."[64] Thus, from the smallest neglect of "holy conversation," caused by seemingly benign parental concern, grew the total corruption of the Quakers' garden and the rank oppression of visible and invisible strangers.

Although Woolman's message remains unsettling, he was a devout Quaker primarily addressing other Quakers whose children were increasingly leaving their religion. Quakers had always argued that "holy conversation," the speech and conduct of the true Christian convert, demanded rejection of all carnal superfluity. To this view, Woolman added a political economy of "holy conversation" which showed concretely how luxury was not only a symptom of personal sin but also the root cause of economic oppression, social disharmony, and the corruption of Quaker children. In addressing other child-centered Quakers, particularly those worried about their own children's disobedience, Woolman repeatedly stressed that the heedless effort to accumulate wealth in order to protect children from the oppression and corruption of carnal strangers was ironically self-defeating; "men may pursue means which are not agreeable to perfect purity, with a view to increase the wealth and happiness of their offspring; and thereby make the way of virtue more difficult to them." Even minor parental corruption created, Woolman argued, irresistibly corrupting household environments for children:

> It appears, by experience, that where children are educated in fullness, ease, and idleness, evil habits are more prevalent, than in common amongst such who are prudently employed in the necessary affairs of life: and if children are not only educated in the way of so great temptation, but have also the opportunity of lording it over their fellow creatures, and being masters of men in their childhood, how can we hope otherwise than that their tender minds will be possessed with thoughts too high for them? which, by continuance, gaining strength will provoke, like a slow current, gradually separating them from (or keeping them from acquaintance with) that humility and meekness in which alone lasting happiness can be enjoyed.[65]

Woolman insisted that Quaker parents would better "leave our children little else but wise instructions, a good example, and the knowledge of some honest employment . . . than laying up treasures for them, which are often a snare, than any real benefit." Instead of worrying about wealth, "did we so improve the [spiritual] gifts bestowed upon us," argued Woolman, "that our children might rejoice in hopes of their being heirs of an inheritance incorruptible."[66]

Woolman thought that social harmony and a common, holy language could be restored in Pennsylvania without abandoning Quaker familialism, child-centeredness, or private property. He clearly insisted, however, that the commercialization and economic growth of Pennsylvania would have to be severely curtailed. All Christians, especially wealthy Quakers, would have to adhere faithfully to the demanding discipline of "holy conversation" in all economic transactions, avoiding the pursuit of luxury for themselves or their children, and examining every economic transaction for complicity in oppression. Woolman was himself a model of vigilant and selfless devotion. In 1756, he closed his lucrative haberdashery shop in Mount Holly, New Jersey, and supported himself and his family by simple tailoring. Testifying against any trade with slave societies, he refused to eat sugar or wear dyes. To testify against the use of English ships in the West Indies trade, he chose to reside, when traveling to England, in steerage, not in a cabin.[67] He refused in England to send letters to his worried family at home because he saw that English "post-boys pursue their business, each one to his stage, all night thro' the winter: some boys, who ride long stages, suffer greatly on winter nights; and, at several, I have heard of their being froze to death."[68] He urged cessation of trade with the West Indies and other slave societies, over half of Pennsylvania's commerce in the 1770s.[69] He advocated the reduction of all international commerce to a draconian minimum until young sailors enjoyed a less arduous and corrupting existence, and he pleaded with Quaker parents not to send their lads to sea.[70] He wanted "those who have large estates" to be "faithful stewards" and lay "no rent, nor interest, nor other demand, higher than consistent with universal love; and those in lower circumstances" to "shun unnecessary expense, even to the smallest articles; and all unite in humbly seeking the Lord . . . ." If Quakers adhered to "holy conversation" and universal empathy in economic matters, "if the leadings of His Holy Spirit were faithfully attended to by His professed followers in general," Woolman promised that "the heathen nations would be exampled in righteousness; a less number of people would be employed on the seas; the channels of trade would be more free from defilement; fewer people would be employed in vanities and superfluities; the inhabitants of cities would be less in number;

those who have much lands would become fathers to the poor; more people would be employed in the sweet enjoyment of husbandry, and in the path of pure wisdom; labour would be an agreeable, healthful employment."[71] Only by a Christian decapitalization of the Delaware Valley economy—a position many Quakers and all republican theorists rejected—could "we experience a restoration," Woolman believed, "of that which was lost at Babel, represented by the inspired prophet in the 'returning of a pure language.'"[72]

THE DEISTIC French republican reformers were neither worried about nor greatly interested in the growth limits of genuine piety within the Quakers' ecclesiastical system or pious anti-commercial Quaker rhetoric like Woolman's. Indeed, few Quaker achievements contributed so centrally to the eventual cooptation and revision of Quaker domesticity as the major familial ideology of the United States than the ending of Quaker expansionism in the mid-eighteenth century and the Quakers' fall from political hegemony. Their fall allowed the Quakers to be accepted as shining, if harmless, examples of private republican virtue, whose system of domesticity could be partially adopted and recommended for republican purposes without contributing to the further strengthening and emboldening of a religious, social, and political colossus.

One of the most endearing social traits that made Americans peculiarly supportive of a republican society was, in Crèvecoeur's opinion, that in America "the various Christian sects introduced wear out and . . . religious indifference becomes prevalent." Toleration and religious pluralism in American society, according to Crèvecoeur, led to the happy dissolution in America of "persecution, religious pride, the love of contradiction . . . ." As Crèvecoeur noted, "zeal in Europe is confined; here it evaporates in the great distance it has to travel; there it is a grain of powder inclosed; here it burns away in the open air and consumes without effect."[73] Instead of through religious zeal and the development of authoritative ministers, Americans would develop their morality, Crèvecoeur hoped, through the happy and prosperous, private familial relations of farming life according to the example set by the Quakers. American society could sustain a republican form of government if it became Pennsylvania writ large. "Can I pass over these reflections," he concluded, "without remembering thy name, O Penn, thou best of legislators, who by thy wisdom of thy laws hast endowed human nature within the bounds of thy province, with every dignity it can possibly enjoy in a civilized state and showed by this singular establishment what all men might be if they would follow thy example."[74] According to Crèvecoeur, it was just as well that Quaker power, or any one religious group's power, no longer prevailed in Pennsylvania.

Brissot also preferred the Quakers as an example more than as a power. The Marquis de Chastellux, reflecting the suspicion many American patriots felt during the Revolution about pacifist and neutralist Quakers, had made a few slighting remarks about the Quakers in his *Travels in North America*. Brissot was furious and immediately issued from London his impassioned *Examen Critique des Voyages . . . de Marquis de Chastellux* (London, 1786). At stake to Brissot was not the mere reputation of a peculiar sect but the defense of the very possibility of a truly republican society. To Brissot, the Quakers were an example of a people who produced exquisite private and public virtue without an authoritative priesthood. They proved that people, at least in a pastoral setting like American, could sustain without overlords sufficient virtue to enjoy republicanism and could refute "the assumption on which European governments are based . . . that man is depraved, unruly, evil, and the fear which the possession of wealth inspires in the rich produces the idea that the poor can be controlled only by chains."[75] Brissot conflated the worthiness of the Quakers with the American people's ability to sustain republicanism. "In vilifying the Quakers, you prevent the good effects of their pious example," accused Brissot, and "in making the people contemptible, you invite their oppressors to rivet their chains." Their imprecision in doctrine, their undramatic worship services, and their loss of political power and ambition, made the Quakers all the more attractive to Brissot. Their success and example, he thought, rested almost solely upon their charismatic form of family life, the element he wanted to adapt and even export. "Considering all the characteristics of the Society of Friends, you will agree," he noted, "that the government ought to make every effort to bring about its establishment in France . . . their example could serve to regenerate our morals, without which liberty cannot be preserved for long, even if it is won without them."[76]

As they traveled throughout North America in the 1760s and 1780s, Crèvecoeur and Brissot were thus far more eager to celebrate the comparative Quaker-led moral and material prosperity of the middle colonies or states than to explore the complexities and ironies of the reformation of Quakerism. Crèvecoeur, and especially Brissot, disliked slavery and the southern colonies' or states' political economy. "Everything in Maryland and in Virginia," noted Brissot, "bears the stamp of slavery: the parched soil, the badly managed farming, the ramshackled houses, and the few scrawney cattle that look like walking skeletons." Even esteemed Virginia planters "live in a kind of tawdry luxury." "The general picture we saw in Maryland," he continued, "was one of uncultivated or poorly cultivated land, occasional large fields of Indian corn, people with pale, drawn, and feverish faces, naked Negroes, and wretched huts."[77] According to Brissot and Crèvecoeur, the South's moral and political economy could not sustain a republican society.

Despite its economic difficulties in the second half of the eighteenth century and its heritage of persecution, Crèvecoeur and Brissot generally endorsed the suitability of more tolerant eighteenth-century New England life for republicanism. Because of their inability to develop a prosperous, pluralistic society, "I know it is fashionable to reflect on them," noted Crèvecoeur, "but I respect them for what they have done; for the accuracy and wisdom which they have settled their territory; for the decency of their manners; for their early love of letters; their ancient college, the first in this hemisphere; for their industry, which to me, who am but a farmer is the criterion of everything. There never was a people, situated as they are, who with so ungrateful a soil, have done more in so short a time." The economic difficulties of New England were due, according to Crèvecoeur, not to New England manners or morals, but to the fact that "great parts of the colony of Massachusetts and Connecticut have cost more in clearing than the land was worth."[78]

Although aware of the economic deficits of New England, Brissot had even a higher opinion of New England land and farming than Crèvecoeur. In 1788, he thought Boston was in a vigorous state of economic renewal, and that the surrounding farmlands, and especially the lands of the Connecticut Valley, were well cultivated. He thought, however, that the economic recovery of New England was being seriously hampered by the inhabitants' discontent, particularly their mania for emigration. While speaking to John Adams at Braintree, Brissot was disappointed that "Mr. Adams complained that land around Boston was expensive and that it did not yield a profit proportionate to its value. Since the return amounts, in his estimate, to three per cent, he found it more profitable to invest in government stocks, which bring in six per cent." "I was astonished to learn that land is so expensive," noted Brissot, "particularly as I knew that so much was for sale because of the two kinds of emigration that are ruining this state. Besides the emigration to the West, I have been told that the region of Maine, to the North, is increasing in population at the expense of Massachusetts." And Brissot lamented, "the desire to better one's lot has poisoned the contentment of even the inhabitants of Connecticut."[79]

While endorsing the manners of the New Englanders, Crèvecoeur and Brissot held no doubts that the middle colonies' or states', especially Pennsylvania's, economy and society would serve as the foundation and model for the new republic. "Examine this flourishing province in whatever light you will," wrote Crèvecoeur, "the eyes as well as the mind of an European traveller are equally delighted because a diffusive happiness appears in every part, happiness which is established on the broadest basis. The wisdom of Lycurgus and Solon never conferred on man one half of the blessings and uninterrupted prosperity which the Pennsylvanians now possess. . . ."[80] Brissot was certain that "Philadelphia may be considered the metropolis of the United States. It is certainly the most beautiful and best-built city in the nation, and also the wealthiest, though not the most ostentatious. Here you find more well-educated men, more knowledge of politics and literature, more political and learned societies than anywhere else in the United States. Many other American cities are older but Philadelphia quickly surpassed them all." "Such ideas spring naturally to mind," he wrote, "on a market day in Philadelphia, for this market is without a doubt one of the finest in the world." Brissot was perhaps over impressed by the variety, vigor, order, cleanliness, quiet, and implicit lessons of the grand Philadelphia market. "Here is one of the most striking effects of habit," he observed, "a habit inspired by the Quakers, who have implanted morality in this country, the habit of performing everything quietly, reasonably, and above all without injury to anyone and without need for the intervention of a magistrate."[81] Agreeing with Crèvecoeur, Brissot argued, ". . . I firmly believe that Pennsylvania does not owe its prosperity merely to . . . geographical advantages, but rather to the private morals of the inhabitants; to the universal toleration which has been practiced here since the very foundation of the colony; to the Quakers' simplicity and thrift; to their firm virtues; and to their industry, which, concentrated on two activities, farming and trade, has necessarily produced better and faster results than other sects have achieved."[82] These philosophes hoped that a Pennsylvania type of society of Quaker-like households—though not a Quaker-dominated society—would spread throughout New England and even the South. This was also essentially the ideal of later New England family reformers like Lydia Maria Child and Louisa May Alcott. Through such exchanges, appreciations, and misperceptions, some of the hard-earned family wisdom of radical northwestern British livestock farmers entered the culture of the new nation.

For their part, the Quakers' fall from power and their knowledge of inherent impediments to additional growth made them accepting of the tutorial, rather than power, role the philosophes would have them play in the emerging republican societies of the eighteenth century. Held in suspicion and contempt by American Whigs during the Revolution, the Quakers were eager for a good press and positive role in the new order. On December 9, 1780, Anthony Benezet, the great Quaker abolitionist and reformer, accosted Marquis de Chastellux at breakfast in Philadelphia, complained about the Whigs' persecution of pacifist Quakers, asked him to protect Quakers in Rhode Island, where French forces were stationed, and asked Chastellux's "permission to send me some pamphlets of his making, which were principally apologies for his sect . . . and he did not fail to send them to me the next morning." Benezet's salesmanship notwithstanding, Chastellux's subsequent *Travels in North America* were critical of the Quaker's role in the American Revolution.[83]

In 1788, Delaware Valley Quaker leaders courted Brissot de Warville with more charm and energy. In praising the Quakers in his *Travels*, Brissot admitted that "I have tried as much as possible not to be influenced by the flattering manner in which they received me because of their gratitude for the apology of their sect which I published."[84] In that year, 1788, Philadelphia Friends translated and published Brissot's pro-Quaker, republican tract, *A Critical Examination of the Marquis of Chastellaux's Travels in North America*. Brissot was invited to tour and lodge within Chester County Quaker farmhouses, to see intimately the daily workings of a charismatic Quaker household. And when Brissot was recuperating from stomach problems apparently caused by eating too much pure Chester County Quaker food, Warner Mifflin, the reforming Quaker abolitionist, paid him a visit. "I am Warner Mifflin,' he said, 'I have read the book in which thou defendest the cause of

Friends, and in which thou preachest the principles of universal benevolence. I learned that thou wast here, and I have come to see thee. Besides, I love thy nation. . . ."[85] Mifflin took Brissot to visit "Miss Ameland, whom [Mifflin] was to marry in a few days," and Samuel Ameland, "one of the richest and most philanthropic of Friends, . . . treated me with the greatest cordiality," Brissot reported, "offering me his houses, his horses, his carriage, and everything that belonged to him."[86] Thomas Mifflin invited Brissot to his lovely house opposite the Schuylkill Falls where Brissot met "an old Quaker who said that he took particular pleasure in shaking my hand because I resembled Anthony Benezet. This resemblance was later confirmed by other Quakers."[87] Never before had pious Quakers courted a stubborn deist as if he were a beautiful saint.

If deistical, republican reformers wanted to try to extract domesticity from the Quakers' ecclesiastical system and revise it for secular, republican expansion—and wished the Quakers to play the roles of examples and advisers—Quaker leaders, while they certainly would have loudly objected thirty years earlier, had now no objection whatsoever to such a cooptation. In return for status and a platform from which to exercise the Quaker conscience within the new republican society, Quaker leaders would try to be helpful and also would remain relatively silent about the familial inexperience of republican reformers and especially about the serious problems domesticity had posed to their own religious order and therefore would pose, most probably, to an expanding and increasingly commercialized republican society.[88] As Quakers well knew, marriages between pious Quakers and deists outside of meeting always had to overcome their tincture of corruption.

APPENDIX

Comparative Statistics on
Quaker Families and Communities

TABLE 1 *323 Personal Estates of "Middling" Northwest Men, 1660–91*

Personal Estate (L)	Yeomen		Hus-bandmen		Artisans		All	
	No.	%	No.	%	No.	%	No.	%
Cheshire								
1660, 1681 (104)								
200+	13	37	4	9	2	8	19	18
160–199	5	14	1	2			6	6
120–159	5	14	3	9	7	29	15	14
80–119	4	11	10	22	3	13	17	16
40–79	4	11	15	33	1	4	20	19
0–39	4	11	12	27	11	46	27	26
Total	35		45		24		104	
Median Income (£)	171		70		81.5			
Merionethshire								
1670–1691 (89)								
200+	1	4	1	2			2	2
160–199	3	11	1	2			4	4
120–159	2	7	2	4			4	4
80–119	1	4	5	9	1	17	7	8
40–79	4	14	10	18	1	17	15	17
0–39	17	61	36	65	4	66	57	64
Total	28		55		6		89	
Median Income (£)	36.5		33		36			
Radnorshire								
1675, 1685 (130)								
200+	1	2	1	1			2	2
160–199								
120–159	2	5	1	1			3	2
80–119	2	5	2	2			4	3
40–79	4	10	15	18			19	15
0–39	30	77	64	77	8	100	102	78
Total	39		83		8		130	
Median Income (£)	27		25		10			

Sources: Cheshire County Probate Records, 1660, 1681, Cheshire County Record Office; Merionethshire Probate Records, 1670–1691, National Library of Wales; Radnorshire and Brecknockshire Probate Records, 1675, 1685, National Library of Wales.

TABLE 2 *Patterns of Bequest in 253 Northwest Wills, 1660–91*

Cheshire, 1660–1681 (94)

Personal Estate (£)	Nuclear		Qualified		Extended		Single	
	No.	%	No.	%	No.	%	No.	%
200+	18	64	1	4	7	25	2	7
100–199	16	53	3	10	6	20	5	17
0–99	24	67	1	3	7	19	4	11
Total	58	62	5	5	20	21	11	12

Welsh Counties, 1670–1691 (158)

Personal Estate (£)	Nuclear		Qualified		Extended		Single	
	No.	%	No.	%	No.	%	No.	%
200+	11	85					2	15
100–199	9	47	1	5	7	37	2	11
0–99	59	46	7	6	23	18	38	30
Total	79	50	8	5	30	19	42	26

Sources: Cheshire County Probate Records, 1660, 1681, Cheshire County Record Office; Merionethshire Probate Records, 1670–91, National Library of Wales; Radnorshire and Brecknockshire Probate Records, 1675, 1685, National Library of Wales.

Notes: "Nuclear" is defined as bequeathing 95% or more of the estate to immediate family (spouse, children, grandchildren); "nuclear qualified" is 94–90% of the estate to immediate family; "extended" is less than 90% to immediate family. These bequests are made by married men and women with children or grandchildren; or widowed men and women with children or grandchildren; or married men and women without children. Singles, including bachelors, spinsters, childless widows, and widowers are placed in a separate category because defining a "nuclear" pattern for them was impossible. In making judgments from this data, I assumed that men and women, who had estates of less than £50, yet who followed a nuclear pattern of bequest, did not expect their children to gain independence from the tiny contributions they made to them. Such parents expected their children to attain only positions of clear dependency in the labor and land markets.

TABLE 3 *Entrenched and Emigrant South Welsh and Cheshire Quaker Households 1655–1684*

	No.	%	Surviving children (mean)	Children married as Quakers in home Quarterly M. No.	%	%	Persecution fine mean	jail %
				Cheshire				
Entrenched households	98	67	2.74	86	32	41	£20.4	15
Emigrants (unknown desination)	27	18	3.85			4	£9	4
Emigrants (Pennsylvania)	21	14	4.09			57	£30.41	14
Total	146		3.14			36	£22.4	13
				South Wales				
Entrenched households	21	37	3.85	15	19	24	£3	5
Emigrants (unknown desination)	23	40	3.74			48	£3.4	43
Emigrants (Pennsylvania)	13	23	3.61			61	£6	31
Total	57		3.75			40	£4.3	26

Sources: Register of Cheshire and Staffordshire Quarterly Meeting: Register of Southe Wales and Hereford Quarterly Meeting, Friends House; Joseph Besse, *A Collection of the Sufferings of the People Called Quakers* (London, 1753), passim; Sufferings, South Division of Wales, Entry Book, Film 239, Box 172, Friends House Library; Welsh Accounts of Sufferings 1660–1665, LSF film 237, box 170, Friends House Library; Chester Monthly Meeting Registers; Radnor Monthly Meeting Registers; William Wade Hinshaw, *Encyclopedia of American Quaker Genealogy*, vols. 1–3 (Ann Arbor, Michigan, 1938); Charles H. Browning, *Welsh Settlement of Pennsylvania* (Philadelphia, 1912); Thomas Allen Glenn, *Welsh Founders of Pennsylvania* (Baltimore, 1970); Richard S. Dunn and Mary M. Dunn, eds., *The Papers of William Penn, Volume Two, 1680–1684* (Philadelphia, 1982), pps. 630–664.

TABLE 4 *Wealth, Marriage, and Discipline Among the Quaker Settlers' Children*

Average tax rate (£'s)	Families No.	Children No.	Married out No.	Disowned No.	%	Single No.	Male marriage age (mean)	Female marriage age (mean)
90–100	19	101	3	1	1	15	23	23
70–89	12	76	5	2	3	5	27	24
50–69	11	45	3	2	4	5	27	23
40–49	12	58	15	12	20	9	26	23
30–39	18	81	21	17	20	18	30	28
Total	72	361	47	34		52		

Source: Radnor Men's and Women's Monthly Meeting Minutes, 1681–1745, Chester Men's and Women's Monthly Meeting Minutes, 1681–1745, Friends Historical Library, Swarthmore, Pa.; Chester County Tax Lists, 1715–1765, Pennsylvania Historical Society.

TABLE 5 *Age at Marriage: Delaware Valley Quakers and Andover, Mass.*

Age at marriage	Quakers (Chester, Welsh Tract) No.	%	Andover (second generation) No.	%	Andover (third generation) No.	%
Men						
Under 21	5	5	5	5	6	3
21–24	35	32	36	35	72	32
25–29	30	27	39	38	87	39
30–34	26	23	17	16	39	17
35–39	9	8	4	4	12	5
40 and over	6	5	3	3	8	4
Total	111	100	104	101	224	100
29 and under	70	63	80	77	165	74
30 and over	41	37	24	23	59	26
Women						
Under 21	27	37	29	36	58	28
21–24	22	30	32	40	74	35
25–29	15	20	14	17	48	23
30–34	5	7	3	4	12	6
35–39	2	3	2	3	10	5
40 and over	3	4	1	1	8	4
Total	74	101	81	101	210	101
24 and under	49	67	61	76	132	63
25 and over	25	34	20	25	78	38

Source: Radnor Monthly Meeting Records, Chester Monthly Meeting Records, Friends Historical Library; P. Greven, *Four Generations* (Ithaca, N.Y., 1970), pp. 31–37, 119, 121.

TABLE 6 *Radnor Women's Meeting's Leaders and Participants, 1695–1730*

Name	Positions No.	Quarterly Meeting	Children No.	Married No.	Married Out No.	Land mean acres
Top tier						
Martha Thomas	70	18	6	5	0	1052
Ellen Jones	61	16	5	5	0	1375
Elinor Bevan	45	18	5	4	0	1250
Hannah Humphry	39	9	10	5	1	420
Gainor Robert	31	6	2	1	0	1100
Total	246/58%	67/63%	28	20	1/3.5%	1039
2nd tier						
Elizabeth David	21	5	3	2	0	520
Margaret Miles	20	5	3	3	0	250
Eliz. Thomas	17	4	7	7	1	250
Barbara Bevan	12	7	5	4	0	1200
Total	70/16%	21/20%	18	16	1/5.8%	555
3rd tier						
Margaret Jarman	18	1	5	4	2	750
Ann Jones	13	2	5	4	0	764
Phebe Moore	13	1	4	4	0	250
Margaret Ellis	11	3	6	2	1	unknown
Jane Ellis	11	2	6	3	1	250
Total	66/15%	9/8%	26	17	4/15%	503

4th tier						
Sidney Roberts	9	0	5	3	1	350
Mary Ormes	7	2	3	3	1	150
Ann Roberts	7	3	4	4	2	350
Margaret Lewis	6	3	3	3	0	unknown
Anne Llewellyn	4	2	4	4	0	1100
Total	33/8%	10/9%	19	17	4/21%	488
5th tier						
Jane Edward	3	0	3	3	0	210
Ellen Meredith	2	0	5	5	0	unknown
Jane Morgan	2	0	1	1	0	300
Cath. Richards	2	0	9	9	2	418
Katherine Lewis	1	0	4	3	1	unknown
Sarah Morgan	1	0	5	4	2	460
Mary Humphry	0	0	8	4	1	300
Eliz. Llewellyn	0	0	4	4	1	500
Mary Llewellyn	0	0	4	2	0	200
Elinor Painter	0	0	1	0	0	landless
Hannah Rydderch	0	0	1	0	0	landless
Total	11/3%	0/0%	45	35	7/16%	266

Sources: Radnor Women's Monthly Meeting Minutes, Friends Historical Library; Chester County Probate Records, Chester County Court House; Chester County Deeds, Chester County Court House; Philadelphia County Probate Records, Philadelphia County Deeds, Philadelphia City Hall and Hall-Annex.

TABLE 7 *Wealth and Marriage Discipline: the Second Generation's Children*

Marriage portion	Married in	Married out	Single	% Married in meeting
Women				
£60+	17	1	4	77
£40–59	14	3	2	74
£20–39	18	4	9	58
0–£19	9	8	4	43
Men				
200 acres+	19	3	2	79
100–199 acres	18	6	4	64
10–99 acres	5	9	6	24
landless	9	16	10	26
Total	200			

Sources: Radnor Men's and Women's Montly Meeting Records, Friends Historical Library, Swarthmore, Chester County Deeds, Chester County Probate Records, Chester County Court House; Philadelphia County Deeds, Philadelphia County Probate Records, Philadelphia City Hall and City Hall- Annex.

Notes

Abbreviations

CCCH   Chester County Court House, West Chester, Pennsylvania

CCRO   Cheshire County Record Office, The Castle, Chester, England

CMMR   Chester Monthly Meeting Records

FH   Friends House Library, London

FHS   Friends Historical Society and Library, Swarthmore, Pennsylvania

HSP   Historical Society of Pennsylvania, Philadelphia

NLW   National Library of Wales, Aberystwyth, U.K.

PCH   Philadelphia City Hall, Philadelphia

PCHA   Philadelphia City Hall Annex, Philadelphia

RMMR   Radnor Monthly Meeting Records.

INTRODUCTION Intimate Frontiers

1. T. W. Bamford, *Rise of the Public Schools: A Study of Boys' Public Boarding Schools in England and Wales from 1837 to the Present Day* (London, 1967); Jonathan Gathorne-Hardy, *The Old School Tie: The Phenomenon of the English Public School* (New York, 1978); James McLachlan, *American Boarding Schools: A Historical Study* (New York, 1970).

2. Michael Grossberg, *Governing the Hearth: Law and Family in Nineteenth-Century America* (Chapel Hill, 1985).

3. Leslie A. Fiedler, *Love and Death in the American Novel* (Revised ed., New York, 1966); for domesticity's impact on female friendship, see Carroll Smith-Rosenberg, "The Female World of Love and Ritual: Relations Between Women in Nineteenth-Century America," *Signs*, 1 (Autumn 1975): 1–29.

4. Some of the major studies are Ann Douglas, *The Feminization of American Culture* (New York, 1977); Mary P. Ryan, *Cradle of the Middle Class: The Family in Oneida County, New York, 1790–1865* (Cambridge, U.K. 1981); Nancy Cott, *The Bonds of Womanhood: "Women's Sphere" in New England, 1780–1835* (New Haven, 1977); Kathryn Kish Sklar, *Catharine Beecher: A Study of American Domesticity* (New Haven, 1975); Bernard Wishy, *The Child and the Republic: The Dawn of Early American Child Nurture* (Philadelphia, 1968); Carl N. Degler, *At Odds: Women and the Family in America from the Revolution to the Present* (New York, 1980).

5. Edmund S. Morgan, *The Puritan Family: Religion and Domestic Relations in Seventeenth-Century New England* (Revised ed., New York, 1966).

6. Some of the major studies that describe the course of Quaker history are: H. Barbour, *The Quakers in Puritan England* (New Haven, 1964); W. C. Braithwaite, *The Beginnings of Quakerism* (Revised ed., Cambridge, 1970); W. C. Braithwaite, *The Second Period of Quakerism* (Revised ed., Cambridge, 1961); Christopher Hill, *The World Turned Upside Down* (New York, 1972); Barry Reay, *The Quakers and the English Revolution* (New York, 1985); Richard T. Vann, *The Social Development of English Quakerism 1655–1755* (Cambridge, Mass., 1969); Sydney James, *A People Among Peoples* (Cambridge, Mass., 1963); Frederick Tolles, *Meeting House and Counting House: The Quaker Merchants of Colonial Philadelphia* (Chapel Hill, 1948); J. William Frost, *The Quaker Family in Colonial America* (New York, 1973); Jack D. Marietta, *The Reformation of American Quakerism, 1748–1783* (Philadelphia, 1984). For the population of Quakers in early America and the United States, see Edwin Scott Gaustad, *Historical Atlas of Religion in America* (New York, 1962), 21–25, 92–96, 167, 169. According to Gaustad's calculations, the Quakers in 1750 were the third largest religious body in British North America. The Quakers' 250 meetings (or churches) were outnumbered only by the Congregationalists with 465 churches and by the Episcopalians (Anglicans) with 289 churches. The Quakers had slightly more meetings than the Presbyterians churches (233) and far more than the Baptists (132) and Lutherans (138). Although Quaker communities existed in the southern colonies and New England, slightly over half of the Quaker meetings were consolidated in the middle colonies, particularly Pennsylvania (70 meetings), New Jersey (41 meetings), and New York (20 meetings). By 1850 the Quakers, including Orthodox and Hicksite, had dropped to the eight largest religious body in the United States. The Quaker reformation, beginning around 1755, clearly retarded the growth of Quakerism. Yet, the most dramatic reduction of Quakerism as a numerical power in American religion actually occurred after 1850, just as domesticity spread throughout the nation. According to Gaustad, there were actually more Quaker meetings in 1850 (726) than in 1950 (654). Perhaps once domesticity had become the unofficial spiritual religion of Americans, the American people could simply favor the easier, merchandised, sentimental variety of charismatic household life over the trials and sacrifices of the coopted, genuine article.

7. Earl Leslie Griggs, *Thomas Clarkson: The Friend of Slaves* (London, 1936), 79–90, *passim*; Thomas Clarkson, *A Portraiture of Quakerism* (New York, 1806), I: introduction, 53–54, 101; II: 42; III: 3, 257, 260, 340. See also "Review of Clarkson's *A Portraiture of Quakerism*," *Monthly Review*, 53 (August 1807): 152–66; Lord Jeffrey, "Review of Clarkson's *A Portraiture of Quakerism*," *Edinburgh Review*, 10 (April 1807): 85–102.

8. Jean Jacques Rousseau, *Emile or Education*, ed. and trans. Allan Bloom (New York, 1979).

9. Abbé Raynal, *A Philosophical and Political History of the Settlements and Trade of the Europeans in the East and West Indies* (Dublin, 1784), VI: 28.

10. *Ibid.*, 12.

11. Two studies of the philosophes' view of Quakers are Edith Philips, *The Good Quaker in French Legend* (Philadelphia, 1932); Durand Echeverria, *Mirage in the West: A History of the French Image of American Society to 1815* (Princeton, 1957).

12. Theodore Besterman, *Voltaire* (Chicago, 1976), 127n; see also W. H. Barber, "Voltaire and Quakerism: Enlightenment and inner light," *Studies on Voltaire and the Eighteenth Century*, 24 (1963): 81–91.

13. J. Hector St. John de Crèvecoeur the pseudonym of Michel-Guillaume-Jean de Crèvecoeur, was born at Caen, France, in 1735. He was educated at a Jesuit school, Collège du Mont. In 1755, he served as an officer in the French army in New France, but emigrated to New York in 1759. He traveled widely in the English colonies before buying a farm in New York in 1759. Crèvecoeur remained neutral during the American Revolution. He fled to England, where in 1782 he published his *Letters from an American Farmer*. He later became French consul in New York City. J. P. Brissot de Warville was born in Chartres, France, in 1754. His father was a prosperous restaurant keeper. Brissot studied law and subsequently worked as a law clerk and journalist in Paris. He was imprisoned in 1784 in the Bastille for his republican sentiments. Brissot met and befriended Crèvecoeur in Paris in 1785. He was also a devoted follower of Rousseau, whose *Confessions* he read six times. Brissot's six-month trip to the United States in 1788 was sponsored by French bankers who were interested in American investments. Brissot published a long critique of Marquis de Chastellux's hostile account of American Quakerism in 1786 and his own *New Travels in the United States of America 1788* in Paris in 1791. During the French Revolution, Brissot became chief of the Girondin party. He fell from power in June 1793 and was guillotined on November 1, 1793.

14. J. P. Brissot de Warville, *New Travels in the United States of America 1788*, translated by Mara Soceanu Vamos and Durand Echeverria (Cambridge, Mass., 1964), 162–65.

15. *Ibid.*, 171–72.

16. "The First Purchasers of Pennsylvania, 1681–1685," *The Papers of William Penn*, ed. Richard S. Dunn and Mary M. Dunn (Philadelphia, 1982), II: 630–64. Of the 313 rural buyers of known origins, William Penn recruited only 81 (26 percent) from the Home Counties, the East Midlands, the South-east, and East Anglia combined. These were the wealthiest, most densely populated, and most commercialized agricultural regions in Britain, which served the massive market in burgeoning London. Not only did Penn recruit poorly from these wealthy regions, but from within them, he recruited only three buyers from the Puritan counties—Essex, Suffolk, Norfolk, Cambridgeshire, Lincolnshire—that had supplied many of the emigrants to Massachusetts fifty years before. In contrast, Pen recruited the bulk of his colony's first rural population from upland, provincial regions, most often characterized by pastoral farming, traditions of dispersed settlement, and relatively low population densities. Among his rural customers, 24 came from the Northern Province and Yorkshire (7.6%), 100 from the Southwest (32%), and 108 from the Lancashire and Cheshire region, the West Midlands, and Wales (35%). On a county basis, Cheshire had the most buyers (55) and Wiltshire was second (53). Wales had only 23 first purchasers, but this small number is deceptive. The Welshmen brought

more land (43,130 acres) than the Cheshire buyers (28,500). The small group of Welsh first purchasers were actually agents for at least 73 other Welsh farmers. Probably to attract these likely customers from Wales and the Welsh border country, William Penn asked the Crown to name his colony, "New Wales." A Welsh Crown official, worried that his beloved homeland might become forever associated with a disreputable religious experiment, vetoed the idea. Pen insisted, however, that "Pennsylvania" was derivative from the Welsh language. "William Penn to Robert Turner, 5 March 1681," *ibid.*, 83.

17. Major studies of this type include James T. Lemon, *The Best Poor Man's Country: A Geographical Study of Southeastern Pennsylvania* (Baltimore, 1972); Stephanie G. Wolf, *Urban Village: Population, Community, and Family Structure in Germantown, Pennsylvania 1683-1800* (Princeton, 1976); Wayland Dunaway, *The Scotch-Irish of Colonial Pennsylvania* (Chapel Hill, 1944); Gillian Gollin, *Moravians in Two Worlds: A Study of Changing Communities* (New York, 1967); Ned C. Landsman, *Scotland and Its First American Colony, 1683-1765* (Princeton, 1985); Lucy Simler, "Tenancy in Colonial Pennsylvania: The Case of Chester County," *William and Mary Quarterly* 3rd ser., 43 (Oct. 1986): 542-69.

18. This formulation is not meant to foreclose the possibility of other groups' impact. For example, the development or existence of a form of domesticity in the South, albeit well after the Quakers introduced such a system in Pennsylvania, is a matter of disagreement among southern historians, and in need of additional clarification. See Michael Zuckerman, "William Byrd's Family," *Perspectives in American History*, 12 (1979): 255-311; Daniel Blake Smith, *Inside the Big House* (Ithaca, 1979); Jan Lewis, *The Pursuit of Happiness: Family and Values in Jefferson's Virginia* (New York, 1983).

19. See Gary B. Nash, *Quakers and Politics: Pennsylvania, 1681-1726* (Princeton, 1968).

20. J. Hector St. John de Crèvecoeur, *Letters from an American Farmer*, ed. Albert Stone (New York, 1981; orig. pub. 1782), 54-55.

21. Brissot, *New Travels*, 172, 312.

22. See Gary B. Nash, "Social Development," in *Colonial British America: Essays in the New History of the Early Modern Era*, eds. Jack P. Greene and J. R. Pole (Baltimore, 1984), 238-40; Alice H. Jones, *Wealth of a Nation To Be* (New York, 1980), *passim*.

23. Marietta, *The Reformation of American Quakerism*.

24. Nathaniel Hawthorne, "The Gentle Boy," in *Complete Novels and Selected Tales of Nathaniel Hawthorne*, ed. N. H. Pearson (New York, 1937), 890-911; see careful and insightful discussion in Michael J. Colacurcio, *The Province of Piety: Moral History in Hawthorne's Early Tales* (Cambridge, Mass., 1984), 160-202.

25. M. C. Turpie, "A Quaker Source for Emerson's Sermon on the Lord's Supper," *New England Quarterly*, 17 (1944): 95-101; see also F. B. Tolles, "Emerson and Quakerism," *American Literature*, 10 (1938): 142-65; R. W. Emerson, "The Transcendentalist," *Nature, Addresses, and Lectures*, 339, as quoted in F. B. Tolles, *ibid.*, 165; R. W. Emerson, "George Fox," *The Early Lectures of Ralph Waldo Emerson*, ed. Stephen E. Whicher and Robert E. Spiller (Cambridge, Mass., 1959), I: 182.

26. George Bancroft, *History of the United States from the Discovery of the American Continent* (6th ed., Boston, 1839), II: 337.

27. *Ibid.*, 379.

28. *Journals of Ralph Waldo Emerson,* ed. Edward Waldo Emerson and Waldo Emerson Forbes (Boston and New York, 1909–14), IV: 304.

29. "L. M. Child to E. Carpenter, March 20, 1838," *Letters of Lydia Maria Child,* ed. John G. Whittier (Boston, 1883), 27. See also "L. M. Child to Rev. Doctor Allyn, Sept. 28, 1826," *ibid.,* 9.

30. L. Maria Child, *Letters from New York* (New York, 1850), 24, 149, 161, 212, 268.

31. For example, see Catharine Maria Sedgwick, *A New England Tale* (1822); Eliza B. Lee, *Naomi* (1848). For another New England family reformer influenced by Quakers, see Lewis Perry, *Childhood, Marriage, and Reform: Henry Clarke Wright 1797–1870* (Chicago, 1980).

32. Louisa May Alcott, *Little Women* (New York, 1966; orig. published 1868–69), 266–73.

33. Odell Shephard, *Pedlar's Progress: The Life of Bronson Alcott* (Boston, 1937), 69–71, *passim*; Martha Saxton, *Louisa May: A Modern Biography of Louisa May Alcott* (New York, 1978), 26, 75–77, 84, 234.

34. Louisa May Alcott, *Work: A Story of Experience* (Boston, 1873), 221.

35. *Ibid.,* 243.

36. *Ibid.,* 251.

37. *Ibid.,* 378.

CHAPTER ONE The Middling Roots

1. For studies of southeastern English families, see, for example, Keith Wrightson and David Levine, *Poverty and Piety in an English Village: Terling, 1525–1700* (London, 1979); Alan Macfarlane, *The Family Life of Ralph Josselin, A Seventeenth-Century Clergyman* (Cambridge, 1970). For the use of the resulting models of middling family life in New England studies, see John Demos, *A Little Commonwealth: Family Life in Plymouth Colony* (New York, 1970); Philip J. Greven, Jr., *Four Generations: Population, Land, and Family in Colonial Andover, Massachusetts* (Ithaca, 1970); T.H. Breen, *Puritans and Adventurers: Change and Continuity in Early America* (New York, 1980); David Grayson Allen, *In English Ways: The Movement of Societies and the Transferal of English Local Law and Custom to Massachusetts Bay in the Seventeenth Century* (Chapel Hill, 1981). For the explicit or implicit use of such a model in Pennsylvania studies, which I think a mistaken strategy, see Lemon, *The Best Poor Man's Country*; James A. Henretta, "Families and Farms: Mentalité in Pre-Industrial America," *William and Mary Quarterly,* 3rd Ser., 35 (1978): 3–32; James Lemon, "Comment on James Henretta's 'Families and Farms: Mentalité in Pre-Industrial America,'" with a "Reply" by James A. Henretta, *ibid.,* 37 (1980): 688–700. James Lemon and James Henretta, while arguing about the *mentalité* of Pennsylvania farmers and artisans, have agreed to ignore the possibility that Quakers in Pennsylvania redesigned the English family according to their radical religious thought. Following the current wisdom, they describe the Quaker settlers socially as carriers of traditional "middling" habits of thought, and although they disagree about what that tradition was in every detail, both believe that it necessarily limited the social impact of the settlers' religious faith in the Delaware Valley.

2. Barry Reay, "The Social Origins of Early Quakerism," *Journal of InterDisciplinary History,* 11:1 (Summer 1980): 55–72.

3 "Merioneth Taxpayers of the Tudor and Stuart Period," Leonard Owen, ed., NLW, Ms#18162d; Hearth Tax Montgomeryshire, E. 179.265/7, Public Record Office, London; Charles Browning, *Welsh Settlement of Pennsylvania* (Philadelphia, 1912), passim; Thomas Allen Glenn, *Merion in the Welsh Tract* (Baltimore, 1970, reprint edition), *passim*. Among all 891 households, 96 percent possessed one or two hearths; among 22 Quaker households, 86 percent possessed one or two hearths. The tithe seizures are from "An Account of Particulars of the Sufferings of the People of God Called Quakers on Account of Tithes," film 239, box 172, FH; MS Great Book of Sufferings, FH. The title report figure was multiplied by ten in order to get estimate of income. In 21 cases, estimate was based on average of two or more tithe seizures.

4. Cheshire Registers of Births, Deaths, and Marriages, FH.

5. Few Welsh Quaker emigrants came from even the few Merionethshire market towns, see Browning, *Welsh Settlement*; Glenn, *Merion*.

6. Demos, *A Little Commonwealth*, 183.

7. Mildred Campbell, "Social Origins of Some Early Americans," in *Seventeenth-Century America; Essays in Colonial History*, ed. James Morton Smith (Chapel Hill, 1959), 89. See also her debate, more recently with David W. Galenson: David W. Galenson, "'Middling People' or 'Common Sort'?: The Social Origins of Some Early Americans Reexamined;" "With a Rebuttal by Mildred Campbell," *William and Mary Quarterly* 3rd ser., 35 (1978): 499-540; David Galenson, with a reply by Mildred Campbell, "The Social Origins of Some Early Americans: Rejoinder," *ibid.*, 36 (April 1979): 264-86. The debate centers on the servant lists from Bristol and London, which, while an essential starting point, will never by themselves yield conclusive answers. Historians need to do more ethnographic studies of the relevant villages, towns, and regions in seventeenth-century Great Britain.

8. Daniel Defoe, *A Tour Through the Whole Island of Great Britain* (London, 1724-26), 377.

9. E.B., "A Trip to North Wales" in Howard W. Troyer, ed., *Five Travel Scripts Commonly Attributed to Edward Ward, Reproduced from the Earliest Editions Extant* (New York, 1933, facs. ed.), 15, 17.

10. "The Life and Death of Shreffery ap Morgan" in Roger Thompson, ed., *Samuel Pepys' Penny Merriments, Being a Collection of Chapbooks* (New York, 1977), 200-203.

11. Defoe, *A Tour*, 391; E.B., "A Trip," 17.

12. Peter Laslett, "Clayworth and Cogenhoe," in *Family Life and Illicit Love in Earlier Generations: Essays in Historical Sociology* (Cambridge, 1977), 50-101; K. Wrightson and D. Levine, *Poverty and Piety*, 23.

13. David Hey, *An English Rural Community: Myddle under the Tudors and Stuarts* (Leicester, 1974), *passim*; Richard Gough, *The History of Myddle*, ed. David Hey (London, 1981), *passim*; D. C. Coleman, "Labour in the English Economy of the Seventeenth Century," *Economic History Review*, 2nd ser., 8 (1956): 280-95.

14. For Welsh land and farming, see Frank Emery, "The Farming Regions of Wales" in Joan Thirsk, ed., *The Agrarian History of England and Wales, Volume 4: 1500-1620*, (Cambridge, 1967), 113-60; B. E. Howells, "Pembrokeshire Farming Circa, 1580-1620," *National Library of Wales Journal*, 9 (1955-56): 239-81, 313-37, 413-39; Frank Emery, "West Glamogranshire Farming Circa 1580-1620," *ibid.*, 392-400; David W. Howell, *Land and People in Nineteenth Century Wales* (London, 1977). For Cheshire, see Joan Thirsk, "The Farming Regions of England" in Thirsk, ed., *Agrarian History*, IV: 80-89; C. Stella Davies, *The Agricultural History of*

Cheshire, 1750-1850 (Manchester, 1960), *passim*; J. Howard Hodson, *Cheshire, 1660-1780: Restoration to Industrial Revolution* (Chester, 1973), 70-77; G. Elliott, "Field Systems of Northwest England," in Alan R. H. Baker and Robin A. Butlin, *Studies of Field Systems in the British Isles* (Cambridge, 1973), 42-92; Dorothy Sylvester, *The Historical Atlas of Cheshire* (Chester, U.K., 1958); Dorothy Sylvester, *The Rural Landscape of the Welsh Borderland: A Study in Historical Geography* (London, 1967); Dorothy Sylvester, "Parish and Township in Cheshire and North East Wales," *Journal of Chester and North Wales Archaeological Society*, 54 (1967).

15. Margaret Spufford, *Contrasting Communities: English Villagers in the Sixteenth and Seventeenth Centuries* (Cambridge, 1974), 25-50.

16. John Sheail, "The Distribution of Taxable Population in England and Wales During the Early Sixteenth Century," *Institute of British Geographers Transactions*, 55 (March 1982): 123.

17. Charles Wilson, *England's Apprenticeship 1603-1763* (London, 1971), 363.

18. W. G. Hoskins, "Harvest Fluctuations and English Economic History, 1620-1759," *Agricultural History Review*, 16 (1968): 15-31.

19. Hey, *An English Rural Community*, 1-50; for example of family usage of life-leasehold, see Adam Martindale, *The Life of Adam Martindale, Written by Himself* (Manchester, U.K., 1845), 4-40.

20. *The Coleman Deeds*, compiled by Francis Green (Aberystwyth, U.K., 1921), *passim*; *The Harwarden Deeds*, complied by Francis Green (Aberystwyth, U.K., 1931), *passim*.

21. "Letter from John Lloyd of Ruthin to Edward Lloyd at Oxford, August 1683," quoted in Frank Emery, "The Farming Regions of Wales," in Thirsk, ed., *Agrarian History*, IV: 116-7.

22. D. M. Woodward, "The Chester Leather Industry, 1558-1625," *Transactions of the Historical Society of Lancashire and Cheshire*, 119 (1967): 65-111; D. M. Woodward, "The Overseas Trade of Chester, 1600-1650," *ibid.*, 122 (1971): 23-42; W. B. Stephens, "The Overseas Trade of Chester in the Seventeenth-Century," *ibid.*, 120 (1968): 23-34; Hodson, *Cheshire, 1660-1780*, 137-55; Robert Craig, "Shipping and Shipbuilding in the Port of Chester in the Eighteenth and Early Nineteenth Centuries," *Transactions of the Historical Society of Lancashire and Cheshire*, 71 (1961): 21-60.

23. Defoe, *A Tour*, 394; Peter Clark and Paul Slack, *English Towns in Transition 1500-1700* (Oxford, 1976), 46-61.

24. F. C. Beazley, ed., "Hearth Tax Returns for the City of Chester, 1664-1665," *Publications of the Lancashire and Cheshire Record Society* (now the *Chester Archaeological Society*) new series, 36 (1946); Hodson, *Cheshire, 1660-1780*, 97.

25. William Stout, *The Autobiography of William Stout of Lancaster, 1665-1752* (Manchester, 1967), *passim*.

26. Ebenezer Worchester, ed., *Frodsham Parish Church Register, 1555-1812* (Chester, 1913); *Eccleston Parish Registers, 1593-1899*, CCRO; M. L. Farrall, ed., *Parish Registers of the Holy and Undivided Trinity in the City of Chester, 1532-1837* (Chester, 1896); Rev. G. B. Sandford, ed., *Registers of the Parish of Church Minshull, 1561-1851* (Chester, U.K., 1850); Rev. G. E. Warburton, ed., *Warburton Parish Registers, 1611-1851* (Chester, U.K., 1896); Robert Dickinson, ed., *The Registers of the Parish Church of Gawsworth in the County of Chester* (London, 1955); Fereguson Irvine, ed., *The Register of Bruera Church, Formerly in the Parish of St. Oswald, Chester County, 1662-1812* (London, Parish Register Society, 1910). The distribution

of the sample is Church Minshull 5, Gawsworth 15, Bruera 4, Frodsham 10, Eccleston 4, Chester 13, and Warburton 4.

27. The Cheshire families produced 176 children or 3.75 live births per household; Terling families (1550-1724) had 3.86 live births per household. Fewer Cheshire children survived childhood diseases. The Cheshire families produced an average of 2.34 surviving children; Terling families produced an average of 2.7 surviving children. See, K. Wrightson and D. Levine, *Poverty and Piety*, 60-63.

28. "Parochial Notitiae for the Diocese of St. Asaph, 1681-1687," NLW, SA/Misc./1300-1491. Some of these have been published and edited by Milwyn Griffith in *Montgomeryshire Collections*, 59, 60, 63, 66 (1965-78).

29. Peter Laslett, *The World We Have Lost: England Before the Industrial Age* (New York, 1963), 108.

30. The sixteen parishes are Aberhafesp, Berriew, Betts Cedewain, Castle Caerinion, Cemmes, Darowen, Guildsfield, Hirnant, Landysilio, Landrino, Llandyssil, Llan Elian, Llanyvill, Llanwoddyn, Meifod. In these parishes, there were 1978 households with 8937 people; 3048 or 34% were under eighteenth years of age. The average household size was 4.5 people and, on average, only 1.54 were children. "Parochial Notitiae for the Diocese of St. Asaph, 1681-1687," SA/MISC/ 1300-1491/, NLW.

31. Leonard Owen, "The Population of Wales in the Sixteenth and Seventeenth Centuries," *Transactions of the Honorable Society of Cymmrodorian*, 55 (1959): 99-113.

32. Registers of Meifod Parish Church, Montgomeryshire, 1660-1700, St. Asaph Collections, NLW.

33. "George Lewis, Dogelley, to the Secretary, July 14, 1716" (document #4683) in Mary Clements, ed., *The Correspondence and Minutes of the S.P.C.K. Relating to Wales, 1699-1740* (Cardiff, 1951), 87.

34. "Dr. Joseph Jones, Bangor, to the Secretary, June 20, 1716" (document #4840), *ibid.*, 86.

35. "Humphry Jones, Glassbury, Brecknockshire, to the Secretary, March 23, 1701" (document #4325), *ibid.*, 76.

36. Howell, *Land and People*, introduction.

37. Will of Robert Lord Viscount Chomordeley, Oct. 23, 1681, Cheshire Probate Records, CCRO.

38. Will of William Vaughan, Esquire, Towyn, Sept. 18, 1677, Merionethshire Probate Records, NLW.

39. See for example, Will of William Higginson, Allostock, Jan. 18, 1660, CCRO.

40. Will of Thomas Boult, Sandbach, Feb. 12, 1660, Cheshire Probate Records, CCRO.

41. Will of Joseph Whisham, Allostock, July 25, 1681, Cheshire Probate Records, CCRO.

42. Will of Morgan ap David, Towyn, April 1, 1687, Merionethshire Probate Records, NLW.

43. Will of Joseph Buckeley, Houghton, May 17, 1681, Cheshire Probate Records, CCRO.

44. Will of Phillip John Phillip. Llandanock, July 5, 1678, Merionethshire Probate Records, NLW.

45. For example, Howell Williams, husbandman of Lanegrin, Merionethshire, who gave all his estate to his wife and young children. But his daughter

got a marriage portion of 10s; another daughter got £1, and his only son got only £10. Will of Howell Williams, Lanegrin, Feb. 5, 1683, Merionethshire Probate Records, NLW.

46. See for example, Will of John Denison, Wereneter, May 14, 1681, Cheshire Probate Records, CCRO.

47. See for example, Will of William ap Arthur, Llandegrin, Oct. 16, 1678, Merionethshire Probate Records, NLW; Will of Mary Dutton, widow, Overton, Dec. 13, 1660, Cheshire Probate Records, CCRO; Will of James Hease, Preston-on-the-Hill, April 6, 1660, Cheshire Probate Records, CCRO.

48. See Christopher Hill, "Puritan and 'the Dark Corners of the Land,'" in *Change and Continuity in Seventeenth-Century England*, ed. C. Hill (Cambridge, Mass., 1975), 3–47.

49. Few craftsmen lived in the parish. The Myddle economy was relatively poor. David Hey, Myddle's modern historian, found that even the more prosperous and socially ambitious families in Myddle "had only a 50:50 chance of retaining their property over two or three generations." The cottagers were also transient. In such scarcity, the tenant farmers, with their clannish strategies, were the most stable group, forming, as Hey found, "the core of the community, that helped to give it some sense of permanency." D. Hey, *An English Rural Community, passim*; Gough, *The History of Myddle*, 1–24.

50. *Ibid.*, 78.

51. Gough noted, "I hope no man will blame me for not naming every person according to that which he conceives is his right and superiority in the seats in the church, because it is a thing impossible for any man to know." *Ibid.*, 10.

52. *Ibid.*, 117–20.

53. *Ibid.*, 114–16.

54. *Ibid.*, 100–101.

55. *Ibid.*, 112–13.

56. For example, William Preece, son of Griffith ap Reece, "a careful, laborious" tenant farmer who "lived plentifully," was a "soldier in the low countries" who returned to Myddle only to enlist "in the trained bands for this county," and later, when King Charles fled to Shrewsbury in the Civil War, "listed himselfe a soldier in the King's service." *Ibid.*, 133–34.

57. *Ibid.*, 238–39.

58. *Ibid.*, 92–94.

59. *Ibid.*, 153.

60. *Ibid.*, 241–43.

61. *Ibid.*, 106.

62. *Ibid.*, 241–43.

63. *Ibid.*, 246–47.

64. *Ibid.*, 210–11.

65. *Ibid., passim*. Gough fully described 99 of 221 marriages he mentioned. Admittedly his gossip on this matter is statistically suspect. It neither can be assumed that his sample of well-described courtships was random nor determined what alternative method of selection Gough followed. Despite this serious problem, his sample is worth analyzing. Gough was the most inclusive gossip in the seventeenth-century Northwest, and perhaps in England. Initiative in seventeenth-century middling marriages will never be understood by ignoring the best available gossip.

66. For excellent evidence of high affect among sixteenth- and seventeenth-century middling English people, see Michael MacDonald, *Mystical Bedlam: Madness, Anxiety, and Healing in Seventeenth-Century England* (London, 1981), 71-111.

67. Gough, *History of Myddle*, 158-160.

68. *Ibid.*, 124-25.

69. *Ibid.*, 99-103.

70. *Ibid.*, 91-92.

71. *Ibid.*, 138-39.

72. *Ibid.*, 176-81.

73. B. G. Blackwood, *The Lancashire Gentry and the Great Rebellion* (Manchester, U.K., 1978); J. S. Morrill, *Cheshire 1630-1660: County Government and Society During the "English Revolution"* (Oxford, 1974); Ronald Hutton, *The Royalist War Effort, 1642-1646* (London, 1982).

74. Morrill, *Cheshire 1630-1660*; Christopher Hill, "Puritans and 'the Dark Corners of the Land,'" 7-75; C. Hill, "Propagating the Gospel" in H. E. Bell and R. L. Ollard, *Historical Essays 1600-1750 Presented to David Ogg* (London, 1963), 25-59; Geraint H. Jenkins, *Literature, Religion, and Society in Wales 1660-1730* (Cardiff, U.K., 1978), chap. 1; R. C. Richardson, *Puritanism in Northwest England: A Regional Study of the Diocese of Chester to 1642* (Manchester, U.K., 1972); Thomas Richards, *A History of the Puritan Movement in Wales* (London, 1920); Geoffrey Nuttal, *The Welsh Saints, 1640-1660: Walter Cradock, Vavasor Powell, Morgan Llwyd* (Cardiff, U.K., 1957); Thomas Richards, *The Religious Census of 1676* (London, 1927).

75. Gough, *History of Myddle*, 172.

76. John U. Ogbu, "Origins of Human Competence: A Cultural-Ecological Perspective," *Child Development*, 52 (1981), 413-29; M. Cole et al., *The Cultural Impact of Learning and Thinking: An Exploration in Experimental Anthropology* (New York, 1971); R. W. LeVine, *Dreams and Deeds: Achievement Motivation in Nigeria* (Chicago, 1967); A. Inkeles, "Social Structure and the Socialization of Competence" in *Socialization and Schools*, ed. Harvard Education Review (Cambridge, Mass., 1966); idem, "Society, Social Structure, and Child Socialization," in *Socialization and Society*, ed. John A. Causen (Boston, 1968); J. W. Berry, *Human Ecology and Cognitive Style: Comparative Studies in Cultural and Psychological Adaptations* (New York, 1977).

77. For the geographical origins of seventeenth-century Massachusetts settlers, see Charles E. Banks, *Topographical Dictionary of 2885 English Emigrants to New England* (Philadelphia, 1937).

78. George Rosse to the Secretary, Chester, 30 Dec. 1712, in *Historical Collections Relating to the American Colonial Church, Volume 2: Pennsylvania* (Hartford, 1969), 69.

CHAPTER TWO Spiritual Tribalism

1. The following discussion focuses on the majority, "conservative" Quakers, not the radical, more individualistic wing led by James Naylor, who Christopher Hill has likened to Ranters. The radical wing of early Quakerism has rightly gotten much attention lately, which has, however, diverted attention from the radicalism, particularly familial radicalism, of the "conservative" group. See C. Hill, *The World Turned Upside Down*; B. Reay, *The Quakers and the English Revolution*.

2. On Puritan reformers' difficulties in northwestern Britain, see Christopher Hill, "Puritans and 'the Dark Corners of the Land,'" 7-75; idem, "Propagating the Gospel," 25-59; G. Jenkins, *Literature, Religion, and Society in Wales 1660-1730*, chap. 1; R. C. Richardson, *Puritanism in North-West England*, chap. 1.

3. For Cradock's career, see G. Nuttal, *The Welsh Saints, 1640-1660*, 18-27.

4. Walter Cradock, *Glad Tydings from Heaven* (London, 1649), as quoted in Nuttal, *Welsh Saints*, 27.

5. Vavasor Powell, *Saving Faith* (London, 1651), 76.

6. Morgan Llwyd, "The Summer," in *Gweithau Morgan Llwyd* (Aberystwyth, 1931) I: 24.

7. A. N. Palmer, *A History of the Older Nonconformity of Wrexham and Its Neighborhood* (Wrexham, 1888), 29-31.

8. Morgan Llwyd, "A Song of My Beloved Concerning his Vineyard (2nd Month in 1652)," in *Gweithau Morgan Llwyd*, I: 88-91.

9. Nuttal, *Welsh Saints*, 50-60; George Fox, *The Journal of George Fox*, ed. Norman Penney (Cambridge, 1911), I: 141 (published in two volumes; known as *Cambridge Journal*).

10. This interpretation owes much to Morrill, *Cheshire 1630-1660*. For additional discussion of George Booth's Rebellion, see also R. N. Dore, "The Cheshire Rising of 1659," *Transactions of Lancashire and Cheshire Antiquarian Society*, 69 (1958): 43-69. Neither author seems aware or stresses the large number of Quakers on Sir George Booth's estate and therefore they tend to dismiss the fearful anti-Quaker rhetoric of the Booth rebels as mere pretext. For an interpretation that highlights fear of Quakerism, see Reay, *The Quakers and the English Revolution*. For Quakerism in Styall or Pownall Fee, see below.

11. *Cambridge Journal Fox*, II.

12. MacDonald, *Mystical Bedlam*, 217.

13. George Fox, *The Journal of George Fox*, ed. Rufus M. Jones (New York, 1963), 97.

14. Henry J. Cadbury, ed., *George Fox's "Book of Miracles"* (Cambridge, U.K. 1948), *passim*.

15. *Dictionary of American Biography* (New York, 1943) XI: 334; XIV: 118; Edward Bronner, *William Penn's Holy Experiment: The Founding of Pennsylvania, 1681-1701* (Philadelphia, 1956), 39, 44.

16. William Smith, *A New Primmer* (London, 1665), 65.

17. George Keith, *The Benefit, Advantage, and Glory of Silent Meetings* (London, 1670), 20.

18. Richard Farnsworth, *The Spirit of God Speaking in the Temple of God* (London, 1663), 13.

19. Cadbury, ed., *Fox's "Book of Miracles"*, 121-22.

20. George Fox, *A Collection of Many Select and Christian Epistles, Letters, Testimonies Written on Sundry Occasions, by that Ancient, Eminent, Faithful Friend, and Minister of Christ Jesus, George Fox, in two Volumes* (Philadelphia, 1831), II: p. 65.

21. Geoffrey Nuttal, *Studies in Christian Enthusiasm, Illustrated from Early Quakerism* (Wallinford, Pa., 1948), 59.

22. For a fine sociolinguistic analysis of Quaker writings and behaviors, see Richard Bauman, *"Let Your Words Be Few": Symbolism of Speaking and Silence Among Seventeenth-Century Quakers* (Cambridge, U.K., 1983).

23. Joseph Pike, *Some Account of the Life* (London, 1837), 34, 35, 42.

24. Bauman, *"Let Your Words Be Few,"* 43–62.

25. George Keith, *The Magick of Quakerism* (London, 1707), 11.

26. Benjamin Furly, *The World's Honor Detected* (London, 1662), 13.

27. "Roger Haydock of Coppull, A Brief Biography and Ten Original Letters," *Transactions of the Lancashire and Cheshire Antiquarian Society*, 52 (1937): 1–66.

28. Richard Davies, *An Account . . . of Richard Davies*, 15–18.

29. "John Lawson to Margaret Fell and Others," Nov. 1653, Swarthmore MSS., 4, 66, FH; R. Farmer, *The Great Mysteries of Godliness and Ungodliness*, as quoted in Nuttal, *Studies in Christian Enthusiasm*, 61; Fox, *Cambridge Journal*, I: 141, 186, 286; E. Brockbank, *Richard Hubberthorne of Yealand* (London, 1929), 147; Braithwaite, *The Beginnings*, 123–24.

30. "Thomas Holme to Margaret Fell, March 1654," Swarthmore Mss., I: 189; "Thomas Holme to Margaret Fell, Aug. 28, 1655, *ibid.*, Swarthmore Mss., I: 197; Braithwaite, *Beginnings*, 126; Nuttal, *Studies in Christian Enthusiasm*, 53–66.

31. The early Chester Quaker converts were often colorful individualists. For example, in 1655, Richard Sale, a corpulent man, went through Derby barefoot and barelegged, dressed in sack cloth, with ashes on his head, sweet flowers in his right hand and stinking weeds in his left, as a sign. In 1657, almost naked, he went down Eastgate Street, Chester with a lighted candle in his hand at midday in hopes of showing the uselessness of candlelight worship. Braithwaite, *Beginnings*, 105, 126, 216, 388, 392; "Return of Recusants and Nonconformists, 1669," in *Cheshire Sheaf*, 3rd ser., 58 (1963): 22.

32. Norman Penney, ed., *The First Publishers of Truth*, (London, 1907), 18–19; Braithwaite, *Beginnings*, 124–25.

33. "Return of Recusants and Nonconformists, 1669."

34. *Ibid.*; "Quarter Session . . . Records for the County Palatine of Chester, 1559–1760," *Records Society of Lancashire and Cheshire*, 94 (1940): 164; "Hearth Tax, 1664, Cheshire" (microfilm copy), CCRO. The names in the 1664 Hearth Tax for Pownall Fee are given below in sequence. The names in italic type are Quakers; dates in parentheses show the earliest mention in Quaker registers. The numbers are hearths:

William Alcock 2; William Alcock 1; Francis Alcock 1; *John Lamb* 2 (1659); *Richard Smith* 1 (1656); *Mary Worthington* 1 (1658); Humphry Pownall 1; *Thomas Janney* 2 (1660); William Faulkner 1; *William Smith* 1 (1683); *Henry Royle* 1 (1684); *John Burgess* 2 (1663); *Lawrence Pierson* 1 (1654); Jeffrey Burgess 1; James Kellsall 1; *Robert Milner* 1 (1659); *John Worral* 1 (1662); Hugh Pownall 1; *Lawrence Cash* 1 (1680); *Thomas Burgess* 1 (1661); Hugh Worthington 1; John Mather 1; Roger Pierson 1; Katherine Kelsall 1; *Thomas Pott* 1 (1656); *Thomas Pierson* (1683); John Kelsall 1; John Cripping 1; Mr. Thatham 4; William Worrall 2; Edward Dunken 1; Thomas Heyes 1; Katherine Alcock 1; William Newton 1; George Barber 1; William Smith 1; Thomas Heald 1; William Worrall 1; Henry Taylor 1; William Baguley 1; John Pierson 2; Widow Harding 1; James Kellsall 1; William Bowen 1; *John Worthington* 2 (1658); Hugh Coppock 1; Edmund Higginson 2; *Richard Roylance* 1 (1659); John Creator 1; Roger Worthington 2; Richard Cockson 2; Elizabeth Warburton 1; Henry Cliffe 1; Peter Newton 1; Richard Stockton 1; *Edward Pierson* 1 (1673).

35. "Mr. Henry Maurice's Account of Numbers of Churches in Wales and their Pastors," in *Records of a Church of Christ Meeting in Broadmead, Bristol, 1640–1687*, ed. E. B. Underhill (London, 1947), 515.

36. Richard Davies, *An Account of . . . Richard Davies* (6th ed., London, 1825), 13, 17, 18, 34.

37. *Ibid.*, 40–56.

38. *Ibid.*

39. For fear of sex and marriage among early Quakers, see "Richard Weaver to Margaret Fell, 6 Oct. 1655," Swarthmore Mss., I: 91, 97; "Richard Hunter to Margaret Fell, Autumn 1656," *ibid.*, Swarthmore Mss. I: 357; "Richard Hunter to Margaret Fell, Nov. 21, 1656, *ibid.*, Swarthmore Mss., I: 358; Fox, *Cambridge Journal*, II: 154; for good discussion, see Mabel Brailsford, *Quaker Women 1650–1690* (London, 1915), 144–57.

40. Miles Halhead, *Sufferings and Passages* (London, 1690), 8. James Naylor also chose to abandon his wife and children.

41. Braithwaite, *Beginnings*, chap. 4; C. Hill, *World Turned Upside Down*, *passim*.

42. For accounts of Swarthmore Hall experience, see Braithwaite, *Beginnings*, chap. 5; Isabel Ross, *Margaret Fell, Mother of Quakerism* (London, 1949), 8–114, *passim*.

43. "Leeds Journal Testimony to George Fox by Margaret Fox," in George Fox, *Journal* (Leeds, 1836); William Caton, *Life of William Caton*, ed. George Fox (London, 1839), 3.

44. "Leeds Journal Testimony."

45. *Ibid.*

46. Caton, *Life*, 7–10.

47. *Ibid.*

48. "William Caton to Margaret Fell, 1657," Swarthmore Mss., I: 316; Caton Mss., III: 31, as quoted in Ross, *Fell*, 72. Ross also documents the often extravagant affection and esteem many other Quaker itinerants, male and female, expressed for Margaret Fell and her daughters.

49. Caton, *Life*, 7–11.

50. "A. Pearson to Margaret Fell, May 9, 1653," as quoted in Ross, *Fell*, 20–21. See also Halhead, *Sufferings*, 4–6.

51. Simmonds was held responsible by many Quakers and others for "bewitching" James Naylor into making his disastrous symbolic entry into Bristol in 1656, which led to his jailing and maiming. According to Christopher Hill, John Milton was convinced by the Simmonds-Naylor incident to give up on women's equality. Obviously, George Fox disagreed. Christopher Hill, *Milton and the English Revolution* (New York, 1979), 135–36.

52. "Miriam Moss's Testimony," *Journal of the Friends Historical Society*, XIII: 143; Ross, *Fell*, 217n.

53. Cheshire Quaker Registers of Births, Marriages, and Deaths, FH.

54. Fox, *Epistles*, I: 68.

55. *Ibid.*, 34, 79–80, 104, 157. According to a categorization by topic of 361 of George Fox's letters from 1650 to 1679 in George Fox, *A Collection of Many Select and Christian Epistles*, 2 vols. (Philadelphia, 1831), a little more than half of the 22 letters he wrote almost exclusively on marriage and family life were written before 1660. He did greatly increase his interest in disciplinary meetings and monthly meetings after 1660. Nearly 95 percent of 25 letters exclusively on monthly meeting organization were written after 1660. Yet, Fox had largely defined the Quaker household and its role before the Restoration. The monthly meetings were a completion of these definitions.

56. Thomas Hilder, *Conjugal Counsell* (London, 1653), 38.

57. Thomas Lawrence, *Concerning Marriage* (1663); Arnold Lloyd, *Quaker Social History, 1669–1738* (London, 1950), 52.

58. "Joseph Nicolson to Margaret Fell, April 3, 1660," Swarthmore Mss., IV: 107; "Joseph Nicolson to Margaret Fell, July 10, 1660," *ibid.*, IV: 108. Discussed in Brailsford, *Quaker Women*, 146–48.

59. "Thomas Lower to Mary Fell, c. 1667," as quoted in Ross, *Fell*, 208–9.

60. "Daniel Abraham to Rachel Fell, 1681," Thirbeck Mss. 17, as quoted in Ross, *Fell*, 315–16.

61. Caton, *Life*, 27.

62. Lloyd, *Quaker Social History*, 48–52.

63. Newton by Frodsham and Frandley Men's Monthly Meeting Minutes, 4th month, 4th day, 1689; 10th month, 2nd day, 1690, CCRO.

64. Morley Men's Monthly Meeting Minutes, Book I, 1677–98, 5th month, 26th day, 1681, CCRO.

65. As quoted in Vann, *The Social Development of English Quakerism 1655–1755*, 184.

66. See, for example, Radnor Women's Monthly Meeting Minutes, 7th month, 3rd day, 1725, FHS.

67. William Salt, *The Light, The Way, That Children Ought to be Trained up in . . .* (London, 1660), 2.

68. Humphry Smith, "To All Parents on the Face of the Earth" (1st ed., 1660), in his *A Collection of the Several Writings and Faithful Testimonies of that Suffering Servant of God, and Patient Follower of the Lamb. . .* (London, 1683), 123–30.

69. John Field, *Friendly Advice in the Spirit of Love unto Believing Parents* (London, 1688), 2.

70. John Banks, *An Epistle to Friends* (London, 1692), 16–20.

71. Joseph Pike, *Some Account of the Life* (London, 1837), 15, 16, 86. For different readings see Vann, *The Social Development*, 169; and J. William Frost, *The Quaker Family in Colonial America* (New York, 1973), 64–88.

72. George Fox, *A Primer* (London, 1665), 67.

73. Isaac Pennington, "For My Dear Children, 3rd Month, 19th day, 1667," in *Letters of Early Friends*, ed. A. R. Barclay (London, 1841), 397–402.

74. Stephen Crisp, "The Christian Experiences . . . and Writings" in *Friends Library* (Philadelphia, 1845), 243–44.

75. Banks, *An Epistle*, 17.

76. Fox, *A Primer*, 67.

77. John Richardson, *An Account of the Life of that Ancient Servant of Jesus Christ, John Richardson* (Philadelphia, 1845), 110.

78. Fox, *Epistles*, II: 39, 40; "George Fox to Friends, January 30, 1675," as quoted in William Braithwaite, *The Second Period of Quakerism* (London, 1919), 274.

79. Fox, *Epistles*, II: 41, 95, 97.

80. *Ibid.*, 96, 113.

81. As quoted in William Loddington, *The Good Order of Truth Justified* (London, 1685), 8.

82. As he tightened family discipline, Fox met consistently with strong opposition within the Quaker ranks, most famously the Wilkinson-Story schism of 1672–77, following on the heels of the establishment of men's, and particularly women's

meetings. But the Wilkinson-Story opposition was preceded by earlier oppositions to Fox's legal familialism: the Naylorites in 1654–56 and the Perrot division in 1662. In brief, Fox's later development of elaborate disciplinary machinery, the monthly meetings, was an elaboration of his earlier ethical and familial themes, not an abrupt change forced by persecution. The northwestern householders generally followed Fox in these disputes. See Braithwaite, *Beginnings*, 241–78; idem, *The Second Period*, 228–50, 290–323, 360–66, 469–82, 494. Fox's dream was recorded in many register books, see Lloyd, *Quaker Social History*, 111.

83. Anne Whitehead and Mary Elson, *An Epistle for True Unity and Order in the Church of Christ* (London, 1680), 4.

84. Note that the empowered female-maternal sphere was vigorously proposed for over 50,000 British and American Quakers merely a hundred years before time-clock factory discipline or the changing nature of textile production made such social organization by gender role and domesticity plausible. See Cott, *The Bonds of Womanhood*, chap. 1.

85. Newton-by-Frodsham and Frandley Men's Monthly Meeting Minutes, 6th month, 7th day, 1683; 6th month, 5th day 1685, 7th month, 4th day, 1686, CCRO.

86. *Ibid.*, 6th month, 7th day, 1683.

87. *Ibid.*, 9th month, 6th day, 1685.

88. *Ibid.*, 3rd month, 4th day, 1697.

89. Morley Men's Monthly Meeting Minutes, Book I, 1677–98, 9th month, 4th day, 1696, CCRO.

90. *Ibid.*, 12th month, 3rd day, 1696.

91. *Ibid.*, 3rd month, 1st day, 1697; 2nd month, 7th day, 1697.

92. *Ibid.*, 7th month, 7th day, 1698.

93. Anonymous, *The Quaker's Dream or the Devil's Pilgrimage in England* (London, 1655). See also Anonymous, *The Quacking Mountebank or the Jesuit Turned Quaker* (London, 1665).

94. Anonymous, *The Quakers Shaken, or, A Warning Against Quaking, Being . . . A Relation of a Horrid Buggery Committed by Hugh Bisbrown, A Quaker with a Mare* (London, 1655); see also, Sir John Denham, "News from Colchester: or, a Proper New Ballad of certain Carnal Passages betwixt a Quaker and a Colt at Horsely, near Colchester, in Essex," in his *Poetical Works of Sir John Denham* (Edinburgh, 1780), 110–12.

95. Matthew Stevenson, *The Quaker's Wedding* (London, 1671); see also Martin Llewellyn, *Wickham Wakened, or, the Quakers' Madrigal in Rime Doggerel* (London, 1672).

96. Anonymous, *The Secret Sinners* (London, 1675); Anonymous, *The Quaker Turned Jew, Being a True Relation, How an Eminent Quaker in the Isle of Ely, on Monday the 18th of April. . .* (London, 1675); Anonymous, *The Quaker and His Maid* (London); Anonymous, *The Monstrous Eating Quaker* (London, 1675).

97. *The Quaker Turned Jew*.

98. *The Secret Sinners*, as reprinted in Roger Thompson, ed., *Samuel Pepy's Merriments* (New York, 1977), 147–53.

99. See Thompson, ed., *Samuel Pepy's Merriments*, 254–59. *passim*.

100. Thomas Walker, *The Quaker's Opera, As it is Performed at Lee's and Harper's Great Theatrical Booth in Bartholomew-Fair, with the Musick Prefix'd to Each Song* (London, 1728). In this mercenary and poor adaptation of Gay's *A Beggar's Opera*, the Quaker is actually a minor character. His use in the title was

probably meant to woo the multitudes. And, although I have not been able to find the work, the theme apparently continued, William Stewardson, *Spiritual Courtship or the Rival Quakeresses* (London, 1764).

101. "Franklin and the Quakers" and "The March of the Paxton Men" in Leonard W. Labaree, ed., *The Papers of Benjamin Franklin* (New Haven, 1967), XI: 70, 374.

102. See Lawrence Stone, *The Family, Sex, and Marriage in England, 1500–1800* (New York, 1977); Randolph Trumbach, *The Rise of the Egalitarian Family: Aristocratic Kinship and Domestic Relations in Eighteenth-Century England* (New York, 1978). Both historians seek and demonstrate changes in upper-class family life, but neither seeks nor finds thorough domesticity.

103. See Christopher Hill, *John Milton and the English Revolution* (New York, 1979), 135–36.

104. Northwestern British Quaker familialism shows how the debate between the advocates of familial continuity and of discontinuity might be reconciled. The story of the emergence of radical domesticity of British Quakers confirms and partly denies both points of view. The first generation of Quakers in northwestern England from 1650 to 1700 were composed of a small group of relatively poor, tertiary gentry and a large group of farmers and small yeomen. The profound Quaker religious experience of being transformed by the Light certainly heightened or reorganized previous ties and affections. Yet, the emergence of Quaker familialism in northwestern England — the whole idea of establishing a religious society without a trained ministry and based solely on the intimate sharing of religious experience — was unthinkable without the powerful familial affections, customs, and dependencies established in northwestern smallholders' lives and society. Clearly the purest, most sustained form of British domesticity arose from people who were building on plebeian family traditions and who were far in social location from Lawrence Stone's or Philippe Aries's creative, urban, upper classes.

At the same time, just as the development of Quakerism in northwestern Britain was unthinkable without the affections that had long existed among northwestern smallholders, so too was it unthinkable without the importation from more urbanized southeastern England of puritanical ideas of the transforming power of the Holy Spirit. Most northwestern Quakers came directly from the new Puritan communities formed in the 1650s by propagating Puritan ministers like Vavasor Powell and Morgan Llwyd. They were initially sponsored and protected by the Rump Parliament and the occupying troops of Oliver Cromwell. Thus, even the consolidation of the English state played a crucial, if indirect, role in emergence of northwestern Quakerism.

It is also impossible to deny the significant impact which the rise of Quaker faith of the indwelling Holy Spirit, reinforced by thorough Quaker discipline and organization, had upon the familial beliefs and practices of smallholders who became Friends. The impact of these beliefs is clearly documentable in respect to economic, demographic, and childrearing behavior. Thus, although they were transformed and even heightened by being taken over by men and women on the periphery of the English state and of its emerging commercialized, urbanized society, the upper-class familial ideological developments which Aries and more directly, Stone and Trumbach wrote about were not totally alien to the development of popular familial radicalism. See, Philippe Aries, *Centuries of Childhood: A Social History of Family Life* (France, 1960; English edition, 1962); L. Stone, *The Family, Sex, and Marriage in England 1500–1800*; R. Trumbach, *The Rise of the Egalitarian Family*; A. Macfarlane, *Marriage and Love* in *England* (London, 1985); Linda Pollock, *Forgotten Children: Parent-Child Relations from 1500 to 1900* (Cambridge, 1983); Michael MacDonald, *Mystical Bedlam: Madness, Anxiety, and Healing in Seventeenth Century England*; Barbara Hanawalt, *The Ties that Bound: Peasant Families in Medieval England* (New York, 1986); John Gillis, *For Better, For Worse: British Marriages, 1600 to the Present* (New York, 1985); Ralph A. Houlbrooke, *The English Family, 1450–1500* (London, 1984).

CHAPTER THREE A Family of Great Price

1. See Appendix, Table 3, for sources and summary of this statistic. In these calculations, based on the Quakers' records of sufferings, distraints for tithes and church rate unpayment have not been included. This does not pretend to be a definitive account of Quaker sufferings in Cheshire and Wales, which would required review of all relevant English court records, not just the Quaker records. Nevertheless, the Quaker records are sufficiently complete to allow an estimate and a basis for internal comparisons.

2. Cheshire Quarterly Meeting Register of Births, Burials, and Marriages, 1650–1790; South Wales and Hereford Quarterly Meeting Register of Births, Burials, and Marriages, 1650–1820, FH; Wrightson and Levine, *Terling, 1525–1700*, 55–65. The forthcoming work of Richard Vann and David Eversley on the demography of English and Irish Quakers will doubtless tell whether or not such healthy benefits were generally enjoyed by seventeenth-century Quakers. See, D. E. C. Eversley, "The Demography of the Irish Quakers, 1650–1850," in J. M. Goldstrum and L. A. Clarkson, eds., *Irish Population, Economy, and Society: Essays in Honour of The Late K. H. Connell* (Oxford, 1981).

3. Cheshire Quarterly Meeting Register; South Wales and Hereford Quarterly Meeting Register; family reconstructions of Cheshire households as in Chapter One, above.

4. Cheshire Quarterly Meeting Register of Births, Burials, and Marriages, 1650–1790; South Wales and Hereford Quarterly Meeting Register of Births, Burials, and Marriages, 1650–1820, FH.

5. Probate of John Cheshire, Overton, 22 May 1685; Probate of John Croudson, High Leigh, 26 Oct. 1705; Probate of John Bancroft, Etchells, March 7, 1699; Probate of Richard Challenor, Helsby, Oct. 3, 1676; Probate of Richard Challeneor, Helsby, Oct. 3, 1676; Probate of Thomas Clare, Over Whitley, Feb. 6, 1692; Probate of William Gandy, Frandley, Over Whitley, May 12, 1684; Probate of Joseph Endon, Bossley, Sept. 13, 1688; Probate of John Eaton, Over Whitley, Dec. 29, 1684; Probate of William Hall, Lachford, May 8, 1682; Probate of Thomas Burrows, Aston near Budsworth, Jan. 28, 1677; Probate of Robert Milner, Pownall Fee, June 18, 1674; Probate of Thomas Rowland, Acton, Dec. 28, 1693; Probate of Robert Prichard, Horton, March 20, 1685; Probate of John Key, Hale, June 28, 1682; Probate of Peter Pickering, Over Whitley, Sept. 17, 1681; Probate of Thomas Waite, Manley, June 16, 1686; Probate of Arthur Wilcoxson, Manly, Dec. 4, 1693; Probate of John Tapley, Norley, Nov. 3, 1685; Probate of Richard Trafford, Woodhouse, Jan. 17, 1666, CCRO.

6. Emphasis on the role of persecution in transforming Quakerism pervades Quaker historiography. In recent literature, the most subtle use of this argument is Richard T. Vann, *The Social Development of English Quakerism, 1655–1755* (Cambridge, Mass., 1969), 88–121; see also Hugh Barbour, *The Quakers in Puritan England* (New Haven and London, 1964) 70–71, 234–56.

7. Probate of William Crimes, Weverham, June 2, 1720 (will written in 1704), CCRO.

8. Probate of Joseph Endon, Bossley, Sept. 13, 1688, CCRO.

9. Probate of William Gandy, Frandley, Over Whitley, May 12, 1684, CCRO.

10. See for example, Probate of Peter Pickering of Over Whitley, Sept. 17, 1681, CCRO.

11. Eighth month, 3rd day, 1673, North Wales Quarterly Meeting Minutes, LSF, Film 248, box 202, FH.

12. Fifth month, 3rd day, 1695, Morley Men's Monthly Meeting Minutes, Book I, CCRO.

13. Pontymoile—South Division of Wales, Sufferings, Entry Book, film 239, box 172, Glamorganshire Record Office, FH.

14. See Mary Clement, *The S.P.C.K. and Wales, 1699-1740* (London, 1954).

15. In the following comparative listing, the name of the orphan is given first, and then in order: the date of indenture, the funding institution, the term of indenture, the skill to be learned, and the fee paid with the child to the guardian. ANGLICAN-STATE: John Smith, 2 Feb. 1677, Audlem parish, 7 yrs., shoemaker, £1.5; Ralph Mason, 12 March 1682, Audlem parish, 8 yrs., husbandry, gratis; William Taylor, 2 Dec. 1683, Wynbunbury parish, 7 yrs., husbandry, £2.25; Mather Hewitt, 2 Dec., 1683, Wynbunbury parish, 8 yrs., husbandry, £4.5; John Stockdale, 20 April 1685, Wynbunbury parish, 8 yrs., husbandry, £3; George Naylor, 24 June 1692, Wynbunbury parish, 9 yrs., husbandry, £5; Thomas Brown, 25 Dec. 1683, Wynbunbury parish, 7 yrs., weaver, £3; Peter Noden, 13 July 1684, Wynbunbury parish, 6 yrs., glover, £2.5; Joseph Snead, 13 July 1684, Wynbunbury parish, 7 yrs., husbandry, £3; Samuel Darlington, 11 November 1699, Wynbunbury parish, 7 yrs., husbandry, £5; Mary Brownfield, 29 April 1681, Audlem parish, 7 yrs., housewifery, gratis; Mary Smith, 29 April 1681, Audlem parish, 9 yrs., housewifery, £2.5; Ellen Leay, 21 Oct. 1670, Church Hulme parish, 7 yrs., housewifery, £8; Ann Barton, 19 May 1700, Wynbunbury parish, 4 yrs., none cited, £1.5; Abigail Bush, 1 May 1700, Wynbunbury parish, 10 yrs., none cited, £4. QUAKER MEETINGS : David Cadwallader, 9 April 1673, North Wales Quarterly, 7 yrs., tailor, £2.35; Mordecai More, 8 June 1674, North Wales Quarterly, 7 yrs., surgeon, £10; Widow Waite's boy, 6 July 1679, Dolobran Monthly Meeting, 7 yrs., unclear, £5; Margaret Baddiley's child, 18 Sept. 1688, Cheshire Quarterly, 7 yrs., tailor, £6; John Lamb, 11 June 1689, Cheshire Quarterly, 7 yrs., unclear, £6; Henry William, 14 Sept. 1697, Cheshire Quarterly, 7 yrs., tailor, £8; John Burtonwood, 4 April 1681, Frandley Monthly Meeting, 7 yrs., shoemaking, £8; Henry Taylor, 12 Sept. 1699, Cheshire Quarterly, 7 yrs., unclear, £10; Priscilla Lewis, 28 May 1695, Dolobran Monthly Meeting, 7 yrs., housewifery, £2.5; Martha Taylor, 12 Dec. 1699, Cheshire Quarterly, 7 yrs., housewifery, £6.1. Audlem Parish, 1669-1809, records, P113/28, CCRO; Church Hulme, 1670-1801, records, P82/20, CCRO; Wynbunbury parish, indentures and bonds, 1682-1713, P37/22, CCRO; North Wales Quarterly, 1668-1752, LSF, Film 248, 202, Glamorgan County Record Office, FH; Dolobran or Montgomeryshire Monthly Meeting, Men's Minutes, 1693-1714, microfilm #252, box 206, vol. 379, FH; Cheshire Quarterly Men's Meeting Minutes, 1668-1700, CCRO; Newton by Frodsham and Frandley Men's Monthly Meeting Minutes, 1677-1700, CCRO.

16. Eighth month, 3rd day, 1673; 11th month, 26th day, 1674; 11th month, 27th day, 1686; 8th month, 3rd day, 1687, North Wales Quarterly Meeting Minutes, LSF, Film 248, box 202, FH.

17. Church Hulme, 1670–1801, Parish Records, p/82/20, CCRO; 2nd month, 3rd day, 1700, Morley Men's Monthly Meeting Minutes, Book I, 1677–98, CCRO.

18. Tenth month, 14th day, 1712, North Wales Quarterly Meeting Minutes, FH.

19. Third month, 10th day, 1703, South Wales Quarterly Meeting Minutes, FH.

20. Tenth month, 2nd day, 1697; 10th month, 12th day, 1699, Cheshire Quarterly Meeting Minutes, CCRO.

21. Eleventh month, 4th day, 1697, Newton-by-Frodsham and Frandley Men's Monthly Meeting Minutes, CCRO.

22. David Brion Davis, *The Problem of Slavery in the Age of Revolution, 1770–1832* (Ithaca, 1975), 233.

23. My emphasis on the familial crises is not to deny the contributions of other factors, often cited by historians. These incude "worldly asceticism," the debarring of Quakers from traditional avenues of wealth, the use of Quaker families and connections to raise capital, and the psychological strength produced by Quaker childrearing. See, Arthur Raiswick, *Quakers in Science and Industry* (2nd ed., Newton Abbot, 1968), *passim*; Paul H. Emden, *Quakers in Commerce: A Record of Business Accomplishment* (London, n.d.); Isabel Grubb, *Quakerism in Industry before 1800* (London, 1930), *passim*. David S. Landes, *The Unbound Prometheus: Technological Change and Industrial Development in Western Europe from 1750 to the Present* (Cambridge, 1969), 23, 52; T. S. Ashton, *Iron and Steel in the Industrial Revolution* (2nd ed., Manchester, U.K., 1951), chap. 9: "The Ironmasters"; Everett Hagen, *On the Theory of Social Change* (Homewood, Ill., 1962), 305–8.

24. Charles Lloyd II to the Pembertons, 1695, as quoted in Humphry Lloyd, *The Quaker Lloyds in the Inudstrial Revolution* (London, 1975), 36.

25. Tenth month, 2nd day, 1699, Dolobran or Montgomeryshire Men's Monthly Meeting Minutes, microfilm 252, box 206, vol. 379, FH; out of the £31.5 first raised, Charles Lloyd gave £15 and £5. There were ten subscribers in all.

26. Third month, 28th day, 1701, Dolobran Men's Monthly Meeting Minutes, FHL; Lloyd, *The Quaker Lloyds*, 34. However when Kelsall went to Dolgellau in 1714, he was not replaced, suggesting that the school was rapidly shrinking in attendance or that few of the students were Quakers' children.

27. *Ibid.*, 40–47.

28. John Kelsall's notebook and diary is preserved in manuscript at FH.

29. Lloyd, *The Quaker Lloyds*, 46–63.

30. *Ibid.*, 275.

31. Cheshire Quarterly Meeting Register of Births, Burials, and Marriages, 1650–1790; South Wales and Hereford Quarterly Meeting Register of Births, Burials, and Marriages, 1650–1820, FH.

32. E. A. Wrigley, "A Simple Model of London's Importance in Changing English Society and Economy 1650–1750," in Philip Abrams and E. A. Wrigley, *Towns in Societies: Essays in Economic History and Historical Sociology* (New York, 1978), 218.

33. Peter Laslett and J. Harrison, "Clayworth and Cogenhoe," in H. E. Bell and R. L. Ollard (eds.), *Historial Essays 1600–1750, Presented to David Ogg* (London, 1963), 157–84; David Souden, "Movers and Stayers in Family Reconstruction Populations," *Local Population Studies*, 33 (1984): 50–65; Idem, "Migrants and the Population Structure of Later Seventeenth-Century Provincial Cities and Market

Towns," in Peter Clark, ed., *The Transformation of English Provincial Towns, 1600-1800* (London, 1972), 117-63; J. Patten, *Rural-Urban Migration in Pre-Industrial England* (University of Oxford School of Geography Research Paper, 1973); Peter Clark, "Migration in England during the Late Seventeenth and Early Eighteenth Centuries," *Past and Present*, 83 (1979): 57-90; Ann Kussmaul, *Servants in Husbandry in Early Modern England* (New York, 1981), 12-13, 143-47; R. Houston, "Geographical Mobility in Scotland, 1652-1811: Evidence of Testimonials," *Journal of Historical Geography*, 11 (1985): 379-94.

34. Joyce Bankes and Eric Kerridge, eds., *The Early Records of the Bankes Family at Winstanley* (Manchester, U.K., 1973), 21-32, 89-101.

35. Hey, *An English Rural Community: Myddle Under the Tudors and Stuarts*, 70-83.

36. For additional evidence of landlord and tenant relations and patronage in northwestern Britain, see Nicholas Blundell, *The Great Diurnal of Nicholas Blundell of Little Crosby, Lancashire, Volume One, 1702-1711* (Liverpool, n.d.), *passim.*

37. See Appendix: Taable 3, for sources.

38. William Stout, *The Autobiography of William Stout of Lancaster, 1665-1752*, ed. J. D. Marshall (Manchester, U.K., 1967), 141.

39. *Ibid.*, 142.

40. *Ibid.*, 114-47.

41. *Ibid.*, 157, 166.

42. *Ibid.*, 152.

43. *Ibid.*, 124, 129-30.

44. Kelsall, *Diary, passim.*

45. *Ibid.*, I: 165.

46. *Ibid.*, II: 102.

47. *Ibid.*, II: 154.

48. *Ibid.*, II: 206.

49. *Ibid.*, II: 243-47.

50. *Ibid.*, III: 102-7, 124.

51. For the earliest prices, see Richard S. and Mary Maples Dunn et al., eds., *The Papers of William Penn, Volume Two, 1680-1684* (Philadelphia, 1982), 636-57. For excellent account of Penn's financial motives in organizing Pennsylvania, see Richard S. Dunn, "Penny Wise and Pound Foolish: Penn as Businessman," in *The World of William Penn* (Philadelphia, 1986), 37-54. For Penn's religious ideas, see Melvin B. Endy, Jr., *William Penn and Early Quakerism* (Princeton, 1973).

52. William Penn, "Some Account of the Province of Pennsylvania," in Albert Cook Myers, ed., *Narratives of Early Pennsylvania, West New Jersey and Delaware 1630-1707* (Trenton, 1967, rpt. ed.), 98-99.

53. "William Penn to Robert Turner, 5 March 1681," in *Papers of William Penn* II: 83. For Penn's close relations with major Welsh leaders see also the warm, intimate letter, "Richard Davies to William Penn, 7 July 1684," *ibid.*, 561-65; "William Penn to John Blaykling et al., April 1683," *ibid.*, 376; "William Penn to Lord Culpeper, 5 Feb. 1683," *ibid.*, 350; "William Penn to Gulielma Penn and Children, 4 Aug. 1682," *ibid.*, 269-76.

54. Fifth month, 29th day, 1690, North Wales Quarterly Meeting Records, FH.

55. Fourth month, 5th day, 1683; 11th month, 2nd day, 1699, Cheshire Quarterly Meeting Minutes, CCRO.

56. Seventh month, 3rd day, 1698, Yearly Meeting for Wales, microfilm, FH.

57. First month, 3rd day, 1713; 2nd month, 4th day, 1713, Dolobran or Mont-gomeryshire Monthly Meeting Minutes, 1693–1714, microfilm 252, box 206, vol. 379, FH.

58. Braithwaite, *The Second Period*, 21–115.

59. Joseph Besse, *A Collection of the Sufferings of the People Called Quakers for the Testimony of Good Conscience . . . from the Time of their First Being Distinguished by that Name in the Year 1650*, I: 106, 107, 108, 735–59.

60. Kelsall, *Diary*, III: 134–37, 105, 123.

61. James Gough, *Memoirs of the Life, Religious Experiences, and Labours in the Gospel of James Gough* (Philadelphia, 1845), 20, 21.

62. Kelsall, *Diary*: H. Lloyd, *The Quaker Lloyds*, 58–59.

63. Bart Anderson, ed., *The Sharples-Sharpless Family*, 2 vols. (West Chester, Pa., 1966), I: 2–50.

64. Besse,*A Collection*, I: 107; Cheshire Quarterly Meeting Registers; *Papers of William Penn*, II: 647; George Smith, *History of Delaware County, Pennsylvania* (Philadelphia, 1862), 480.

65. "Sufferings for Tithes," Pontymoile, South Division of Wales, Entry Book, Film 239, box 172, FH.

66. *Papers of William Penn*, II: 661; Radnor Monthly Meeting: Births, Deaths, and Marriages, 1682–1750, FHS. See, for example, Will of Morris Llewellyn, Haver-ford, yeoman, Aug. 16, 1714, Philadelphia Wills, Book E, 141, PCH.

67. John Bevan, "John Bevan's Narrative," as quoted in James Levick, "Emi-gration of the Early Welsh Quakers to Pennsylvania," *Pennsylvania Magazine of History and Biography* 4 (1880): 336–44; Browning, *Welsh Settlement*, 25, 33, 63–168.

68. *Dictionary of Welsh Biography*, NLYV, 412.

69. R. Davies, *An Account . . . of the Life*, 121.

70. "Thomas Ellis to George Fox, June 14, 1685," *Journal of Friends Histori-cal Society*, 6: 173–76.

CHAPTER FOUR Quaker Domesticity with the Grain

1. "Dr. Edward Jones to John ap Thomas, 6th month, 26th day, 1682," as quoted in Thomas Allen Glenn, *Merion in the Welsh Tract* (Baltimore, 1970), 66–68. Other new settlers also criticized the Swedes' farming; see Daniel Pastorious, "Fur-ther News from Pennsylvania, January 7, 1684," as quoted in Albert Cook Myers, ed., *Narratives of Early Pennsylvania, West New Jersey, and Delaware, 1630–1707* (New York, 1912), 397.

2. Early Welsh Settler's Bible Notations, quoted in Glenn, *Merion in the Welsh Tract*, 69–70.

3. Thomas Ellis, *A Song of Rejoicing*, quoted in George Smith, *History of Delaware County* (Philadelphia, 1862), 492. The poem was written in Welsh and soon after translated into English by Ellis's neighbor John Humphry.

4. William Penn, "A Further Account of the Province of Pennsylvania, 1685," in Myers, ed., *Narratives*, 264–68.

5. Thomas Budd, *Good Order Established in Pennsylvania and New-Jersey in America, 1685* (New York, 1865, facs. of 1685 ed.), 36–37.

6. "A Letter from Doctor More with Passages Out of Several Letters, 1687," in Myers, ed., *Narratives*, 285.

7. *Ibid.*, 291. For the role of merchants in the Pennsylvania economy, see Thomas M. DoerFlinger, *A Vigorous Spirit of Enterprise: Merchants and Economic Development in Revolutionary Philadelphia* (Chapel Hill, 1986).

8. This conclusion is based upon close inspection of 240 inventories of estate registered between 1660 and 1730 of rural men in Merionethshire and Cheshire, and of Quaker men in Chester County, Pennsylvania. These inventories record all the crops, including those remaining in the fields, and livestock a farmer or rural tradesman owned upon death. Looking at the type of agricultural commodity that had the highest total value in each farmer's inventory, it is clear that farmers changed agricultural priorities quickly in Pennsylvania. As a commentary to the following figures, it should be noted that many men in Pennsylvania who continued to retain cows as their most highly valued commodity were rural artisans. Livestock did not demand as much labor as livestock. The type of agricultural commodity most favored by farmers 1660–1730 were by region:

	Crops	Cows	Dry cattle	Horses	Sheep/ goats
Merioneth, U.K.	2% (2)	38% (31)	35% (28)	1% (1)	23% (19)
Cheshire, U.K.	19% (16)	69% (57)	6% (5)	5% (4)	1% (1)
Chester Co., Pa.	38% (29)	34% (26)	none	26% (20)	2% (1)

For probate inventories, see Philadelphia County Probate Records, PCH; Chester County Probate Records, CCCH; Merionethshire Probate Records, NLW; Cheshire Probate Records, CCRO.

9. Inventory of Robert Lloyd, Merion, Sept. 29, 1714, Philadelphia County Probate, 17, 219, PCHA; Glenn, *Merion*, p. 83.

10. For New England rural economic conservatism, see David Grayson Allen, *In English Ways: The Movement of Societies and the Transferral of English Local Law and Custom of Massachusetts Bay in the Seventeenth Century* (Chapel Hill, 1981); P. Greven, *Four Generations*; Bernard Bailyn, *The New England Merchants in the Seventeenth Century* (New York, 1955); Howard S. Russell, *A Long, Deep Furrow: Three Centuries of Farming in New England* (Hanover, 1976). For economic innovation in the Chesapeake, see Edmund S. Morgan, *American Slavery: American Freedom: The Ordeal of Virginia* (New York, 1975), 108–31; Thad W. Tate and David Ammerman, eds., *The Chesapeake in the Seventeenth Century: Essays on Anglo-American Society and Politics* (Chapel Hill, 1979), *passim*.

11. For a different perception of the settlement pattern of southeastern Pennsylvania, see Lemon, *The Best Poor Man's Country*, 108-9, 218-9. The following economic, familial, and communal analyses are based upon the reconstruction of 72 of some 160 Quaker families in the Welsh Tract and Chester. The sample was randomly taken from the meeting records and checked for economic bias. Thirty-eight out of 91 families were chosen from the Radnor Monthly Meeting (Welsh Tract). According to land records and deeds, the mean acreage of all families was 325.5 with a standard deviation of 228 acres. The 38 families, according to the 1693 tax list, including 11 from the top third, 12 from the middle, and 13 from the bottom third. In Chester Monthly Meeting, 34 family heads were taken from 70 men who signed a testimony in 1688 pledging not to sell rum to the Amerindians, which all Quaker adults were to sign. The earliest wealth assessment for Chester is the list of

landowners and their acreage made in 1699 by "Charles Akom and others" for a map, and recorded in the Chester County Treasurer's book. This shows that the mean acreage of all the 83 households listed was 337 acres, with a standard deviation of 248 acres. The average for the 34 reconstructed families was 417 acres with a standard deviation of 261. If placed in rank order, this listing shows that the sample included 10 from the top third of landowners, 12 from the middle third, 8 from the bottom third, and 4 non-landowners. In general, these samples are representative, though the Chester sample is slightly biased in favor of the wealthier settlers, and therefore provides a slightly more attractive view of Quaker family life than actually existed.

For the reconstructions, the chief records used were Chester Monthly Meeting Marriages, Births, and Deaths, 1692-1870, and Removals, 1701-1871, CMMR, FHS: Chester Men's Monthly Meeting Minutes, 1681-1785; Chester Women's Monthly Meeting Minutes, 1695-1745; Radnor Monthly Meeting Births, Deaths, and Marriages, 1684-1872; Radnor Men's Monthly Meeting Minutes, 1680-1744; Radnor Women's Monthly Meeting Minutes, 1681-1760, FHS. Very helpful was the Gilbert Cope Collection, Pennsylvania Genealogical Society, Historical Society of Pennsylvania, Philadelphia. It consists of a mass of notes (95 volumes) Cope made in the late nineteenth-century for the purpose of serving clients interested in their ancestors. Also of help were George Michner Pearson, *Benjamin and Ester (Furnas) Pearson, the Ancestors and Descendants* (Los Angeles, 1941); George L. Maris and Annie Maris, *The Maris Family in the United States, a Record of the Descendants of George and Alice Maris, 1682-1885* (West Chester, 1885); Gilbert Cope, *Genealogy of the Smedley Descended from George and Sarah Smedley, Settlers in Chester County, Pennsylvania* (Lancaster, 1901); Bart Anderson, ed., *The Sharples-Sharpless Family*, vol. 1 (West Chester, 1966); Morris Llewellyn Cooke, *Morris Llewellyn of Haverford, 1647-1730* (Philadelphia, 1935); Lewis Woodward, *Genealogy of the Woodward Family of Chester County, Pennsylvania* (Wilmington, 1879); Charles Ogden, *The Quaker Ogdens in America: David Ogden of Ye Good Ship "Welcome" and His Descendants, 1682-1897* (Philadelphia, 1898); Thomas Allen Glenn, *Merion in the Welsh Tract* (Baltimore, 1970); Ross Holland Routh, *The Routh Family in America* (El Paso, 1976); no author, *Edward and Eleanor Foulke: Their Ancestry and Descendants: 1698-1898* (Philadelphia, 1899); Arthur N. Jenkins, *The Descendants of Charles Foulke Jenkins* (Philadelphia, 1962); A. Trego Shertzer, *A Historical Account of the Trego Family* (Baltimore, 1884); Henry Hart Beeson, *The Mendenhalls: A Genealogy* (Houston, 1969); David Loth, *Pencoyd and the Roberts Family* (New York, 1960); Walter Lee Sheppard, Jr., ed., *Passengers and Ships Prior to 1684* (Baltimore, 1970); William Wade Hinshaw, *Encyclopedia of American Quaker Genealogy*, 5 vols. (Ann Arbor, 1938); Clarence V. Roberts, *Early Friends Families of Upper Bucks with Some Accounts of Their Descendants* (Philadelphia, 1912); T. Mardy Rees, *A History of the Quakers in Wales and Their Emigration to North America* (Carmarthen, 1925); William Heiss, ed., *Quaker Biographical Sketches of Ministers and Elders, and Other Concerned Members of the Yearly Meetings of Philadelphia, 1682-1800* (Indiana, Pa., 1972). Almost all of these works can be found at the Historical Society of Pennsylvania.

12. "Thomas Ellis to George Fox, June 12, 1685, Dublin," *Journal of the Friends Historical Society*, 6 (1909): 173-74.

13. Radnor Monthly Meeting Removal Certificates Received, 1681-1695, RMMR, FHS.

14. Fox, *Epistles*, II: 101.

15. Chester Men's Monthly Meeting Minutes, 6th month, 27th day, 1750, FHS.

16. Radnor Men's Monthly Meeting Minutes, 11th month, 16th day, 1694, FHS.

17. Chester Men's Monthly Meeting Minutes, 6th month, 6th day, 1700, FHS.

18. Radnor Men's Monthly Meeting Minutes, 3rd month, 4th day, 1695, FHS.

19. Chester Men's Monthly Meeting Minutes, 2nd month, 3rd day, 1719, FHS.

20. Radnor Men's Monthly Meeting Minutes, Radnor Women's Monthly Meeting Minutes, Chester Men's Monthly Meeting Minutes, Chester Women's Monthly Meeting Minutes, 1683-1725, FHS; Jack Marietta, "Ecclesiastical Discipline in the Society of Friends, 1685-1776 (Ph.D. dissertation, Stanford, 1968); Susan Forbes, "Twelve Candles Lighted" (Ph.D. dissertation, 1975, University of Pennsylvania). Jack Marietta found similar figures for a number of other Pennsylvania Monthly Meetings, and Susan Forbes found that over 75 percent of the disownments in another Chester County Meeting, New Garden, related to marriage. See also Marietta, *The Reformation of American Quakerism.*

21. Based on Radnor and Chester Monthly Meeting Records. See also Lloyd, *Quaker Social History*, 48-62; Frost, *The Quaker Family in Colonial America*, 150-83.

22. "Benjamin and Ann Mendenhall to Owen and Mary Roberts, 6th month, 20th day, 1716," in Howard M. Jenkins, ed., *Historical Collections Relating to Gwynedd* (Philadelphia, 1884), 342-43.
Beloved Friends,
Owen Roberts and Mary his wife,
Our love is unto you, and to your son and daughter. Now this is to let you understand that our son Benjamin had made us acquainted that he has a kindness for your daughter Lydia, and desired our consent thereon, and we having well considered of it and knowing nothing in our minds against this preceeding therein, have given our consent that he may proceed orderly, that is to have your consent, and not to proceed without it. And it is our desire that you will give your consent. Also now, as touching place that we have given him for to settle on, we shall say but little at present.
Ellis Lewis knows as well of our minds and can give you as full account of it, as we can if we were with you, but if you will be pleased to come down, we shall be very glad to see you, or either of you, and then you might satisfy yourselves. Now we desire you when satisfied, to return us an answer, in the same way as we have given you our minds.
No more, but our kind love to you and shall remain your loving Friends,
Benjamin and Ann Mendenhall
[This marriage was accomplished in less than a year.]

23. Chester Women's Monthly Meeting Minutes, 7th month, 28th day, 1713, FHS.

24. Radnor Women's Monthly Meeting Minutes, 7th month, 3rd day, 1725, FHS.

25. Radnor Men's Monthly Meeting Minutes, 3rd month, 4th day, 1700, FHS.

26. "Minutes of the Welsh Tract, 1702," Land Bureau, Harrisburg, Pennsylvania; Chester County Treasurer's Book, 1685-1716, Chester County Historical Society, West Chester.

27. "Commisioner's Minutes of the Welsh Tract, 1702"; Chester County Treasurer's Book, 1685-1718; Chester County Deeds, 1681-1690, CCCH; Philadelphia County Deeds, 1631-1790, PCH.

28. In determining the size of southeastern Pennsylvania Quaker farmers' land accumulations, deeds as well as wills must be thoroughly inspected. Exclusive

inspection of wills and inventories will under-represent the proper figure by half. First generation Quaker fathers conveyed about 50 percent of their land to their sons by deeds. Family reconstitutions greatly helped in the search for deeds. The land accumulations conveyed to children by deed and will of 53 Quaker settlers in the Welsh Tract and Chester, all of whom died before 1736, were as follows:

50-199 acres	*200-399 acres*	*400-799 acres*	*800+ acres*
9% (5)	19% (10)	42% (22)	30% (16)

See, Philadelphia County Deeds, Philadelphia Wills and Inventories, PCH, PCHA; Chester County Deeds, Chester County Wills and Inventories, CCCH.

29. Will of Joseph Baker, Aug. 25, 1724, Chester County Wills, CCCH; Will of Francis Yarnell, 6th month, 6th day, 1721, Chester County Wills, A-124, CCCH.

30. Chester County Probate Records, 1681-1790, CCCH; Philadelphia County Inventories, 1681-1790, PCHA.

31. Will and Inventory of Edmund Cartledge, 2nd month, 2nd day, 1703, Chester County Probate Records, A-143, CCCH.

32. For use of slave labor in wheat farming, see Paul G. Clemens, *The Atlantic Economy and Colonial Maryland's Eastern Shore: From Tobacco to Grain* (Ithaca, 1980), 222-23.

33. "Robert Pyle's Testimony (1698)," in Henry J. Cadbury, ed., "An Early Anti-Slavery Statement," *Journal of Negro History*, 22: 492-93.

34. "Cadwallader Morgan's Testimony, 1700," in Henry Cadbury, ed., "Another Early Quaker Anti-Slavery Document," *Journal of Negro History*, 27: pp. 210-15.

35. Edward Turner, *The Negro in Pennsylvania: Slavery, Freedom, 1639-1861* (New York, 1911), 60-75; David Brion Davis, *The Problem of Slavery in Western Culture* (Ithaca, 1966), 315.

36. Jean R. Soderlund, *Quakers and Slavery: A Divided Spirit* (Princeton, 1983), 68-86. This is the best book on the subject.

37. Chester Men's Monthly Meeting Acknowledgments, 10th month, 2nd day, 1693, Cope Copy, HSP.

38. Chester Men's Monthly Meeting Acknowledgments, 1st month, 4th day, 1740, HSP.

39. Chester Women's Monthly Meeting Minutes, 2nd month, 30th day, 1716; Chester Men's Monthly Minutes, 10th month, 29th day, 1717; 3rd month, 2nd day, 1721, FHS.

40. In the Radnor Men's Meeting landed wealth was common among the leadership, but a somewhat stronger correlation existed between leadership and obedient children. Obviously landed wealth, obedient children, and leadership were inextricably tied. Leadership was determined by counting each man's monthly meeting assignments. The distribution of land among 87 male leaders and non-leaders between 1683 and 1685 in the Welsh Tract was as follows:

Leadership	*top 10%*	*20%*	*30%*	*40%*	*50%*	*60%*	*70%*	*80%*	*90%*
Mean acres	745	356	395	312	227	280	233	160	212
St. dev.	25	189	370	240	119	482	60	34	32

Notice the small standard deviations from the mean at the top and bottom of the leadership, and the enormous deviations from the mean in the middle.

The relation between male meeting leadership and children's behavior in 53 first-generation households was also very strong:

Leadership	top quartile	2nd quartile	3rd quartile	bottom quartile
Radnor	5% of children married out	13%	10%	25%
Chester	11% of children married out	25%	20%	18%

See, Radnor Men's Monthly Meeting Minutes, 1681–1715, Chester Men's Monthly Meeting Minutes, 1681–1715, FHS; Land Commissioner's Minutes of the Welsh Tract, 1702, Bureau of Land Records, Harrisburg, Pennsylvania,; Philadelphia County Deeds, Philadelphia County Wills and Inventories, PCH, PCHA; Chester Chester County Deeds, Chester County Wills and Inventories, CCCH.

41. Chester Men's Monthly Meeting Minutes, 5th month, 30th day, 1705; 10th month, 3rd day, 1728, FHS.

42. Radnor Men's Monthly Meeting Minutes, 9th month, 3rd day, 1701; 7th month, 2nd day, 1716, FHS.

43. Radnor Men's Monthly Meeting Minutes, 6th month, 21st day, 1733; 6th month, 3rd day, 1732; 9th month, 2nd day, 1726; 8th month, 1st day, 1741, FHS.

44. Goshen Men's Monthly Meeting Minutes, 3rd month, 21st day, 1733; 6th month, 3rd day, 1732, 9th month, 2nd day, 1726; 8th month, 1st day, 1741, FHS.

45. The relationship between wealth and obedience—and relative poverty and disobedience—was also evident, when precise marriage portions to daughters and family land grants to sons were inspected. Among 81 female children of the first generation in the Welsh Tract and Chester, whose monetary portions could be ascertained, the distribution was as follows:

	Married in	Spinster	Married out
£40–£150 portion	19	2	1
£0–£39 portion	37	9	13

Among 84 male children of the first generation in the Welsh Tract and Chester, whose land gifts from their parents could be ascertained, the distribution was as follows:

	Married in	Bachelor	Married out
200+ acres	57	3	4
50–199 acres	4	3	13

See, Philadelphia County Wills, 1681–1776, Philadelphia County Deeds, 1681–1776, PCH; Chester County Wills, 1681–1765, Chester County Deeds, 1681–1765, CCCH; Radnor Men's Monthly Meeting Minutes, 1681–1755, Chester Men's Monthly Meeting Minutes, 1681–1755, FHS.

46. Morgan, *Puritan Family*, 65–86; James Axtell, *The School upon a Hill: Education and Society in Colonial New England* (New Haven, 1974), 160–200.

47. Greven, *Four Generations*, 72–99, 139.

48. *Ibid.*, 111.

49. *Ibid.*, 68.

50. "Deed of Ralph Lewis to his son," April 15, 1707, Chester County Deeds, CCCH.

51. The land distributed to sons by 40 settling Andover households and 53 settling Quaker Welsh Tract and Chester County households was as follows:

	500+ acres	*200–499 acres*	*0–200 acres*
Welsh Tract and Chester	67% (35)	23% (12)	10% (5)
Andover	5% (2)	28.5% (11)	67% (27)

See, Philadelphia County Deeds, Philadelphia County Wills and Inventories, PCH, PCHA; Chester County Deeds, Chester County Wills and Inventories, CCCH; Greven, *Four Generations*, 58, *passim*.

52. Greven, *Four Generations*, 144–45.

53. See also John Waters, "The traditional World of the New England Peasants: A View from Seventeenth Century Barnstable," *The New England Historical and Genealogical Register*, 130 (1976). Waters also found similar differences between inheritance patterns of Quakers and Puritans living in seventeenth-century Barnstable.

54. For example, Ralph Lewis, who came over as a servant to John Bevan, gave deeds to three of his sons before or just after marriage. In 1707, he sold to his son Abraham at marriage a 200-acre tract for £60. Samuel Lewis, another son, bought 250 acres from his father for £60 in 1709. A deed three years later showed that his debt to his father was paid off in 1712, the year he married. Deeds of Thomas Minshall to sons, 2nd month, 3rd day, 1706; 8th month, 23rd day, 1707, Philadelphia County Deeds, A-172, A-203, PCH; Deeds of Ralph Lewis to sons, October 6, 1709, 4th month, 2nd day, 1712, Chester County Deeds, B-342, C-326, CCCH.

55. Deeds of Philip Yarnell to his sons, Dec. 8, 1724, Feb. 27, 1725, Chester Coutny Deeds, E-513, F-43, CCCH; Will of Philip Yarnell, 6th month, 14th day, 1733, Chester County Wills, CCCH.

56. For confirming analysis of a wider range of data without ethnographic context, see Robert V. Wells, "Quaker Marriage Patterns in a Colonial Perspective," *William and Mary Quarterly*, 3rd series, 29 (1972).

57. Deeds of Edward Foulke, Senior, to Evan Foulke, Dec. 15, 1725, Philadelphia County Deeds, 1-14-248, PCH.

58. "Edward Foulke, Senior, to his children," c. 1735, Cope Collection, F-190, Genealogical Society Reading Room, HSP; also reprinted in *Edward and Eleanor Foulke: Their Ancestry and Descendants: 1698–1898* (Philadelphia, 1899, private edition in HSP).

59. "Walter Faucit's Dying Speech, 1704," Cope Collection, F-23, HSP.

60. For economic scarcity, conflict, and witchcraft in Salem, Mass., see Paul Boyer and Stephen Nissenbaum, *Salem Possessed: The Social Origins of Witchcraft* (Cambridge, Mass., 1974). See also John Demos, *Entertaining Satan* (New York, 1983).

61. There is no book on "wheat" to compare with the many works on tobacco, sugar and rice. Early American historians prefer the exotic. For the extension of the

wheat trade out of the Delaware Valley, see Clemens, *The Atlantic Economy and Colonial Maryland's Eastern Shore*. As of 1770, bread and flour was the second most important export from the British continental colonies (including Newfoundland, the Bahamas, and Bermuda). The principal port of export was Philadelphia, where this immensely important trade had been first organized. U.S. Bureau of the Census, *Historical Statistics of the United States, Colonial Times to 1970*, 2 vols. (Washington, D.C., 1975), II: 1183-84.

62. See note 10, above.

63. J. Hector St. John de Crèvecoeur, *Letters from an American Farmer and Sketches of 18th-Century America*, Albert E. Stone, ed. (New York, 1981, orig. pub. 1782), 53-55.

CHAPTER FIVE Quakers on Top

1. "Mr. Robert Suder to the Governor, November 20, 1698," in *Historical Collections Relating to the American Colonial Church, Volume 2: Pennsylvania*, 9-12.

2. Nash, *Quakers and Politics, passim*.

3. See Herbert William Fitzroy, "The Punishment of Crime in Provincial Pennsylvania," *Pennsylvania Magazine of History and Biography*, 60 (1936): 242-69; Joseph Henry Smith, *Appeals to the Privy Counsel, from the American Plantations* (New York, 1950), 243.

4. *Minutes of the Provincial Counsel of Pennsylvania, Colonial Records* (Harrisburg, 1934), III: 40-42.

5. Winifred Trexler Root, *The Relations of Pennsylvania with the British Government 1696-1715* (New York, 1912), 234 and seq..

6. Based on Lemon, *Best Poor Man's Country*, 23, 126; Edwin S. Gaustad, *Historical Atlas of Religion in America* (New York, 1962); Alan Tully, *William Penn's Legacy: Politics and Social Structure in Provincial Pennsylvania, 1726-1755* (Baltimore, 1977), 55-60. Tully's is the best description of Quaker political hegemony; see also Joseph E. Illick, *Colonial Pennsylvania: A History* (New York, 1976); Hermann Wellenruether, *Glaube und Politik in Pennsylvania, 1681-1776* (Cologne, 1972); Richard Bauman, *For the Reputation of Truth: Politics, Religion, and Conflict Among Pennsylvania Quakers, 1750-1800* (Baltimore, 1971); John J. Zimmerman, "Benjamin Franklin and the Quaker Party, 1755-1756," *William and Mary Quarterly*, third series, 20 (1963): 416-39; Jack Marietta, "Conscience, the Quaker Community, and the French and Indian War," *Pennsylvania Magazine of History and Biography*, 95 (1971): 3-27; Frederick Tolles, *Meeting House and Counting House: The Quaker Merchants of Colonial Philadelphia, 1683-1763* (Chapel Hill, 1948); Nash, *Quakers and Politics*. An introduction to various historians' views of deference in eighteenth-century American politics can be found in Michael G. Kammen, ed., *Politics and Society in Colonial America* (2nd ed., New York, 1978).

7. See Alan Tully's tables, *William Penn's Legacy*, 55-60.

8. *Ibid.*, 83.

9. "Richard Peters to Thomas Penn, Oct. 2, 1756," Pennsylvania Proprietary Correspondence, Vol. 8; "Governor George Thomas to Thomas Penn, Oct. 27, 1741," Pennsylvania Proprietary Correspondence, Vol. 3, HSP.

10. John Murrin, "Political Development," in *Colonial British America: Essays in the New History of the Early Modern Era*, eds. Jack Greene and J. R. Pole (Baltimore, 1984), 438-40.

11. Tully, *William Penn's Legacy*, 109-11.

12. *Ibid.*, 85.

13. Jerome Wood, *Conestoga Crossroads, Lancaster, Pennsylvania, 1730-1790* (Harrisburg, 1979), 112.

14. Ethyn Williams Kirby, *George Keith, 1638-1716* (New York, 1942), *passim*. For previous interpretations of the Keithian schism, see J. William Frost, "Unlikely Controversialists: Caleb Pusey and George Keith," *Quaker History*, 84 (1975): 2-44; and J. William Frost, *The Keithian Controversy in Early Pennsylvania* (Norwood Pa., 1979), introduction. Frost's article and his introduction to his book of primary sources provide thorough and lucid discussions of the theological issues in the controversy, and ample proof, given the heat and persistence of the theological debate, that the controversy was centered upon religious doctrine. Frost does not attempt to explain, however, why the theological points raised were so emotionally charged. Edward J. Cody, "The Price of Perfection: The Irony of George Keith," *Pennsylvania History*, 39 (Jan. 1972): 1-19, also emphasizes the role of religious commitment. Two historians who, I think, wrongly, de-emphasize the centrality of emotionally laden theological issues, but who provide excellent data and insights on social, economic, ecclesiastical and political causes, contexts, and ramifications are Gary Nash, *Quakers and Politics*, 144-61, and Jon Butler, "'Gospel Order Improved,' The Keithian Schism and the Exercise of Quaker Ministerial Authority in Pennsylvania," *William and Mary Quarterly*, 3rd ser., 31 (July 1974): 431-52. However, in a subsequent piece, Jon Butler, "Into Pennsylvania's Spiritual Abyss: The Rise and Fall of the Late Keithians," *Pennsylvania Magazine of History and Biography* (April 1977), 151-70, Butler superbly traces the religious careers and ideas of the Keithians after the schism, and, by so doing, proves the importance of religious ideas to the controversy itself. Ned Landsman, "Revivialism and Nativism in the Middle Colonies: The Great Awakening and the Scots Community in East New Jersey," *American Quarterly*, 34 (Summer 1982): 153-59, recognizes an ethnic dimension to the schism, not previously seen. Kirby, *George Keith, 1638-1716*, 47-94, provides a good narrative and the interpretation that Keith never was theologically and emotionally attuned to Quaker spiritualism. My interpretation attempts to make use of the valid contributions of all of this work.

15. Kirby, *George Keith, passim*.

16. While not insisting on the indispensibility of knowledge and faith in the historical Christ to all mankind, the anti-Keithians, Jennings and Pusey, noted that right-thinking Pennsylvanians thought, as Thomas Lloyd affirmed at the school house debates, "that he did believe it our duty who had the advantage of having the holy scriptures, and hearing the faith preached, to receive and believe it." Keith furiously rejected Lloyd's qualified position and dubbed him a "devout heathen." As reported in Samuel Jennings, *The State of the Case* (London, 1694), 11-3.

17. Francis Makemie, *An Answer to George Keith's Libel* (Boston, 1691), 22.

18. Letter of George Keith, as printed in George Whitehead, *The Power of Christ Vindicated* (London, 1708), 233-37.

19. George Keith, *A Plain Short Catechism for Children and Youth* . . . (Philadelphia, 1690), 8, 9.

20. "Gospel Order and Discipline," printed in Frost, *The Keithian Controversy*, a. 13-20. For a different reading of this document, see Jon Butler, "Gospel Order

Improved,' The Keithian Schism and the Exercise of Quaker Ministerial Authority in Pennsylvania," *William and Mary Quarterly*, 3rd ser., 31 (July 1974): 431–52.

21. "Minutes of the Meeting of Ministers, Philadelphia, 4th Month, 17th day, 1694," in Frost, *The Keithian Controversy*, 53–5.

22. *Ibid.*, 55.

23. George Keith, *The Presbyterian and Independent Visible Churches in New England and Elsewhere Brought to the Test* (Philadelphia, 1689), 84–90.

24. John Delavel is not named as the tattle-tale in Keith's *Truth and Innocency Defended Against Calumny and Defamation in a Late Report Spread Abroad Concerning the Revolution of Humane Souls* (Philadelphia, 1691). I believe Delavel was the tattle-tale, however. In that work, Keith accused the tattle-tale of using the exact same oath ("as God was in Heaven, it was true") which he accused John Delavel of explicitly using, among other Quaker leaders' infelicities, in Keith's *An Account of the Great Divisions* (London, 1692), 13. It is possible, of course, that between 1690 and 1692 John Delavel used the exact same oath in Keith's hearing that the tattle-tale, another person, had used earlier. Nonetheless, it is more likely that John Delavel was the tattle-tale. Circumstantial evidence is also strong. In *Truth and Innocency Defended*, Keith identified the tattle-tale as a confidant. In other works, he identified John Delavel as an early adherent of his efforts who later turned against them. John Delavel was a merchant who became a Quaker through the love of a woman and after being an early ally of Keith, Delavel had strong motives for proving his orthodoxy to his influential Quaker father-in-law by seriously wounding Keith. See also George Keith, *The Heresie and Hatred . . . Charged Upon the Innocent Justly Returned Upon the Guilty* (Philadelphia, 1693).

25. See, for example: "Query 85: Seeing the Scripture saith, 'everyone shall reap, what he hath sown, and all shall receive according to the deeds done in the body, good or evil,' Gal.6.7, Rom.2.6.. Is is not apparant, that all children that dye in their infancy, before they have wrought good or evil in that body, must either have lived before, or shall live after, or both, if their 12 revolutions or hours be not finished?" See also, "Query 165: Do all that dye in infancy go to heaven, seeing we perceive in some infants very bad and perverse inclinations? And if all that dye in infancy go to heaven, were it not an advantage for men generally to dye in that state? But how can any go to heaven unless they be spiritually regenerated or sanctified, which certainly all infants are not . . . Besides, if all infants were from the womb sanctified and regenerated, would they not more commonly show the fruits and effects of it, when they were come to some age?" Mercurius van Helmont, *Two Hundred Queries Concerning the Revolution of Humane Souls* (London, 1684), 101, 134.

26. The tattle-tale (John Delavel?) as quoted in George Keith, *Truth and Innocency Defended*, 5. Most bibliographies date this work, 1692, but J. William Frost found that the copy at the Friends' Historical Library, Swarthmore contained the notation, "Samuel Miles his book 12-5-1691." As Frost noted, "this would make the pamphlet the earliest to appear after the controversy began." J. William Frost, "UnLikely Controversialists: Caleb Pusey and George Keith," *Quaker History*, 84 (1975): 26, and, *The Keithian Controversy*, introduction.

27. Keith, *Truth and Innocency Defended*, 1,4,7,9, 26–27.

28. On Pusey's background and career, see Frost, "Unlikely Controversialists."

29. Caleb Pusey, *Proteus Ecclesiasticus* (Philadelphia, 1703), 2,7; see also George Keith, *The Spirit of the Railing Shimei and of Baal's Four Hundred Lying Prophets Entered into Caleb Pusey* (New York, 1703), and "Caleb Pusey's Account of Pennsylvania," *Quaker History*, 64 (1975): 116.

30. Caleb Pusey also helped define precisely the theological position of the Pennsylvania Quaker majority. The issue was not, Pusey noted, the derivation of the inner Light from the historical Christ, upon which all agreed, but the epistemological question of what a genuine convert needed to know in order to be saved. As Pusey noted, "our Friends did never deny but dearly own what our blessed Lord and Saviour [did] for us in suffering outwardly for our sins, rising again for our justification, ascending into heaven, and of his being our advocate with the Father, etc." Nor did Pennsylvania Quakers differ with Keith on the epistemological point that adult or near adult men and women in Christian societies had to know and believe about Christ and what he did in order to be saved. Jennings and Pusey noted that right-thinking Pennsylvanians believed that Quaker adults and near adults must know about the historical Christ. The epistemological issue was confined solely to infants or young children and heathens. As Pusey noted, "the question betwixt G.K. and our Friends was not whether faith in Christ without was necessary to our salvation to whom it was made known, but whether it was universally necessary to all mankind." Caleb Pusey, *George Keith Once More Brought to the Test* (Philadelphia, 1703), 2-7.

31. Kirby, *George Keith*, 62-79; Frost, *The Keithian Controversy*, introduction.

32. George Keith, *An Account of the Great Divisions Amongst the Quakers in Pennsylvania, and etc., as Appears by their own Book, here Following, Printed 1692, and Lately Come from Thence, Entitled, viz. The Plea of the Innocent Against the False Judgment of the Guilty* (London, 1692), 5-24.

33. Keith also forced Pennsylvania Quaker ministers to define their position on the substance of the body of Christ after resurrection. This issue related directly to the religio-psychological or soteriological issue of what any true convert had to know and had to believe about Christ. From what he considered irrefutable biblical evidence, Keith held "that Christ's body that was crucified and buried without us rose again without us and is now in Heaven without us." In other words, although Christ's body was more glorious in heaven than it had been on earth, the heavenly body retained its previous substance; and although Christ's previously incarnated body and soul in heaven were not the Godshead, his soul and body were "most gloriously united therewith." Why did Keith make a fuss about this doctrine of the continuity of substance between Christ's earthly and heavenly bodies? Both Keith and his opponents held to the mysterious doctrine of the Trinity—that the Father, Son, and Holy Ghost were distinct yet simultaneously the same and inseparable. Thus, if Christ's heavenly body and earthly body shared the same substance, no man or woman or child could possess the saving holy spirit or inner light, on the logic of the Trinity, without partaking—meaning without having knowledge and faith in— the historical Christ whose body was the same as Christ's heavenly body and of a piece inseparably with the Holy Spirit. During the early stages of the schism, Keith had learned that many Pennsylvania Quaker ministers believed that Christ's body had been spiritualized during or after resurrection. During the Stockdale and Fitzwater debates, for example, the important Quaker minister, Arthur Cooke, had called Keith, "Muggletonian for affirming that Christ had the true body of man in heaven,

the which body was not everywhere." If Christ's body had, in fact, changed substance during or after the resurrection, even on the logic of the Trinity, a man, woman, or child could possess the saving Holy Spirit of Inner Light without any explicit or implicit knowledge of the existence, life, or events surrounding the historical Christ, whose earthly and historical body was not of the same substance as that in the Trinity. A spiritualized version of Christ's body after the resurrection thus legitimized the Pennsylvania Quaker farmers' dominant reliance in childrearing on "holy conversation" in lieu of catechisms, early literacy, and scriptural gospel sermons. Thus, in the first official theological refutation of Keith's positions by a Pennsylvania Quaker, Caleb Pusey argued that Keith's sharp views on the resurrection were not clearly supported by biblical text and were consequently "notional." Frost, "Unlikely Controversialists," stresses this issue. George Keith, *A Testimony Against that False and Absurd Opinion Which Some Hold, viz. That all True Believers . . . Immediately After the Bodily Death Attain to . . . Resurrection* (Philadelphia, 1692); Keith, *An Account of the Great Divisions . . .* , 9; Caleb Pusey, *A Modest Account from Pennsylvania* (London, 1696), 24–30.

34. Kirby, *George Keith*, 62–79; Frost, *The Keithian Controversy*, introduction.

35. William Bradford, the printer the Quaker magistrate-ministers had hired to print their material, turned Keithian and dedicated the only press in Philadelphia to the publication of Keithian tracts. For printing and selling without a license Keith's "Appeal from the Twenty-eight Judges," The Quaker magistrate-ministers jailed Bradford, confiscated part of his print, and also jailed his distributor, John McComb, a Scottish tavern-keeper. For publicly calling Thomas Lloyd and other magistrate-ministers "devout heathens" and other names, they also indicted, tried, and found Keith and some of his advocates guilty of "speaking slightingly of a magistrate." In the colorful trial, Keith argued that he abused these men only as Quakers, Christians, and ministers, but had due respect for them as magistrates. He was nevertheless fined. For their part, the Keithians published attacks berating Quaker ministers for involving themselves in the magistracy, bankrolling a privateering expedition against smugglers, and sanctioning slavery and the slave trade. Finally, in 1693 the Keithians built a speakers' gallery for themselves at the end of the Philadelphia Meetinghouse opposite the magistrate-ministers'· gallery. During "silent worship" Keithians and anti-Keithians shoved and harangued one another, and zealous followers on both sides then proceeded to destroy each others' galleries with hammers and saws. Kirby, *George Keith, passim*; Frost, *The Keithian Controversy, passim*.

36. Samuel Jennings, *The State of the Case* (London, 1694), 10–15.

37. Nash, *Quakers and Politics*, 153–61.

38. Butler, "Into Pennsylvania's Spiritual Abyss," 151–70.

39. Radnor Monthly Meeting Records, FHS; Chester County Tax Lists (microfilm), HSP.

40. Landsman, "Revivalism and Nativism," 153–54; Landsman, "The Scottish Proprietors and the Planning of East New Jersey," in Michael Zuckerman, ed. (Philadelphia, 1982), 65–89.

41. Nash, *Quakers and Politics*, 157; Hannah Roach, "Philadelphia Business Directory, 1690," *Pennsylvania Genealogical Magazine*, 23 (1693): 95–129.

42. Inasmuch as Keith was the most lustrous Quaker in late seventeenth-century Pennsylvania and New Jersey, claimed the mantle of Quaker orthodoxy

through much of the schism, and advanced the most logical, scripturally supported, and elegantly phrased arguments, Keith's limited appeal must also be analyzed. From the dominant northwestern British and Welsh Quaker minister-magistrates, Keith drew only a small minority of Quakers, 20 percent at most. The northwestern British Quaker minister-magistrates' and their allies theological and intellectual defense must be given some credit for containing the damage Keith posed to their hegemony. Although self-admittedly intellectually overmatched, they created a workable rhetorical defense by vividly reminding the populace of "revolving" infants, berating Keith for his lack of charity to established Quaker ministers, highlighting his fickliness on major theological issues over his career, and composing a plausible, if incomplete, version of Christian theology supporting childrearing through "holy conversation." More significantly, although the colony's politics and legal system was in frequent turmoil, and although many Scottish, poor English and Welsh households were excluded or subordinated (not to mention Indians, Blacks, and non-Quaker Europeans), the Quaker minister-magistrates did lead by 1690 a workable society of unusually profitable mixed-wheat farms with ample land reserves supporting, well-ordered, loving households which created moral, industrious children, who even Keith thought looked deceptively like Christians. At least, he thought the Quakers' children were growing up as *"devout"* or *"virtuous"* heathens."

The case of William Cuerton of Haverford shows how the colony's dynamic economic, familial, and religious affairs, encouraged by the Lloydian leadership, combined to help create and then reclaim a Keithian household. After receiving only 150 acres from his father, Richard Cuerton, William married Mary Couborn at Chester in 1689. By 1694, he already had two children (eventually he and Mary would have six surviving children). Cuerton went into debt to support them. Because he was occasionally dunned through the monthly meeting, Cuerton did not advance in the Welsh Tract meeting hierarchy. Apparently internalizing and being humiliated by the regime of "holy conversation," Cuerton joined the Chirst-centered Keithians in 1694. Radnor Monthly Meeting visiting commitees, led by John Bevan, now made much of Cuerton and helped to restore him financially and spiritually. Cuerton began to feel better about himself and his household. In 1700, Cuerton rejoined Radnor Friends and gave them a paper, "confessing that he was drawn away with George Keith and company, and acknowledging the Lord's mercy unto him, in visiting him, and making him sensible of his goodness, and drawing him again to his people." Free of financial and spiritual debt, Cuerton moved to a larger farm in 1713 at Duck Creek. In 1720 he became a Quaker elder. A tinge of his former apostasy remained. In 1721 Cuerton held the wedding of his daughter Elizabeth to a non-Quaker "in his own dwelling house." The Duck Creek Meeting discovered that Cuerton was initially "not willing to sign a paper so full as Friends would have it until he is convinced by Scripture that the proceedings in relation to his daughter's marriage is an offense against God." However, Cuerton was now so positively involved in Quaker community life that he soon gave them a full acknowledgment of sin. Positive involvement for self and children in the prosperous and moral development of the Delaware Valley made the northwestern Quaker leaders' most effective arguments. Radnor Men's Monthly Meeting Minutes, 1st month, 3rd day, 1713; Radnor Men's Monthly Meeting Minutes, 4th month, 13th day, 1700: Duck Creek Monthly Meeting Minutes, 1st month, 4th day, 1722; 11th day, 21st day, 1722, FHS.

43. Kirby, *George Keith*, 60-110, *passim*.

44. *Ibid.*, 113-24; H.P. Thompson, *Thomas Bray* (London, 1954), 41-42, 48, 107; W.K. Lowther Clarke, *A History of the S.P.C.K.* (London, 1959), 9-11, 13.

45. Thompson, *Thomas Bray*, 2-42.

46. "Mr. Rosse to Mr. Chamberlayne, Chester, Jan. 22, 1711," in *Historical Collections Relating to the American Colonial Church, Volume 2: Pennsylvania*, 68.

47. Thompson, *Thomas Bray*, 10-5.

48. *Ibid.*, 15-25.

49. *Ibid.*, 125-37; George Keith, *A Journal of Travels from New Hampshire to Caratuck on the Continent of North America* (London, 1706), reprinted in *Protestant Episcopal Historical Society Collections*, I (New York, 1851). For an insightful interpretation of the Anglican and Quaker rivalry in the Delaware Valley that stresses ecclesiastical organization, see Jon Butler, *Peace, Authority, and the Origins of American Denominational Order: The English Churches in the Delaware Valley, 1680-1730* (Philadelphia, 1973).

50. "The Vestry of Chester, Alias Uplands, in Pennsylvania, to the Society, 1704," in *Historical Collections Relating to the American Colonial Church, Volume 2, Pennsylvania*, 23.

51. "Address from St. Paul's Church in Chester, Pa., 1706," in *ibid.*, 28, 29, 30.

52. "Vestry of Chester to the Society, Sept. 1, 1709," *ibid.*, 53, 54.

53. "Mr. Rosse to Mr. Chamberlayne, Chester, Jan. 22, 1711," *ibid.*, 68.

54. "Mr. Humphreys to the Secretary, Chester, Nov. 30, 1719," *ibid.*, 68.

55. George Smith, *History of Delaware County* (Philadelphia, 1862), 409, 468, 483, 489, 495, 507. For origins of Welsh Tract and Chester Quakers and Anglicans, see Walter Sheppard, ed., *Passengers and Ships, Prior to 1684* (Baltimore, 1970); RMMR; CMMR; George Smith, *History of Delaware County, Pennsylvania* (Philadelphia, 1862), 400 and *passim*.

56. "List of Landholders, 1689," "List of Taxables, 1695," in Gilbert Cope, *History of Chester County, Pennsylvania* (Philadelphia, 1881), 31-34. See also manuscript tax assessments: 1693, Chester County, Miscellaneous Papers, HSP; Lemon, *Best Poor Man's Country*, 219.

57. For the Anglicans, 55 families were reconstructed from a random sample of families mentioned in records of St. Martin's, St. John's, St. Paul's, St. David's, HSP.

58. Removal Certificate of Ralph Lewis, 6th month, 18th day, RMMR, FHS; Will of Ralph Lewis, September 19, 1712, E-313, Philadelphia County Will Books, PCH; Deed, Ralph Lewis to Evan Lewis, 6th month, 8th day, 1705, F-202, Chester County Deed Books, CCCH; Deed, Ralph Lewis to Samuel Lewis, September 6, 1712, C-326, Chester County Deed Books, CCCH.

59. Based upon family reconstitutions and inspection of wills and deeds, 72 households 1681-1745 distributed the following amounts of land to their children:

	400+ acres	200-300 acres	0-199 acres
Quakers	73% (38)	17% (17)	10% (5)
Anglicans	10% (2)	43% (9)	47% (10)

See, Chester County Wills and Inventories, Chester County Deeds, CCCH; Philadelphia County Wills and Inventories, Philadelphia County Deeds, PCH, PCHA.

60. For the Wade family there are at least ten sales and rents, at very low rates, recorded in Chester County Deed Books, 1681–1735, CCCH.

61. The Anglican families included in this analysis were those of Thomas Smith, George Culin, Andrew Rawson, Peter Eliot, William Martin, and Thomas Powell. They had a mean personal estate of £242, 4.7 children, 2.3 sons, and bought on average 269 acres. The Quaker families included were those of James Pugh, William Jenkins, Owen Evan, Robert David, Joseph Baker, Peter Taylor, and Humphry Ellis. They had a mean personal estate of £129, 5.9 children, 3.1 sons, and bought an average of 631 acres. See Chester County Wills and Inventories, Chester County Deeds, CCCH; Philadelphia County Wills and Inventories, Philadelphia County Deeds, PCH, PCHA.

62. For example, Andrew Rawson died intestate, Feb. 2, 1731. He had a personal estate of £215 6s 16d, including a bond of £47. Inventory of Andrew Rawson, Feb. 2, 1731, Inventory no. 931, Chester County Inventories, CCCH.

63. Deed, Thomas Dawson and uxor to Abraham Dawson, Nov. 1746, A-434, Chester County Deed Books, CCCH.

64. Will of Thomas Dawson, July 11, 1748, E-18, Chester County Will Books, CCCH.

65. Will of Abraham Dawson, Aug. 26, 1760, G-51, Chester County Will Books, CCCH.

66. Chester County Wills, CCCH; Philadelphia County Wills, PCH.

67. Gwynedd Men's Monthly Meeting Minutes, 12th month, 13th day, 1730, FHS. The Gwynedd Meeting was originally part of the Radnor Monthly Meeting.

68. For exact figures, see Marietta, "Ecclesiastical Discipline in the Society of Friends," Appendix. See also Marietta, *The Reformation of American Quakerism.*

69. In order to compare domestic living arrangements, the estate inventories of Quaker and Anglican households with almost identical personal estates and family sizes were closely compared, particularly in regard to bedding. The four Anglican households 1681–1735 all had personal estates from £100 to £199, as did the six Quaker households 1681–1735. The Anglican households included those of Evan Evans (1731), Morgan Hughes (1727), John Test (1718), and John Evans (1739). The Quaker households included those of William Jenkins (1712), Richard Woodward (1706), Owen Evan (1723), Joseph Baker (1735), Peter Taylor (1720), and Humphrey Ellis (1712). The Anglicans had an average of 3.75 children and the Quakers an average of 5.5 children. The Anglicans spent an average of £7 on bedding; the Quakers an average of £15.3. The Anglicans spent £1.86 per child; the Quakers spent £2.78 per child. See Chester County Wills and Inventories, CCCH; Philadelphia County Wills and Inventories, PCH, PCHA.

70. Inventory of Peter Eliot, Jan. 4, 1769, no. 1103, Chester County Inventories, CCCH.

71. Inventory of Morris Llewellyn, Oct. 4, 1749, Philadelphia County Inventories, PCHA.

72. Peter Bewind Schiffer, *The Chester County Historical Society* (Exton, Pa., 1971); George Vaux, "Rees Thomas and Martha Awbrey, Early Settlers in Merion," *Pennsylvania Magazine of History and Biography,* 13 (1889): 292–97.

73. Radnor Men's Monthly Meeting Minutes, 8th month, 3rd day, 1726, FHS..

74. In the following analysis, 43 Chester County Anglican householders and 72 Chester and Welsh Tract Quaker householders were checked against the defendants in all debt cases in the Chester County Court records and all complaints concerning debt in the Radnor and Chester Monthly Meetings, 1714-39:

	6+ cases	4-5 cases	2-3 cases	1 case	zero cases
Anglicans	7% (3)	11% (5)	5% (2)	19% (8)	58% (25)
Quakers	3% (2)	4% (3)	8% (6)	10% (7)	75% (54)

See, Chester Court of Common Pleas, dockets, 1714-39, CCCH; Radnor Men's Monthly Meeting Minutes, 1681-1735, Chester Men's Monthly Meeting Minutes, 1681-1735, FHS. I am clearly indebted to Lucy Simler who provided access to this material, which she was in the process of organizing.

75. Chester Men's Monthly Meeting Minutes, 5th month, 3rd day, 1723; Executions, June 1, 1722, Chester Court of Common Plea Records, CCCH.

76. Chester Court of Common Pleas, Dockets, 1714-1735, CCCH.

77. Indictments, Feb. 3, 1730, Chester County Court of Common Plea Records; Dockets, May 27, 1718, Feb. 3, 1719, Docket Books, CCCH.

78. Dockets, 1716, 1725, Docket Books, Chester County Court of Common Pleas, CCCH.

79. Execution, Sept. 2, 1731, Chester County Court of Common Pleas Records, CCCH.

80. Docket, 3rd month, 1732, Docket Books, Chester County Court of Common Plea Records, CCCH.

81. The Quakers even received a meaningful dividend in lower childhood mortality and greater fertility. The Radnor and Chester Monthly Meeting records are sufficiently detailed to allow an estimation of family size, and they can be supplemented by deeds, intestate records, and wills. Based on a total of seventy-two reconstructed Quaker families in Radnor and Chester Meetings in the first generation, the average number of Quaker children per family to reach twenty-one years of age was 4.73 in the Welsh Tract and 5.65 in Chester. By contrast, thirty-one Anglican families, for which documentation can be provided, had an average of 3.77 children who were born between 1681 and 1730 and who reached adulthood.

Wealth satisfactorily explains this sliding scale of family size. The Chester Quakers were richer than the Welsh Quakers, and in the long run the Anglican families became poorer than both. Significantly, compared with family sizes in Cheshire and Wales, the Pennsylvania Anglicans did better: the Quakers simply did better still. Among 44 middling families living in five Cheshire towns between 1660 and 1730, the average family had just 2.44 children reach 21 years of age. The middling Cheshire families were far poorer on average than any of the Pennsylvania groups. Additionally, the limited expectations the churchmen displayed in economic areas for their children may have seeped into early child care; doubtless the Quakers' deep concern for children did. Indeed, as Robert Wells has shown, Pennsylvania Quakers would later decide to control growing family sizes in order to have enough resources and time for each individual child. In the 1760s the resources of Pennsylvania finally appeared finite. But in 1740 it was clear which family system paid more easily and bountifully. St. Paul's; St. David's; St. Martin's; St. John's; RMMR; CMMR.

82. Comparative wealth was investigated by tax assessments and by personal estates according to probate inventories. The distribution of average tax assessments of Anglican and Quaker families in Chester and the Welsh Tract 1715-35 was as follows:

	60£+	*40-59£*	*20-39£*	*0-19£*
Quakers	27% (14)	9% (5)	41% (21)	23% (12)
Anglicans	0 (0)	7% (3)	48% (19)	45% (18)

The distribution by personal estate, 1681-1740, was similar:

	400£+	*300-399£*	*200-299£*	*100-199£*	*0-99£*
Quakers	15% (2)	20% (8)	15% (6)	38% (15)	12% (5)
Anglicans	7% (2)	11% (3)	23% (6)	15% (4)	44% (12)

See, Chester County Tax List (microfilm), HSP; Chester County Inventories, CCCH; Philadelphia County Inventories, PCHA (Anglicans and Quakers from Merion township were excluded from tax analysis, since Merion was in Philadelphia County, where comparable tax lists for this period do not exist).

83. "Mr. Nicholls to Mr. Hodges, Chester, April 30, 1704," *Historical Collections*, 19.

84. Evan Evans, "The State of the Church in Pennsylvania, Most Humbly Offerred to ye Venerable Society . . . ," Oct. 18, 1707, *ibid.*, 36.

85. "An Account or History of the Building of St. Paul's Church in Chester, June 21, 1714," *ibid.*, 78-80.

86. "The Clergy of Pennsylvania to the Secretary, Chichester, October 24, 1723," *ibid.*, 131.

87. "Mr. Rosse to the Secretary, Chester, Dec. 30, 1712," *ibid.*, 69.

88. "Mr. Rosse to Mr. Chamberlayne, Chester, Jan. 22, 1712," *ibid.*, 67.

89. "Mr Currey to the Secretary, Radnor, March 31, 1760," *ibid.*, 281, 282.

90. He also noted, "I had 4 communicants on Christmas day and only 6 on Easter Sunday," "Mr. Thompson to the Secretary, Chester, April 23, 1752," *ibid.*, 185-86.

91. He also noted, "I was never more amazed than after a prepartion sermon and six weeks' notice given them of the sacrament to be administered on Christmas day I found but three communicants . . . : on Easter Sunday but four and two of them the same, and on Whit-Sunday at Concord the same." "Mr. Craig to the Secretary, Chester, July 27, 1760," *ibid.*, 290-91.

92. For Anglicanism in Philadelphia, see Deborah Gough, "Pluralism, Politics, and Power Struggle: The Church of England in Colonial Philadelphia, 1695-1789" (Ph.D. dissertation, University of Pennsylvania, 1978).

93. Patricia U. Bonomi and Peter R. Eisenstadt, "Church Adherence in Eighteenth-Century British American Colonies," *William and Mary Quarterly*, 3rd ser., 39 (April 1982), 245-86, argues that Anglican Church attendance was strong in the eighteenth-century South; Rhys Isaac, "Evangelical Revolt: The Nature of the Baptists' Challenge to the Traditional Order in Virginia, 1765 to 1775," *William and Mary Quarterly*, 3rd ser., 31 (July 1974), 345-68, argues that Anglicans held cultural hegemony in Virginia until 1765; Bruce E. Steiner, "Anglican Office Holding in Pre-

Revolutionary Connecticut: The Parameters of New England Community," *William and Mary Quarterly*, 3rd ser., 31 (July 1974), 369–406, documents the strength and acceptance by 1760 of Anglicanism in the Connecticut countryside.

94. "The author of this publication concludes with the wish," wrote Mittelberger with unintended irony, "that the British nation might take to heart the spiritual as well as the material condition of its brethren, and might help to put them in the position of forming a constant bulwark in America against all enemies." Little did he know how hard the Anglican Church had tried. Gottlieb Mittelberger, *Gottlieb Mittelberger's Journey to Pennsylvania in the Year 1750 and Return to Germany in the Year 1754* (Cambridge, Mass., 1960), 47–48, 52–53.

95. Gary Nash, *The Urban Crucible: Social Change, Political Consciousness, and the Origins of the American Revolution* (Cambridge, Mass., 1979), 403, 407, 409, 411; idem, "Social Development," in *Colonial British America: Essays in the New History of the Early Modern Era*, 239–40; U.S. Bureau of Census, *Historical Statistics of the United States: Colonial to 1790*, 2 vols. (Washington D.C., 1975) II: 1168, 1176–77, 1183–84; see also, Fred Anderson, "A People's Army: Provincial Military Service in Massachusetts During the Seven Years' War," *The William and Mary Quarterly*, 3rd ser., 40 (Oct. 1983); 500–529; he estimates that over 30 percent of all the Massachusetts men born between 1725 and 1745 volunteered as "provincials" in the Seven Years' War. Military service was the only way most of the men could raise enough capital to marry and settle down as small artisans and farmers.

96. For inheritance patterns in the Chesapeake, see Edward S. Morgan, *American Slavery-American Freedom* (New York, 1975), 170–71; Robert E. and B. Katherine Brown, *Virginia 1705-1756: Democracy or Aristocracy* (East Lansing, Mich., 1964), 81–83. During the seventeenth-century, Chesapeake inheritance patterns were often dictated by the orphan court and were otherwise irregular due to a staggering death rate among young and middle-aged parents, a consequence probably of malarial infection of much of the population, see Lorena S. Walsh, "'Till Death Us Do Part,' Marriage and Family in Seventeenth-Century Maryland," and Darrett B. and Anita H. Rutman, "'New-Wives and Sons-in-Laws': Parental Death in a Seventeenth-Century Virginia County," in *The Chesapeake in the Seventeenth-Century: Essays on Anglo-American Society and Politics*, eds. Thad W. Tate and David L. Ammerman (Chapel Hill, 1979), 126–82. For southern values, see Michael Zuckerman, "William Byrd's Family," *Perspectives in American History*, 12 (1979), 255–311; Bertram Wyatt-Brown, *Southern Honor: Ethics and Behavior in the Old South* (New York, 1982); Jan Lewis, *The Pursuit of Happiness: Family and Values in Jeffersonian Virginia* (New York, 1983); Daniel Blake Smith, *Inside the Great House: Planter Family Life in Eighteenth-Century Chesapeake Society* (Ithaca, 1980). For New England, see Greven, *Four Generations*; John Waters, "The Traditional World of the New England Peasants: A View from Seventeenth-Century Barnstable," *The New England Historical and Genealogical Register*, 19.

97. For eighteenth-century political economy, see Drew R. McCoy, *The Elusive Republic: Political Economy in Jeffersonian America* (Chapel Hill, 1980); "Richard Jackson to Benjamin Franklin, June 17, 1755," in *Papers of Benjamin Franklin*, Leonard Labaree, ed. (New Haven, 1959-), VI: 171; J. P. Brissot de Warville, *New Travels in the United States of America, 1788*, Durand Echeverria, ed. (Cambridge, Mass., 1964, originally published 1791), 253–61, 339; Crèvecoeur, *Travels in Pennsylvania and New York*, Percy G. Adams, trans. and ed. (New York, 1961 rpt. ed.).

CHAPTER SIX Wives—Ministers—Mothers

1. For a critical overview and bibliography of modern literature on colonial American women, see Mary Beth Norton, "The Evolution of White Women's Experience in Early America," *The American Historical Review*, 89 (June 1985): 593–619.

2. Removal Certificate of Ellis Pugh, Merionethshire, 10th month, 5th day, 1685, Garthgnvor Meeting, Radnor Removal Certificates, FHS.

3. Removal Certificate of John ap Bevan and Barbara, his wife, 2nd month, 7th day, 1683, Llantrisant Meeting, Radnor Removal Certificates, FHS.

4. Removal Certificate of Griffith John, widower, 8th month, 6th day, 1690, Tyddyn y Gareg Meeting, Radnor Removal Certificates, FHS.

5. Removal Certificate of Hugh Griffith, widower, 12th day, 5th month, 1696, Hendre Mawr Meeting, Radnor Removal Certificates, FHS.

6. Removal Certificate of John ap Bevan and Barbara, his wife.

7. Removal Certificate of William Lewis, his wife, and family, 5th month, 5th day, 1683, Treverig Monthly Meeting, Radnor Removal Certificates, FHS.

8. Removal Certificate of Cadwallader Morgan of Gwernfell, and family, 6th month, 15th day, 1683, Radnor Removal Certificates, FHS.

9. Chester Women's Monthly Meeting Minutes, 6th month, 27th day, 1711, FHS.

10. Gottlieb Mittelberger, *Journey to Pennsylvania*, eds. and trans., Oscar Handlin and John Clive (Cambridge, Mass., 1960), 93.

11. Laurel Thatcher Ulrich, *Good Wives: Image and Reality in the Lives of Women in Northern New England, 1650–1750* (New York, 1982); for a passionate, well-documented denunciation of seventeenth-century Puritan males' treatment of women, see also Lyle Koehler, *A Search for Power: the "Weaker Sex" in Seventeenth-Century New England* (Urbana, 1980). For other views on Quaker women in colonial America, see Mary Maples Dunn, "Saints and Sisters: Congregational and Quaker Women in the Early Colonial Period," *American Quarterly*, 30 (1978): 582–601; Mary Maples Dunn, "Women of the Light," in *Women of America: A History*, eds. Carol Ruth Berkin and Mary Beth Norton (Boston, 1979), 115–33; Frost, *The Quaker Family in Colonial America*, 183, *passim*. The transmission of Delaware Valley female culture to New England will not be discussed in this book. Students of New England women's dramatic nineteenth-century adaptation of "true womanhood" are aware of local Quaker influences on their New England female authors and reformers, but limit the importance of these models of alternative womanhood because of the marginality of Quakers and other religious sectarians in New England. Fair enough, but what about Philadelphia? Should the leading women of that city and its hinterlands—Quakers and Quaker descendants become Episcopalians—be forgotten simply because they were wealthier and lived in a wealthier region than did their New England sisters? Much of the New England women's sentimental literature was published through the Lippincott press and *Godey's Lady's Book* in Philadelphia, which in the crucial days of the early republic was literally America's capital city. Even proper Bostonians like Henry Adams had to admit that in those days Philadelphia and its mainlines were grander and more central than Dover, New Hampshire or Utica, New York. For the New England view, see Ulrich, *Good Wives*, 233–35; Ann Douglas, *The Feminization of American Culture* (New York, 1977), 126–27 and chap. 4, *passim*; Barbara Welter, "The Feminization of American Religion: 1800–1860," in *Insights and Parallels*, ed. William L. O'Neill (Minneapolis, 1973), 305–31.

For nineteenth-century Delaware Valley women see, Joan M. Jensen, *Loosening The Bonds: Mid-Atlantic Farm Women, 1700–1850* (New Haven, 1986).

12. In order to assess Quaker women's economic activities comparatively, equipment used and commodities produced by women were inspected in 37 Chester and Welsh Tract Quaker households' inventories of estate between 1700 and 1710 and 54 such households between 1730 and 1740. These findings were compared with Laurel Thatcher Ulrich's findings for 95 Essex County, Massachusetts, inventories of estate in 1700 and 92 in 1730. In 1700–1710 the comparison was as follows:

	cows	churns and presses	sheep	spinning wheels	looms	flax
Essex Co.	64%	14%	45%	46%	6%	12%
Chester Co.	75%	19%	59%	43%	3%	13%

In 1730–40 the comparison was as follows:

	cows	churns and presses	sheep	spinning wheels	looms	flax
Essex Co.	57%	10%	39%	39%	13%	18%
Chester Co.	83%	23%	81%	63%	7%	24%

See, Laurel Thatcher Ulrich, *Good Wives*, 16; Chester County Wills and Inventories, CCCH; Philadelphia County Wills and Inventories, PCH, PCHA.

13. "Matthew Roberts' Accounts, 8th month, 15th day, 1724, Philadelphia County Orphan Court Records, PCH.

14. Philadelphia County Orphan Court Records, Accounts, PCH; Chester County Orphan Court Records, Accounts, CCCH.

15. "Matthew Roberts' Accounts."

16. For other legal-economic restrictions of Pennsylvania wives and widows, see Marylynn Salmon, "Equality or Submersion? *Feme Covert* Status in Early Pennsylvania," in *Women of America* Berkin and Norton, eds., 115–33.

17. In order to assess the widow's role in executing her deceased husband's estate comparatively, I examined the following: 78 wills from North Wales, 1660–90; 55 wills from Cheshire, England, 1670–90; 80 wills from Essex County, Massachusetts, 1664–74; and 83 wills of Quakers from Chester and the Welsh Tract, Pennsylvania, 1683–1730. Only wills of men leaving widows were counted and assessed. The distribution was as follows:

	only executive	joint executive	not executive	overseers
Wales, 1660–90	64%	21%	15%	15%
Cheshire, 1670–90	18%	42%	40%	11%
Essex, Mass., 1664–74	55%	17.5%	27.5%	50%
Chester, Pa., 1683–1730	25%	53%	22%	43%

See, Merionethshire wills and inventories, St. Asaph's wills and inventories, NLW; Cheshire Wills and Inventories, CCRO; *Probate Records of Essex County, Massachusetts*, vol. 2, 1665-74 (Salem, Mass., 1917), *passim*; Chester County wills and inventories, CCCH; Philadelphia County Wills and Inventories, PCH, PCHA.

18. James Swaffer's Will, Feb. 1, 1715, Chester County Wills, CCCH.

19. Andrew Job's Will, 3rd month, 2nd day, 1722, Chester County Wills, CCCH.

20. See note 17, above.

21. "Estate of Ralph Ellinwood of Beverly (1674)," in *The Probate Records of Essex County, Massachusetts* (Salem, Mass., 1917, spec. ed.), II: 412-13. For a close study of some colonial Massachusetts widows, see Alexander Keyssar, "Widowhood in Eighteenth-Century, Massachusetts: A Problem in the History of the Family," *Perspectives in American History*, 8 (1974): 83-119. For other studies, see Kim Lacy Rogers, "Relicts of the New World: Conditions of Widowhood in Seventeenth-Century New England," in *Women's Being, Woman's Place: Female Identity and Vocation in American History*, ed. Mary Kelley (Boston, 1979), 32-33; David Evan Narrett, "Patterns of Inheritance in Colonial New York City, 1664-1775: A Study in the History of the Family" (Ph.D. diss., Cornell University, 1981); Linda E. Speth, "More than Her 'Thirds': Wives and Widows in Colonial Virginia," in *Women, Family, and Community in Colonial America: Two Perspectives* (New York, 1983); John E. Crowley, "Family Relations and Inheritance in Early South Carolina," *Histoire Sociale/Social History*, 17 (1984): 46.

22. "Estate of John Chaney of Newbury (1672)," in *The Probate Records of Essex County*, II: 258-59.

23. "Estate of John Turner of Salem, 1680," *ibid.*, III: 399-401.

24. Miss Dorothy Lapp, ed., *"Enterys of the Orphans Court" of Chester County, Pennsylvania 1716-1730, 1732-1734* (Danboro, Pa., 1973), I: 43-44; II: 19-56.

25. *Ibid.*, I: 26-40; for the lack of such cases in Massachusetts, see Keyssar, "Widowhood," 111.

26. Lapp, ed., *"Enterys of the Orphans Court" of Chester County*, I: 4-11.

27. In order to assess comparatively the role of gender in court selected and minor selected guardians in Massachusetts and Chester County, Pa., I analyzed Essex County, Mass., court records from 1665 to 1681, during which time 13 guardians were selected by the court and 38 guardians were chosen by the minors themselves; the Suffolk County, Mass., court records from 1671 to 1680, during which time 21 guardians were selected by the court and 22 by the minors; the Chester County court records from 1716 to 1730, during which time 24 guardians were selected by the court and 19 by minors; and the Chester County court records from 1747 to 1761, during which time 302 guardians were selected by the court and 174 by minors. There was no regional variation in the distributions by gender among guardians chosen by the minors themselves:

	Essex *1665-1681*	*Suffolk* *1671-1680*	*Chester* *1716-30*	*Chester* *1747-61*
Male	95%	95%	95%	96%
Female	5%	5%	5%	4%

There were, however, significant regional variations in the distribution of gender among guardians chosen by the court for minors under fourteen years of age:

	Essex 1665–1681	Suffolk 1671–1680	Chester 1716–30	Chester 1747–61
Male	77%	86%	96%	99%
Female	23%	14%	4%	1%

See, *The Probate Records of Essex County, Massachusetts*, II, 1665–1674; III:, 1675–1681 (Salem, Mass., 1917, 1920), *passim*; *Records of the Suffolk County Court, 1671–1680*, part 2 (Boston, 1933), *passim*; Lapp, ed., *"Enterys of the Orphans Court"* of *Chester County, passim.*

28. Benjamin Franklin, *Autobiography* portrays his problems in Boston but also the help he received from many men in Philadelphia and the region. For frequent references to Quaker elders who helped orphans, see *A Collection of Memorials Concerning Divers Deceased Ministers and Others of the People Called Quakers* (Philadelphia, 1787), *passim*. For example, see the Gwynedd Monthly Meeting, Pennsylvania memorial of John Evans (1689–1756) which noted, "a considerable part of his time was spent in assisting widows, and the guardianship of orphans, which, though laborious to him, was of much advantage to them." *Ibid.*, 177; Thomas Jones (d. 1727), son of John ap Thomas, left a cache of letters concerning his guardianship of several fatherless children in Wales, see Glenn, *Merion in the Welsh Tract*, 300.

29. "Isaac Norris to Joseph Pike, 12th month, 25th day, 1708-9," in Mrs. Deborah Logan, ed., *Correspondence Between William Penn and James Logan, Secretary of the Province of Pennsylvania, and Others, 1700–1750* (Philadelphia, 1872), II: 320–21.

30. "Isaac Norris to Jeffrey Pinnell, 1st month, 6th day, 1701," *ibid.*, I: 40.

31. "William Penn to James Logan, 11th month, 4th day, 1701, *ibid.*, I: 76.

32. "William Penn to James Logan, 4th month, 21st day, 1702, *ibid.*, I: 116.

33. "Rees Thomas to William Awbrey, 2nd Month, 29th day, 1695," as quoted in Glenn, *Merion in the Welsh Tract*, pp. 312-13.

34. Gabriel Thomas, "An Historical and Geographical Account of the Province and Country of Pennsylvania; and of West-New-Jersey in America" (London, 1698), in Albert Cook Myers, ed., *Narratives of Early Pennsylvania, West New Jersey, and Delaware, 1630–1707*, 332.

35. Radnor Women's Monthly Meeting Minutes, 1st month, 4th day, 1705 to 12th month, 2nd day, 1706, FHS.

36. Radnor Women's Monthly Meeting Minutes, 7th month, 3rd day, 1706, FHS.

37. Glenn, *Merion in the Welsh Tract*, 35, 63, 98–110; Browning, *Welsh Settlement of Pennsylvania*, 73, 130, 133, 190, 296, 480.

38. Glenn, *Merion in the Welsh Tract*, 303-14, 261-75; Howard M. Jenkins, *The Family of William Penn, Founder of Pennsylvania, Ancestry, and Descendants* (Philadelphia, 1899), 47-128.

39. "Early Baptist Records," in George Smith, *History of Delaware County, Pennsylvania* (Philadelphia, 1862), 543–44.

40. Daniel Scott Smith, "Parental Power and Marriage Patterns: An Analysis of Historical Trends in Hingham, Massachusetts," *Journal of Marriage and the Family* (Aug. 1973), 419–28.

41. Chester Women's Monthly Meeting Minutes, 1st month, 28th day, 1709; 2nd month, 30th day, 1711; Radnor Women's Monthly Meeting Minutes, 2nd month, 7th day, 1715, FHS.

42. Radnor Women's Monthly Meeting, 5th month, 27th day, 1721, FHS.

43. See, for example, Radnor Women's Monthly Meeting Minutes, 3rd month, 2nd day, 1700; 1st month, 4th day, 1702; 7th month, 3rd day, 1704, FHS. The skills and procedures women used in visiting can be assessed from various entries in *A Collection of Memorials*. For example, the Gwynedd Monthy Meeting noted of Alice Griffith (d. 1749), "she was well qualified for that weighty service of visiting families, having, at such opportunities, to communicate of her own experiences, and tell what God had done for her soul; and under a good degree of divine influence would often be drawn forth in opening divine mysteries, as if she had been in a large assembly, as many witnesses can testify, that have been sensibly reached, yea baptized by her religious visits; at which she was mostly full of good matter, well adapted and suitable to the different circumstances of individuals and families." *Ibid.*, 141–44. Other elders specialized in marriage counseling.

44. Radnor Women's Monthly Meeting Minutes, 11th month, 3rd day, 1712, FHS.

45. Radnor Women's Monthly Meeting Minutes, 8th month, 2nd day, 1734; 3rd month, 5th day, 1735, FHS.

46. Radnor Women's Monthly Meeting Minutes, 8th month, 3rd day, 1721; 9th month, 4th day, 1721, FHS.

47. Radnor Women's Monthly Meeting Minutes, 12th month, 3rd day, 1720, FHS.

48. Chester Men's Monthly Meeting Minutes, 3rd month, 8th day, 1720, FHS: "women complain of M.T. of Springfield for keeping idle, dissolute company to ye scandal of her sex."

49. Chester Women's Monthly Meeting Minutes, 3rd month, 30th day, 1713, FHS.

50. Chester Men's Monthly Meeting Minutes, 8th month, 31st day, 1720, FHS: ". . . and the women Friends having labored with her ineffectually for her reformation request assistance to disown her."

51. Radnor Women's Monthly Meeting Minutes, 5th month, 2nd day, 1726, FHS.

52. Society of Friends, *A Collection of Elegiac Poems Devoted to the Memory of the Late Virtuous and Excellent Matron and Worthy Elder in the Church of Christ of the Society of Friends, Martha Thomas, Late Wife of Rees Thomas of Merion of the County of Philadelphia in the Province of Pennsylvania and Daughter of William Awbrey of Llanelieu in the County of Brecknock in Great Britain who Departed this Life the 7th of the 12 Month 1726–1727* (Philadelphia, 1727). I have not been able to locate a copy of this work.

53. The following is a summary of the social-economic positions of major Chester and rural Philadelphia County female Quaker ministers, 1690–1775:

Name	Year Married	Husband's town place by taxes	Township
Sarah Worrall	1714	1st of 25	Edgemont
Dorothy Yarnell	1694	2nd of 25	Edgemont
Alice Pennell	1701	3rd of 25	Edgemont
Mary Pennell	1710	1st of 30	Middletown
Mary Smedley	1727	6th of 30	Middletown
Rebecca Minshall	1707	2nd of 29	Providence
Margaret Ellis	1696	unknown	Merion
Grace Lloyd	1703	1st of 69	Chester
Jane Hoskens	1738	7th of 69	Chester
Elizabeth Levis	unknown	19th of 98	Kennett
Elizabeth Ashbridge	1746	3rd of 66	Goshen
Margaret Miles	c. 1686	1st of 34	Radnor
Elizabeth Richards	1726	15th of 29	Tredeffryn
Susanna Lightfoot	1763	2nd of 73	Pikeland

See, Radnor Women's Monthly Meeting Minutes, 1693-1765; Chester Women's Monthly Meeting Minutes, 1706-65, FHS; Chester County Tax Lists; Philadelphia County Tax Lists, HSP.

54. Anonymous, *An Account of the Religious Experience and Some of the Trials, of that Faithful Servant and Minister of the Gospel, Susanna Lightfoot, with Particulars of Her Last Illness and Dying Sayings, Compiled from the Testimony Given by Friends in America, and From the Minutes Kept by Her Husband, and an Intimte Friend, who Attended upon Her* (Manchester 1844), *passim*; Chester County Tax Lists, 1715-70, HSP.

55. Jane Hoskens, *An Account of the Life, Suffering, Exercises, and Travels of that Faithful Servant of Christ, Jane Hoskens* (Philadelphia, 1833), 2.

56. *Ibid.*, 4-5.

57. *Ibid.*, 11.

58. *Ibid.*, 11-13.

59. *Ibid.*, 21.

60. *Ibid.*, 28.

61. *Ibid.*, 30.

62. *Ibid.*, 35-41.

63. "Some Account of the Life, Sufferings, and Exercises of Elizabeth Ashbridge," in John and Isaac Comly, eds., *Friends' Miscellany Being a Collection of Essays and Fragments, Biographical, Religious, Epistolary, Narrative, and Historical* (Philadelphia, 1833-39), V: 1-8, 12.

64. *Ibid.*, 24.

65. *Ibid.*, 27, 28.

66. *Ibid.*, 32, 34-38.

67. *Ibid.*, 38-42.

68. *Ibid.*, 40-48; Chester County Tax Lists 1715-70, HSP.

69. *A Collection of Memorials*, 234-38.

70. *Ibid.*, 143.

71. *Ibid.*, 132.

72. *Friends' Miscellany*, VIII: 337.

73. *A Collection of Memorials*, 187.

74. *Ibid.*, 38–41.

75. *Ibid.*, 54–56.

76. *Ibid.*, 152–54.

77. "Margaret Bishpam's Instructions to her Daughters, Mount Holly, New Jersey, 1782," in *Friends' Miscellany*, VII: 337–40.

78. *Ibid.*, 35–41.

79. Hoskens, *An Account*, 5.

80. *A Collection of Memorials*, 143.

81. *Friends' Miscelleny*, IX: 97.

82. *Ibid.*, II: 383–84.

83. "Extracts from Ann Whitall's Diary," in Hannah Whitall Smith, *The Story of His Life* (Philadelphia, 1879), 14–21.

84. *Friends' Miscellany*, IX: 97.

85. *Ibid.*, 97–98.

86. *A Collection of Memorials*, 212–14.

87. "Elizabeth Levis's Letters to Her Children, 1774," *Friends' Miscellany*, VII: 370–74.

88. *A Collection of memorials*, 184–86. For Philadelphia Quaker elite's reluctance to use corporal punishment, see *Correspondence Between Penn and Logan*, I: 203, 283, 293; II: 82.

89. *Friends' Miscellany*, VI: 158–69.

90. *Ibid.*, IV: 170–71.

91. *Ibid.*, X: 5, 8, 12.

92. "Dr. John Fothergill to Susanna Fothergill, 3rd month, 24th day, 1739," in *Chain of Friendship: Selected Letters of Dr. John Fothergill of London, 1735–1780*, eds. Betsy Corner and Christopher Booth (Cambridge, Mass., 1971), 51.

CHAPTER SEVEN Saints and Republicans

1. The best book on the Pennsylvania Quakers' reformation in the mid and late eighteenth century is Jack D. Marietta, *The Reformation of American Quakerism, 1748–1783* (Philadelphia, 1984). This chapter particularly relies heavily on Professor Marietta's comprehensive study of Pennsylvania Quaker monthly meeting discipline—over 10,000 cases. It differs, however, with his acceptance of the reformers' depiction of the second generation as in religious and moral declension. It argues that the second generation's problems arose less from their spiritual laxity than from socio-economic circumstances and the contradictions within the Quaker family system.

2. *Some Account of the Lives and Religious Labours of Samuel Neale and Mary Neale* (London, 1845), 347–48.

3. George Crosfield, ed., *Memoirs of the Life and Gospel Labours of Samuel Fothergill* (Liverpool, 1858), 167, 187, 218, 240, 281–82.

4. *Ibid.*, 216.

5. *Ibid.*, 206–7.

6. *Ibid.*, 189.

7. *Ibid.*, 335.

8. Inventory of George Smedley, Middletown, 6th month, 12th day, 1766, #2335, Chester County Probates, CCRO.

9. Will of George Smedley, Willistown, 2nd month, 28th day, 1723, Chester County Wills, A-148, CCRO; Inventory of George Smedley, Willistown, 10th month, 4th day, 1723, Chester County Inventories, #162, CCRO.

10. Gwynedd Men's Monthly Meeting Minutes, 12th month, 3rd day, 1730, FHS; Radnor Men's Monthly Meeting Minutes, 9th month, 2nd day, 1760; 11th month, 3rd day, 1770, FHS.

11. Radnor Men's Monthly Meeting Minutes, 8th month, 13th day, 1759, FHS.

12. Goshen Men's Monthly Meeting Minutes, 8th month, 16th day, 1749, FHS.

13. Concord Men's Monthly Meeting Minutes, 12th month, 7th day, 1736; 1st month, 7th day, 1737; 2nd month, 4th day, 1737; 3rd month, 1st day, 1738; 2nd month, 3rd day, 1738, FHS.

14. Chester Men's Monthly Meeting Minutes, 5th month, 2nd day, 1738; 2nd month, 27th day, 1734, FHS.

15. Chester Men's Monthly Meeting Minutes, 1st month, 4th day, 1747; 3rd month, 1747; 4th month, 1747, FHS.

16. Goshen Men's Monthly Meeting Minutes, 12th month, 15th day, 1747, FHS.

17. For methodology of family reconstructions and collation and linking with other records, see note 11 in Chapter 4, above.

18. Inventories from CCCH and PCHA. To ensure proper religious identification, all inventories used were those linked to reconstructed families.

19. "Daniel Humphry's Will, April 7, 1735," Philadelphia County Wills, E-327, PCH.

20. For example, in 1685, when the price of wheat was 3.5 shillings per bushel, the partly cleared 197-acre plantation of Richard Few, a Quaker farmer of Chester township, was evaluated at £170 or about 17 shillings per acre. In 1685, it cost about £85 or 485 bushels of wheat to purchase a 100-acre plantation with buildings and improvements, and only some 80 bushels to purchase 100 unimproved acres. By 1740, however, a 300-acre Providence plantation cost 2,727 bushels of wheat, or 909 bushels of wheat per 100 acres. The large change in the ratio shows why these families failed to convert their productivity into the purchase of large tracts. "Richard Few's Inventory, 10th month, 12th day, 1686," Philadelphia County Inventories, 2-28, PCHA; "Peter Taylor's Inventory, April 23, 1740," Chester County Inventories, #701, CCCH. The land prices were taken from study of 200 Chester County and Philadelphia County inventories of estate. The wheat prices were taken from Bezanson et al., *Prices in Colonial Pennsylvania* (Philadelphia, 1935), *passim*.

	Improved land per acre	Unimproved land per acre	Wheat per bushel
1685–89	£0-10-0	£0-4-10	3.5s
1690–1709	£1-6-8	£0-10-8	5.2s.
1710–29	£1-6-0	£0-14-0	3.08s.
1730–49	£1-10-7	£0-15-9	3.7s.
1750–70	£3-2-1	£0-17-0	4.9s.

21. In order to assess changes in land use and production, 124 inventories of estate of Chester and rural Philadelphia Quaker households were examined:

Rich households ($£400+$)	n	Crop mean	Livestock mean	Average production
1st generation	14	£36.5	£77	£113.5
2nd generation	26	£30.7	£78	£113.7
Upper middling ($£300-399$)				
1st generation	7	£31	£55	£86
2nd generation	15	£26.3	£67.8	£94.1
Middling ($£200-299$)				
1st generation	27	£15.8	£39.2	£55
2nd generation	17	£22.4	£45.7	£68.1
Lower middling ($£50-199$)				
1st generation	8	£9.7	£33.7	£43.4
2nd generation	10	£15.5	£15.3	£38.8

See, Philadelphia County Inventories, PCHA; Chester County Inventories, CCCH.

22. The comparative inequalities by quartile of wealth among first- and second-generation Welsh Tract and Chester Quaker households were as follows (probates were linked to reconstituted households):

	Land	Personal wealth
Top quartile of wealth		
1st generation	48.5%	49%
2nd generation	54%	59%
2nd quartile of wealth		
1st generation	26%	25%
2nd generation	22%	23%
3rd quartile of wealth		
1st generation	18%	16%
2nd generation	15%	12%
Bottom quartile of wealth		
1st generation	7.5%	10%
2nd generation	9%	6%
Number of inventories and wills	117	151

See, Philadelphia County Wills and Inventories, PCHA; Chester County Wills and Inventories, CCCH.

23. "Ellis Davies's Inventory, 2nd month, 3rd day, 1774," Chester County Inventories, CCCH.

24. "Thomas Pennell's Inventory, May 17, 1750," Chester County Inventories, # 1276, CCCH.

25. "John Carter's Inventory, July 26, 1760," Chester County Inventories, # 1868, CCCH.

26. "Inventory of William Pennell, Oct. 7, 1757," Chester County Inventories, #1671, CCCH.

27. Based on study of inventories linked to family reconstructions.

28. "Goshen Town Book, 1718–1870," Chester County Historical Society, West Chester, Pennsylvania.

29. *The Autobiography of Benjamin Franklin,* ed. Leonard W. Labaree et al. (New Haven, 1964), 108, 111–12, 117, 120, 122, 123; *Pennsylvania Gazette,* May 6, 13, 1731.

30. Larry Dale Gragg, *Migration in Early America: The Virginia Quaker Experience* (Ann Arbor, 1980), 21, 37, 77, *passim.*

31. "Thomas Pennell's Inventory, May 17, 1750," Chester County Inventories, #1276, CCCH; "William Trego's Inventory, Sept. 29, 1768," Chester County Inventories, CCCH.

32. "Jacob Vernon's Inventory, 3rd month, 30th day, 1740," Chester County Inventories, #1281, CCCH; "John Davis's Iventory, Oct. 5, 1749," Chester County Inventories, #1274, CCCH.

33. "Morris Llewellyn's Inventory, Oct. 4, 1749," Philadelphia County Inventories, #107, PCHA; "Peter Worrall's Inventory, 7th month, 25th day, 1772," Chester County Inventories, #2698, CCCH.

34. "Thomas Yarnell's Inventory, June 16, 1764," Chester County Inventories #2159, CCCH.

35. The 19 families consist of the families of John Evans, Thomas Foulke, Daniel Humphry, Robert Jones, Thomas Jones, Isaac Minshall, Owen Owen, Robert Owen, Joseph Pennell, William Pennell, Edward Roberts, Owen Roberts, Thomas Smedley, John Edge, John Worrall, Edward Woodward, Thomas Pennell.

36. "Isaac Minshall's Inventory, Feb. 1, 1731," Chester County Inventories, #406, CCCH: "Isaac Minshall's Will, Jan. 13, 1731," Chester County Wills A-347, CCCH; "Chester Men's Monthly Meeting Minutes, 4th month, 28th day, 1742," FHS.

37. "Daniel Humphry's Will, April 7, 1735," Philadelphia County Wills E-347, PCH; "Daniel Humphry to Samuel Humphry, deed, 6th month, 3rd day, 1729," Philadelphia County Deeds, R-401, PCH.

38. "Jacob Edge's Will, 12th month, 2nd day, 1705," Chester County Wills, A-97, CCCH.

39. Thomas Smedley's Will, March 25, 1758," Chester County Wills, E-213, CCCH.

40. These 18 families consist of the families of Stephen Jenkins, Joshua Hoopes, Nathan Hoopes, John Owen, George Smedley, William Trego, Jacob Malin, John Morgan, Enoch Walker, Francis Yarnell, Cadwallader Foulke, Griffith Llewellyn, William Pusey, Thomas Parry, Robert Roberts, William David, Hugh Evans.

41. "George Smedley and uxor, deed, Jan. 12, 1761," Chester County Deeds D-2-67, CCCH; Chester Men's Monthly Meeting Minutes, 10th month, 31st day, 1763, FHS; Chester County Taxes, Chester County Historical Society, West Chester, Pennsylvania; George Smedley's Will, December 8, 1766," Chester County Wills, e-408, CCCH; "George Smedley, Jr.'s Will, December 8, 1766," Chester County Wills, E-410, CCCH.

42. The 28 families include the families of Samuel Lewis, John Maris, Thomas Massey, Lawrence Pierson, Hugh Pugh, John Pugh, Samuel Richards, Peter Taylor,

William Thomas, Daniel Walker, John Yarnell, Benjamin Ellis, Evan Evans, Benjamin Humphry, John Jarman, Abraham Lewis, Rees Thomas, Aaron Roberts, William David, James Massey.

43. Goshen Men's Monthly Meeting Minutes, 2nd month, 20th day, 1758; 10th month, 17th day, 1750; 1st month, 15th day, 1759; 6th month, 3rd day, 1772, FHS.

44. "T.E.'s Will, May 16, 1760," Philadelphia County Wills, L-449, PCH: Radnor Men's Monthly Meeting Minutes, 4th month, 1749; 11th month, 1748, FHS.

45. B.H.'s Will, Jan. 17, 1738, Philadelphia County Wills, F-87, PCH; Radnor Men's Monthly Meeting Minutes, 4th month, 1749; 11th month, 3rd day, 1748, FHS.

46. The eight families included the families of Stephen Ogden, Jacob Trego, Samuel Ogden, Sublimus Ellis, Moses Martin, John Taylor, James Trego, Thomas Woodward.

47. For M. M. family discipline, see Chester Men's Monthly Meeting Minutes, 6th month, 27th day, 1744; 2nd month, 30th day, 1750; 4th month, 29th day, 1741; 9th month, 18th day, 1745; 7th month, 14th day, 1747; 4th month, 27th day, 1737; Goshen Women's Monthly Meeting Minutes, 7th month, 15th day, 1754; Chester Women's Monthly Meeting Minutes, 3rd month, 30th day, 1737, FHS.

48. For the "freemen" category, see Chester County Tax Lists, 1715–75, HSP.

49. Marietta, *The Reformation of American Quakerism, 1748–1783*, 73.

50. *Ibid.*, 75–77.

51. *Ibid.*, *passim.*

52. Jean R. Soderlund, *Quakers and Slavery: A Divided Spirit* (Princeton, 1985), 170–91; J. William Frost, "The Origins of the Quaker Crusade Against Slavery: A Review of Recent Literature," *Quaker History*, 67 (1978): 56–58.

53. Soderlund, *Quakers and Slavery*, 148–72.

54. Marietta, *The Reformation of American Quakerism*, 150–202; Hermann Wellenreuther, *Glaube und Politik in Pennsylvania, 1681–1776* (Cologne, 1972), 430–41; James H. Hutson, "Benjamin Franklin and Pennsylvania Politics, 1751–1755: A Reappraisal," *Pennsylvania Magazine of History and Biography*, 93 (1969): 303–71; James H. Hutson, *Pennsylvania Politics, 1746–1770: The Campaign for Royal Government* (Princeton, 1972), 41–121, *passim.*; Arthur J. Mekeel, *The Relation of the Quakers to the American Revolution* (Washington, D.C., 1979); Benjamin H. Newcomb, *Franklin and Galloway: A Political Partnership* (New Haven, 1972); Sydney V. James, *A People Among Peoples* (Cambridge, Mass., 1963), *passim.*

55. Marietta, *The Reformation of American Quakerism*, 49, 63.

56. John Woolman, *The Works of John Woolman* (Philadelphia, 1775), 386–87.

57. *Ibid.*, 139–40.

58. *Ibid.*, 47, 336, 337.

59. *Ibid.*, 149.

60. *Ibid.*, 389–91.

61. *Ibid.*, 353–54.

62. *Ibid.*, 353.

63. *Ibid.*, 393.

64. *Ibid.*, 284.

65. *Ibid.*, 267.

66. *Ibid.*, 266–67.

67. *Ibid.*, 205.

68. *Ibid.*, 231.

69. *Ibid.*, 198.

70. *Ibid.*, 209, 211, 213, 226-27.

71. *Ibid.*, 406-7.

72. *Ibid.*, 358.

73. Crèvecoeur, *Letters from an American Farmer*, 73-74.

74. *Ibid.*, 92.

75. Brissot de Warville, *Examen Critique des Voyages dans l'Amérique Septentrionale, de m. le Marquis de Châtellux* (London, 1786), 1-4.

76. Brissot, *New Travels in the United States*, 334.

77. *Ibid.*, 237, 339, 347; Crèvecoeur, *Letters from an American Farmer*, 166-79.

78. *Ibid.*, 68, 264.

79. Brissot, *New Travels in the United States*, 93, 102, 103, 112, 119.

80. Crèvecoeur, *Letters from an American Farmer*, 187.

81. Brissot, *New Travels in the United States*, 199, 253, 257.

82. *Ibid.*, 261-62.

83. Marquis de Chastellux, *Travels in North America in the Years 1780, 1781, and 1782*, Ed. and trans. Howard C. Rice, Jr. (Chapel Hill, 1963; orig pub. 1786), I: 165-68.

84. Brissot, *New Travels in the United States*, 299.

85. *Ibid.*, 165, 167.

86. *Ibid.*, 194.

87. *Ibid.*, 203.

88. For other views of the Quaker reconciliation with American republicanism, see James, *A People Among Peoples*; and Marietta, *The Reformation of American Quakerism, 1748-1783*.

Index